Dictionary of Mythology Folklore and Symbols

by

Gertrude Jobes

Part 3 - Index

The Scarecrow Press, Inc.
New York 1962

L.C. Card No. 61-860

With affection
to my sister
Augusta Cantor
and to the memory of
Arthur Cantor

CONTENTS

PREFACE

When Gertrude Jobes showed me the manuscript of her Dictionary of Mythology, Folklore, and Symbols, I suggested that as a librarian I would find it helpful if there were a subject index to tabulate the names and attributes of gods, heroes, and abstractions.

Now two years later, Mrs. Jobes surprises me with such a tool. The approximately 22,000 listings in this useful index are divided into two categories. The first part lists deities and mythological characters by their fields of interest. The second part similarly lists mythological affiliations, attributes and things.

Now one can see at a glance one hundred and three personal names associated with music, ranging from the Teutonic, to the Japanese, to the Zuni, to the Celtic, to the Inca. Or, grouped together, one finds fifty island abodes within the broader category of Other Worlds, and spread among equally diverse cultures.

The presentation of this Index is a fitting key to accelerate the use of the Dictionary. It will be extremely useful to librarians, scholars, and indeed to crossword puzzle workers.

A.P. DeWeese
The New York Public Library

ACKNOWLEDGEMENTS

Ever since I have been old enough to use Room 315, the great reading room of the New York Public Library, it has been a second home to me. Most of the research for my Dictionary of Mythology, Folklore and Symbols was accomplished there. When Mr. DeWeese, the Library's Chief of Information, suggested that the Dictionary should be supplemented by a topical guide, the thought of further cutting into time usually devoted to poetry or fiction writing terrified me. But the need nagged, and to free myself of the idea, I organized these tables. An entry may refer to a positive or negative aspect of the category under which it is listed. Each number under "Page" in the tables refers to the page in my Dictionary of Mythology, Folklore and Symbols on which details, such as legends, genealogy, functions, symbolic meaning of activities, etc. may be found.

I would like to say that I am grateful not only to the many fine departments of the New York Public Library, but to Yale University Library, the Library of Congress, to those libraries that sent books on loan to Milford, and to Miss Virginia Walters and the other librarians at the Taylor Library of Milford, Connecticut, for their ever ready assistance.

Gertrude Jobes

Milford, Conn.
May, 1962

ABBREVIATIONS USED IN THIS WORK

Abys.	Abyssinian
Afr.	African
Alas.	Alaskan
Algon.	Algonquin
Am. Folk.	American Folklore
Am. Ind.	American Indian
Am. Lit.	American Literature
Ang-Sax.	Anglo-Saxon
Apal. Ind.	Apalachian Indian
Arm.	Armenian
As. Min.	Asia Minor
Arab.	Arabian
Argen.	Argentine
Assyr.	Assyrian
Assyr-Baby.	Assyro-Babylonian
Astron.	Astronomy
Athap.	Athapascan Indian
Aus.	Australian
Baby.	Babylonian
Basum.	Basumbwa
Bav.	Bavarian
Belg.	Belgian
Bol.	Bolivian
Braz.	Brazilian
Brit. Col.	British Columbian
Bryth.	Brythonic
Bud.	Buddhist
Bulg.	Bulgarian
Burm.	Burmese
Bush.	Bushman
Caba.	Cabalism
Calif.	California Indian
Carib.	Caribbean
Caro. Is.	Caroline Islands
Carol.	Carolingian
Carth.	Carthagenian
Cel.	Celtic
Cey.	Ceylonese
Chald.	Chaldean
Chath. Is.	Chatham Islands
Chib.	Chibcha Indian
Chick.	Chickasaw Indian
Chil.	Chilean
Chin.	Chinese
Chip.	Chippewa Indian
Christ.	Christian
Cowich.	Cowichian Indian
Croa.	Croatian
Daho.	Dahoman
Dan.	Danish
Dict.	Dictionary
E. Afr.	East African
Egy.	Egyptian
Eng.	English
Ethiop.	Ethiopian
Euro.	European
Fin.	Finnish
Fin-Ug.	Finno-Ugric
Folk.	Folklore
Fr.	French
Germ.	German
Gil. Is.	Gilbert Islands
Gk.	Greek
Gk/Baby.	Greek name of a Babylonian deity
Guar.	Guarayo Indian
Guate.	Guatemalan
Hawa.	Hawaiian
Hebr.	Hebrew

Hebr-Christ.	Hebraeo-Christian
Herv. Is.	Hervey Island
Hidat.	Hidatsa Indian
Hin.	Hindu
Hotten.	Hottentot
Huama.	Huamachuco (Peru)
Ice.	Icelandic
Illy.	Illyrian
Ind.	Indian
Ind-Chin.	Indo-Chinese
Indo.	Indonesian
Iroq.	Iroquois Indian
Is.	Island
Ital.	Italic
Jap.	Japanese
Kor.	Korean
Lib.	Libyan
Lib-Egy.	Libyan & Egyptian
Lit.	Literature
Lithu.	Lithuanian
Malay.	Malayan
Marq.	Marquesan
Marsh.	Marshall Island
Mass.	Massachusetts Indian
Med.	Medieval
Medit.	Mediterranean
Mel.	Melanesian
Men.	Menominee Indian
Meso.	Mesopotamian
Mex.	Mexican
Micro.	Micronesian
Mong.	Mongolian
Mos.	Moslem
N.A.I.	North American Indian
Nav.	Navaho Indian
N. Guin.	New Guinean
N. Heb.	New Hebrides Islands
N. Zeal.	New Zealand
Nica.	Nicaraguan
Norw.	Norwegian
Oc.	Occult
Pac. Coast	Pacific Coast Indians
Para.	Paraguayan
Pers.	Persian
Peru.	Peruvian Indians
Philip.	Philippine Islands
Philis.	Philistine
Phoen.	Phoenician
Phryg.	Phrygian
Poly.	Polynesian
Portu.	Portuguese
Pota.	Potawatomi Indian
Rom.	Roman
Rom/Cel.	Roman name for a Celtic deity
Rus.	Russian
S.A.I.	South American Indian
Sax.	Saxon
Scan.	Scandinavian
Scot.	Scottish
Sem.	Semitic
Serb.	Serbian
Serb-Croa.	Serbo-Croatian
Siam.	Siamese
Sib.	Siberian
Slav.	Slavonic
So. Is.	Society Islands
Solom. Is.	Solomon Islands
Span.	Spanish
Sum.	Sumerian
Swed.	Swedish
Tahi.	Tahitian
Teut.	Teutonic

Thomp. Riv.	Thompson River Indians
Tib.	Tibetan
Trans.	Transvaal
Tsim.	Tsimshian Indian
Tupi. Guar.	Tupi-guarani Indian
Tup. Ind.	Tupinamba Indian
Van. Is.	Vancouver Island Indian
W. Ind.	West Indian
W.U.S. Ind.	Western United States Indian
Yura	Yuracari Indian
Zoro.	Zoroastrian

SYMBOLS USED IN THIS WORK

A	=	Androgynous
E	=	Eunuch
F	=	Female
F/A	=	Female with androgynous aspects
F-F	=	A pair, both female
F-M	=	A pair, one female, one male
M	=	Male
M/A	=	Male with androgynous aspects
M/F	=	A supernatural, in some areas worshiped as male, in other areas worshiped as female
M, F	=	A supernatural class composed of males and females
M-F	=	A pair, one male, one female
M-M	=	A pair, both male
+	=	Addenda

PART A

Table of Deities, Heroes, and Personalities

Index to Deities, Heroes, and Personalities

	Culture	Sex	Page
ABANDONED CHILD (EXPOSED, FATAL CHILD. ALSO SEE RENOUNCED BY PARENT)			
Abraham	Hebr., Mos.	M	17
Achaemenes	Pers.	M	24
Achilles	Gk.	M/A	25
Adonis	Gk.	M	34
Aegisthus	Gk.	M	39
Aesculapius	Rom.	M	41
Amadis	Span.	M	78
Amphion	Gk.	M	88
Ariel	Eng.	M	125
Arthur	Bryth.	M	132
Asclepius	Gk.	M	136
Atalanta	Gk.	F	148
Attis	Phyrg.	M	154
Byat Ta	Ind-Chin.	M	264
Byat Twe	Ind-Chin.	M	1445
Cyrus	Pers.	M	403
Dionysus	Gk.	M	447
Erichthonius	Gk.	M	519
Eumolpus	Gk.	M	530
Finn MacCoul	Cel.	M	570
Fleance	Eng.	M	1032
Frey	Norse	M	609
Gilgamesh	Sum.	M	656
Grettir	Ice.	M	374a
Gwion Bach	Cel.	M	701
Hagan	Germ.	M	707
Havelock	Dan.	M	732
Heracles	Gk.	M	752
Hercules	Rom.	M	759
Hirugo	Jap.	M	774
Horus	Egy.	M	792
Iamus	Gk.	M	815
Ion	Gk.	M	837
Ishmael	Hebr.	M	843
Jason	Gk.	M	866
Joshua	Hebr.	M	889
Kao Hsin	Chin.	M	908

Abandoned child (cont.)	Culture	Sex	Page
Karna	Hin.	M	910
Krishna	Hin.	M	945
Linus	Gk.	M	998
Llew Llaw Gyffes	Bryth.	M	1005
Maui	Poly.	M	1077
Mordred	Bryth.	M	1122
Moses	Hebr.	M	1126
Neleus	Gk.	M	1161
Oedipus	Gk.	M	1198
Paris	Gk.	M	1238
Pelias	Gk.	M	1250
Perseus	Gk.	M	1257
Philandrus	Gk.	M	1262
Phylacides	Gk.	M	1266
Pradyumna	Hin.	M	1290
Priapus	Gk.	M	1292
Pryderi (Gwri)	Bryth.	M	1298
Rama	Hin.	M	1321
Remus	Rom.	M	1332
Romulus	Rom.	M	1346
Sargon I	Meso.	M	1400
Scyld	Ang-Sax.	M	1409
Semiramis	Assyr.	F	1415
Shwe Pyin Nyi-Naung	Ind-Chin.	M	1445
Siegfried	Germ.	M	1448
Sigurd	Norse	M	1451
Stigande	Ang-Sax.	M	1494
Taliesin	Bryth.	M	1528
Tammuz	Baby.	M	1530
Telephus	Gk.	M	1542
Tenedos	Gk.	M	1264
Theseus	Gk.	M	1554
Zal	Pers.	M	1715
Zethus	Gk.	M	1718
Zeus	Gk.	M	1719

ABSTRACTIONS, MISCELLANEOUS			
Algea (pain)	Gk.	F	68
Ara (curses)	Gk.	F	116
Areta (virtue)	Gk.	F	121
Boulaios (assemblies)	Gk.	M	1720
Cacia (vice)	Gk.	F	265
Cratos (power)	Gk.	M	378
Eleos (pity)	Gk.	M	+
Eleutherois (liberator)	Gk.	M	1720
Kairos (psychological moment)	Gk.	M	+

	Culture	Sex	Page
Litae (prayers)	Gk.	F	1002
Meable (disgrace)	Cel.	F	405
Odin (wishes)	Norse	M	1195
Philotes (desire)	Gk.		1264
Pistios (oaths)	Gk.	M	1720
Saint Thomas (skepticism)	Christ.	M	1382
Sharbda (slanderer)	Baby.		1431
Sol (perfect balance)	Bryth.	M	1471
Sophrosyne (moderation)	Gk.	F	1476
Spes (hope)	Rom.	M	1481
Sphinx (mystery)	Eg., Gk.	F	1482
Sraddha (faith)	Hin.	F	1487
Styx (oath)	Gk.	F	1502
Susa-no-wo (impetuousness)	Jap.	M	1512
Syn (denial)	Norse	F	1522
Tagtug (sin)	Sum.	M	1524
T'ai I Ching (evolution)	Chin.	M	1525
Tapas (ardor)	Hin.	M	1533
Telete (rites)	Gk.	F	+
Valkyrie (wishes)	Norse	F	1636
Vor (prudence, vows)	Norse	F	1658
Yaotl (enemy)	Mex.	M	1701
Yaotlnecoc (enemy)	Mex.	M	1701
Yaotzin (enemy)	Mex.	M	1701
Yedidah (vitality)	Caba.		1703
Zadkiel (intercession, prayer)	Hebr, Christ.	M	1714
Zelus (zeal)	Gk.	M	1717
Zeus (partiality)	Gk.	M	1719
Zophar (cynicism)	Hebr.	M	1734

ABYSS (CHAOS, VOID. ALSO SEE PRIMORDIAL)

	Culture	Sex	Page
Aaba	Sum.		9
Abyss	Gk.		20
Ageb	Egy.		48
Anshar	Baby.	M	101
Apsu	Baby.	M	115
Basmu	Sum.	M	185
Chaos	Gk.		312
Domnu	Cel.	F	460
Engur	Baby.	M	511
Gandarewa	Pers.	M	625
Girtablili	Baby.	M	660
Kishar	Baby.	F	933
Kore-te-whiwhia	Poly.	M	942
Ku Shen	Chin.		953

Abyss (cont.)	Culture	Sex	Page
Labbu	Sum.	M	957
Lachamu	Baby.	F	961
Lachmu	Baby.	M	961
Lady of Abyss	Baby.	F	962
Leviathan	Hebr.		989
Mahasahasrapramardani	Bud.	F	1044
Monad	Chin.	A	1116
Mummu	Sum.	M	1136
Mushussu	Sum.	M	1139
Nu	Egy.	A	1184
Omorka	Baby.	F	1208
Pa-hra	Egy.	M	1226
Po	Poly.	F	1281
Tai-kih	Chin.	A	1525
Te Kore	N. Zeal.	A	1541
Tiamat	Baby.	F	1570
Tomoye	Jap.	A	1586
Ugallu	Sum.	M	1620
Uridimmu	Sum.	M	1629
Yamutbal	Sum.	M	1700
Ymir	Norse	M	1708
Zerpanitum	Baby.	F	1718
Zu	Baby., Sum.	M	1734

ADJUSTMENT OF UNIVERSE (SEE ORDER)
ADVENTURER (SEE QUESTER, TRAVELER, WANDERER)
AERONAUT (SEE FLIGHT)
AFTERWORLD (SEE UNDERWORLD)

AGRICULTURE (ALSO SEE FERTILITY)			
Abu	Sum.	M	20
Acantum	Mex.	M	22
Actaeon	Gk.	M	28
Agras	Fin-Ug.	M	51
Airya (Iraj)	Pers.	M	57
Aka-kanet	Chil.	M	59
Albina	Gk.	F	63
Alphito	Gk.	F	76
Amaethon	Bryth.	M	78
Ame-waka-hiko	Jap.	M	85
Asari	Baby.	M	135
Ashnan	Sum.	F	139
Attis	Phryg.	M	154
Bacchus	Gk., Rom.	M	170
Belun	Rus.	M	201

	Culture	Sex	Page
Bodhidharma	Bud.	M	233
Byggvir	Norse	M	264
Cachimana	Orinoco	M	265
Cadmus	Gk.	M	266
Cailleach	Scot.	F	269
Cain	Christ, Heb, Mos.	M	269
Calakomanas	Pueblo	F	272
Carpo	Gk.	F	293
Caswallawn	Bryth.	M	296
Celeus	Gk.	M	302
Ceres	Rom.	F	305
Cerridwen	Bryth.	F	305
Chicomecoatl	Mex.	F	322
Chloe	Gk.	F	328
Churl	Norse	M	337
Cinteotl	Mex.	M/F	341
Combalus	Syrian	M	361
Conaire	Cel.	M	363
Convector	Rom.	M	369
Cormac MacArt	Cel.	M	371
Creirwy	Cel.	F	379
Criosphinx	Egy.	M	382
Cueravaperi	Mex.	F	396
Cybele	Phryg.	F	400
Danu	Cel.	F	104
Demeter	Gk.	F	429
Demogorgon	Christ.	M	431
Dendrites	Gk.	M	432
Deo	Gk.	F	432
Deohako	Seneca	F	433
Dionysus	Gk.	M	447
Diwrnach	Cel.	M	454
Dumuzi	Sum.	M	476
Du'uzu	Sum.	M	478
Elisha	Hebr.	M	504
Elphin	Cel.	M	506
Enmeshara	Sum.	M	512
Eochaid Airem	Cel.	M	513
Eochaid Ollathair	Cel.	M	513
Erechtheus	Gk.	M	518
Eremon	Cel.	M	518
Erichthonius	Gk.	M	519
Ermenrich	Germ.	M	522
Esus	Cel.	M	526
Eurystheus	Gk.	M	533

	Culture	Sex	Page
Evander	Rom.	M	533
Faunus (Inuus)	Rom.	M	552
Fulla	Norse	M	616
Gaea	Gk.	F/A	621
Ga'n	Apache Ind.		625
Gandayah	Iroq.		626
Gefjon	Dan.	F	637
Gilling	Norse	M	657
Gluskap	Algon.	M	664
Groa	Norse	F	692
Gyges	Gk.	M	703
Ham	Hebr.	M	713
Hamaguchi Gohei	Jap.	M	714
Hamori	Jap.	M	716
Han Hsiang-Tzu	Chin.	M	722
Harmonia	Gk.	F	727
Hayk	Arm.	M	734
Hou Chi	Chin.	M	794
Hreidmar	Norse	M	797
Hyacinthus	Gk.	M	809
Hyas	Gk., Phryg.	M	810
Idakeru	Jap.	M	818
Ihi-yori-hiko	Jap.	M	822
Inari-m'yojim	Jap.	F	827
Ingun (Yngvi)	Norse	F	831
Ira (Irra)	Hin.	F	838
Ishullanu	Assyro-Baby.	M	845
Issachar	Hebr.	M	848
Italus	Ital.	M	848
Itzamna	Mex.	M	850
Kavi Usan	Pers.	M	914
Kayanu-hime	Jap.	F	915
Ksetrasya	Hin.	M	947
Kubera	Hin.	M	948
Kushi-nada-hime	Jap.	F	953
Labraid	Cel.	M	960
Lamech	Hebr.	M	967
Lityerses	Gk.	M	1003
Llevelys	Bryth.	M	1004
Logris	Bryth.	M	1009
MacCecht	Cel.	M	1033
Maira-Monan	Tup. Ind.	M	1047
Maneros	Egy.	M	1057
Mesgegra	Cel.	M	1094
Midas	Gk.	M	1099
Minerva	Ital.	F	1106

	Culture	Sex	Page
Minyas	Gk.	M	1107
Mitosh-no-kami	Jap.	M	1112
Naboth	Heb.	M	1146
Nabu	Baby.	M	1146
Nacien	Bryth.	M	1146
Namo	Carol.	M	1152
Naphtali	Hebr.	M	1154
Niezguinek	Slav.	M	1168
Ningirsu	Sum.	M	1172
Nithud	Swed.	M	1176
Noah	Hebr.	M	1177
Numa Pompilius	Rom.	M	1185
Oannes	Baby., Chald., Phoen.	M	1190
Oeneus	Gk.	M	1198
Oenomaus	Gk.	M	1199
Oilioil	Cel.	M	1202
Pandion	Gk.	M	1232
Payetome	Braz.	M	1245
Pay Zume	Para.	M	1245
Picumnus	Rom.	M	1269
Picus	Rom.	M	1269
Pilumnus	Rom.	M	1273
Quirinus	Ital.	M	1314
Rongo	Poly.	M	1347
Sa-Kalama	Baby.	M	1389
Salus	Rom.	F	1392
Saritor	Rom.	M	1401
Sarpedon	Gk.	M	1401
Shen Nung	Chin.	M	1434
Sterculius	Ital.	M	1494
Sume	Braz.	M	1506
Sunasira	Hin.	M	1509
Sylvanus	Rom.	M	1521
Teyrnon	Bryth.	M	1549
T'ien Tsu	Chin.	M	1572
Triptolemus	Gk.	M	1598
Tros	Gk.	M	1600
Urvara	Hin.	M	1630
Viracocha	Inca	M	1652
Ya-Daganu	Sem.	M	1697
Zume	W. Ind.	M	1735

	Culture	Sex	Page
AIR (ATMOSPHERE, BREATH, SPACE)			
Aer (Aero)	Gk.	F	41
Aethre	Gk.	F	42
Akasa	Hin.	A	1236
Amen	Egy.	M	83
Anhoret	Egy.	M	97
Ariel	Med. Lit.	M	124
Aslog	Norse	F	141
Baal	Sem.	M	167
Boyg	Norw.		239
Buddhadakini	Bud.	F	257
Dakinis	Bud.	F	408
Eri	Cel.	F	519
Erinyes	Gk.	F	520
Geniti Glinne	Cel.	F	645
Hadad	Sem.	M	705
Harlequin	Euro. Lit.	M	726
Hehu	Egy.	M	742
Helle	Gk.	F	748
Hera	Gk.	F	752
Hsi Wang Mu	Chin.	F	800
Ilmatar	Fin.	F	824
Incubus	Folk.	F	828
Iodhi	Slav.	M, F	836
Itshi	Sib.	M	849
Jakis	Jap.		862
Jumala	Fin.	M	895
Karmadakini	Bud.	F	910
Kihunai	Hupa Ind.		927
Kneph	Egy.	M	937
Liu Tsung	Chin.	M	1003
Makaravaktra	Bud.	F	1047
Mandarava	Bud.	F	1056
Murgi	Baltic	M, F	1137
Niu	Egy.	M	1176
Odin	Norse	M	1195
Onouris	Egy.	M	97
Padmadakini	Bud.	F	1225
Panis	Hin.	M	1233
Parabrahma	Hin.	A	1236
Phrixus	Gk.	M	1267
Pierides	Gk.	F	1269
Podoga	Slav.	M	1281
Prana	Hin.	M, F	1291
Raphael	Hebr.	M	1323
Ratnadakini	Bud.	F	1324

	Culture	Sex	Page
Rksavaktradakini	Bud.	F	1342
Saramaya	Hin.	M	1399
Sarvabuddhadakini	Bud.	F	1401
Sciron	Gk.	M	1407
Shu	Egy.	M	1443
Siddha	Hin.	M	1447
Simhavaktra	Bud.	F	1455
Sylph	Med. Lit.	M, F	1521
Tara	Bud.	F	1534
Tefenet	Egy.	F	1541
Te-more-tu	Maori	M	1543
Tengu	Jap.	M	1545
Thagyas	Ind-Chin.		1551
Thriae	Gk.	F	1566
Trita Aptya	Hin.	M	1599
Tung Wang Kung	Chin.	M	1607
Vajradakini	Bud.	F	1634
Vajravarahi	Bud.	F	1635
Vanir	Norse	M, F	1638
Vasistha	Hin.	F	1641
Vayu	Hin.	M	1642
Visvadakini	Hin.	F	1655
Visvavasu	Hin.	M	1447
Vyaghravaktradakini	Bud.	F	1660
Whai-tua	N. Zeal.		1674
Wunschelwybere	Germ.	F	1693
Zadkiel	Hebr.	M	1714

ALE (SEE WINE)
ALPHABET INVENTOR (SEE CULTURE HERO)
ANGEL (SEE SPIRIT)
ANGER (SEE WRATH)
ANGUISH (SEE PAIN)
ANIMAL KEEPER (GAME KEEPER, HERDSMAN)

Admetus	Gk.	M	33
Aegipan	Gk.	M/F	38
Anahit	Arm.	F	90
Apollo	Gk.	M	110
Ashima	Sem.	M	139
Bhava	Hin.	M	208
Bodb	Cel.	M	232
Charidotes	Gk.	M	313
Ch'ien Niu	Chin.	M	322
Ching Yuh	Kor.	M	759
Chlevnik	Rus.		328

	Culture	Sex	Page
Colin Clout	Eng.	M	356
Damoetas	Rom.	M	410
Damon	Rom.	M	410
Damona	Cel.	F	410
Daonus	Baby.	M	414
Daphnis	Gk.	M	414
David	Hebr.	M	417
Doeg	Hebr.	M	455
Dogedoi (Toklok)	Sib.	M	458
Endymion	Gk.	M	511
Epaphus	Gk.	M	514
Epimelian	Gk.	F	516
Epona	Cel.	F	517
Etana	Sum.	M	527
Eumaeus	Gk.	M	529
Faunus	Rom.	M	552
Faustulus	Rom.	M	553
Flidais	Cel.	F	583
Friuch	Cel.	M	613
Ganyklos	Lith.	M	627
Geush Urvan	Zoro.	F	652
Gid-kuzo	Fin-Ug.	M	655
Giolla Deacair	Cel.	M	659
Glaucus	Gk.	M	662
Goibniu	Cel.	M	670
Govetter	Norw.	M	680
Gufittar	Lapp	M	695
Gwydion	Bryth.	M	702
Gymir	Norse	M	704
Hafra-drottin	Norse	M	1561
Hecate	Gk.	F	740
Heimdal	Norse	M	743
Helios	Gk.	M	747
Heracles of Oeta	Gk.	M	755
Heracles of Tiryns	Gk.	M	756
Hercules	Rom.	M	759
Hermes	Gk.	M	760
Hippona	Gk.	F	774
Jabal	Hebr.	M	855
Jethro	Hebr.	M	877
Jubal	Hebr.	M	891
Kavya Usanas	Hin.	M	914
Kekri	Fin-Ug.	M	916
Kengiu (Hikoboshi)	Jap.	M	916
Khensu	Egy.	M	923
Kingu	Baby.	M	932

	Culture	Sex	Page
Kosla-kuguza	Fin-Ug.	M	943
Kosla-kuva	Fin-Ug.	F	943
Kudai	Sib.	M	948
Laban	Hebr.	M	957
Lahar	Sum.	F	964
Lampetia	Gk.	F	969
Lot	Hebr.	M	1014
Lufu	Basum.	M	1022
Luot-hozjik	Lapp	F	1025
Lyceus	Gk.	M	1027
Mamurius Veturius	Rom.	M	1052
Marduk	Assyr-Baby.	M	1065
Meliades	Gk.	F	1085
Moccus	Rom./Cel.	M	1114
Moses	Hebr.	M	1126
Mulla	Cel.	M	1135
Mutunus	Rom.	M	1142
Nabal	Hebr.	M	1145
Nagasvaraja	Bud.	M	1148
Nana	Sum.	F	1152
Nanda	Hin.	M	1152
Nannar	Baby.	M/A	1153
Ninamaskug	Sum.	M	1170
Ninsubur	Sum.	M	1173
Ninurta (Nikilim)	Sum.	M	1174
Niu Lang	Chin.	M	1176
Nules-murt	Fin-Ug.	M	1185
Ochall Ochne	Cel.	M	1193
Palaemon	Rom.	M	1227
Pales	Ital.	A	1228
Pan	Gk.	M	1230
Paris	Gk.	M	1238
Peter Klaus	Germ.	M	1259
Phyllis	Rom.	F	1268
Picus	Rom.	M	1269
Poeas	Gk.	M	1281
Poseidon	Gk.	M	1288
Poshaiyanne	Pueblo	M	1288
Pots-hozjik	Rus.	F	1289
Pots-hozjin	Rus.	M	1289
Priapus	Gk.	M	1292
Proteus	Gk.	M	1297
Pusan	Hin.	M	1305
Rohina	Hin.	F	1345
Rongoteus (Rukotivo)	Fin-Ug.	M	1347
Rucht	Cel.	M	1353

Animal Keeper (cont.)	Culture	Sex	Page
Rudiobus	Cel.	M	1353
Saint Blaise	Christ.	M	1365
Saint Patrick	Christ.	M	1378
Sarakka	Lapp	F	1399
Sarama	Hin.	F	1399
Shem	Hebr.	M	1433
Shepherd Boy	Chin.	M	1435
Shulamite	Hebr.	F	1444
Sibzianna	Baby.	M	1530
Silvanus	Rom.	M	1453
Sin	Assyr.	M	1456
Solbon	Sib.	M	1471
Strephon	Eng.	M	1500
Sulbundu	Sib.	M	1505
Sumugan	Sum.	M	1507
Surabhi	Hin.	F	1511
Tammuz	Baby.	M	1530
Terah	Hebr.	M	1546
Thjalfi	Norse	M	1560
Thyrsis	Gk., Rom.	M	1570
Tiamat	Baby.	F	1570
Tityrus	Gk., Rom.	M	1580
Tura	Pers.	M	1608
Usching	Baltic	M	1631
Vitsa-kuguza	Fin-Ug.	M	1656
Vitsa-kuva	Fin-Ug.	F	1656
Vohu Manah	Zoro.	M	1657
Volos (Ganyklos)	Rus.	M	1657
Yang Ching	Chin.	M	1700

ANIMAL NURSED OR SAVED

Name	Culture	Sex	Page
Achilles	Gk.	M	25
Aegisthus	Gk.	M	39
Amphion	Gk.	M	88
Asclepius	Gk.	M	136
Atalanta	Gk.	F	148
Cyrus	Pers.	M	403
Gilgamesh	Sum.	M	656
Heracles	Gk.	M	752
Horus	Egy.	M	792
Hou Chi	Chin.	M	794
Iamus	Gk.	M	815
Jason	Gk.	M	866
Kao Hsin	Chin.	M	908
Maugis	Frankish	M	1077
Neleus	Gk.	M	1161

	Culture	Sex	Page
Paris	Gk.	M	1238
Pelias	Gk.	M	1250
Philandrus	Gk.	M	1262
Phylacides	Gk.	M	1267
Ptolemy I	Egy.	M	1187
Remus	Rom.	M	1332
Romulus	Rom.	M	1346
Semiramis	Gk.	M	1415
Telephus	Gk.	M	1542
Tiri	Braz.	M	1576
Ymir	Norse	M	1708
Yu	Chin.	M	1711
Zal	Pers.	M	1715
Zethus	Gk.	M	88
Zeus	Gk.	M	1719

ARCHER (SEE MARKSMAN)
ARCHITECT (SEE ARTISAN)
ARHAT (SEE SPIRIT)

ARTISAN (ARCHITECT, SMITH)

Alberich	Norse	M	62
Alfar	Norse	M	67
Amatsu-mara	Jap.	M	843
Andvari	Norse	M	95
Argus	Gk.	M	122
Asvid	Norse	M	146
Atabyrius	Gk.	M	147
Baba, Mustapha	Arab.	M	168
Boshintoi	Sib.	M	237
Brok	Norse	M	251
Cabiri	Phryg.	M	265
Credne	Cel.	M	379
Culann	Cel.	M	396
Curetes	Gk.	M	398
Cyclops	Gk.	M	400
Dactyli	Gk.	M	404
Daedalus	Gk.	M	404
Dai Dalos	Gk.	M	406
Dainn	Norse	M	407
Diancecht	Cel.	M	442
Duergar	Norse	M	475
Dulb	Cel.	M	476
Ea	Baby.	M	481
Egil	Norse	M	493
Elath-Iahu	Sem.	M	498

	Culture	Sex	Page
Elf	Norse	M, F	502
Enki	Assyr., Baby., Sum.	M	511
Foland	Norse	M	589
Gavida	Cel.	M	635
Gavidjeen Go	Cel.	M	635
Gobhan Saer	Cel.	M	666
Goibniu	Cel.	M	670
Govannon	Bryth.	M	680
Hengest	Norse	M	750
Hephaestus	Gk.	M	751
Hlebard	Norse	M	776
Ilmarinen	Fin-Ug.	M	824
Ishi-kori-dome	Jap.	F	843
Ivalde	Norse	M	850
Kavya Usanas	Hin.	M	914
K'daai Maqsin	Yakut	M	915
Khensu	Egy.	M	923
Khnemu	Egy.	M	924
Kuan-de	Ind-Chin.	M	947
Kudai-bakshy	Yakut	M	948
Kuski-banda	Baby.	M	482
Lamech	Hebr.	M	967
Lord of Sesennu	Egy.	M	1013
Luchta	Cel.	M	1020
Lug	Cel.	M	1022
Mahagiri	Ind-Chin.	M	1042
Mamurius Veturius	Rom.	M	1052
Manawyddan	Bryth.	M	1056
Miach	Cel.	M	1097
Mimi	Germ.	M	1105
Mulciber	Rom.	M	1135
Ngawn-wa Magam	Burm.	M	1167
Nibelung	Norse	M	1167
Nun-ura	Baby.	M	1186
Oberon	Eng.	M	1192
P'an Ku	Chin.	M/A	1233
Perillus	Gk.	M	1255
Ptah	Egy.	M	1299
Pygmalion	Gk.	M	1306
Rbhus (Ribhus)	Hin.	M	1326
Regin	Norse	M	1330
Schilbung	Norse	M	1407
Sek-ya	Ind-Chin.	M	1414
Sethlaus	Ital.	M	1421
Sindre	Norse	M	1457

	Culture	Sex	Page
Slagfin	Norse	M	1466
Sucellos	Cel.	M	1503
Svald	Norse	M	1514
Svarog	Slav.	M	1514
Svartalfar	Norse	M	1514
Tagtug (Tibir)	Sum.	M	1524
Tawiscara	Huron	M	1539
Telchines	Cretan	M	1541
Telyaveli	Baltic	M	1542
Thaah	Mex.	M	1550
Thjasse	Norse	M	1560
Thoth	Egy.	M	1562
Torx	Arm.	M	1590
Troll	Norse	M	1600
Trophonius	Gk.	M	1600
Tubal-Cain	Hebr.	M	1606
Tvastr	Hin.	M	1611
Unferth	Ang-Sax.	M	1625
Usanas	Hin.	M	1631
Vaja	Hin.	M	1634
Varuna	Hin.	M	1639
Vibhvan	Hin.	M	1648
Visvakarman	Hin.	M	1655
Volund	Norse	M	1658
Vulcan	Rom.	M	1659
Wayland	Ang-Sax.	M	1670
ASTRAL			
Adar	Baby.	M	31
Agas Xenas Xena	Chinook		45
Allat	Sem.	F	69
Anael	Oc.	M	645
Anat	Sem.	F	91
Anat Bethel	Hebr.	A	92
Andrew	Christ.	M	93
Andromeda	Gk.	F	94
Anshar	Baby.	M	101
Antinous	Rom.	M	103
Anunaki	Baby.		105
Aphrodite	Gk.	A	108
Apisirahts	Blackfeet	M	109
Arcas	Gk.	M	118
Arcturus	Fin-Ug.	M	119
Ariadne	Gk.	F	123
Arion	Gk.	M	125
Arishis	Hin.	M	125

	Culture	Sex	Page
Arsa	Syrian	F	130
Arsu	Sem.	F	1490
Asclepius	Gk.	M	136
Asher	Hebr.	M	138
Ashera	Sem.	F	138
Asshur	Assyr.	M	143
Astarte	Phoen.	F	144
Astraea	Gk.	F	145
Astraeus	Gk.	M	145
Asvins	Hin.	M	146
Athtar	Abys.	F	151
Auriga	Gk.	M	158
Azizos	Arab.	M	166
Azizu	Sem.	M	166
Bartholomew	Christ.	M	183
Bel	Baby.	M	196
Beltis	Baby.	F	201
Benjamin	Hebr.	M	202
Boahje-naste	Fin-Ug.	M	230
Bootes	Gk.	M	236
Bright Star	Pawnee	F	1460
Bu	Mel.	M	254
Buto	Jap.	M	263
Cabiri	Phryg.	M	265
Caleb	Hebr.	M	273
Callisto	Gk.	F	278
Cassiopeia	Gk.	F	294
Castor and Pollux	Gk.	M	295
Celaeno	Gk.	F	301
Cepheus	Gk.	M	304
Cetus	Gk.	M	306
Chang	Chin.	M	311
Ch'ien Niu	Chin.	M	322
Chih Nu	Chin.	F	323
Chiron	Gk.	M	327
Chiun (Remphan)	Hebr.	M	327
Chnuphis	Gnostic	M	328
Christ	Christ.	M	1491
Citallicue	Mex.	M	344
Citlalatonic	Mex.	M	344
Cygnus	Gk.	M	401
Cynosura	Gk.	F	402
Dan	Hebr.	M	410
Dhruva	Hin.	M	439
Dioscuri	Gk.	M	449
Dogai	Mel.	F	458

	Culture	Sex	Page
Electra	Gk.	F	499
Enceladus	Gk.	M	510
Eosphorous	Gk.	M	514
Ephraim	Hebr.	M	515
Erichthonius	Gk.	M	519
Erigone	Gk.	F	520
Fravashi	Pers.	M	608
Fu Shen	Chin.	M	618
Gad	Hebr.	M	620
Gimini	Rom.	M	643
Gendenwitha	Iroq.	M	644
Girtablili	Baby.	M	660
Gudanna	Assyr-Baby.	M	694
Helice	Gk.	F	747
Heosphorus	Gk.	M	751
Heracles	Gk.	M	752
Hercules	Rom.	M	759
Hermes	Gk.	M	760
Hesperus	Gk.	M	765
Hestia	Gk.	F	765
Houri	Mos.	F	795
Hsiu Chi	Chin.	F	1711
Hyades	Gk.	F	809
Hydra	Gk.	M	810
Hydrus	Gk.	M	810
Icarius	Gk.	M	817
Innini	Sum.	F	832
Ishtar	Assyr-Baby.	F	844
Isis	Egy.	F	845
Issachar	Hebr.	M	848
Ivalde (Slagfin)	Norse	M	850
James the Great	Christ.	M	862
James the Less	Christ.	M	862
John	Christ.	M	884
Judah	Hebr.	M	892
Judas	Christ.	M	892
Judas Iscariot	Christ.	M	892
Jupiter	Rom.	M	896
Kara Khan	Mong.	M	909
Knights of the Round Table	Bryth.	M	938
Koshin	Jap.	M	943
Kudai	Sib.	M	948
Kudai-jajutshi	Mong.	M	948
Kuei-Sing	Chin.	M	949
Kulilu	Baby.	M	951
Kuribu	Sum.	M	952

	Culture	Sex	Page
Kusariqqu	Baby.	M	953
Levi	Hebr.	M	988
Lucifer	Rom.	M	1020
Maera	Gk.	M	1037
Manasseh	Hebr.	M	1055
Manco Capac	Inca	M	1056
Marduk	Baby., Sum.	M	1065
Maritchi	Chin.	F	1067
Mars	Rom.	M	1069
Matthew	Christ.	M	1076
Melanippe	Gk.	F	1085
Mercury	Rom.	M	1091
Merope	Gk.	F	1093
Monimos	Arab.	M	1117
Myojo-Tenshi	Jap.	M	1142
Nabu	Baby.	M	1146
Nagelfare	Norse	M	1148
Nanai	Baby.	F	1152
Nanchi-lao-jen	Chin.	M	1442
Naphtali	Hebr.	M	1154
Neptune	Rom.	M	1163
Nergal	Assyr-Baby.	M	1164
Nibhaz	Avite	M	1167
Ningishzida	Sum.	M	1172
Ninib	Assyr-Baby.	M	1173
Ninlil	Sum.	F	1173
Ninsubur	Sum.	M	1173
Ninurta	Sum.	M	1174
Noh Ek	Mex.	F	1179
Norma	Rom.	F	1180
Nu	Chin.	F	1184
Nuter Dua	Egy.	M	1187
Oannes	Baby., Phoen.	M	1190
Oetaeus	Gk.	M	1199
Ophiuchus	Gk.	M	1212
Orion	Gk.	M	1215
Orvandel's Toe	Norse	M	1217
Otava & Otso	Finnish	M	1220
Ovillus	Gk.	M	1221
Ox Leg	Egy.		1223
Pegasus	Gk.		1248
Pei-chi Chen Chun	Chin.	M	1249
Perkune Tete	Baltic	M	1257
Perseus	Gk.	M	1257
Peter	Christ.	M	1379
Philip	Christ.	M	1380

	Culture	Sex	Page
Phoenix	Egy.		1265
Phosphorus	Gk.	M	1266
Pirua	Inca	M	1275
Pleiades	Gk.	F	1279
Poia	Blackfeet	M	1281
Prajapati (Mrga)	Hin.	A	1290
Quetzalcoatl	Mex.	M	1312
Ratri	Hin.	F	1324
Regulus	Rom.	M	1331
Reuben	Hebr.	M	1334
Rishis	Hin.	M	1340
Romulus	Rom.	M	1346
Sa'd	Arab.	M	1360
Sa'dan	Arab.	F	1360
Sani	Hin.	M	1397
Santa Claus	Christ.	M	1397
Saturn	Rom.	M	1403
Satyabhama	Hin.	F	946
Shou Hsing	Chin.	M	1442
Shou Shen	Chin.	M	1442
Shu & Tefenet	Egy.	M, F	1444
Shulpae	Baby.	M	1444
Sibzianna	Baby.	M	1530
Sidi	Mos.	M	1447
Simeon-Levi	Hebr.	M	1454
Simon Zelotes	Christ.	M	1381
Sirius (Sothis)	Rom.		1459
Skanda	Hin.	M	1464
Solbon	Sib.	M	1471
Solbon	Yakut	F	1471
Stella Maris	Christ.	F	1493
Sterope	Gk.	F	1494
Sukra	Hin.	M	1505
Swan	Rom.		1516
Taehti	Fin.	M	1524
Tara Bai	Hin.	F	1534
Taurus	Gk.	M	1538
Tengri	Buriat	M	1545
Tezcatlipoca	Mex.	M	1549
Thein	Burm.	M	1553
Thjasse	Norse	M	1560
Thomas	Christ.	M	1560
T'ien Kou	Chin.	M	1571
Tishtrya	Pers.	M	1577
Tlauizcalpantecutli	Mex.	M	1582
Tonacatecutli	Mex.	M	1586

Astral (cont.)	Culture	Sex	Page
Torem	Sib.	M	1589
Torem-Talmas	Sib.	M	1589
Tou-mu	Chin.	F	1591
T'si Tsiang	Chin.	M	1604
Tungk-pok	Ostiak	M	1607
Ugallu	Sum.	M	1620
Unas	Egy.	M	1623
Uranus	Gk.	M	1627
Urgel	Yakut	M	1629
Uridimmu	Baby.	M	1629
Vanand	Pers.	M	1638
Venus	Rom.	A	1644
Veraldar-Nagli	Scan.	M	1645
Veralden-Olmai	Lapp	M	1645
Vesper	Rom.	M	1647
Virgo	Rom.	F	1653
Vrihaspatic	Hin.	M	1659
Wabanang	Men.	M	1660
Wabung Annung	Algon.	M	1661
Warrior (Great Star)	Pawnee	M	1491
Wen Ch'ang	Chin.	M	1673
Wyungare	Aus.	M	1694
Xaman Ek	Mex.	M	1695
Xipe Totec	Mex.	M	1696
Yang Ch'eng	Chin.	M	1700
Yazata	Zoro.	M	1702
Yu Shih	Chin.	M	1713
Zadkiel	Hebr.	M	1714
Zamama	Baby.	M	1715
Zebulun	Hebr.	M	1717
Zu	Baby., Sum.	M	1734
ATHLETICS (GAMES, WRESTLING)			
Agoneus	Gk.	M	50
Castor and Pollux	Gk.	M	295
Chiron	Gk.	M	327
Dascylus	Gk.	M	416
Dionysus	Gk.	M	447
Dioscuri	Gk.	M	449
Doryphorus	Gk.	M	465
Hermes	Gk.	M	760
Jupiter Capitolinus	Rom.	M	896
Kerkuon	Gk.	M	919
Luka-kane	Hawa.	M	1024
Luna	Rom.	F	1025
Nomi-no-sukune	Jap.	M	1179

	Culture	Sex	Page
Palaemon	Gk.	M	1227
Phocus	Gk.	M	1541
Togakushi	Jap.	M	1584
Ullerus	Norse	M	1622
ATTENDANT			
Ganymede	Gk.	M	627
Hebe	Gk.	F	739
Heka	Egy.	M	744
Ilithyiae	Gk.	F	823
In-ab	Baby.	M	827
Iolaus	Gk.	M	836
Ishi-kori-dome	Jap.	F	843
Jejamo-karpo	Bud.	F	871
Kaguhana	Jap.	M	902
Kimpurushas	Hin.	M	928
Kittu (Kettu)	Assyr-Baby.	M	1110
Kuei Hsin	Chin.	M	1673
Lichas	Gk.	M	991
Loegaire	Cel.	M	1008
Lofn	Norse	F	1008
Ma-ku	Chin.	F	1048
Maruts	Hin.	M	1071
Matali	Hin.	M	1074
Maudgalyayama & Sariputra	Bud.	M	1077
Mesharu	Baby.	M	1094
Mi-li	Chin.	M	1102
Mirume	Jap.	F	1110
Misharu	Phoen.	M	1110
Myrmidon	Gk.	M	1142
Naiades	Gk.	F	1148
Napaeae	Gk.	F	1154
Nereids	Gk.	F	1164
Nymph	Gk.	F	1188
Ol	Bryth.	M	1204
Palinurus	Rom.	M	1228
Panisc	Gk.	M	1233
Peitho	Gk.	F	1249
Pelops	Gk.	M	1251
Phobos	Gk.	M	1265
Poinae	Gk.	F	1281
Sanjaya	Hin.	M	1397
Sattakurodzusagai-ai	Yakut	M	1402
Sbires	Mos.	M	1404
Seraph	Hebr. Christ.	M	1417

Attendant (cont.)	Culture	Sex	Page
Shimbei	Jap.	M	1437
Silenus	Gk.	M	1453
Sjofn	Norse	F	1463
Snorta	Norse	F	1470
Syn	Norse	F	1522
Thunderbird	Am. Ind.	M	1568
T'ien-lung	Chin.	M	1673
Tiphys	Gk.	M	1575
Ti-ya	Chin.	M	1673
Tros	Gk.	M	1600
Ubyr	Gk.	M	1619
Udo	Sumu Ind.	M	1620
Ukhat	Baby.	F	1621
Upali	Bud.	M	1626
Valkyrie	Norse	F	1636
Vasu	Hin.	M	1641
Vor	Norse	F	1658
Vyaghravaktradakini	Bud.	F	1660
Wiglaf	Ang-Sax.	M	1680

AXIS (SKY OR WORLD SUPPORT)

Agamedes	Gk.	M	44
Aloidae	Gk.	M	71
Amala	Tsim.	M	79
Ama-no-minaka	Jap.	M	80
Ame-no-mi-hashira	Jap.	M	1272
Anhoret	Egy.	M	97
Atlas	Gk.	M	152
Baiame	Aus.	M	173
Boshintoi	Sib.	M	237
Hyas	Gk.	M	810
Indra	Hin.	M	829
Jurojin	Jap.	M	898
Kerkuon	Gk.	M	919
Kuei Shen	Chin.	M	949
Kuni-no-mi-hashira	Jap.	F	1272
Kurma	Hin.	M	952
Mandishire	Sib.	M	1057
Nagaitcho	Calif. Ind.	M	1147
Nanchi-lao-jen	Chin.	M	1442
Nordre	Norse	M	1180
Onouris	Egy.	M	97
Osiris	Egy.	M	1218
Pei-chi Chen Chun	Chin.	M	1249
Perikionios	Gk.	M	1255
Picus	Rom.	M	1269

Ptah-tanen	Egy.	M	1300
Ra	Egy.	M/A	1314
Rehua	Poly.	M	1331
Ru	Poly.	M	1352
Shina-tsu-hiko	Jap.	M	1438
Skambha	Hin.	M	1464
Talus	Gk.	M	1529
Tane	Poly.	M	1531
Teharonhiawagon	Iroq.	M	1541
Telamon	Gk.	M	1541
Tharonhiawakon	Iroq.	M	1552
Tu	Poly.	M	1604
Turtle	N.A.I.	M	1610
Varaha	Hin.	M	1638
Zacharias	Mos.	M	1714

BANSHEE (SEE DEMON)

BEAUTY

Achilles	Gk.	M/A	25
Acis	Gk.	M	26
Adonis	Gk.	M	34
Agnar	Norse	M	49
Alexis	Rom.	M	67
Anchises	Rom.	M	93
Andromeda	Gk.	F	94
Angus	Cel.	M	97
Antinous	Rom.	M	103
Aphrodite	Gk.	F	108
Apollo	Gk.	M	110
Ara	Arm.	M	116
Attis	Phryg.	M	154
Badoura	Arab.	F	172
Balder	Norse	M	174
Baldwin	Carol.	M	175
Benten	Jap.	F	203
Benzaiben	Oc.	M	203
Blodeuwedd	Bryth.	F	226
Bres	Cel.	M	246
Creirwy	Cel.	F	379
Cuchulainn	Cel.	M	393
Devorgilla	Cel.	F	436
Eloah Va-daath	Caba.	M	506
Emer	Cel.	F	508
Endymion	Gk.	M	511
Eros	Gk.	M	522
Europa	Gk.	F	531

	Culture	Sex	Page
Findabair	Cel.	F	568
Fraoch	Cel.	M	607
Frey	Norse	M	609
Freya	Norse	F	610
Galatea	Gk.	F	623
Ganymede	Gk.	M	627
Gaya Maretan	Pers.	M	636
Gerd	Norse	F	647
Gilgamesh	Sum.	M	656
Graces	Gk.	F	681
Gualdrada	Ital.	F	693
Guinevere	Bryth.	F	696
Hallgerda	Ice.	F	712
Havfrue	Dan.	F	732
Havmand	Dan.	M	732
Hebe	Gk.	F	739
Helen	Gk.	F	745
Helios	Gk.	M	747
Heloise	Fr.	F	749
Hnoss	Norse	F	776
Horae	Gk.	F	786
Houri	Mos.	F	795
Hulderfolk	Norse	M, F	803
Hyacinthus	Gk.	M	809
Hylas	Gk.	M	811
Hyperion	Gk.	M	812
Iodama	Gk.	F	836
Iris	Gk.	F	839
Kama	Bud., Hin.	M	905
Krishna	Hin.	M	945
Lakshmi	Hin.	F	965
Lamia	Gk.	F	967
Leilah	Pers.	F	982
Lilith	Hebr.	F	994
Maia	Gk.	F	1046
Mermaid	Euro.	F	1093
Mirabella	Eng.	F	1108
Miranda	Eng.	F	1296
Nakula	Hin.	M	1150
Nanna	Norse	F	1153
Narcissus	Gk.	M	1155
Niamh	Cel.	F	1167
Ningyo	Jap.	F	1173
Nymph	Gk.	F	1188
Odatis	Pers.	F	1194
Okuni-nushi	Jap.	M	1204

	Culture	Sex	Page
Orion	Gk.	M	1215
Otohime	Jap.	F	1202
Pandora	Gk.	F	1232
Paris	Gk.	M	1238
Penthesilea	Gk.	F	1253
Peri	Pers.		1255
Phaon	Gk.	M	1261
Phra Naret	Siam.	F	1267
Psyche	Gk.	F	1299
Puskara	Hin.	M	1305
Queen of Sheba	Hebr.	F	1311
Rakshasa	Hin.	F	1320
Rymenhild	Eng., Fr.	F	1355
Sadhadiva	Hin.	M	1360
Sandde-bryd-angel	Bryth.	M	1396
Sarah (Sarai)	Hebr.	F	1399
Sarasvati	Hin.	F	1400
Satan	Hebr-Christ.	M	1402
Semiramis	Assyr.	F	1415
Sepd	Egy.	M	1417
Siegfried	Germ.	M	1448
Si She	Chin.	F	1459
Sri	Hin.	F	1487
Susanna	Hebr.	F	1512
Swanhild	Germ.	F	1517
Sylph	Med.	F	1521
Tadzio	Germ.	M	1524
Tammuz	Baby.	M	1530
Thalia	Gk.	F	1551
Tilottama	Hin.	F	1574
Tipherath	Caba.	M	1575
Veele	Serb.	F	1643
Venus	Rom.	F	1644
Wunschelwybere	Germ.	F	1693
Yama-uba	Jap.	F	1700
Ye-hime	Jap.	F	1202
Yu Nu	Chin.	F	1424
Zairivairi	Pers.	M	1715
Zmay	Serb.	M	1722

BEGGAR (ALSO SEE POVERTY)

	Culture	Sex	Page
Guy of Warwick	Eng.	M	700
Irus (Arnaeus)	Gk.	M	841
Odysseus	Gk.	M	1196
Penelophon (Zenelophon)	Eng.	F	1252
Saint Alexis	Christ.	M	1362

Beggar (cont.)	Culture	Sex	Page
Sukuyan	Trinidad	F	1505

BENEVOLENCE (SEE MERCY, VIRTUE)

BETRAYED

Aeetes	Gk.	M	37
Agamemnon	Gk.	M	44
Apollo	Gk.	M	110
Ariadne	Gk.	F	123
Arsinoe	Gk.	F	130
Brynhild	Norse	F	253
Christ	Christ.	M	330
Curoi MacDaire	Cel.	M	398
Cycnus	Gk.	M	401
Deidamia	Gk.	F	426
Deiphobus	Gk.	M	426
Enipeus	Gk.	M	511
Fergus mac Roich	Cel.	M	561
Finn mac Coul	Cel.	M	570
Gorlois	Bryth.	M	679
Hagar	Hebr.	F	707
Iole	Gk.	F	836
Lamia	Gk.	F	967
Leda	Gk.	F	980
Llew Llaw Gyffes	Bryth.	M	1005
Minos	Gk.	M	1107
Naoise	Cel.	M	1154
Nisus	Gk.	M	1176
Octavius	Rom.	F	1194
Palamedes	Gk.	M	1227
Procis	Gk.	F	1294
Samson	Hebr.	M	1394
Siegfried	Germ.	M	1448
Sigurd	Norse	M	1451
Suinin	Jap.	M	1504
Tahmurath	Pers.	M	1525
Ushnach Clan	Cel.	M	1631

BETRAYER

Ariadne	Gk.	F	123
Blathnat	Cel.	F	225
Blodeuwedd	Bryth.	F	226
Brunhild	Germ.	F	253
Brynhild	Norse	F	253
Clytemnestra	Gk.	F	351
Conchobar	Cel.	M	364

	Culture	Sex	Page
Deianeira	Gk.	F	425
Delilha	Hebr.	F	427
Eriphyle	Gk.	F	520
Helen	Gk.	F	745
Helenus	Gk.	M	746
Ishtar	Assyr-Baby.	F	844
Medea	Gk.	F	1082
Rhiannon	Bryth.	F	1336
Sahobime	Jap.	F	1361
Scylla	Gk.	F	1409
Semiramis	Assyr.	F	1415
Tyro	Gk.	F	1618

BEWITCHMENT (SEE MAGIC)

BLINDNESS (BLIND)

Dhritarashtra	Hin.	M	439
Hoder	Norse	M	778
Kui	N. Zeal.	F	949
Mi-saru	Jap.	M	1118
Mordu	Bryth.	M	1123
Oedipus	Gk.	M	1198
Oryithus and Crambis	Gk.	M-M	1264
Phineus	Gk.	M	1264
Plutus	Gk.	M	1280
Polydectus	Gk.	M	1264
Polydorus	Gk.	M	1264
Polyphemus	Gk.	M	1284
Shabriri	Hebr.	M	1428
Thamyris	Gk.	M	1551
Tiresias	Gk.	M/A	1576
Tobit	Hebr.	M	1583
Zedekiah	Hebr.	M	1717

BODY USED IN CREATION

Andalma-Muus	Tatar	M	93
Angoi	Borneo	M	96
Apsu	Sum.	M	115
Areop-enap	Nauru	M	120
Awonawilona	Zuni	A	162
Cipactli	Mex.	M	1312
Gaya Maretan	Pers.	M	636
Geush Urvan	Pers.		652
Giaiael	Taino	M	653
Hahness	Chinook	M	708
Kingu	Baby.	M	932

Body used in creation (cont.)	Culture	Sex	Page
Kvaser	Norse	M	954
Louquo	Carib.	M	1016
Manzashiri	Mong.	M	1062
Ophion	Gk.	M	1211
P'an Ku	Chin.	M/A	1233
Purusa	Hin.	A	1305
Ra	Egy.	M/A	1314
Tiamat	Baby.	F	1570
Tuna	Poly.	M	1607
Ur-kuh	Pers.		1629
Ymir	Norse	M	1708
Zagreus	Cretan	M	1715

BOUNDARIES

Agyieus	Gk.	M	51
Herkeios	Gk.	M	1719
Horios	Gk.	M	1719
Jupiter Terminus	Rom.	M	897
Numa Pompilius	Rom.	M	1185
Silvanus	Rom.	M	1453
Terminus	Rom.	M	1547

BRAVERY (SEE VALOR)
BREEZE (SEE WIND)
BUFFOONERY (SEE REVELRY)
BURIED HEAD (SEE PROTECTOR)
CANDOR (SEE VIRTUE)

CANNIBALISM (ALSO SEE CHILD DEVOURER)

Atreus	Gk.	M	153
Baba-yaga	Rus.	F	168
Bilu	Burm.	M	211
Bugbear	Euro.		258
Bunyip	Aus.		261
Dalhan	Arab.	M	409
Enim	Gnostic	M, F	509
Glaucus	Gk.	M	662
Goblin	Euro.	M	666
Harpaluke	Gk.	F	728
Jezinky	Slav.	F	879
Kai-tangata	Maori	M	1674
Kholumolumo	Bantu	M	925
Khosodam	Sib.	F	925
Koyorowen	Aus.	M	944
Kui	N. Zeal.	F	949

	Culture	Sex	Page
Kurriwilban (Yaho)	Aus.	F	953
Laestrygones	Gk.	M	963
Lamme	Sum.	F	968
Lycaon	Gk.	M	1027
Makutu	N. Zeal.	M	1048
Minotaur	Gk.	M	1107
Nona	Chath. Is.		1539
Pisacas	Hin.		1275
Polyphemus	Gk.	M	1284
Punegusse	Sib.	M	1301
Rakshasa	Hin.	M, F	1320
Shuten Doji	Jap.	M	1444
Sneneik	W.U.S. Ind.	F	1470
Tantalus	Gk.	M	1533
Taranis	Cel.	F	1534
Tauni-kapi-kapi	N. Guin.	M	1538
Tereus	Gk.	M	1546
Thyestes	Gk.	M	1569
Tsonoqoa	N.A.I.	F	1604
Tzitzimime	Mex.	F	1618
Ubyr	Fin-Ug.	M	1619
Ulala	Haida	M	1621
Unas	Egy.	M	1623
Wanga	E. Afr.	M	1664
Whaitari	Maori	F	1674
Windigo	Algon.	M	1683
Xipe Totec	Mex.	M	1696
Zagreus	Cretan	M	1715

CARRION EATER

Buso	Poly.	M	262
Ker	Gk.	F	917

CATACLYSM (SEE UNIVERSAL RUIN)
CELESTIAL (SEE SKY)
CHANCE (SEE FORTUNE)

CHASTITY (VIRGINITY)

Aemilia	Rom.	F	40
Ann	Christ.	F	99
Artemis	Gk.	F	131
Astraea	Gk.	F	145
Athena	Gk.	F	150
Ayesha	Mos.	F	164
Baau	Phoen., Sum.	F	168
Belit-Ilani	Sum.	F	197

Chastity (cont.)	Culture	Sex	Page
Belit-Itani	Assy-Baby.	F	198
Benedict	Christ.	M	202
Bona Dea	Rom.	F	234
Britomart	Eng.	F	250
Britomartis	Gk.	F	250
Cailleach	Scot.	F	269
Camilla	Rom.	F	281
Chaabu	Sem.	F	307
Chalchiutlicue	Mex.	F/A	308
Chasca	Inca	F	316
Chimalman	Mex.	F	325
Daeira	Gk.	F	404
Diana	Rom.	F	441
Dughdhova	Zoro.	F	1734
Fatima	Mos.	F	552
Fortuna Virgo (Muliebris)	Rom.	F	596
Galahad	Bryth.	M	622
Gefjon	Norse	F	637
Graces	Gk.	F	681
Houri	Mos.	F	795
Ilmatar	Fin.	F	824
Io	Gk.	F	835
Ishtar	Assyr-Baby.	F	844
Isis	Egy.	F	845
Juno Caelestis	Rom.	F	895
Leilah	Pers.	F	982
Licinia	Rom.	F	991
Lucretia	Rom.	F	1021
Maire	Cel.	F	1047
Makh	Assyr-Baby.	F	1048
Mary	Christ.	F	1072
Maya	Hin., Bud.	F	1080
Metsanneitsyt	Fin.	F	1097
Muskrat	Algon.	F	1140
Nana	Sum.	F	1152
Nanna	Norse	F	1153
Neith	Lib., Egy.	F	1161
Nin Ella	Baby.	F	1172
Ninhursag	Sum.	F	1173
Ninlil	Sum.	F	1173
Ninmah	Baby.	F	1173
Ninsikilla	Sem.	F	1042
Nu	Chin.	F	1184
Nu	Egyp.	A	1184
Padmasambhava	Tib.	M	1225
Parsifal	Germ.	M	1239

	Culture	Sex	Page
Parthenos	Gk.	F	1240
Parvati	Hin.	F	1241
Persephone	Gk.	F	1257
Proserpina	Rom.	F	1296
Rana-Neidda	Lapp	F	1322
Rhea Silvia	Rom.	F	1335
Rishyacringa	Hin.	M	1341
Rose of Sharon	Christ.	F	1349
Sabina	Ital.	F	1357
San Ch'ing	Chin.	M	1395
Shulamite	Hebr.	F	1444
Silvia	Rom.	F	1454
Sita	Hin.	F	1460
Sylph	Med.	M, F	1521
Tai Yuan	Chin.	A	1527
Tanit	Carth.	F	1532
Taurica	Gk.	F	1538
Uatlan	Kiche	F	1619
Uazit	Egy.	F	1619
Vila	Serb-Croa.	F	1650
Virgin Mary	Christ.	F	1653
Virgin of Jasper	Chin.	F	1653
Virginensis	Rom.	F	896

CHILDBIRTH

	Culture	Sex	Page
Ajysit	Sib.	F	58
Al	Pers.	M, F	60
Anahit	Arm.	F	90
Anjea	Aus.		99
Arianrhod	Cel.	F	123
Artemis	Gk.	F	131
Bast	Egy.	F	185
Befind	Cel.	F	195
Bes	Egy.	M	205
Bubastis	Egy.	F	254
Carmenta	Rom.	F	291
Chalchiutlicue	Mex.	F	308
Chang Sien	Chin.	M	311
Chthonius	Gk.	M	334
Ch'uang-kung	Chin.	M	335
Ch'uang-mu	Chin.	F	335
Cuichi Supai	Ecuador		396
Deverra	Rom.	F	+
Dharti Mai	Hin.	F	439
Diana	Rom.	F	441
Dzajaga	Mong.	F	481

	Culture	Sex	Page
Egeria	Rom.	F	491
Eileithyia	Gk.	F	496
Epet (Tueret, Ueret)	Egy.	F	514
Frigg	Norse	F	612
Harinegamesi	Hin.	M	726
Hecate	Gk.	F	740
Hekt	Egy.	F	745
Hera	Gk.	F	752
Horae	Gk.	F	786
Ilithyiae	Gk.	F	823
Intercidona	Rom.	F	+
Israfil	Mos.	M	847
Itoki	Nica.	F	849
Itzcuinan	Mex.	F	850
Ix-chel	Mex.	F	852
Jaik-khan	Sib.	M	861
Jajutsi	Mong.	M	861
Jingu (birth control)	Jap.	F	880
Jordegumma	Swed.	F	887
Juksakka	Lapp	F	894
Juno	Rom.	F	895
Khensu	Egy.	M	923
Khotun	Yakut	F	925
Kildisin	Fin-Ug.	F	927
Kwan	Siamese		955
Kwan-yin	Chin.	F/A	955
Kybai-khotun	Yakut	F	956
Lamastu	Sum.	F	966
Levana	Rom.	F	988
Lochia	Gk.	F	1007
Lucina	Rom.	F	1020
Luonnotar	Fin.	F	1025
Madderakka	Lapp	F	1035
Mater Matuta	Ital.	F	1074
Meskhenet	Egy.	F	1094
Moakkibat, Al	Mos.		70
Mylitta	Chald.	F	1142
Nannar	Baby.	M/A	1153
Nemesis	Gk.	F	1162
Ninhursag	Sum.	F	1173
Ninkarraka	Baby.	F	1173
Ninsun	Baby.	F	1174
Nintu	Sum.	F	1174
Oho-iwa-daimyojin	Jap.	M	1202
Picumnus	Rom.	M	1269
Pilumnus	Rom.	M	1269

Childbirth (cont.)	Culture	Sex	Page
Postverta	Rom.	F	1288
Prorsa	Rom.	F	1296
Puah	Hebr.	F	1439
Quetzalcoatl	Mex.	M	1312
Rodjenice	Croa.	F	1344
Sarakka	Lapp	F	1399
Sarpanitum	Baby.	F	1401
Sasthi	Hin.	F	1401
Sekhet	Egy.	F	1414
Shekinah	Caba.	F	1432
Shen Mu	Chin.	F	1434
Shiphrah	Hebr.	F	1439
Suratan-tura	Chuvash	M	1511
Tanit	Carth.	F	1532
Ta-urt	Egy.	F	1538
Thepla	Arm.	M	1554
Tonacacihuatl	Mex.	F	1586
Ubugami	Jap.	M	1619
Uksakka	Lapp	F	1621
Upis	Gk.	F	+
Vagtanus	Rom.	M	1633
Virbius	Rom.	M	1652
Yamano-kami	Jap.		1699
Yohualticetl	Anahuac	F	1709

CHILD DEVOURER (ALSO SEE CANNIBALISM)			
Cronus	Gk.	M	384
Eresichthon	Gk.	M	518
Hariti	Hin.	F	726
Kishibojin	Jap.	F	933
Mary	Hebr.	F	1072
Meulen	Braz.	M	1097
Moloch	Carth.	M	1115
Narwoje	Papuan		1156
Saturn	Rom.	M	1403
Tereus	Gk.	M	1546

CHILD IMMOLATED OR SLAIN			
Astyanax	Gk.	M	145
Bacab	Mex.	M	170
Conlaoch	Cel.	M	367
Demophoon	Gk.	M	432
Dryas	Gk.	M	473
Dylan	Cel.	M	480
Gwern	Cel.	M	701

Child immolated (cont.)	Culture	Sex	Page
Gwion Bach	Cel.	M	701
Hadubrand	Germ.	M	770
Hippolytus	Gk.	M	773
Iphigenia	Gk.	F	838
Isaac	Hebr.	M	841
Itylus	Gk.	M	849
Itys	Gk.	M	850
Jephthah's Daughter	Hebr.	F	872
Learchus	Gk.	M	149
Lugaid	Cel.	M	1023
Meleager	Gk.	M	1085
Nyctimus	Gk.	M	1187
Pelops	Gk.	M	1251
Pentheus	Gk.	M	1253
Pleisthenes	Gk.	M	153
Randver	Norse	M	1322
Scamandrius	Gk.	M	1405
Sinfjotle	Norse	M	1457
Suhrab	Pers.	M	1504
Tenes	Gk.	M	1545

CHILD IMMOLATOR OR SLAYER			
Abraham	Hebr.	M	17
Aedon	Gk.	F	37
Agamemnon	Gk.	M	44
Agave	Gk.	F	46
Agelaus	Gk.	M	48
Ahaz	Hebr.	M	52
Alcmene	Gk.	F	65
Althea	Gk.	F	77
Amylion	Fr.	M	89
Arianrhod	Cel.	F	123
Arthur	Bryth.	M	132
Athamas	Gk.	M	149
Atreus	Gk.	M	153
Atthis	Gk.	F	154
Brutus, Lucius Junius	Rom.	M	253
Cerridwen	Bryth.	F	305
Conall	Cel.	M	363
Cuchulainn	Cel.	M	393
Erechtheus	Gk.	M	518
Finn mac Coul	Cel.	M	570
Giaia	Taino	M	653
Gudrun	Norse	F	694
Harpaluke	Gk.	F	728
Hecuba	Gk.	F	741

	Culture	Sex	Page
Heracles	Gk.	M	752
Herod	Christ.	M	763
Hildebrand	Germ.	M	770
Idomeneus	Gk.	M	820
Ino	Gk.	F	833
Ishtar	Assyr-Baby.	F	844
Jephthah	Hebr.	M	872
Jormunrek	Norse	M	887
Kamsa	Hin.	M	907
Kinharigan	Borneo	M	932
Lycaon	Gk.	M	1027
Lycurgus	Gk.	M	1028
Magna Mater	Phryg.	F	1040
Medea	Gk.	F	1082
Philomela	Gk.	F	1263
Procne	Gk.	F	1294
Rustam	Pers.	M	1355
Salmoneus	Gk.	M	1391
Sam	Pers.	M	1392
Seuechorus	Sum.	M	656
Signy	Norse	M	1451
Silvia (Rhea Silvia)	Rom.	F	1454
Tantalus	Gk.	M	1533
Theseus	Gk.	M	1554
Uranus	Gk.	M	1627

CHIVALRY (SEE NOBILITY)

CLOUD (ALSO SEE MOISTURE)

	Culture	Sex	Page
Aebh	Cel.	F	37
Aed	Cel.	M	37
Aegis	Gk.	F	38
Ahi	Hin.	M	52
Ahmed, Prince	Arab.	M	53
Alcyone	Gk.	F	65
Alcyoneus	Gk.	M	65
Aloidae	Gk.	M	71
Apsaras	Bud.	F	115
Ardan	Cel.	M	1154
Bayard	Med.	M	187
Benkei	Jap.	M	202
Cherub	Hebr.	M	319
Chiron	Gk.	M	327
Chokanipok	Algon.	M	328
Chrysomallus	Gk.	M	334
Conn	Cel.	M	564
Cycnus	Gk.	M	401

Cloud (cont.)	Culture	Sex	Page
Fenrir	Norse	M	560
Fiachra	Cel.	M	564
Fionnuala	Cel.	F	571
Freya	Norse	F	610
Gandarewa	Pers.	M	625
Gandharva	Hin.	M	626
Giolla Deacair	Cel.	M	659
Golden Fleece	Gk.		673
Gottfried	Germ.	M	1009
Heidrun	Norse	F	743
Hesperides	Gk.	F	765
Houssain	Arab.	M	1038
Hyades	Gk.	F	809
Iphicles	Gk.	M	837
Iztac Mixcoatl	Mex.	M	854
Japheth	Hebr.	M	1177
Lichas	Gk.	M	991
Luchta	Cel.	M	1020
Lung-Wang	Chin.	M	1025
Mixcoatl	Mex.	M	1113
Narwoje	Papuan		1156
Navagvas	Hin.	M	1158
Nephele	Gk.	F	1163
Paravataksha	Hin.	M	1237
Parjanya	Hin.	M/A	1238
Philomela	Gk.	F	1263
Pleiades	Gk.	F	1279
Prsni	Hin.	F	1297
Rgvedic	Hin.	M	1335
Sao-ts'ing-niang	Chin.	F	1398
Sarsaok	Pers.		1401
Shem	Hebr.	M	1177
Shen Mu	Chin.	F	1434
Sisiutl	Kwakiutl	M	1459
Stymphalides	Gk.		1502
Tai Shan	Chin.	F	1526
Taygete	Gk.	F	1539
Thrud	Norse	F	1567
Toyo-kumo	Jap.	M	1592
Typhon	Gk.	M	1617
William of Cloudeslee	Eng.	M	1680
Wunschelwybere	Germ.	F	1693
Yaai	Van. Is.		1697
Yun Chung Chun	Chin.	M	1713

CLOWN (SEE FOOL)

	Culture	Sex	Page
COLD (SEE FROST)			
COMIC (SEE REVELRY)			
CONFLAGRATION (SEE UNIVERSAL RUIN)			
CONSORT OF FEMALE KIN			
Adon	Phoen.	M	33
Adonis	Gk.	M	34
Arthur	Bryth.	M	132
Athar	Sem.	M	150
Attis	Phryg.	M	154
Ba-neb-tettu	Egy.	M	764
Bata	Egy.	M	186
Brahma	Hin.	M	240
Bres	Cel.	M	1023
Conchobar	Cel.	M	364
Dumuzi	Sum.	M	476
Dyaus	Hin.	M	479
Elatha	Cel.	M	498
Enlil	Baby., Sum.	M	512
Eochaid Airem	Cel.	M	513
Erebus	Gk.	M	518
Eshmun	Phoen.	M	525
Faunus	Rom.	M	552
Frey	Norse	M	609
Fu Hsi	Chin.	M	615
Gwydion	Bryth.	M	702
Haoshyangha	Pers.	M	723
Herod Antipas	Christ.	M	763
Hyperion	Gk.	M	812
Iapetus	Gk.	M	816
Ioskeha	Huron	M	837
Izanagi	Jap.	M	853
Jupiter	Rom.	M	896
Karu	Jap.	M	911
Kingu	Baby.	M	932
Klumenos	Gk.	M	728
Labraid	Cel.	M	960
Lamerock	Bryth.	M	967
Lan-yein	Burm.	M	972
Lil	Sum.	M	994
Lothar	Cel.	M	1023
Lugaid	Cel.	M	1023
Mars	Rom.	M	1069
Mashya	Pers.	M	1072
Melkarth	Phoen.	M	1086

Consort of female kin (cont.)	Culture	Sex	Page
Nar	Cel.	M	1023
Nareau	Gil. Is.	M	1156
Nesu	Sem.	M	1042
Oceanus	Gk.	M	1193
Oedipus	Gk.	M	1198
Oho-to-no-ji	Jap.	M	1202
Omo-daru	Jap.	M	1208
Osiris	Egy.	M	1218
Sampsa	Fin-Ug.	M	1394
Shu	Egy.	M	1443
Shulpae	Baby.	M	1444
Sigmund	Norse	M	1449
Surya	Hin.	M	1511
Taaroa	Poly.	M	1522
Tammuz	Baby.	M	1530
Tane	Poly.	M	1531
Tangaroa	Maori	M	1531
Thyestes	Gk.	M	1569
Tii	Marq.	M	1573
Tlaloc Tecutli	Mex.	M	1581
Tsuki-yomi	Jap.	M	1604
Uhiji-ni	Jap.	M	1620
Wigan	Philip.	M	1679
Yima	Pers.	M	1707
Zeus	Gk.	M	1719
CONSORT OF MALE KIN			
Amaterasu	Jap.	F	81
A-mong	Burm.	F	972
Aphrodite	Gk.	F	108
Arianrhod	Cel.	F	123
Aruru	Sum.	F	133
Astarte	Phoen.	F	144
Ate	As. Min.	F	149
Aya-kashikone	Jap.	F	163
Baau	Phoen., Sum.	F	168
Belili	Sum.	F	197
Belit-sheri	Assyr.	F	198
Bellona	Rom.	F	200
Berenice	Egy.	F	204
Bugan	Philip.	F	258
Ceto	Gk.	F	306
Chalchiutlicue	Mex.	F	308
Clothru	Gk.	F	349
Cybele	Phryg.	F	400
Dechtire	Cel.	F	423

	Culture	Sex	Page
Eri	Cel.	F	519
Ess	Cel.	F	525
Euryphassa	Gk.	F	532
Freya	Norse	F	610
Frigg	Norse	F	612
Guzhak	Pers.	F	723
Gwyar	Bryth.	F	702
Harpaluke	Gk.	F	728
Hera	Gk.	F	752
Heru-pa-kaut	Egy.	F	764
Hina	Poly.	F	771
Hine-ahu-one	Poly.	F	772
Hine-itau-ira (Hine-nui)	Poly.	F	772
Ila	Hin.	F	823
Innini	Sum.	F	832
Ishtar	Assyr-Baby.	F	844
Isis	Egy.	F	845
Izanami	Jap.	F	853
Jocasta	Gk.	F	882
Jord	Norse	F	887
Juno	Rom.	F	895
Kobine	Gil. Is.	F	1156
Lumimu-ut	Indo.	F	1024
Magna Mater	Phryg.	F	1040
Mama	Baby.	F	1050
Mama Ogllo	Inca	F	1051
Mashyoi	Pers.	F	1072
Morgause	Bryth.	F	1123
Myrrha	Gk.	F	1142
Nekhebet	Egy.	F	1161
Nephthys	Egy.	F	1163
Ninlil	Sum.	F	1173
Ninsikilla	Sem.	F	1042
Nu Kua	Chin.	F	1185
Nyx	Gk.	F	1188
Oh-to-no-be	Jap.	F	1202
Papa	Maori	F	1235
Perdix	Gk.	A	1254
Saho-bime	Jap.	F	1361
Sarah	Hebr.	F	1399
Shuhiji	Jap.	F	1444
Signy	Norse	F	1451
Tefenet	Egy.	F	1541
Tethys	Gk.	F	1548
Theia	Gk.	F	1553
Tiamat	Baby.	F	1570

Consort of male kin (cont.)	Culture	Sex	Page
Yimeh	Pers.	F	1707

CONSTELLATION (SEE ASTRAL)
CONTEMPLATION (SEE MEDITATION)

CONTENTMENT

Aglaos	Gk.	M	48
Hotei	Jap.	M	794
Maitreya	Bud.	M	1047
Mi-li	Chin.	M	1102
Pou-t'ai	Chin.	M	1290

CONTENTION (SEE STRIFE)

CORRELATIVES (COUPLINGS, TWINS.
* INDICATES THEY ARE ENEMIES)

AA	Used in Art	M-M	9
Aac and Coh*	Mex.	M-M	9
Aaron & Moses	Hebr.	M-M	10
Abaangui & Zaguaguayu	Para.	M-M	11
Acarnan & Amphoterus	Gk.	M-M	22
Achilles & Patroclus	Gk.	M-M	25
Aegyptus & Danaus	Gk.	M-M	39
Aeson & Pelias*	Gk.	M-M	42
Agamedes & Trophonius	Gk.	M-M	44
Aglaopheme & Thelxiepia	Gk.	F-F	1458
Agnar & Geirrod*	Norse	M-M	49
Agras (god of twins)	Fin-Ug.	M	51
Ahans	Hin.	M-M	52
Ahayuta Achi	Zuni	M-M	52
Airya & Tura*	Pers.	M-M	57
Akambou & Yris	Carib.	M-M	59
Alcis	Norse	A-A	64
Aleyn & Mot	Sem.	M-M	67
Aloidae	Gk.	M-M	71
Amphion & Zethus	Gk.	M-M	88
Amyclaean Brothers	Gk.	M-M	89
Anakes	Gk.	M-M	90
Aokeu & Ake*	Poly.	M-M	106
Apocatequil & Piguero*	Inca	M-M	109
Apollo & Artemis	Gk.	M-F	110
Apollo & Hermes	Gk.	M-M	110
Arikute & Ariconte*	Braz.	M-M	124
Artegal & Elidure	Bryth.	M-M	130
Ashim-Bethel	Sem.	M-F	139
Asmund & Asvitus*	Norse	M-M	141

	Culture	Sex	Page
Asvins	Hin.	M-M	146
Atreus & Thyestes	Gk.	M-M	153
Auxo & Hegemone	Gk.	F-F	681
Axieros (Axiocersa)	Gk.	M-M	163
Babes in the Woods	Folk.	M-F	302
Baldur & Loki*	Norse	M-M	174
Balin & Balan*	Bryth.	M-M	175
Belenus & Brennius	Bryth.	M-M	197
Belus & Agenor	Gk.	M-M	201
Biton & Cleobis	Gk.	M-M	220
Bootes & Erectheus	Gk.	M-M	236
Bride & Bridegroom	Hebr.	F-M	248
Byat Twe & Byat Ta	Ind-Chin.	M-M	1445
Cacus & Caca	Ital.	M-F	265
Cain & Abel*	Hebr.	M-M	269
Calais & Zetes	Gk.	M-M	272
Carpo & Thallo	Gk.	F-F	786
Castor & Pollux	Gk.	M-M	295
Caut & Cautopat	Pers.	M-M	300
CC	Used in Art	M-M	300
Chanun & Woi-shun	Burm.	M-M	312
Charybdis & Scylla	Gk.	F-F	316
Ch'en Ch'i & Cheng Lung	Chin.	M-M	318
Ch'in Shu-pao & Yu Ch'ih Ching-te	Chin.	M-M	326
Christ & Sophia	Christ.	M-F	1475
Chrysaor & Pegasus	Gk.	M-M	334
Cleta & Phaenna	Gk.	F-F	681
Coatrischic & Guatauva	Zuni	M-M	352
Conn & Fiachra	Cel.	M-M	367
Damon & Pythias	Rom.	M-M	410
Dasra & Nasatya	Hin.	M-M	416
Dioscuri	Gk.	M-M	449
Dylan & Llew Llaw	Bryth.	M-M	480
Eber & Eremon	Cel.	M-M	488
Electryon & Sthenelus*	Gk.	M-M	1494
Ephialtes & Otus	Gk.	M-M	515
Eros & Anteros*	Gk.	M-M	522
Etalak & Latarak	Sum.	M-M	1174
Eteocles & Polynices*	Gk.	M-M	527
Evnissyen & Nissyen*	Bryth.	M-M	536
Fat the Flasher & Tan the Dawn	Chin.	M-M	550
Fenja & Menja	Norse	F-F	560
Fjaler & Galar	Norse	M-M	578
Florismart & Roland	Carol.	M-M	585

	Culture	Sex	Page
Fravak & Fravakain	Pers.	M-F	608
Friuch & Rucht*	Cel.	M-M	613
Gemini	Rom.	M-M	643
Gilgamesh & Eabani	Baby.	M-M	656
Glaucus & Sarpedon	Gk.	M-M	662
Gluskap & Malsum*	Algon.	M-M	664
God & Sophia	Gnostic	M-F	1475
Gog & Magog*	Bryth.	M-M	669
Grettir & Illuga*	Ice.	M-M	374a
Grettir & Thorir*	Ice.	M-M	374a
Gwalchmei & Mordred*	Bryth.	M-M	700
Gwydion & Gilvaethwy	Bryth.	M-M	702
Gwyn & Gwyrthur*	Bryth.	M-M	703
Habil & Jumella	Arab.	M-F	269
Hadding & Gudhorn*	Norse	M-M	705
Hahgwehdiyu & Hahgweh-daetgah*	Iroq.	M-M	708
Haitsi-Aibeb & Gama*	Hotten.	M-M	711
Ham & Shem*	Hebr.	M-M	713
Hamlet & Laertes*	Eng.	M-M	714
Haoshyangha & Guzak	Pers.	M-F	723
Hastshehogan & Hastshey-alti*	Nav.	M-M	730
Helen & Clytemnestra	Gk.	F-F	745
Heracles & Eurystheus*	Gk.	M-M	752
Heracles & Iphicles	Gk.	M-M	752
Heracles & Philoctetes	Gk.	M-M	752
Heracles & Poeas	Gk.	M-M	752
Hesperus & Heosphorus	Gk.	M-M	765
Hidimva & Surpanakha	Hin.	M-F	1511
Ho-Ho	Chin.	M-M	779
Horus & Set*	Egy.	M-M	792
Hrothgar & Helgi	Ang-Sax.	M-M	798
Hun Ahpu & Xbalanque	Kiche	M-M	806
Hus Brothers	Wintun	M-M	808
Hypnus & Thanatos	Gk.	M-M	813
Hyuki & Bil	Norse	M-F	814
Idas & Lynceus (The Apharetidae)	Gk.	M-M	818
Ihoh	Caba.	M-F	822
Ioskeha & Tawiscara*	Huron	M-M	837
Isaac & Ishmael*	Hebr.	M-M	841
Ishtar & Shamash	Assyr-Baby.	F-M	844
Isis & Nephthys	Egy.	F-F	845
Jacob & Esau*	Hebr.	M-M	858
Kabibonokka & Shawano	Algon.	M-M	900

	Culture	Sex	Page
Kabil & Aclima	Mos.	M-F	269
Kabil & Habil*	Mos.	M-M	269
Kastor & Polydeukes	Gk.	M-M	912
Keresaspa & Thraetaona	Pers.	M-M	918
Kettu & Misharu	Baby.	M-M	1110
Kowwituma & Watsusi	Zuni	M-M	944
Kukumatz & Tochipa	Yuman	M-M	950
Laksmana & Satrughna	Hin.	M-M	1321
Lempo & Sukkamielli	Fin.	M-F	982
Llew Llaw & Gronw Pebyr*	Bryth.	M-M	1005
Lucifer & Michael*	Christ.	M-M	1020
Luxman & Rama	Hin.	M-M	374a
Maasewe & Uyuuyewe	Sia	M-M	1031
Mahaitiac & Tsakakaitiac	Hidat.	M-M	1043
Manabhozho & Chichiabos*	Algon.	M-M	1054
Manabush & Wolf*	Men.	M-M	1054
Mashu & Mashtu	Baby.	M-M	1072
Mashya & Mashyoi	Pers.	M-F	1072
Maudgalyayana & Sariputra	Bud.	M-M	1077
Messou & Lynx*	Pota.	M-M	1054
Michabo & Chokanipok*	Algon.	M-M	1098
Michael & Satan*	Christ.	M-M	1377
Misharu & Kittu	Phoen.	M-M	1110
Misor & Sydyk	Phoen.	M-M	1521
Mitra & Varuna	Hin.	M-M	1112
Modi & Magni	Norse	M-M	1114
Monker & Nakir	Mos.	M-M	1117
Mors & Somnus	Rom.	M-M	1125
Nakula & Sadhadiva	Hin.	M-M	1150
Nasatya & Dasra	Hin.	M-M	1156
Nayanezgani & Thobadzistshini	Nav.	M-M	1159
Neleus & Pelias*	Gk.	M-M	1161
Ningirsu & Ninsubur	Sum.	M-M	1174
Ninsubur & Ningishzida	Sum.	M-M	1173
Nipinoukhe & Pipounoukhe	Algon.	M-M	1175
Nowutset & Utset*	Sia	F-F	1513
Numitor & Amulius*	Rom.	M-M	1185
Nynnyaw & Peibaw	Cel.	M-M	1188
Ohousu & Wousu	Jap.	M-M	1202
Orestes & Pylades	Gk.	M-M	1214
Ormuzd & Ahriman*	Zoro.	M-M	1216
Oryithus & Crambis	Gk.	M-M	1264
Osiris & Isis	Egy.	M-F	1218
Osiris & Set.*	Egy.	M-M	1218
Owain & Mabon	Bryth.	M-M	1221
Pachacamac & Con*	Inca	M-M	1224

	Culture	Sex	Page
Pachacamac & Vichama*	Inca	M-M	1648
Palici	Ital.	M-M	1228
Pelethites & Cherethites	Hebr.	M-M	1249
Peleus & Telamon	Gk.	M-M	1250
Perez & Zarah	Hebr.	M-M	1716
Phaethon & Cycnus	Gk.	M-M	401
Philandrus & Phylacides	Gk.	M-M	1262
Picumnus & Pilumnus	Rom.	M-M	1269
Polydectus & Polydorus	Gk.	M-M	1264
Pookonghoya & Balongahoya	Hopi	M-M	1286
Proetus & Acrisius*	Gk.	M-M	1295
Prometheus & Epimetheus*	Gk.	M-M	1295
Pyrocles & Musidorus	Eng.	M-M	1307
Qat & Marawa*	Mel.	M-M	1309
Quetzalcoatl & Tezcatlipoca*	Mex.	M-M	1312
Rama & Bharata	Hin.	M-M	374a
Rehoboam & Asa*	Hebr.	M-M	1331
Rigsbumo & Srogbdag	Tib.	F-M	1339
Rinaldo & Orlando*	Ital.	M-M	1339
Roland & Oliver*	Carol.	M-M	1345
Romulus & Remus*	Rom.	M-M	1346
Satanael & Christ*	Bulg.	M-M	1402
Shen Shu & Yu Lu	Chin.	M-M	1434
Shesemtet & Shesmu	Egy.	F-M	1435
Shiphrah & Puah	Hebr.	F-F	1439
Shu & Tefenet	Egy.	M-F	1444
Shu Yu & Yu Lei	Chin.	M-M	1445
Shwe Pyin Nyi-Naung	Ind-Chin.	M-M	1445
Siegmund & Sieglind	Germ.	M-F	302
Silenus & Midas	Gk.	M-M	1453
Simeon & Levi	Hebr.	M-M	1455
Simurgh & Camrosh	Pers.	M-M	1456
Siyakmak & Nashak	Pers.	M-F	1463
Solomon & Asmodeus*	Hebr.	M-M	1472
Solomon & Shulamite	Hebr.	M-F	1472
Spaul & Queenah*	Cowich.	M-M	1480
Spenjaghrya & Vazishta*	Pers.	M-M	1481
Spenta Mainyu & Ahriman*	Zoro.	M-M	1481
Sunawavi & Coyote (or Wolf)*	Ute	M-M	1509
Sunda & Upasunda	Hin.	M-M	1509
Sunna & Nanna	Norse	F-F	1510
Tagaro the Wise & Tagaro the Fool*	Banks Is.	M-M	1524
Tagaro & Suqematua*	New Heb.	M-M	1524
Tangaroa & Vatea*	Herv. Is.	M-M	1532
Tazh & Tazhak	Pers.	M-F	1539

	Culture	Sex	Page
Theseus & Pirithous	Gk.	M-M	1554
Thierry & Guy of Warwick	Eng.	M-M	700
Tigranes & Tigranuki	Arm.	M-F	1573
To-kabinana & To-Karvuvu*	Mel.	M-M	1584
Tow & Tow-us-tussin*	Haida	M-M	1592
Triptolemus & Demophoon	Gk.	M-M	1598
Trung-trac & Trung-nhi	Ind-Chin.	F-F	1602
Tsui Goab & Gaunab*	Hotten.	M-M	1604
Tsunuguhi & Ikuguhi	Jap.	M-F	1604
Tyltyl & Mytyl	Belg.	M-F	1144
Uhiji & Shuhiji	Jap.	M-F	1620
Umashiashikabi & Amenotoko	Jap.	M-F	1527
Umunlua & Umunesiga*	Sum.	M-M	1623
Vali & Vidar	Norse	M-M	1636
Vohu Manah & Aka Manah*	Zoro.	M-M	1657
Votan & Yalahau*	Mex.	M-M	1658
Wabun & Kabun	Algon.	M-M	1660
Yab-Yum	Bud.	M-F	1697
Yama-Yami	Hin.	M-F	1699
Yang-Um	Kor.	M-F	1700
Yang-Yin	Chin.	M-F	1700
Yappan & Yaotl	Mex.	M-M	1701
Yehl & Kanook*	Alas.	M-M	1703
Yima & Spityura*	Pers.	M-M	1707
Yima & Yimeh	Pers.	M-F	1707
Yo & In	Jap.	M-F	1708
Yoskeha & Tawiscara*	Iroq.	M-M	1710
Zinsu & Zinsi	Daho.	M-M	1720

COUNSELOR

Bikki	Norse	M	211
Egeria	Rom.	F	491
Fylgia	Norw.	M	619
Fylgukona	Norw.	F	619
Gaga	Baby.	M	621
Hanuman	Hin.	M	723
Jethro	Hebr.	M	877
Matali	Hin.	M	1074
Mentor	Gk.	M	+
Metis	Gk.	F	1096
Mordecai	Hebr.	M	1122
Mummu	Baby.	M	1136
Nestor	Gk.	M	1165
Samuel	Hebr.	M	1394
Sugiwara	Jap.	M	1504
Tenjin	Jap.	M	1545

Counselor (cont.)	Culture	Sex	Page
Ucalegon	Gk.	M	1619
Unferth	Ang-Sax.	M	1625
Vertumnus	Rom.	M	1646
Yu Huang	Chin.	M	1712

COUPLINGS (SEE CORRELATIVES)
COURAGE (SEE VALOR)

COWARDICE			
Acres, Bob	Eng.	M	27
Azhi Dahaka	Pers.	M	165
Chen Tsung	Chin.	M	318
Herfjotur	Norse	F	759
Mark (March)	Bryth.	M	1068
Martano	Ital.	M	1070
Nym	Eng.	M	1088
Panurge	Fr.	M	1235
Sganarelle	Fr.	M	1427

COWHERD (SEE ANIMAL KEEPER)
CRAFTINESS (SEE CUNNING)

CRAFTS (COMMERCE, TRADE, WORKERS)			
Chao San Niang	Chin.	F	313
Crispin, Saint	Christ.	M	382
Cyllenius	Gk.	M	401
Daikoku	Jap.	M	401
Ebisu	Jap.	M	489
Ekchuah	Mex.	M	497
Fuku	Jap.	M	616
Hermes	Gk.	M	760
Ho-Ho	Chin.	M	779
Kuan-ti	Chin.	M	947
Kudai-bakshy	Yakut	M	948
Liu Pei	Chin.	M	1003
Lu Tung-pin	Chin.	M	1026
Mercury	Rom.	M	1091
Minerva	Rom.	F	1106
Nari	Jap.	A	1156
Nindubarra	Sum.	M	1171
Nomi no Sukune	Jap.	M	1179
Nun-ura	Baby.	M	1181
Poseidon	Gk.	M	1288
Quetzalcoatl	Mex.	M	1312
Rajah Kidar (Bir Badr)	Hin.	M	1320

	Culture	Sex	Page
Saint Thomas	Christ.	M	1382
Shen Nung	Chin.	M	1434
Shiho-tsuchi	Jap.	M	1437
Sien-tsan	Chin.	F	1448
Sumiyoshi	Jap.	M	1506
Tacatecutli	Mex.	M	1523
Tagtug (Tibir)	Sum.	M	1524
Valmiki	Hin.	M	1637
Vanir	Norse	M, F	1638
Vertumnus	Rom.	M	1646
Xipe Totec	Mex.	M	1696
Yacatecutli	Mex.	M	1697
Zalambur	Mos.	M	1715

CREATOR

	Culture	Sex	Page
Aa (Aos)	Chald.	M	9
Afraid of Nothing	N.A.I.	F	+
Archon	Gnostic	M	119
Arddha-nari	Hin.	A	119
Areop-enap	Nauru	M	120
Areskoui	Iroq.	M	121
Arohi-rohi	Maori	M	128
Ataguju	Huama.	M	147
Atahocan	Algon.	M	147
Atanua	So. Is.	F	148
Atea	So. Is.	M	149
Atman	Hin.	M	152
Avalokitesvara	Bud.	M	160
Awonawilona	Zuni	M/A	162
Aya-kashiko	Jap.	F	163
Baal	Sem.	M	167
Baiyuhibi	Indo.	M	173
Bekotshidi	Nav.	M	193
Bel	Baby.	M	196
Boorala	Aus.	M	236
Brahma	Hin.	M	240
Buga	Sib.	M	258
Bumba	Af.	M	260
Burkhan	Sib.	M	261
Byamee	Aus.	M	264
Cagn	Bush.	M	269
Ceos	Gk.	M	303
Chaac	Mex.	M	307
Chagan-Shukuty	Sib.	M	307
Chaos	Gk.		312
Chepera	Egy.	M	318

	Culture	Sex	Page
Chicomexochit	Mex.	M	322
Chiminagagua	Chibcha	M	+
Chimizigagua	Bogata	M	232
Chinnigchinich	Calif.	M	326
Chinun Way Shun	Burm.	M	899
Chokmah	Caba.	A	667
Codoyanape	Chinook	M	+
Condor	Inca	M	365
Coyote	N.A.I.	M	377
Cronus	Gk.	M	384
Dagon	Sem.	A	406
Daksha	Hin.	M	408
De-ai	Gil. Is.	F	422
De-Babou	Gil. Is.	M	422
Dhatr	Hin.	M	439
Dhyanibodisattvas	Bud.	M	440
Dinewan	Aus.	F	445
Dis	Cel.	M	450
Ea	Assyr., Baby., Sum.	M	481
Ea-pe	Ind-Chin.	M	484
Ehlaumel	Yuki Ind.	M	494
El	Hebr.	M	497
Elohim (Eloah)	Hebr.	M	506
Es	Fin-Ug.	M	523
Esaugeteh Emissee	Creek Ind.	M	524
Eugpamolak Manobo	Bagobo	M	529
Fe'e	Poly.	M	558
Fenja & Menja	Norse	F	560
Finuweigh	Indo.	M	571
Freydis	Am. Lit.	F	611
Fro (Friuja)	Norse	M	613
Gucumatz (Qucumatz)	Guate.	M	1311
Gudatrigakwitl	Wiyote	M	694
Hahgwehdiyu	Iroq.	M	708
Hastshehogan	Nav.	M	730
Hastsheyalti	Nav.	M	730
Hatuibwari	Mel.	M	732
Haweniyo	Iroq.	M	733
Heqet (Heket)	Egy.	F	752
Her-shef	Egy.	M	763
He-who-invites	Jap.	M	766
Hiranyagarbha	Hin.	M	774
Hkun Hsang L'rong	Ind-Chin.	M	775
Hnitma-Dawgyi & Min Magaye	Ind-Chin.	F-M	776

	Culture	Sex	Page
Hometeuli	Mex.	M	784
Huntin	Ewes (Af.)	M	1453
Iapetus	Gk.	M	816
Idoiho	So. Is.	M	820
Ihoh	Caba.	M	822
Ikanam	Chinook	M	+
Ilmatar	Fin.	F	824
Ioskeha	Huron	M	837
Izamna	Mex.	M	853
Izanagi	Jap.	M	853
Izanami	Jap.	F	853
Janardana	Hin.	M	863
Jehovah	Hebr.	M	870
Ka	Burm.	M	899
Kala	Hin.	M	903
Kala-siva	Hin.	M	903
Kali	Hin.	F	903
Kalki	Hin.	M	904
Kane	Poly.	M	908
Karali	Hin.	F	909
Karei	Malay.	M	910
Kasyapa	Hin.	M	912
Kathatakanave	Walapai	M	912
Katonda	Uganda	M	913
Khepera	Egy.	M	924
Khnemu	Egy.	M	924
Kiehtan	Mass.	M	927
Kinharigan	Borneo	M	932
Kitshi-Manitou	Chip.	M	935
K'mukamtch	Klamath	M	936
Kobine	Gil. Is.	F	1156
Ku	Hawa.	M	947
Kukumatz & Tochipa	Yuman	M	950
Kumush	Modoc	M	951
Kururumany	Braz.	M	953
Kutku	Sib.	M	954
Lajnan	Micro.	M	964
Ligobund	Micro.	F	994
Loa	Marshall	M	1006
Loder	Norse	M	1007
Loki	Norse	M	1010
Lubumba	Bantu	M	1020
Lukelang	Caro. Is.	M	1024
Lumawig	Poly.	M	1024
Madumba	Calif.	M	1036
Mah	Sem.	F	1042

	Culture	Sex	Page
Mahasthamaprata	Bud.	M	1044
Maira-Monan	S.A.I.	M	1047
Maitreya	Bud.	M	1047
Mama	Sum.	F	1050
Manabhozho	Algon.	M	1054
Mandishire	Sib.	M	1057
Manuai	Admir.	M	1062
Marawa	Mel.	M	1064
Marduk	Assyr., Baby.	M	1065
Maui	Poly.	M	1077
Mazda	Pers.	M	1081
Mbamba (Kiara)	Af.	M	1081
Mbir (Miracucha)	S.A.I.	M	1081
Mehrem	Arab.	M	1084
Melu	Indo.	M	1087
Messou	Pota.	M	1095
Michabo	Algon.	M	1098
Mother Chuber	Sum.	F	1128
Mula Dyadi	Poly.	M	1135
Mummu	Sum.	M	1136
Mundilfore	Norse	M	1136
Mustamho	Mojave	M	1140
Nagaitcho	Calif.	M	1147
Nankilstlas	Haida	M	1153
Nareau	Gil. Is.	M	1156
Nascakiyetl	Tlingit	M	1156
Ne-kilst-luss	Haida	M	1161
Nesaru	Caddoan	M	1165
Ninurta	Sum.	M	1174
Nudimmud	Baby.	M	1184
Nu Kua	Chin.	F/A	1185
Numi-torem	Fin-Ug.	M	1185
Nurrudere	Aus.	M	1186
Nwali	Banyai	M	1187
Nyankopong	Ashantis	M	1187
Nzame (Njambi)	Congo	A	1188
Obagat	Pelew Is.	M	1191
Odin	Norse	M	1195
Old Man Coyote	Crow Ind.	M	1205
Old One	Thomp. Ri.	M	+
Ometecutli	Mex.	M	1208
Omo-daru and Aya-kashiko	Jap.	M-F	1208
Onitsu-nu	Jap.	M	1210
Ophion	Gk.	M	1211
Ormuzd	Zoro.	M	1216
Otshirvani	Sib.	M	1220

	Culture	Sex	Page
Pachacamac	Inca.	M	1224
Pandora	Gk.	F	1232
Panggu	Mel.	M	1233
P'an Ku	Chin.	M/A	1233
Pariacaca	Inca	M	1237
Phanes	Cel.	M	1261
Po	Poly.	F	1281
Pomonus (Pupdike)	Ital.	M	1285
Prajapati (Prakriti)	Hin.	A	1290
Prometheus	Gk.	M	1295
Protogonos	Gk.	A	1297
Ptah	Egy.	M	1299
Pundjel	Aus.	M	1301
Purushottama	Hin.	M	1305
Qabauil	Kiche	M	1308
Qat	Mel.	M	1309
Qeb	Egy.	M	1309
Qoluncotun	W. U. S. Ind.	M	1309
Quetzalcoatl	Mex.	M	1312
Quikinna'qu (Kutq, Kurkil)	Sib.	M	1313
Quoots-hooi	Chinook	F	1314
Ra	Egy.	M/A	1314
Ratnapani	Bud.	M	1324
Ratnasambhava	Bud.	M	1324
Recaranus	Rom.	M	1327
Rhea	Gk.	F	1335
Rigi	Micro.	M	1339
Rinaggon & Iri	Borneo		1339
Samantabdahra	Bud.	M	1393
Sesa	Hin.	M	1420
Sholmo	Sib.	M	1442
Sibu	Antilles	M	1445
Silver Fox	Calif.	M	1454
Sophia	Gnostic	F	1475
Spenta Mainyu	Zoro.	M	1481
Sucellos	Cel.	M	1503
Sunawavi	Ute	M	1509
Susanowo	Jap.	M	1512
Sussistinnako	Sia	M	1513
Taaroa	Poly.	M	1522
Tagaro the Wise	Banks Is.	M	1524
T'ai I Ching	Chin.	M	1525
Taikomol	Calif.	M	1526
Takaro	N. Heb.	M	1527
Tane	Poly.	M	1531
Tangaroa	Poly.	M	1531

	Culture	Sex	Page
Tawiscara	Huron	M	1539
Tchue	Bush.	M	1540
Teharonhiawagon	Iroq.	M	1541
Tem	Egy.	M	1542
Teyocoyani	Mex.	M	1549
Tezcatlipoca	Mex.	M	1549
Thaah	Mex.	M	1550
Thoth	Egy.	M	1562
Tiamat	Baby.	F	1570
Tiermes	Lapp	M	1572
Tii	Marq.	M	1573
Tiki	Maori	M	1573
Tiki-ahua	Marq.	M	1573
Tilo	Baronga	M	1573
Tiri	Brazil.	M	1576
To-kabinana	Mel.	M	1584
Tokay	Inca	M	1584
Tonacatecutli	Mex.	M	1586
Tuchaipa (Kwikumat, Mayoha)	Yuman Ind.	M	1606
Tukma	Juaneno Ind.	M	1606
Turtle	N.A.I.	M	1610
Tutu	Baby.	M	1611
Tvastr	Hin.	M	1611
Uhubaput	Sumu Ind.	M	1621
Ulgen	Tatar	M	1622
Vana Mothers	Norse	F	1638
Vasuki	Hin.	M	1641
Ve	Norse	M	1643
Vili	Norse	M	1650
Viracocha	Inca	M	1652
Vishnu	Hin.	A	1654
Vishnu-Narayana	Hin.	A	1655
Visvakarman	Hin.	M	1655
Visvapani	Bud.	M	1655
Wakan	Siouan		1662
Wati Kutjara (Men Iguana)	Aus.	M	1669
Wolaro	Aus.	M	1688
Wu-chi	Chin.	A	1693
Yelafaz	Micro.	M	1703
Yimantuwing-yai	Calif.	M	1707
Yo	Jap.	M	1708
Yoskeha	Iroq.	M	1710
Yryn-ajy-tojon	Sib.	M	1710
Zerpanitum	Baby.	F	1718

CROSSROADS	Culture	Sex	Page
Artemis	Gk.	F	131
Diana	Rom.	F	441
Ganesa	Hin.	M	627
Hecate	Gk.	F	740
Hermes	Gk.	M	760
Hsing Shen	Chin.	M	799
Jizo	Jap.	M	881
Lares Compitales	Rom.	M	974
Matrs	Hin.	F	1076
Quadriviae	Rom.	F	686
Sae-no-kami	Jap.	M	1360
Shozuga-no-baba	Jap.	F	1443
Trivia	Gk.	F	1599

CRUELTY			
Aeife	Cel.	F	39
Amestris	Pers.	F	85
Anakim	Hebr.		91
Ashura	Jap.	M	140
Bres	Cel.	M	246
Dirce	Gk.	F	450
Doeg	Hebr.	M	455
Drag-gs'ed	Tib.	M	467
Emathion	Gk.	M	507
Herod	Christ.	M	763
Herod Antipas	Christ.	M	763
Igigi	Assyr-Baby.		821
Ino	Gk.	F	833
Jenghis Khan	Mon.	M	872
Jezebel	Hebr.	F	879
Joab	Hebr.	M	881
Kaika	Hin.	F	902
Kunigunde	Germ.	F	952
Likho	Slav.	F	994
Mezentius	Ital.	M	1097
Minos	Gk.	M	1107
Moloch	Carth.	M	1115
Nabis	Spartan	M	1146
Nero	Rom.	M	1164
Ope	Norse	M	1211
Phalaris	Gk.	M	1261
Pilate	Rom.	M	1271
Rephaim	Hebr.	M	1332
Sargon II	Assyr.	M	1400
Satan	Hebr-Christ.	M	1402
Saul	Hebr.	M	1404

Cruelty (cont.)	Culture	Sex	Page
Semiramis	Assyr.	F	1415
Shesmu	Egy.	M	1435
Sisyphus	Gk.	M	1459
Su	S.A.	F	1502
Tachi	Chin.	F	1523
Tope	Norse	M	1588
Umunesiga	Sum.	M	1623
Ur-Nina	Sum.	M	1630
Yalahau	Mex.	M	1698
Yuriaku	Jap.	M	1713
Zeus	Gk.	M	1719
CUCKOLD			
Acastus	Gk.	M	22
Amphitryon	Gk.	M	88
Chrysale	Fr.	M	333
Diomedes	Gk.	M	446
Elcmar	Cel.	M	498
Enipeus	Gk.	M	511
Hephaestus	Gk.	M	751
John Tamson's (Thomson's) Man	Scot.	M	885
Lot	Bryth.	M	1014
Menelaus	Gk.	M	1089
Sui Jen	Jap.	M	1504
Vulcan	Rom.	M	1659
CULTURE HERO (SEE ALSO PROGENITOR)			
Abaangui & Zaguaguayu	Guar.	M-M	11
Academus	Gk.	M	21
Acarnan & Amphoterus	Gk.	M	22
Achaemenes	Pers.	M	24
Achaeus	Gk.	M	24
Ahayuta Achi	Zuni	M	52
Ailill	Cel.	M	55
Airya (Iraj)	Pers.	M	57
Amaethon	Bryth.	M	78
Amarud	Baby.	M	80
Ammon	Hebr.	M	86
Amphictyon	Gk.	M	87
Arcas	Gk.	M	118
Argus	Gk.	M	122
Armenak	Arm.	M	128
Ascanius	Rom.	M	136
Atse Hastin	Nav.	M	153

	Culture	Sex	Page
Bellerophon	Gk.	M	199
Benjamin	Hebr.	M	202
Bi-Har	Bud.	M	211
Brea	Cel.	M	244
Brute	Bryth.	M	253
Cadmus	Gk.	M	266
Cain	Christ., Hebr., Mos.	M	269
Camber	Bryth.	M	280
Can	Mex.	M	283
Cecrops	Gk.	M	301
Christ	Christ.	M	330
Cin-an-ev	Ute	M	339
Comizahual	Honduras	F	362
Coyote	N.A.I.	M	377
Cuchulainn	Cel.	M	393
Cuculcan	Mex.	M	396
Curicaberis	Mex.	M	398
Dan	Hebr.	M	410
Danaus	Gk.	M	411
Dardanus	Gk.	M	415
Dido	Rom.	F	444
Dionysus	Gk.	M	447
Ea	Baby.	M	481
Elatha	Cel.	M	498
Enna	Cel.	M	512
Eochaid Airem	Cel.	M	513
Ephraim	Hebr.	M	515
Evander	Rom.	M	533
Fu Hsi	Chin.	M	615
Hammurabi	Baby.	M	716
Haoshyangha	Pers.	M	723
Hayk	Arm.	M	734
Heimdal	Norse	M	743
Hengest	Ang-Sax.	M	750
Heracles of Oeta	Gk.	M	755
Hermes	Gk.	M	760
Hiawatha	N.A.I.	M	767
Hou Chi	Chin.	M	794
Hsi-ling Shih	Chin.	F	799
Hu	Bryth.	M	800
Huang Ti	Chin.	M	801
Hu Gadarn	Welsh	M	802
Huitziton	Mex.	M	803
Hypsistos	Gk.	M	813
Ingunar	Norse	M/A	610

	Culture	Sex	Page
Ion	Gk.	M	837
Ioskeha	Huron	M	837
Isaac	Hebr.	M	841
Ishmael	Hebr.	M	843
Issachar	Hebr.	M	848
Italapas	Chinook	M	+
Italus	Ital.	M	848
Itzamna	Mex.	M	850
Izanagi	Jap.	M	853
Jamshid	Pers.	M	863
Jimmu Tennu	Jap.	M	880
Kali	Hin.	F	903
Kanaan	Hebr.	M	907
Kao Hsin	Chin.	M	908
Kettu (Kittu) & Misharu	Baby.	M-M	1110
Kiaklo	Zuni	M	926
Kukulcan	Mex.	M	950
Ku-yu	Mojave	M	954
Laki-oi	Borneo	M	965
Lamech	Hebr.	M	967
Latinus	Rom.	M	975
Lelex	Gk.	M	982
Lycaon	Gk.	M	1027
Maira-Monan	Tup. Ind.	M	1047
Mama Ogllo	Inca	F	1051
Manco Capac	Inca	M	1056
Manuscithra	Pers.	M	1062
Marduk	Assyr-Baby.	M	1065
Maui	Poly.	M	1077
Melissa	Gk.	F	1086
Michabo (Messon)	Algon.	M	1098
Minos	Gk.	M	1107
Mitsotsozini	Pokomo	M	1113
Monotaro	Jap.	M	1118
Nabhi	Jain	M	1146
Nabu	Baby.	M	1146
Nauplius	Gk.	M	1158
Nidaba	Sum.	F	1168
Nimrod	Baby.	M	1170
Ninigi	Jap.	M	1173
Ninus	Gk/Baby.	M	1174
Numa Pompilius	Rom.	M	1185
Nurrudere	Aus.	M	1186
Ogma	Cel.	M	1200
Ogyrvran	Bryth.	M	1201
Old One	Thomp. Riv.	M	+

	Culture	Sex	Page
Pachacamac	Inca	M	1224
Palamedes	Gk.	M	1227
Pelasgus	Gk.	M	1249
Phoroneus	Gk.	M	1266
Poshaiyanne	Pueblo	M	1288
Prometheus	Gk.	M	1295
Ptah	Egy.	M	1299
Qat	Mel.	M	1309
Quetzalcoatl	Mex.	M	1312
Remus	Rom.	M	1332
Reuben	Hebr.	M	1334
Romulus	Rom.	M	1346
Sandan	As. Min.	M	1396
Sarpedon	Gk.	M	1401
Saul	Hebr.	M	1404
Scamandrius	Gk.	M	1405
Scef	Norse	M	1406
Selk	Egy.	M	1415
Shedad	Mos.	M	1432
Shem	Hebr.	M	1433
Shun	Chin.	M	1444
Sidon	Hebr.	M	1447
Simha	Ceylon	M	1455
Sisyphus	Gk.	M	1459
Sivirri	Aus.	M	1461
Skjolding	Norse	M	1465
Sneferu	Egy.	M	1470
Sugiwara	Jap.	M	1504
Taaut	Phoen.	M	1523
Tages	Ital.	M	1524
Tahmurath	Pers.	M	1525
Taikomol	Calif.	M	1526
Taliesin	Bryth.	M	1528
Tamoi	Tupi-Guar.	M	1531
T'ang	Chin.	M	1531
Tawhaki	Chath. Is.	M	1539
Tchue	Bush.	M	1540
Telchines	Cretan	M	1541
Tenjin	Jap.	M	1545
Teucer	Gk.	M	1549
Theseus	Gk.	M	1554
Thoth	Egy.	M	1562
Tigernmas	Cel.	M	1572
Tigranes	Arm.	M	1573
To-Kabinana	Mel.	M	1584
Ts'ang Chieh	Chin.	M	1602

Culture Hero (cont.)	Culture	Sex	Page
Ts'an Nu	Chin.	F	1603
Uazale	Paressi Ind.	M	1619
Unktomi	Siouan	M	1626
Ur-Nammu	Sum.	M	1630
Urukagina	Sum.	M	1630
Van-Xuong	Ind. Chin.	M	1638
Viracocha	Inca	M	1652
Votan	Mex.	M	1658
Wainamoinen (Vainamoinen)	Fin.	M	1661
Wen Ch'ang	Chin.	M	1673
Wisakketjak	Micmac Ind.	M	1686
Xbalanque	Kiche	M	1695
Xelas	Lummi Ind.	M	1695
Yao	Chin.	M	1701
Yimantuwingyai	Calif.	M	1707
Yin-chen-hsin	Chin.	M	1707
Yu	Chin.	M	1711
Yu Huang	Chin.	M	1712
Zebulun	Hebr.	M	1717

CUNNING (ALSO SEE TRICKSTER)

Fan Li	Chin.	M	548
Forgall	Cel.	M	594
Gizo	Hausa	M	660
Gylfe	Swed.	M	704
Loki	Norse	M/A	1010
Malengin	Eng.	M	1050
Odysseus	Gk.	M	1196
Outis (Noman)	Gk.	M	1221
Pandora	Gk.	F	1232
Patelin	Fr.	M	1243
Paul Bunyan	Am. Lit.	M	1244
Penelope	Gk.	F	1252
Rebecca	Hebr.	F	1326
Reynard	Med.	M	1334
Rinaldo	Ital.	M	1339
Satyr	Gk.	M	1403
Semiramis	Assyr.	F	1415
Sidrophel	Eng.	M	1447
Siegfried	Germ.	M	1448
Sigurd	Norse	M	1451
Sisyphus	Gk.	M	1459

CURIOSITY

Agib	Arab.	M	48
Hiko-Hohodemi	Jap.	M	769

	Culture	Sex	Page
Maui	Poly.	M	1077
Orpheus	Gk.	M	1216
Pandora	Gk.	F	1232
Paul Pry	Eng.	M	1244
Psyche	Gk.	F	1299
Raymond	Fr.	M	1325
Semele	Gk.	F	1415
Tane	Poly.	M	1531
Urashima Taro	Jap.	M	1628
DANCE			
Ame-no-Uzume	Jap.	F	83
Anshar	Baby.	M	101
Apsaras	Bud.	F	115
Balmarcodes	Phoen.	M	176
Bharata	Hin.	M	208
Bowa	Tib.		238
Castor & Pollux	Gk.	M	295
Choni	Tib.		329
Citapati	Bud.		344
Corybantes	Phryg.	M	375
Cotytto	Gk.	F	376
Curetes	Gk.	M	398
Dactyli	Gk.	M	404
David	Hebr.	M	417
Dioscuri	Gk.	M	449
Elf	Norse		502
Elle-folk	Norse	F	505
Faun	Rom.	M	552
Frau Frigg	Germ.	F	608
Gahe	Apache Ind.		622
Gandharva	Hin.	M	626
Harlequin	Fr.	M	726
Kachinas	Zuni	M	900
Korybantes	Phryg.	M	943
Kouretes	Gk.	M	944
Kumush	Modoc	M	951
Ludki (Krasnoludi)	Serb.		1021
Luka-kane	Hawa.	M	1024
Macuilxochitl	Mex.	M	1035
Maid Marian	Bryth.	F/A	1046
Maruts	Hin.	M	1071
Nag-pa	Tib.	M	1148
Nataraja	Hin.	M	1461
Natesa	Bud.	M	1157
Nix	Teut.	M	1176

Dance (cont.)	Culture	Sex	Page
Nixe	Teut.	F	1176
Nymph	Gk.	F	1188
Otafuku	Jap.	F	1219
Pan	Gk.	M	1230
Pasithea (Aglaia)	Gk.	F	1241
Pixy	Eng.	M, F	1277
Polyidus	Gk.	M	1284
Pundjel	Aus.	M	1301
Qat	Mel.	M	1309
Robin Hood	Eng.	M	1343
Saint George	Christ.	M	1370
Saint Vitus	Christ.	M	1383
Salii	Rom.	M	1390
Salome	Christ.	F	1391
Sarube	Jap.		1401
Satyr	Gk.	M	1403
Shojo	Jap.	M	1441
Silenus	Gk.	M	1453
Silvanus	Rom.	M	1453
Siva	Hin.	M	1461
Stutly, Will	Eng.	M	1502
Tapio (Vir-ava)	Fin.	A	1534
Terpsichore	Gk.	F	1547
Tezcatlipoca	Mex.	M	1549
Thandu (Tandu)	Hin.	M	1552
Tom the Piper	Eng.	M	1585
Troll	Germ.	M, F	1600
Typanom	Siam.	M	1617
DARKNESS			
Aac	Mex.	M	9
Aeetes	Gk.	M	37
Aegisthus	Gk.	M	39
Aeson	Gk.	M	42
Ahriman	Zoro.	M	53
Alberich	Norse	M	62
Alce	Gk.		63
Aleus	Gk.	M	66
Alfar	Norse	M	67
Alkha	Mon.		69
Alv	Norse	M	77
Alviss	Norse	M	78
Amen-Khnum	Egy.	M	83
Amulius	Rom.	M	1185
Angra Mainyu	Zoro	M	97
Anshar	Baby.	M	101

	Culture	Sex	Page
Antaeus	Gk.	M	101
Any-any-any-ha	Cowich.	M	105
Apep	Egy.	M	107
Apocatequil	Inca	M	109
Aram	Arm.	M	117
Arimans	Pers.	M	124
Astraeus	Gk.	M	145
Atli	Norse	M	152
Azdahah	Arm.	M	165
Babes in Woods	Folk.	M-F	169
Balan (Brennius)	Bryth.	M	174
Balor	Celt.	M	176
dBan-mgon	Bud.	M	178
Bath Chorim	Sem.		186
Bel Enlil	Baby.	M	197
Belial	Eng.	M	197
Bharata	Hin.	M	208
Bjorno-Hoder	Norse	M	221
Black Arky	Cel.	M	222
Buto	Egy.	F	263
Cain	Christ., Hebr., Mos.	M	269
Cairima	Pers.	M	271
Calatine	Cel.	M	272
Camaxtli	Mex.	M	279
Cassiopeia	Gk.	F	294
Castor	Gk.	M	295
Ceos	Gk.	M	303
Cheng Wu	Chin.	M	318
Cichol the Footless	Cel.	M	338
Cimmerii	Gk.	M, F	339
Cinteotl	Mex.	M	341
Creon	Gk.	M	380
Deiphobus	Gk.	M	426
Dhritarashtra	Hin.	M	439
Dokkalfar	Norse	M	458
Dopkalfar	Norse	M	464
Dylan	Norse	M	480
Eabani	Sum.	M	482
Eber	Cel.	M	488
Eire	Cel.	F	496
Elcmar	Cel.	M	498
Emathion	Gk.	M	507
Emen	Egy.	M	508
Enkidu	Sum.	M	512

	Culture	Sex	Page
Eo-anu	Cel.	F	513
Erc	Cel.	M	518
Erebus	Gk.	M	518
Esau	Hebr.	M	524
Eteocles	Gk.	M	527
Euryale	Gk.	F	532
Feng	Dan.	M	559
Fenrir	Norse	M	560
Ferdia	Cel.	M	560
Fergus macRoy	Cel.	M	561
Firbolgs	Cel.	M	571
Fomhair	Scot.	M	590
Fomor	Cel.	M	590
Forgall	Cel.	M	594
Furina	Ital.	F	618
Geryon	Gk.	M	647
Giukings	Norse	M, F	660
Golagras	Bryth.	M	670
Golerotheran	Bryth.	M	674
Goll mac Morna (Aod)	Cel.	M	674
Gorgon	Gk.	F	678
Gorlois	Bryth.	M	679
Green Knight	Bryth.	M	689
Gronw Pebyr	Bryth.	M	692
Gucumatz (Qucumatz)	Kiche	M	694
Gudhorn	Norse	M	694
Gunnar	Norse	M	698
Gunther	Norse	M	698
Hag	Scot.	F	707
Hahgwehdaetgah	Seneca	M	708
Halfdan	Norse	M	712
Ham	Hebr.	M	713
Hansel & Gretel	Folk.	M-F	+
Hathor	Egy.	F	730
Hati (eclipse)	Norse		731
Hecate	Gk.	F	740
Hector	Gk.	M	741
Hehut	Egy.	F	742
Helge	Norse	M	746
Hine-i-tau-ira (Hine-nui)	Poly.	F	772
Hoder	Norse	M	778
Hogne	Norse	M	779
Holofernes	Hebr.	M	893
Hrodvitnir	Norse	M	798
Hromund	Norse	M	798
Huang T'ien Shang Ti	Chin.	M	801

	Culture	Sex	Page
Hun-ahpu & Xbalanque	Kiche	M-M	806
Hunhun-ahpu	Kiche	M	807
Hydra	Gk.	M	810
Hymir	Gk.	M	811
Iku-tama-yori-hime	Jap.	F	822
Ilus	Gk.	M	825
Indech	Cel.	M	828
Indra	Hin.	M	829
I-qong	Mel.	M	838
Ishbibenob	Hebr.	M	843
Ishmael	Hebr.	M	843
Ismene	Gk.	F	847
Itztli	Mex.	M	850
Ixtlilton	Mex.	M	853
Jinn & Jinniyeh	Mos.	M, F	880
Jotun	Norse	M	890
Judas Iscariot	Christ.	M	892
Kalamahakala	Bud.	M	903
Kamsa	Hin.	M	907
Kanook	Alas.	M	908
Kanva (eclipse)	Hin.	M	908
Kauravas	Hin.	M	913
Kek (Emen)	Egy.	M	915
Kekuit	Egy.	F	916
Kerhet	Egy.	F	918
Kneph	Egy.	M	937
Koshchei	Fin.	M	943
Kostey	Slav.	M	944
Kubera	Hin.	M	948
Kveldrida	Norse	F	954
Lachamu	Baby.	F	961
Lachmu	Baby.	M	961
Laius	Gk.	M	964
Laodamas	Gk.	M	972
Laomedon	Gk.	M	972
Latona	Rom.	F	975
Leda	Gk.	F	980
Leto	Gk.	F	986
Lilith	Hebr.	F	994
Lilithu	Baby.	F	995
Lilu	Baby.	M	995
Llyr	Bryth.	M	1006
Longinus	Christ.	M	1011
Losy	Mon.	M	1013
Lot	Bryth.	M	1014
Louhi	Lapp	F	1016

	Culture	Sex	Page
Lucifer	Christ.	M	1020
Lynge	Norse	M	1029
Maanegarm (eclipse)	Norse	M	1031
Makha	Hin.	M	1048
Mark (March)	Bryth.	M	1068
Marocael	Taino	M	1068
Mastiphal	Oc.	M	1074
Maui	Poly.	M	1077
Medb	Bryth.	F	1082
Medusa	Gk.	F	1084
Meilichios	Gk.	M	1084
Melwas	Bryth.	M	1087
Memnon	Gk.	M	1088
Mictlantecutli	Mex.	M	1099
Midgard Serpent	Norse		1100
Minotaur	Gk.		1107
Mo-li Hung	Chin.	M	601
Mordu	Bryth.	M	1123
Morna	Cel.	M	1124
Mushussu	Sum.	M	1139
Nanga	Poly.	M	1153
Naraka	Hin.	M	1155
Nat	Norse	F	1157
Neleus	Gk.	M	1161
Nephthys	Egy.	F	1163
Nibhaz	Sem.	M	1167
Nichard	Germ.	M	1168
Nipa	Algon.	F	1175
Nithhoggr	Scan.	M	1176
Nor	Norse	M	1180
Nox	Rom.	F	1183
Nut	Egy.	F	1187
Nuter Dua	Egy.	M	1187
Nuye	Jap.		1187
Nyctimus	Gk.	M	1187
Nyx (Nox)	Gk.	F	1188
Octriallach	Cel.	M	1195
Oegishialm	Norse	M	1198
Oenopion	Gk.	M	1199
Og	Hebr.	M	1200
Pa-hra	Egy.	M	1226
Palleneos	Gk.	M	1229
Pandarus	Gk.	M	1232
Panis	Hin.	M	1233
Panoptes	Gk.	M	1234
Perez	Hebr.	M	1255

	Culture	Sex	Page
Phylacides	Gk.	M	1267
Poeas	Gk.	M	1281
Poko-ha-rua-te-po	Poly.	F	1282
Polybus	Gk.	M	1283
Polydorus	Gk.	M	1284
Polyphemus	Gk.	M	1285
Potiphar	Heb., Mos.	M	1289
Praxidikae	Gk.	F	1291
Priam	Gk.	M	1292
Proetus	Gk.	M	1295
Puck	Eng.	M	1300
Pwcca	Welsh	M	1300
Pwyll	Bryth.	M	1306
Pygmalion	Gk.	M	1306
Queenah	Cowich.	M	1312
Rafusen	Jap.	F	1317
Rahab	Hebr.	F	1318
Rahu & Ketu (eclipse)	Hin.	M	1318
Ratri	Hin.	F	1324
Ravana	Hin.	M	1324
Regin	Norse	M	1330
Remus	Rom.	M	1332
Rephaim	Hebr.	M	1332
Ryence	Bryth.	M	1335
Saehrimner	Norse	M	1360
Searbhan Lochlannach	Cel.	M	1411
Set (Sut)	Egy.	M	1420
Sharvan	Cel.	M	1431
Shesmu	Egy.	M	1435
Shu	Egy.	M	1443
Sichaeus	Rom.	M	1446
Siggeir	Norse	M	1449
Sisera	Hebr.	M	1459
Skoll (eclipse)	Norse	M	1465
Sokar	Egy.	M	1471
Sosondowah	Iroq.	M	1476
Spenjaghrya	Iroq.	M	1481
Sreng	Cel.	M	1487
Stheno	Gk.	F	1494
Strophius	Gk.	M	1501
Styx	Gk.	F	1502
Suddhodana	Bud.	M	1503
Summanus	Ital.	M	1506
Susanowo	Jap.	M	1512
Svarbhanu (eclipse)	Hin.	M	1514
Taepo	N. Zeal.		1524

Darkness (cont.)	Culture	Sex	Page
Tanaoa	So. Is.	M	1531
Tawiscara	Iroq.	M	1539
Te-po	N. Zeal.		1546
Tezcatlipoca	Mex.	M	1549
Thaukt (Thokh)	Norse	F/A	1552
Thorir of Garth	Ice.	M	+
Tima-te-kore	Poly.	F	1235
Tiresias	Gk.	M/A	1576
Titlacauan	Mex.	M	1578
Ti-tsang	Chin.	M	1580
Tityus	Gk.	M	1580
Tlacauepan	Mex.	M	1581
Tlaloc Tecutli	Mex.	M	1851
Tow-us-tussin	Haida	M	1592
Triglav	Slav.	M	1597
Triptolemus	Gk.	M	1598
Tuiren	Cel.	M	1606
Turkish Knight	Med. Lit.	M	1608
Turnus	Rom.	M	1609
Uazit	Egy.	F	1619
Ucalegon	Gk.	M	1619
Uriah	Hebr.	M	1629
Uther Pendragon	Bryth	M	1632
Varns (eclipse)	Norse	M	1639
Varuna	Hin.	M	1639
Vibhandaka	Hin.	M	1648
Virabhadra	Hin.	M	1652
Vitzilopochtli	Mex.	M	1656
Vlkodlak (eclipse)	Slav.	M	1656
Vrtra	Hin.	M	1659
Vukub-cakix	Kiche	M	1659
Wang-gon	Tib.	M	1665
Whiro	Poly.	M	1676
Xuthus	Gk.	M	1697
Yalahau	Mex.	M	1698
Yama	Bud., Hin.	M	1699
Yami	Hin.	F	1700
Yoalliehecatl	Mex.	M	1708
Yoamaxtli	Mex.	M	1708
Yohualticetl	Anahuac	F	1709
Yspaddeden Penkawr	Bryth.	M	1711
Zedekiah	Hebr.	M	1717
Zeus	Gk.	M	1719

DAWN			
Aarvak	Norse		10

	Culture	Sex	Page
Aethre	Gk.	F	42
Ahans	Hin.	M	52
Ahi	Egy.	F	52
Andromeda	Gk.	F	94
Antiope	Gk.	M	103
Aphrodite	Gk.	F	108
Aponibolinayen	Philip.	F	111
Argynnis	Gk.	F	123
Ariadne	Gk.	F	123
Arjuni	Hin.	M	126
Aruna	Hin.	M	133
Arusha	Hin.	M	134
Asvins	Hin.	M	146
Ataentsic	Huron	F	147
Atalanta	Gk.	F	148
Atanua	So. Is.	F	148
Athena	Gk.	F	150
Athra	Gk.	F	151
Atthis	Gk.	F	154
Auge	Gk.	F	156
Aurora	Rom.	F	158
Ausera	Slav.	F	159
Ayar Cachi	Inca	M	163
Bhrigu	Hin.	M	209
Bochica	Bogata Ind.	M	232
Brynhild (Brunhilda)	Norse	F	253
Cabha	Hebr.	F	265
Chalciope	Gk.	F	309
Charis	Gk.	F	314
Chasca	Inca	F	316
Chih Nu	Chin.	F	323
Chiminizagagua	Chib.	M	325
Citlallatonac	Mex.	M	344
Clytemnestra	Gk.	F	351
Coronis	Gk.	F	374
Danae	Gk.	F	411
Daphne	Gk.	F	414
Deirdre	Cel.	F	426
Devorgilla	Cel.	F	436
Eos	Gk.	F	514
Eostre (Ostara)	Ang-Sax.	F	514
Etalak & Latarak	Sum.	M	1174
Europa	Gk.	F	531
Euryclea	Gk.	F	532
Eurydice	Gk.	F	532
Euryphassa	Gk.	F	532

	Culture	Sex	Page
Ganymede	Gk.	M	627
Gourgourgahgah	Aus.	M	680
Graces	Gk.	F	681
Guinevere	Bryth.	F	696
Gullinkambi	Norse	M	697
Gullintami	Norse	M	697
Gwyar	Bryth.	F	702
Harits	Hin.	M/F	726
Hebe	Gk.	F	739
Heimdal	Norse	M	743
Helen	Gk.	F	745
Hero	Gk.	F	762
Hjordis	Norse	F	775
Horae	Gk.	F	786
Horus	Egy.	M	792
Hueytonantzin	Mex.	F	802
Huruing Wuhti	Hopi	F	808
Iamus	Gk.	M	815
Igerna	Bryth.	F	821
Ingeborg	Ice.	F	831
Ino	Gk.	F	833
Iole	Gk.	F	836
Iseult	Bryth.	F	842
Itonia	Gk.	F	849
Itys	Gk.	M	850
Jael	Hebr.	F	860
Jocasta	Gk.	F	882
Judith	Hebr.	F	893
Lampetus	Gk.	M	969
Leah	Hebr.	F	978
Ljosalfar	Norse	M	1004
Lord of Sesennu	Egy.	M	1013
Lyonors (Liones)	Bryth.	F	1029
Marici	Bud.	F	1067
Marpessa	Gk.	F	1068
Mater Matuta	Ital.	F	1074
Maya	Bud.	F	1080
Medea	Gk.	F	1082
Menoeceus	Gk.	M	1089
Merope	Gk.	F	1093
Minerva	Ital.	F	1106
Miranda	Eng.	F	1296
Morgan le Fay	Bryth.	F	1123
Nausicaa	Gk.	F	1158
Neamhuain Clann	Cel.	M	1159
Nehes	Egy.	M	1161

	Culture	Sex	Page
Nimue	Bryth.	F	1170
Ningishzida & Ninsubur	Sum.	M-M	1172
Ninudzalli	Sum.	F	696
Odatis	Pers.	F	1194
Orihime	Jap.	F	1215
Orthros	Gk.	M	1217
Pallas	Gk.	F	1228
Pay Zume	Para.	M	1245
Phyllis	Gk.	F	1267
Pollux	Gk.	M	295
Prabhasa	Hin.	M	1641
Protogenia	Gk.	F	1297
Psyche	Gk.	F	1299
Quetzalcoatl	Mex.	M	1312
Rhiannon	Bryth.	F	1336
Sadb	Cel.	F	1360
Sakut	Sum.	M	1389
Salma	Sem.	M	1391
Sanjna	Hin.	F	1397
Sarama	Hin.	F	1399
Saranyu	Hin.	F	1400
Sati	Hin.	F	1402
Sieglinde	Germ.	F	1448
Signy	Germ.	F	1451
Sleeping Beauty	Folk.	F	1467
Suhrab	Pers.	M	1504
Swanhild	Germ.	F	1517
Talatumsi	Pueblo	F	1528
Tan	Chin.	M	1531
Te-ata	N. Zeal.		1541
Techu	Egy.	M	1540
Telemachus	Gk.	M	1542
Telyaveli	Baltic	M	1542
Tereus	Gk.	M	1546
Thesan	Ital.	M	1554
Thisbe	Rom.	F	1560
Thora	Norse	F	1561
Thoth	Egy.	M	1562
Tiphys	Gk.	M	1575
Tlalecutli	Mex.	M	1581
Tobias	Hebr.	M	1582
Togakushi	Jap.	M	1584
Tuag	Cel.	F	1605
Tung Chun	Chin.	M	1607
Tung Fang So	Chin.	M	1607
Tyro	Gk.	F	1618

Dawn, (cont.)	Culture	Sex	Page
Uathach	Cel.	F	1619
Urvasi	Hin.	F	1630
Ushapati	Hin.	M	1631
Ushas	Hin.	F	1631
Vijaya Sakti	Bud.	F	1649
Vikramaditya	Hin.	M	1650
Vinata	Hin.	F	1650
Wabanang	Men.	M	1660
Wabasso	Pota.	M	1660
Wabun	Algon.	M	1660
Xiuhtecutli	Mex.	M	1696
Zarah	Hebr.	M	1716
Zasis	Lithu.		1716
Zipacna	Kiche	M	1721
Zora	Illy.	F	1734
Zuhe	Bogata Ind.	M	232
Zume	W. Ind.	M	1735

DAY (SEE DAWN, GLOAMING, LIGHT)

DEATH (ALSO SEE UNDERWORLD)

Abaddon	Hebr.	M	11
Adad-ea (ferryman)	Baby.	M	29
Adam	Hebr., Mos.	M	29
Adrammelech	Caba.	M	35
Aeacus (judge)	Gk.	M	37
Ahhazu	Sum.	M	52
Ah Puch	Mex.	M	53
Ahriman	Zoro.	M	53
Ame-no-ko-ya-ne-no-mikoto	Jap.	M	83
Amen-Ra	Egy.	M	83
Amenti Genii	Egy.	M	84
Ammit	Egy.	F	86
Amset	Egy.	M	89
Anaye	Nav.	M	92
Angoi	Borneo	M	96
Angra Mainyu	Zoro.	M	97
Anhoret	Egy.	M	97
Ankou	Brittany	M	99
Anpu	Egy.	M	100
Antaka	Hin.	M	102
Anubis (pathfinder)	Egy.	M	105
Anunaki (judge)	Baby.	M	105
Anunnaki (judge)	Sum.	M	105
Apaukkyit Lok	Burm.	M	107
Apis	Egy.	M	109

	Culture	Sex	Page
Apollo	Gk.	M	110
Apuat (pathfinder)	Egy.	M	115
Arad-ea (ferryman)	Baby.	M	117
Arimans	Pers.	M	124
Arsan-duolai	Yakut	M	130
Ataentsic (Eagentci)	Huron	F	147
Azrael	Heb., Mos.	M	166
Baba Yaga	Rus.	F	168
Baloo	Aus.	M	176
Banba	Cel.	F	178
Banshee	Cel.	F	179
Beatrice (guide)	Ital.	F	191
Beli	Bryth.	M	197
Bellerophon	Gk.	M	199
Bhadrakali	Hin.	F	207
Bile	Cel.	M	211
Bowa	Tib.		238
Bozaloshtah	Slav.	F	239
Bragi	Norse	M	240
Bran	Bryth.	M	241
Brigit (keening)	Cel.	F	249
Brynhild	Norse	F	253
Buarainech	Cel.	M	254
Cacce-Jielle	Mon.	A	265
Camazotz	Mex.	M	279
Carvara	Hin.	M	293
Chakekenapok	Pota.	M	308
Charon (ferryman)	Egy., Gk.	M	315
Chen Wu (T'ien Pao)	Chin.	M	1572
Chibiabos	Algon.	M	321
Ch'in-Kuang (judge)	Chin.	M	326
Chipiapoos	Pota.	M	326
Chitragupta (judge)	Hin.	M	327
Choni	Tib.		329
Chos-rgyal Phyi-sgrub	Tib.	M	329
Christ (guide)	Christ.	M	330
Chthonius (guide)	Gk.	M	334
Chuan-lun Wang (guide)	Chin.	M	335
Cichol the Footless	Cel.	M	338
Citapati	Bud.		344
Couatlicue	Mex.	F	376
Coyote	N.A.I.	M	377
Cupay	Peru.	M	397
Dagon (judge)	Assyr.	A	406
Dainn	Norse	M	407
Dharma	Hin.	M	438

	Culture	Sex	Page
Dolphin (guide)	Gk.		459
Duamutef	Egy.	M	474
Eckhardt	Germ.	M	490
Emma (judge)	Jap.	M	509
Enki	Assyr., Baby., Sum.	M	511
Eopuco	Mex.	M	53
Erebus	Gk.	M	518
Ereshkigal	Baby.	F	518
Erlik-khan	Mong.	M	521
Erlking	Germ.	M	522
Etraphill	Mos.	M	528
Eumenides	Gk.	F	529
Euronymous	Med. Lit.	M	431
Folkvitr	Norse	F	1637
Fomhair	Scot.	M	590
Fomor	Cel.	M	590
Four Horsemen of Apocalypse	Christ.	M	604
Frau Holle (guide)	Germ.	F	608
Fravashi (guide)	Pers.	M	608
Freya	Norse	F	610
Gabriel	Christ., Hebr., Mos.	M	619
Gabriel's Hounds	Bryth.		620
Gama (Goub)	Hotten.	M	624
Gandreid	Norse		626
Garbh Ogh	Cel.	F	628
Gilgamesh (judge)	Sum.	M	656
Gjallar Horn	Norse		660
Gjoll	Norse		661
Gorgopa	Gk.	F	679
Grim Reaper	Folk.	M	691
Gwrach Y Rhibyn	Bryth.		702
Gwyn	Bryth.	M	703
Habergeis	Tyrolian		705
Hades	Gk.	M	706
Hanhau	Yucatec Ind.	M	722
Hapi	Egy.	M	724
Harbard (ferryman)	Norse	M	725
Harpies	Gk.	F	728
Hathor	Egy.	F	730
Havfrue	Dan.	F	732
Hel	Norse	F	745
Hera	Gk.	F	752
Herfjotur	Norse	F	759
Herjan's Disir	Norse	F	1637

	Culture	Sex	Page
Herla (Hertyr)	Scan.	M	1196
Hermes (guide)	Gk.	M	760
Herne	Eng.	M	762
Hjalmmeyjar	Norse	F	1637
Holde	Germ.	F	780
Horus (judge)	Egy.	M	792
Hotoke	Jap.	M	794
Hototogisu (guide)	Jap.		794
Hrafna-God	Norse	M	797
Hringerd	Norse	F	798
Htamenmas	Tib.	F	800
Huergo	Span.	M	802
Hus Brothers	Wintun	M	808
Iha-naga-hime	Jap.	F	822
Iris	Gk.	F	839
Israfil	Mos.	M	847
Itoki	Nica.	F	849
Ixtab	Mex.	F	853
Izanami	Jap.	F	853
Jaik-khan	Sib.	M	861
Jamshid	Pers.	M	863
Jupiter	Rom.	M	896
Jurupari	Braz.	M	898
Kaguhana	Jap.	M	902
Kala	Hin.	M	903
Kalamahakala	Bud.	M	903
Kala Siva	Hin.	M	903
Kalma	Fin.	M	904
Kalunga	Angola	M	905
Kande Yake	Ceylon	M	907
Kara	Norse	F	909
Karei (judge)	Malay.	M	910
Kebehsenuf	Egy.	M	915
Kelpi	Scot.	M	916
Ker	Gk.	F	917
Kerimas	Tib.	F	918
Khensu	Egy.	M	923
Khentamenti	Egy.	M	923
Khosodam	Sib.	F	925
Khulater	Sib.	M	926
Kiousa	Florida Ind.	M	932
Kiyamat-tora	Fin-Ug.	M	935
Korka-murt	Fin-Ug.	M	942
Kuinyo	Aus.	M	949
Kurdaitcha	Aus.		952
Kururumany	Braz.	M	953

	Culture	Sex	Death Page
Laki Tenengan	Borneo	M	965
Latura	Indo.	M	976
Lethe	Gk.	F	986
Lha-mo-kar-po	Tib.	F	989
Libitina	Rom.	F	991
Lilu	Baby.	M	995
Littur	Norse	M	1003
Llyr	Bryth.	M	1006
Loup-Garou	Fr.	M	1016
Lufu	Basum.	M	1022
Maat (guide, judge)	Egy.	F	1031
Mahakala	Hin.	M	1043
Mampes (guide)	Malay.		1052
Mana	Rom.	F	1054
Manannan	Cel.	M	1054
Manat	Sem.	F	1056
Manawyddan	Bryth.	M	1056
Manes	Rom.		1058
Marawa	Mel.	M	1064
Masauwu	Hopi	M	1072
Mate	Banks Is.	M	1074
Matrs	Hin.	F	1076
Matu'u-ta'u-ta'ua	Tahi.		1077
Medr	Arab.	M	1083
Megaera	Gk.	F	1084
Meliagraunce	Bryth.	M	1086
Mercury (guide)	Rom.	M	1091
Michael (judge)	Christ.	M	1099
Mictlantecutli (Tzontemoc)	Mex.	M	1099
Midas (judge)	Gk.	M	1099
Minos (judge)	Gk.	M	1107
Minotaur	Gk.	M	1107
Miru	Hawa.	M	1110
Mirume (judge)	Jap.	F	1110
Mithra	Pers.	M	1112
Mitra (judge)	Hin.	M	1112
Modgudur	Norse	F	1114
Mo-li Shou	Chin.	M	1115
Monker (judge)	Mos.	M	1117
Moqwaio	Men.	M	1122
Mora	Slav.	F	1122
Morana	Slav.	F	1122
Morc	Cel.	M	1122
Morgan le Fay	Bryth.	F	1123
Morrigu	Cel.	F	1125
Mors	Rom.	M	1125
Mrtyu	Hin.	M	1132

	Culture	Sex	Page
Nakir (judge)	Mos.	M	1150
Namtaru	Assyr-Baby.	M	1152
Namuci	Hin.	M	1152
Nanga	Poly.	M	1153
Nasnas	Arab.	M	1156
Nasu	Zoro.	F	1157
Navky	Slav.		1158
Neheb-kau	Egy.	F	1160
Nekedzaltara	Tinne Ind.		1161
Nekyomanteion	Gk.	M	1161
Nephthys	Egy.	F	1163
Nergal (judge)	Assyr-Baby.	M	1164
Nerrivik	Eskimo	F	1164
Nessus	Gk.	M	1165
Nipa	Algon.	F	1175
Nirrti	Hin.	F	1175
Nut	Egy.	F	1187
Nuter Dua (ferryman)	Egy.	M	1187
Octriallach	Cel.	M	1194
Odin (ferryman)	Norse	M	1195
Okuni-nushi	Jap.	M	1204
Olofat	Caro. Is.	M	1206
Orc	Ital.		1213
Orcus	Ital.	M	1213
Osiris (judge)	Egy.	M	1218
Osk-meyjur	Norse	F	1637
Pau-puk-keewis (Pauguk)	N.A.I.	M	1244
Pepezu	Yura.	M	1254
Persephone	Gk.	F	1257
Peter	Christ.	M	1259
Phemios	Gk.	M	1262
Phlegyas (ferryman)	Ital.	M	1264
Phonoi	Gk.	M	1266
Pisacas	Hin.	M	1275
Pluto	Rom.	M	1280
Plutus	Gk.	M	1280
Pohjan-akka	Fin.	M	1281
Poloznitsa	Fin-Ug.	F	1283
Poludnica	Rus.	F	1283
Procrustes (Damastes)	Gk.	M	1295
Proserpina	Rom.	F	1296
Pryderi	Bryth.	M	1298
Psychopompus (guide)	Gk.	M	1299
Pusan (guide)	Hin.	M	1305
Rabisu	Baby.	M	1316
Rail	Pelew Is.	M	1319

	Culture	Sex	Page
Rakshasa	Hin.	M, F	1320
Rashnu (judge)	Zoro.	M	1323
Resheph (Mot)	Phoen.	M	1333
Rhadamanthus (judge)	Gk.	M	1335
Rhot-Amenti (judge)	Egy.	M	1337
Rudra	Hin.	M	1353
Rudrani	Hin.	F	1353
Rutu	Lapp	M	1355
Saint Hubert	Christ.	M	1680
Saint Julian (ferryman)	Christ.	M	1373
Samael	Caba.	M	1393
Sarvitr	Norse	F	1637
Satan	Hebr-Christ.	M	1402
Schal-jime	Tatar	M	1407
Sebek	Egy.	M	1412
Sedna	Eskimo	F	1413
Sedu	Baby.	M	1413
Serapis	Egy.	M	1418
Shinje-chhol-gyal (judge)	Tib.	M	1438
Shozuga-no-baba	Jap.	F	1443
Shulmus	Mong.	M	1444
Shuten Doji	Jap.	M	1444
Shvaz	Arm.	M	1445
Sitnapishtim	Baby.	M	1461
Sokar	Egy.	M	1471
Spider Woman	N.A.I.	A	1483
Sraoscha (judge)	Zoro.	M	1487
Styx	Gk.	F	1502
Susanowo	Jap.	M	1512
Tagaro the Fool	Banks. Is.	M	1524
Tamek-vui	Fin-Ug.	M	1530
Tamoi	Tupi-Guar.	M	1531
Tanga Tanga	Inca	M	1532
Taranis	Cel.	F	1534
Taripaca (judge)	Inca	M	1535
Tathagata	Bud.	M	1537
Tchue	Bush.	M	1540
Teimatini	Mex.	M	1541
Tena-ranide	Athap.		1544
Teoyaomiqui	Mex	M	1546
Tepeyollotl	Mex.	M	1546
Tezcatlipoca (judge)	Mex.	M	1549
Thanatos	Gk.	M	1551
Thaye	Burm.	M	1552
Thoth (judge, pathfinder)	Egy.	M	1562
Tima-te-kore	Poly.	F	1235

	Culture	Sex	Page
Tir	Mos.	M	1576
Ti-tsang	Chin.	M	1580
Tiur (pathfinder)	Arm.	M	1581
Tlatecutli	Mex.	M	1581
Tofana	Ital.	F	1583
To-karvuvu	Mel.	M	1584
Triptolemus (judge)	Gk.	M	1598
Ts'in-kuan-wang (judge)	Chin.	M	1603
Tuamatef	Egy.	M	1605
Tuonetar (Manator)	Fin-Ug.	F	1608
Tuoni (Mana)	Fin-Ug.	M	1608
Tupilaq	Greenland	M	1608
Turnface (ferryman)	Egy.	M	1609
Twrch Trwyth (Porcus Troit)	Bryth.	M	1616
Up-uauat (pathfinder)	Egy.	M	1627
Urd	Norse	F	1628
Ursanapi (ferryman)	Baby.	M	1630
Valfather	Norse	M	1636
Valkjosandi	Scan.	M	1636
Valkyrie	Norse	F	1636
Valmeyjar	Norse	F	1637
Valtam	Norse	M	1643
Vata	Papuan		1641
Vederaj	Fin-Ug.		1643
Vediovis	Ital.	M	1643
Vetala	Hin.	M	1648
Vichama	Inca	M	1648
Vidhatr	Hin.	M	1649
Vila	Serb-Croa.	F	1650
Virgil (guide)	Ital.	M	1652
Vu-murt	Fin-Ug.	A	1660
Vut-oza	Fin-Ug.	M	1660
Walleyneup	Aus.	M	1663
Walumbe	Uganda	M	1664
Whaitari	Maori	F	1674
Whiro	Poly.	M	1676
Witch of Endor	Hebr.	F	1687
Wryd	Ang-Sax.	F	1628
Xipe Totec (pathfinder)	Mex.	M	1696
Xolotl (pathfinder)	Mex.	M	1697
Yabme-akka	Lapp	F	1697
Yalahau	Mex.	M	1698
Yama	Hin.	M	1699
Yama-uba	Jap.	F	1700
Yami	Hin.	F	1700
Yatai (Yahsang Kahsi)	Ind-Chin.	F	1702

Death (cont.)	Culture	Sex	Page
Yatawm (Tahsang Kahsi)	Ind-Chin.	M	1702
Yebegen	Tatar	M	1703
Yemma (judge)	Jap.	M	1705
Yen-lo Wang	Chin.	M	1705
Yima	Pers.	M	1707
Yomo-tsu-shiko-me	Jap.	F	1709
Yuki-onne	Jap.	F	1712
Yum Cimil	Mex.	M	1713
Zmei Goruinich	Slav.	M	1722

DEBAUCHERY (SEE OBSCENITY)

DECAY			
Atharna	Cel.	M	150
Avagddu	Cel.	M	160
Avernucus	Rom.	M	162
Azariah	Hebr.	M	164
Cathbad	Cel.	M	298
Dithyrambos	Gk.	M	452
Eresichthon	Gk.	M	518
Eriphyle's Veil & Jewels	Gk.		521
Fulla	Norse	F	616
Gilvaethwy	Bryth.	M	657
Harmonia's Veil & Jewels	Gk.		727
Harpies	Gk.	F	728
Hniker	Norse	M	776
Mordu	Bryth.	M	1123
Nasu	Zoro.	F	1157
Niddhogge	Norse	M	1168
Robigus	Rom.	M	1343
Tlaelquani	Mex.	F	1581
Tlazolteotl	Mex.	F	1582

DECEIT (HYPOCRISY. ALSO SEE TRAITOR)			
Ananeas	Christ.	M	91
Apate	Gk.		107
Archimago	Eng.	M	119
Arimans	Pers.	M	124
Asura	Hin.	M	146
Ate	Eng.	F	149
Barmecide	Arab.	M	182
Breg	Cel.	F	405
Drauga	Zoro.	M	470
Druj	Pers.	M, F	472
Duessa	Eng.	F	475

	Culture	Sex	Page
Ermenrich	Norse	M	522
Lucullus	Gk.	M	1021
Meng	Cel.	F	405
Mitothin	Norse	M	1112
Modo	Eng.	M	1114
Munchausen, Baron	Germ.	M	1136
Nibelung	Norse	M	1167
Olofat	Caro. Is.	M	1206
Rudra	Hin.	M	1353
Sapphira	Christ.	F	1398
Satan	Hebr-Christ.	M	1402
Schilbung	Norse	M	1407
Sinon	Gk.	M	1457
Sut	Mos.	M	1513
Taliesin	Welsh	M	1528
Talus	Gk.	M	1529
Tartuffe	Fr.	M	1536
Tom Pepper	Eng.	M	1585
Uso-dori	Jap.	F	1631
Wisakketjak	Micmac Ind.	M	1686
Zalambur	Mos.	M	1715

DEFORMED (SEE MAIMED)
DELUGE (SEE UNIVERSAL RUIN)

DEMON

Abasy	Yakut		12
Abbadona	Germ.	M	12
Abigor	Med. Lit.	M	16
Abiku	Yoruba	M	16
Abonsam	Guinea	M	17
Abtagigi	Sum.	F	20
Abyzu	Christ.	F	21
Acham	Oc.	M	24
Adamastor	Portu.	M	30
Adrammelech	Caba.	M	35
Adversary, The	Christ.	M	36
Aegeon	Gk.	M	38
Aeife	Cel.	M	39
Aello	Gk.	F	40
Aeshma	Zoro.	M	41
Afiti	Afr.	M	43
Afrasiyab	Pers.	M	43
Afrit (Afreet)	Arab.	M	44
Agdistis	Gk.	A	46
Ahl At-tral	Mos.	M	53

	Culture	Sex	Page
Ahlmakoh	Van. Is.	M	53
Ahriman	Zoro.	M	53
Aigamuchab	Hotten.	M	55
Ailo	Hebr.	F	56
Akhtya	Pers.	M	1709
Al	Pers.	M, F	60
Ala	Sum.	A	60
Alad	Baby.	M	61
Alastor	Gk.	M	62
Albasta	Tatar	F	62
Albin	Mong.	M	63
Alecto	Gk.	F	68
Alocer	Oc.	M	71
Alrinach	Eastern	F	76
Alu	Sum.	M	77
Alukah	Hebr.		77
Amaimon	Med. Lit.	M	78
Amarum	Ecuadoran	M	80
Amine	Arab.	F	86
Anakhai	Mong.	M, F	90
Anammelech	Oc.	M	91
Anaye	Nav.	M	92
Andhaka	Hin.	M	93
Andras	Oc.	M	93
Angerboda	Norse	F	96
Annis	Bryth.	F	100
Antichrist	Christ.	M	102
Anunaki	Baby.	M, F	105
Apollyon	Christ.	M	111
Ara	Gk.	F	116
Aratis	Hin.		117
Ardad	Pers.	M	119
Ardat Lili	Sum.	F	119
Ariel	Caba.	M	124
Arimaspians (Ahrimanes)	Gk.	M	124
Asakku	Baby.	M	135
Ascaroth	Med. Lit.	M	136
Ashmedai	Hebr.	M	139
Ashmodel	Med. Lit.	M	139
Ashura	Jap.	M	140
Asmodeus	Hebr.	F	141
Astaroth	Caba.	M	144
Asto-vidhotu	Pers.	M	145
Asuang	Philip.	M	145
Asura	Hin.	M	146
Auld Ane	Scot.	M	147

	Culture	Sex	Page
Auld Clootie	Scot.	M	157
Auld Hornie	Scot.	M	157
Aulne	Norse	M	157
Avezuha	Christ.	F	162
Awar	Mos.	M	162
Azazel	Hebr., Mos.	M	165
Baal	Med. Lit.	M	431
Baalberith	Med. Lit.	M	431
Baal Chanan	Caba.	M	167
Badb	Cel.	F	171
Bajang	Ind-Chin.		173
Bake (Inangi-I-Bake)	Indo.	F	174
Bakemono	Jap.	M	174
Banshee	Cel.	F	179
Barghest (Barquest)	Eng.	M	181
Beelpeor (Baal-peor)	Hebr.	M	194
Beelzebub (Baalzebub)	Hebr., Christ.	M	194
Behemoth	Hebr.	M	196
Bel Enlil	Baby.	M	197
Belial	Hebr.	M	197
Belphegor	Caba.	M	200
Ben Nefilim	Sum.	M	+
Berchta	Christ.	F	203
Bhut	Hin.	M, F	209
Bilu	Ind-Chin.	M	211
Bithia	Mong.	F	220
Bjerg Folk	Norse	M, F	479
Bogey	Folk.	M	234
Bucon	Oc.	M	255
Bugbear	Folk.	M	258
Buninka	Mong.	M	261
Bushyasta	Zoro.	M	262
Celaeno	Gk.	F	301
Cercopes	Gk.	M	301
Chamos	Oc.	M	432
Ch'ih Yeo	Chin.	M	323
Christmas People	Fin-Ug.	M, F	333
Clootie	Scot.	M	349
Co-hon	Ind-Chin.		355
Continh	Ind-Chin.	F	368
Corrigan	Christ.	F	374a
Cuchi	Aus.	M	393
Curupira	Braz.	M	399
Cyhiraeth	Bryth.	F	401
Daemons	Gk.	M	405
Daeva (Div)	Zoro.	M	405

	Culture	Sex	Page
Dagon	Christ.	M	406
Dahhak	Pers.	M	406
Danavas	Hin.	M	412
Dasas	Hin.	M	416
Deber	Sem.	M	+
Deil	Scot.	M	426
Demeter	Gk.	F	429
Demogorgon	Christ.	M	431
Dev	Arm.	M	434
Devil	Hebr-Christ.	M	435
Diabolus	Eng.	M	440
Dimme-kur	Sum.	M	445
Dir	Pers.	M	450
Djinn	Mos.	M	454
Dodo	Bush.	M, F	455
Dogai	Mel.	F	458
Dokkalfar	Norse	M	458
Dore-le (Dam-c'an)	Tib.	M	409
Drac	Fr.	M	467
Druhs	Hin.	M	471
Duende	Span.	M	475
Duffy (Duppy)	W. Ind.	M	418
bDul-rgyal	Tib.	M	476
Eblis (Azazel)	Mos.	M	489
Ekajata	Bud.	F	496
Ekimmu	Baby.		497
Elf	Norse	M	502
Emin	Hebr.		509
Eric (Old Eric)	Christ.	M	519
Erinyes	Gk.	F	520
Erlik	Tator	M	521
Erlking	Germ.	M	522
Eruncha	Aus.	M	523
Etimmu	Baby.	M, F	528
Euronymous	Med. Lit.	M	431
Fallen Angel	Hebr-Christ.	M	546
Fata	Ital.	F	550
Fata Morgana	Ital.	F	550
Fjalar	Norse	M	578
Flaga	Norse	M	581
Flibbertigibbet	Eng.	M	583
Freya	Christ.	F	610
Friar Rush (Bruder Rausch)	Germ.	M	611
Fuda-hegashi	Jap.	M	615
Funa-yurei	Jap.	M, F	617
Furies	Rom.	F	617

	Culture	Sex	Page
Gaki	Jap.	M, F	622
Galar	Norse	M	623
Gallu	Sum.	M	624
Gama (Goub)	Hotten.	M	624
Gamaliel	Caba.	M	624
Gandreid	Norse	M, F	626
Gaunab (Ga-gorib)	Hotten.	M	634
Gayal	Hin.	M	636
Gello	Gk.	F	638
Gelou	Hebr-Christ.	F	638
Gelu	Rumanian	M	638
Gentle Annie	Scot.	F	645
Ghaddar	Arab	M	652
Ghost	Universal	M, F	652
Ghoul	Arab.	M	653
Gian ben Gian	Arab.	M	653
Gigim	Sum.	M	655
Glaisrig	Manx	F	661
Glaistig	Manx	F	661
Glam	Norse	M	661
Gnome	Gk.	M	664
Goblin	Fr.	M	666
Gog & Magog	Eng., Hebr., Mos.	M-M	669
Golem	Caba.	M	674
Gombo	Tib.	M	674
Gremlin	Eng.	M	689
Gri-bdog (Di-do)	Tib.	M	690
Grimalkin	Med. Lit.	F	691
Gwragedd Annwn	Christ.	F	702
Gwyllion	Bryth.	F	703
Hag	Scot.	F	707
Hangie	Scot.	M	157
Hanpa	Sum.	M	722
Hariti	Hin.	F	726
Harut & Marut	Mos.	M-M	729
Hidimva	Hin.	M	768
Hiisi	Fin-Ug.	M	769
Hisa Females	Jap.	F	775
Hob	Eng.	M	776
Hobgoblin	Eng.	M	778
Hobomokko	N.A.I.	M	778
Hold	Germ.		780
Holde	Germ.	F	780
Horei	W. Afr.	M	787
Hornie	Scot.	M	157

	Culture	Sex	Page
Hpi	Ind-Chin.	M	797
Huard	Brittany	M	801
Huergo	Span.	M	802
Hugon	Fr.	M	803
Humbaba	Baby.	M	804
Hunter, The	Christ.	M	807
Hutgin	Med. Lit.	M	431
Hyrokkin	Norse	F	813
Igart Bat Mahlat	Hebr.	F	821
Igigi	Assyr-Baby.		821
Ilu Limnu	Assyr.	M	825
Imp	Ang-Sax.	M	826
Incubus	Med. Lit.	M	828
Irra	Assyr-Baby.	M	841
Itzpapalotl	Mex.	M	850
Jann	Arab.	M	863
Jhoting	Hin.	M	879
Jinn	Arab., Mos.	M	880
Jinniyeh	Arab., Mos.	F	880
Kabandha	Hin.	M	900
Kaitabha	Hin.	M	902
Kala	Bali	M	903
Kalavatri	Hin.	M	903
Kali	Hin.	F	903
Kalu Kumara Yaka	Shinhalese	M	905
Kamsa	Hin.	M	907
Kappa	Jap.	M	909
Kelpi	Scot.	M	916
Keremet	Rus., Sib.	M	917
Khnathaiti	Pers.	F	918
Kimidins	Hin.	M	928
Kine-kine-boro	Indo.	M	928
Knecht Ruprecht	Germ.	M	937
Kobal	Oc.	M	432
Kobold	Germ.	M	939
Kormos	Mong.	M	943
Kui	N. Zeal.	F	949
Kumbhandas	Hin.	M	951
Kung-kung	Chin.	M	1185
Kupai	Inca	M	952
Labartu	Assyr.	F	957
Labasu	Sem.	M	957
Lady of the Woods	Eng.	F	905
Lamastu	Sum.	F	966
Lamia	Gk.	F	967
Laminak	Basque	M	968

	Culture	Sex	Page
Lamme	Sum.	F	968
Lammikin	Scot.	M	968
Lamyroi	Gk.	M	969
Langsuyar	Malay.	F	971
Larvae	Rom.	M	974
Lemures	Rom.		982
Leonard	Med. Lit.	M	984
Leviathan	Med. Lit.	M	431
Lilim	Sem.	M, F	994
Lilith	Hebr.	F	994
Lilithu	Sum.	F	995
Lilu	Baby.	M	995
Lucifer	Christ.	M	1020
Lucifuge	Caba.	M	1020
Lutin	Folk.	M	545
Madhu	Hin.	M	1035
Maga-tsumi	Jap.	M	1037
Mahagiri	Ind-Chin.	M	1042
Mahu	Scot.	M	1046
Mamit	Sum.	F	1051
Mammon	Syrian	M	1051
Manito	Algon.	M	1058
Mara	Bud.	M	1063
Marakayikas	Jap.	M	1063
Marka	Hin.	M	1068
Martinet	Med. Lit.	M	432
Masan	Hin.	M	1072
Master Leonard	Med. Lit.	M	1073
Mastiphal	Med. Lit.	M	1074
Matche-Manito	Algon.	M	1058
Mazainyon	Pers.	M	1081
Mazzikim	Sem.	M	+
Melchom	Med. Lit.	M	432
Mephistopheles	Med. Lit.	M	1091
Metakorab	Mel.	F	1095
Misroch	Med. Lit.	M	432
Moloch	Caba.	M	1115
Monaciello	Folk.	M	545
Mora	Slav.	F	1122
Mormo	Gk.	F	1124
Morvran	Bryth.	M	1126
Mrtyu	Hin.	M	1132
Muckle-mouth Meg	Eng.	F	1133
Mudgegong	Aus.	M	1133
Mullin	Med. Lit.	M	432
Mumbo Jumbo	W. Afr.	M	1136

	Culture	Sex	Page
Mwenembago	Uzaramo	M	1142
Nag-Pa	Tib.	M	1148
Nahema	Oc.	M	1148
Namtaru	Assyr-Baby.	M	1152
Namuci	Bud., Hin.	M	1152
Naonghaithya	Zoro.	M	1154
Nasargiel	Hebr.	M	1156
Nasu	Zoro.	F	1157
Navky	Slav.	M, F	1158
Nephilim	Hebr.	M, F	1163
Nergal	Med. Lit.	M	431
Ngoyama	Burm.	M	1167
Nhangs	Arm.	F	1167
Nick	Eng.	M	1168
Nicklen Ben	Scot.	M	1168
Nickneven	Scot.	F	+
Ninamaskug	Sum.	M	1170
Nitne Kamui	Ainu	M	1176
Nix	Teut.	M	1176
Nixe	Teut.	F	1176
Nocnitz	Rus.	F	1179
Nybras	Oc.	M	432
Oaf	Scan.	M	1189
Ocypete	Gk.	F	1194
Oghuz	Asian	M	1200
Ogre	Germ.	M	1201
Old Adam	Eng.	M	30
Old Bendy	Eng.	M	1205
Old Boy	Eng.	M	1205
Old Clootie	Scot.	M	1205
Old Davy	Eng.	M	436
Old Driver	Eng.	M	1205
Old Eric	Norse	M	519
Old Gentleman	Eng.	M	1205
Old Gooseberry	Eng.	M	1205
Old Harry	Eng.	M	729
Old Horny	Eng.	M	1205
Old Ned	Eng.	M	1205
Old Nick	Eng.	M	1168
Old One	Eng.	M	1205
Old Poker	Eng.	M	1205
Old Scratch	Scot.	M	1409
Old Serpent	Eng.	M	1205
Old Simmie	Eng.	M	1205
Oni	Jap.	M	1209
Ope	Norse	M	1211

	Culture	Sex	Page
Otgon	Iroq.		1220
Pa'ewa	Solom. Is.	M	999
Pari	Mel.	M	1237
Pephredo	Gk.	F	1254
Peri	Pers.		1255
Perkele	Fin.	M	1256
Phorcys	Germ.	M	1266
Pipru	Hin.	M	1275
Pisacas	Hin.	M	1275
Plat-eye	W. Ind.		1279
Pluto	Med. Lit.	M	431
Podarge	Gk.	F	1281
Polevik	Rus.	M	1283
Pooka	Cel.	M	1286
Preta	Hin.	M/F	1292
Prince of Darkness	Christ.	M	1293
Procrustes	Gk.	M	1295
Prosperpine	Med. Lit.	F	431
Puck	Eng.	M	1300
Pura	Hebr.	M	+
Putana	Hin.	F	1305
Puuk	Esthonian	M	1305
Pwcca	Welsh	M	1300
Rabisu	Baby.	M	1316
Ragamoffyn	Eng.	M	1317
Rahu & Ketu	Hin.	M-M	1319
Ravana	Hin.	M	1324
Red Devil Tiger	Tib.	M	1328
Remphan	Hebr.	M	1332
Rigs-bu-mo	Tib.	F	1339
Rimmon	Med. Lit.	M	432
Rksavaktra-dakini	Bud.	F	1342
Rokuro-kubi	Jap.	F	1345
Ruah Kardeyako	Sem.	M	+
Ruah Kezarit	Sem.	M	+
Ruah Tegazit	Sem.	M	+
Ruah Zelachta	Sem.	M	+
Ruah Zenanim	Sem.	M	+
Ruhim	Sem.	M	+
Ruotta	Lapp	M	1354
Rutu	Lapp	M	1355
Saalah	Arab.	M	1356
Saivo Men & Maids	Lapp	M, F	1389
Samael	Hebr.	M	1393
Samhanach	Scot.	M	1393
Sanda	Hin.	M	1395

	Culture	Sex	Page
Satan	Hebr-Christ.	M	1402
Satanael	Sib.	M	1402
Sathariel	Caba.	M	1402
Sauru	Zoro.	M	925
Schratt	Germ.	M	1409
Scrat	Teut.	M	1409
Scritta	Ang-Sax.	M	1409
Scylla	Gk.	F	1409
Sed	Hebr.	M	1412
Sedit	Wintun	M	1413
Seidhkoma	Norse	F	1413
Seidhmahr	Norse	M	1413
Seirim	Hebr.	M	1413
Semjaza	Med. Lit.	M	546
Setek	Slovenian	M	1421
Shabriri	Hebr.	M	1428
Shahapet	Arm.	M	1428
Shaitan	Mos.	M	1429
Shedim	Hebr.	M	1432
Shibbeta	Hebr.	F	1436
Shitkur	Mong.	M	1439
Sholmo	Sib.	M	1442
Shulmus	Mong.	M	1444
Shura	Jap.	M	1444
Shuten Doji	Jap.	M	1444
Shvaz	Arm.	M	1445
Shvod	Arm.	M	1445
Shwe Myet-Hna	Ind-Chin.	F	1445
Siren	Gk.	F	1458
Skratti	Scan.	M	1465
Skritek	Slovenian	M	1465
Sojobo	Jap.	M	1471
Sphinx	Gk.	F	1482
Srin-po	Tib.	M	1487
Srog-bdag	Tib.	M	1339
Stryge	Med. Lit.		1501
Succor-Benoth	Med. Lit.	M	432
Succuba	Med. Lit.	F	1503
Suksendal	Fin-Ug.	A	1505
Sukuyan	Trinidad	F	1505
Supay	Inca	M	1510
Sycorax	Eng.	F	1521
Taepo	N. Zeal.	M	1524
Tamamo-no-maye	Jap.	F	1529
Tan-ma (bsTan-ma)	Tib.	F	1532
Tase	Burm.	M, F	1537

	Culture	Sex	Page
Tawiscara	Huron	M	1539
Tengu	Jap.	M	1545
Tervils	Norw.	M	1547
Thabet	Burm.	F	1550
Thamuz	Med. Lit.	M	431
Thepla	Arm.	M	1554
Timi	Hebr.	M, F	1574
Titan	Gk.	M, F	1577
Togarini	Caba.	M	1584
Tom Poker	Eng.	M	1585
Tom Titevil	Christ.	M	1585
Tomomori	Jap.	M	1586
Tope	Norse	M	1588
Torx	Arm.	M	1590
Triptopatores	Gk.	M	1599
Troll	Norse	M	1600
Trow	Scot.	M	1600
Tsan-rgyal	Tib.	M	1603
Tshindi	Nav.	M	1603
Tupilaq	Greenland	M	1608
Twanjiraka	Aus.	M	1611
Typhoeus	Gk.	M	1617
Ubyr	Fin-Ug.	M	1619
Ulrica	Ital.	F	1622
Umkovu	Afr.		1623
Uor	Yakut	M, F	1626
Uphir	Med. Lit.	M	1627
Upir	Slav.		1627
Urgan	Folk.	M	1628
Utgard-Loki	Norse	M	1632
Utumo	Fin-Ug.		1632
Vaetter	Dan.	M, F	1633
Vatak	Zoro.	F	1641
Velchanos	Cretan	M	1644
Verdelet	Med. Lit.	M	1645
Vice	Eng.	M	1648
Vinayaka	Bud.	M	1650
Virudaka	Bud.	M	1654
Vjedogonja	Slav.	M, F	1656
Vlkodlak	Slav.	M	1656
Volos (Ganyklos)	Rus.	M	1657
Wanga	E. Afr.	M	1664
Wayland	Christ.	M	1670
Wen Kamui	Ainu	M	1673
Willis	Germ.	F	1681
Witch of Endor	Hebr.	F	1687

Demon (cont.)	Culture	Sex	Page
Wudes Heer (Wade)	Norse	M	1693
Wu Kuang Ching	Chin.	M	1693
Yaka	Cey.	M	1698
Yama-omba	Jap.	F	1699
Yech	Am. Ind.	M	1703
Yogini	Hin.	F	1708
Yorka	Surinam		1710
Yurupari	Braz.	M	1713
Zimwi	Afr.	M	1720
Zluidni	Slav.	M	1722
Zombi	Haitian	M, F	1734

DEMON SLAYER (SEE FOE OF DEMONS)
DESPISED (SEE RENOUNCED BY PARENT)

DESTROYER			
Adharma	Hin.	M	32
Androktasiai	Gk.	F	94
Apollo	Gk.	M	110
Bhairava	Hin.	M	208
Brimo	Mong.	F	249
Byleipt	Norse	M	264
Caena-maergha	Pers.	M	267
Charybdis & Scylla	Gk.	F-F	316
Chimera	Gk.	F	325
Cronus	Gk.	M	384
Dibbara (Lubara)	Baby.		443
Echidna	Gk.	F	489
Erin-bird	Sum.		520
Fenja & Menja	Norse	F	560
Gandarewa	Pers.	M	625
Gibil	Baby., Sum.	M	512
Glam	Norse	M	661
Gore	Slav.	M	678
Hara	Hin.	M	724
Hathor	Egy.	F	730
Heracles	Gk.	M	752
Hercules	Rom.	M	759
Hermes	Gk.	M	760
Hnickar (Nickar)	Norse	M	776
Jahi	Zoro.	F	861
Janardana	Hin.	M	863
Kala	Hin.	M	903
Kala-Siva	Hin.	M	903
Kali	Hin.	F	903
Kalki	Hin.	M	904

	Culture	Sex	Page
Karali	Hin.	F	909
Kasyapa	Hin.	M	912
Kengida	Baby., Sum.	M	512
Khensu	Egy.	M	923
Khwai-hemm	Bush.	M	926
Ki-gulla	Baby.	M	927
Kingaluddda	Baby., Sum.	M	512
Kingu	Baby.	M	932
Kirttimukha	Hin.	M	933
Kulilu	Baby.	M	951
Kusariqqu	Baby.	M	953
Labbu	Sum.	M	957
Loki	Norse	M/A	1010
Mahadeva	Hin.	M	1042
Mahrkusha	Pers.	M	1046
Malkosh	Pers.	M	1050
Maruts	Hin.	M	1071
Mother Chuber	Sum.	F	1128
Mudje-Monedo	Chip.	M	935
Narfi	Norse	M	1156
Oghuz	Asian	M	1200
Pachacamac	Inca	M	1224
Perses	Gk.	M	1257
Phanes	Cel.	M	1261
Phra In Suen	Siam.	M	1267
Siva	Hin.	M	1461
Sobk	Egy.	M	1470
Suqe-matua	N. Heb.	M	1511
Surtr	Norse	M	1511
Susanowo	Jap.	M	1512
Tentetemic	Mex.	M	1546
Thunderbird	Am. Ind.	M	1568
Tiamat	Baby.	F	1570
Uddagubba	Baby., Sum.	M	512
Umu-dapruti	Baby.		1623
Urd	Norse	F	1628
Utgard-Loki	Norse	M	1632
Vii	Serb.	M	1649
Vlkodlak	Slav.	M	1656
Wyrd	Ang-Sax.	F	1694
Yaotl	Mex.	M	1701
Zainigav	Arab.	M	1715
Zerpanitum	Baby.	F	1718
Ziz (Ziv)	Hebr.		1721

	Culture	Sex	Page
DETHRONED BY KIN (SEE SLAIN BY KIN)			
DETHRONER OF KINSMAN (SEE SLAYER OF KINSMAN)			
DEVIL (SEE DEMON)			
DEVOTION (SEE LOYALTY)			
DEW (SEE MOISTURE)			

DIRECTION (c=center, e=east, n=north, s=south, w=west)

Name	Culture	Sex	Page
Agni (n)	Hin.	M	49
Airya (e)	Pers.	M	1608
Amrtadhara & Sakti (n)	Bud.	M-F	89
Amset (n)	Egy.	M	89
Ao-jun (w)	Chin.	M	106
Ao-K'in (s)	Chin.	M	106
Ao-Kuang (e)	Chin.	M	106
Ao-Shun (n)	Chin.	M	106
Aquila (n)	Rom.	M	116
Argestes (e)	Gk.	M	1683
Arimans (n)	Pers.	M	124
Auna (n)	Eskimo		601
Auster (s)	Rom.	M	159
Axieros (Axiocersa) (all)	Gk.	M	163
Ayar Aucca (s)	Inca	M	164
Ayar Cachi (e)	Inca	M	163
Ayar Manco (n)	Inca	M	164
Ayar Uchu (w)	Inca	M	164
Azure Dragon (e)	Chin.		166
Bacabab (all)	Mex.	M	170
Bach-ho (w)	Chin.	M	1226
Billing (w)	Norse	M	211
Bishamon (n)	Jap.	M	220
Black Tortoise (n)	Chin.		223
Boreas (n)	Gk.	M	236
Buto (n)	Egy.	F	263
Cairima (w)	Pers.	M	1608
Cardea (all)	Rom.	F	290
Castor (w)	Gk.	M	295
Cathena (w)	Mojave	F	298
Chaacs (all)	Mex.	M	307
Chalchiutlicue (w)	Mex.	F	308
Cheng Wu (n)	Chin.	M	318
Cherubim (all)	Hebr.	M	319
Ch'i-lin (w)	Chin.	A	1488
Ch'ing Lung (e)	Chin.		601
Christ (e)	Christ.	M	330

	Culture	Sex	Page
Chu Ch'ieh (s)	Chin.		335
Chu-dieu (s)	Chin.		335
Colla (s)	Inca	M	356
Con (s)	Inca	M	363
Corus (nw)	Rom.	M	374a
Daikoku (n)	Jap.	M	407
Dajoji (w)	Iroq.	M	408
Dark Warrior (n)	Chin., Jap.		416
Delling (e)	Norse	M	427
Dhartarastra (e)	Bud.	M	439
Dogs of Foh (w, e)	Chin.	M-F	458
Dogs of Foo (w, e)	Jap.	M-F	458
Duamutef (w)	Egy.	M	474
El of Gebal (all)	Sem.	M	497
Eurus (e, se)	Gk., Rom.	M	532
Ezekiel (all)	Heb.	M	541
Favonius (w)	Rom.	M	553
Feng-huang (s)	China		1488
Gymir (e)	Norse	M	704
Ham (s)	Hebr.	M	713
Hamsika (s)	Hin.	F	716
Hapi (s)	Egy.	M	724
Haptok Ring (n)	Zoro.	M	724
Hastshehogan (w)	Nav.	M	730
Hastsheyalti (w)	Nav.	M	730
Hathor (w)	Egy.	F	730
Hawo-gang-zang (w)	Tib.	M	1129
Henk-Nisesui (e)	Egy.	M	1683
Horus (all)	Egy.	M	792
Horus's four sons (all)	Egy.	M	793
Hsi Wang Mu (w)	Chin.	F	800
Huang T'ien Shang Ti (n)	Chin.	M	801
Hueytecpatl	Mex.	M	802
Huitzilopochtli (s)	Mex.	M	803
Hutchaiui	Egy.	M	1683
Huyen-thien (n)	Ind-Chin.	M	808
Indra (e)	Hin.	M	829
Ioskeha (e)	Huron	M	837
Itzamna (e)	Mex.	M	850
Ixcuin	Mex.	M	852
Janus (all)	Ital.	M	864
Japheth (n)	Hebr.	M	865
Jehovah (s)	Hebr.	M	870
Jikoku-ten (e)	Jap.	M	879
Jokwa (w)	Jap.	F	885
Kabibonokka (n)	Algon.	M	900

	Culture	Sex	Page
Kabun (w)	Algon.	M	900
Kauna (s)	Eskimo		601
Kebehsenuf (w)	Egy.	M	915
Khentamenti (w)	Egy.	M	923
Komoku-ten (w)	Jap.	M	941
Krishna (all)	Hin.	M	945
Kubera (n)	Hin.	M	948
Kuei-lung (e)	Chin.		949
Kuei-shen (n)	Chin.		949
Kul-lha-sha-ri (s)	Tib.	M	1129
Lung (e)	Chin.	F	1488
Mahamantranu-sarini (e)	Bud.	F	1043
Mahamayrui (n)	Bud.	F	1043
Mahapratisara (s)	Bud.	F	1044
Mahasahasrapramardani (c)	Bud.	F	1044
Mahasitavati (w)	Bud.	F	1044
Manco Capac (n)	Inca	M	1056
Marishiten (all)	Jap.	M	1067
Messon (e)	Algon.	M	1095
Michabo (e)	Algon.	M	1098
Mictlantecutli (n)	Mex.	M	1099
Mo-li Ch'ing (e)	Chin.	M	1115
Mo-li Hai (w)	Chin.	M	1115
Mo-li Hung (s)	Chin.	M	601
Mo-li Shou (n)	Chin.	M	1115
Mudjekeewis (w)	N.A.I.	M	1133
Nahurak (w)	Pawnee	M	1148
Nanacatltzatzi	Mex.	M	1152
Nanihehecatli	Mex.	M	1153
Neago (s)	Seneca	F	1159
Ninib (s)	Assyr-Baby.	M	1173
Nordre (n)	Norse	M	1180
Notus (s)	Gk.	M	1183
Oyan-do-ne (e)	Seneca	M	1223
Pah (w)	Pawnee	F	1226
Pai Hu (w)	Chin.		1226
Palato (n)	Rom.	F	1227
Pauna (e)	Eskimo	M	601
Pay Zume (e)	Para.	M	1245
Pei-chi Chen Chun (n)	Chin.	M	1249
Periscii (n)	Gk.		1256
Pinahua (w)	Inca	M	1273
Pindola (w)	Chin.	M	274
Pinto-lo-po-lo-t'o-she (w)	Chin.	M	1274
Pohjan-akka (n)	Fin.	M	1281
Pollux (e)	Gk.	M	295

	Culture	Sex	Page
Qehui (n)	Egy.	M	1683
Quetzalcoatl (e)	Mex.	M	1312
Ra (e)	Egy.	M	1314
Raphael (e)	Gnostic	M	1323
Ravana (c)	Hin.	M	1324
Rudra (n)	Hin.	M	1353
Sakuru (e)	Pawnee	M	1389
Salma (e)	Sem.	M	1391
Salmaone (e)	Aegean	F	1391
Sarvakamadugha (n)	Hin.	F	1401
Satavesˎ (w)	Zoro.	M	1402
Sauna (w)	Eskimo	M	601
Seiobo (w)	Jap.	F	1413
Set (s, w)	Egy.	M	1420
Shawano (s)	Algon.	M	1431
Shehbui (s)	Egy.	M	1683
Shem (c)	Hebr.	M	1433
Shen Pao (w)	Chin.	M	1434
Shutu (sw)	Baby.	F	1445
Siva (all)	Hin.	M	1461
Somber Warrior (n)	Chin., Jap.		1474
Ssu Ling (all)	Chin.	M	1488
Subhadra (w)	Hin.	F	1503
Surupa (e)	Hin.	F	1511
Sut (s, w)	Egy.	M	1513
Suvetar (s)	Hin.	F	1513
Tahuantin Suyu Kapac (all)	Inca	M	1525
Tai-yo Tati (e)	Chin.	M	1527
Tamon-ten (n)	Jap.	M	1531
Taranis (w)	Cel.	M	1534
Tenetemic	Mex.	M	802
Tezcatlipoca (e, n, s)	Mex.	M	1549
Thang-lha (n)	Tib.	M	1129
Tishtrya (e)	Pers.	M	1577
Titlacauan (n)	Mex.	M	1578
Tlaloc Tecutli (e)	Mex.	M	1581
Tobosaku (e)	Jap.	M	1583
Tokay (e)	Inca	M	1584
Too-lux (s)	Chinook	M	1587
Tran-vu (n)	Ind-Chin.	M	1593
T'si Tsiang (n)	Chin.	M	1604
Tung Hai (e)	Chin.	M	1607
Tung Huang Tai I (e)	Chin.	M	1607
Tung Wang Kung (e)	Chin.	M	1607
Tura (s)	Pers.	M	1608
Uzziel (s)	Christ.	M	1633

Direction (cont.)	Culture	Sex	Page
Vaisravana (n)	Bud.	M	1634
Vanand (w)	Pers.	M	1638
Varuna (w)	Hin.	M	1639
Vayu (nw)	Hin.	M	1642
Vermilion Bird (s)	Chin., Jap.	M	1646
Vijaya Sakti (e)	Bud.	F	1649
Virudhaka (s)	Bud.	M	1654
Virupaksa (w)	Bud.	M	1654
Voltumna (se)	Ital.	M	1658
Wabanang (e)	Men.	M	1660
Wabasso (nw)	Pota.	M	1660
Wabun (e)	Algon.	M	1660
Weiwobo (w)	Jap.	F	1672
Xipe Totec (w)	Mex.	M	1696
Yahualliehecca tl (w)	Mex.	M	1698
Yama (s)	Bud.	M	1699
Yamantakasakti (s)	Tib.	F	1699
Ya-o-gah (n)	Seneca	M	1701
Yar-lha-shang-Po (e)	Tib.	M	1129
Yo (s)	Jap.	M	1708
Yogini (all)	Hin.	F	1708
Zadkiel (all)	Hebr-Christ.	M	1384
Zephyrus (w)	Gk.	M	1718
Zocho-ten (s)	Jap.	M	1722
Zume (e)	W. Ind.	M	1735

DISCORD (SEE STRIFE)

DISEASE (PESTILENCE)			
Azhi Dahaka	Pers.	F	472
Bath Chorim	Sem.		186
Ben Nefilim	Sem.	M	+
Bennu	Baby.	M	202
Bushyansta	Zoro.	M	262
Ciuateteo	Mex.	F	346
Cuchi	Aus.	M	393
Deber	Sem.		+
Dibbara (Lubara)	Baby.	M	443
Drauga	Pers.	F	472
Druj	Pers.	F	472
Ekibiogami	Jap.	M	497
Epimetheus	Gk.	M	516
Etimmu	Baby.	M, F	528
Febris	Rom.	M	557
Four Horsemen of Apocalypse	Christ.	M	601
Gandhari	Hin.	F	626

	Culture	Sex	Page
Gigim	Sum.	M	655
Gilgamesh	Sum.	M	656
Gozu-tenwo	Jap.	M	680
Grahas	Hin.	M, F	682
Hadui	Iroq.	M	707
Harpies	Gk.	F	728
Hel	Norse	F	745
Hminza	Burm.		1537
Irra	Assyr-Baby.	M	841
Jakis	Jap.		862
Jalyogini	Hin.	M	862
Ketu	Hin.	M	920
Khin-ort	Sib.	M	924
Kuda	Hebr.	M	948
Kukulcan	Mex.	M	950
Labartu	Assyr.	F	957
Laimos	Gk.	M	964
Lamastu	Sum.	F	966
Lamme	Sum.	F	968
Leprea	Gk.	F	985
Lha-mo-kar-po	Tib.	F	989
Libu	Baby.	M	991
Lilu	Baby.	M	995
Long Meg	Bryth.	F	1012
Louhi	Lapp	F	1016
Lua	Ital.	F	1019
Maahiset	Fin-Ug.		1030
Ma-mo	Tib.	F	1052
Mariamma	Hin.	F	1067
Masan	Hin.	M	1072
Matrs	Hin.	F	1076
Meg (Long Meg, Mons Meg)	Eng.	F	1084
Mindi	Aus.		1106
Moloch	Sem.	M	1115
Moravaya Panna	Slav.	F	1122
Morc	Cel.	M	1122
Namtaru	Assyr-Baby.	M	1152
gNan	Tib.		1152
Nasu	Pers.	F	472
Nergal	Assyr-Baby.	M	1164
Notus	Gk.	M	1183
Oni	Jap.	M	1209
Paluc Cat	Bryth.	F	1230
Pandora	Gk.	F	1232
Pazuzu	Sum.	M	1245
Preta	Hin.		1292
Qetebh Meriri	Hebr.		1309

Disease (cont.)	Culture	Sex	Page
Rail	Pelew Is.	M	1319
Resheph	Phoen.	M	1333
Roga	Hin.	M	1699
Rudra	Hin.	M	1353
Rudrani	Hin.	F	1353
Rutu	Lapp	M	1355
Saint Vitus	Christ.	M	1383
Shitala	Bengali	F	1439
Sidanu	Baby.		1447
Sitala	Hin.	F	1460
Smintheus	Gk.	M	111
Tase	Burm.		1537
Tena-ranide	Athap.		1544
Tengri, Black	Buriat	M	1545
Tezcatlipoca	Mex.	M	1549
Thabet	Burm.	F	1550
Thaye	Burm.	M, F	1552
Thepla	Arm.	M	1554
Timi	Hebr.	M, F	1574
Tou-shen	Chin.	M	1591
Triglav	Slav.	M	1597
Tsunuguhi	Jap.	M	1604
Tupilaq	Greenland	M, F	1608
Unk-ta-he	Dakota Ind.	M	1626
Ura	Sum.	M	1627
Vaisravana	Bud.	M	1634
Vata	Papuan		1641
Vetehinen	Rus.		1648
Xipe Totec	Mex.	M	1696
Yaksa	Bud.	M	1698
Yaotzin	Mex.	M	1701

DISORDER (SEE STRIFE)

DIVINATION

Abaris	Gk.	M	12
Abu-bekr	Mos.	M	20
Aesacus	Gk.	M	41
Agabus	Christ.	M	44
Agastya	Hin.	M	45
Aggeus	Heb.	M	48
Agni	Hin.	M	49
Amergin	Cel.	M	84
Amos	Heb.	M	87
Amphiaraus	Gk.	M	87
Amphilochus	Gk.	M	88

	Culture	Sex	Page
Anna	Christ.	F	99
Apollo	Gk.	M	110
Arishis	Hin.	M	125
Aruns the Etruscan	Rom.	M	133
Asaph	Heb.	M	135
Asdente	Ital.	M	137
Asita	Bud.	M	140
Atri	Hin.	M	153
Augurs	Rom.	M	156
Baalberith	Hebr.	M	167
Badb	Cel.	F	171
Balaam	Hebr.	M	174
Bangma	Hin.	M	178
Bara	Baby.	M	180
Bharadvaja	Hin.	M	208
Bhrigu	Hin.	M	209
Black Tortoise	Chin.	M	223
Bona Dea	Rom.	F	234
Brigit	Cel.	F	249
Brynhild	Norse	F	253
Calchas	Gk.	M	272
Camaean Sibyl	Gk.	F	279
Camenae	Rom.	F	281
Cassandra	Gk.	F	294
Cazotte	Oc.	M	300
Cethlionn	Cel.	F	306
Chiron	Gk.	M	327
Chryseis	Gk.	F	334
Chyavana	Hin.	M	337
Cumaean Sibyl	Rom.	F	396
Daniel	Hebr.	M	413
Dasagvas	Hin.	M	416
Deborah	Hebr.	F	422
Dee	Cel.	F	424
Delphicia	Cel.	F	428
Delphic Oracle	Gk.	F	428
Dharmapala of gNas-c'um	Tib.	M	438
Dionysus	Gk.	M	447
Dodona's Black Pigeon	Gk.		455
Don Quixote	Span.	M	462
Draugr	Norse	M	470
Droll	Norse	M	471
Eckhardt	Germ.	M	490
Egeria	Rom.	F	491
Elijah	Hebr.	M	503
Enmenduranna	Sum.	M	512

	Culture	Sex	Page
Eurypylus	Gk.	M	532
Ezekiel	Hebr.	M	541
Fedelm	Cel.	F	557
Fergus the Eloquent	Cel.	M	561
Finn Eger	Cel.	M	570
Frey	Norse	M	609
Fu Hsi	Chin.	M	615
Gad	Hebr.	M	620
Gefjon	Norse	F	637
Glaucus	Gk.	M	662
Gollveig	Norse	F	743
Grifir	Norse	M	691
Gunasarman	Hin.	M	698
Habakkuk	Hebr.	M	705
Haggai	Hebr.	M	708
Han Hsiang-tzu	Chin.	M	722
Heid	Norse	F	743
Helenus	Gk.	M	746
Heracles of Oeta	Gk.	M	755
Hermes	Gk.	M	760
Hosea	Hebr.	M	793
Hud	Mos.	M	802
Huitzilopochtli	Mex.	M	803
Huitziton	Mex.	M	803
H'uraru	Pawnee	F	808
Iamus	Gk.	M	815
Idmon	Gk.	M	820
Ilu-tashmit	Baby.	M	825
Isaiah	Hebr.	M	842
Israel	Hebr.	M	847
Iuturna	Ital.	F	850
Jamshid	Pers.	M	863
Jeremiah	Hebr.	M	873
Jizo	Jap.	M	881
Joel	Hebr.	M	883
John the Baptist	Christ.	M	1372
Jonah	Hebr.	M	886
Joseph (Yusuf)	Hebr., Mos.	M	888
Joshua	Hebr.	M	889
Jotham	Hebr.	M	890
Kalchas	Gk.	M	903
Kanva	Hin.	M	908
Katmir	Mos.	M	913
Kavi	Indo-Iranian	M	914
Kevalins	Hin.	M	920
Khidv	Mos.	M	924

	Culture	Sex	Page
King Goldemar (Vollmar)	Germ.	M	929
Korotangi	N. Zeal.		943
Kuei-shen	Chin.		949
Kui-gyal-po	Tib.	M	949
Kutsa	Hin.	M	954
Lamha	Sum.	M	482
Laocoon	Gk., Rom.	M	972
Lao Tze	Chin.	M	973
Lemuel	Hebr.	M	982
Levarcham	Cel.	F	988
Li T'ieh-kuai	Chin.	M	1002
Ludki (Krasnoludi)	Serb.		1021
Lug	Cel.	M	1022
Luke	Christ.	M	1374
Lu-tung-pin	Chin.	M	1026
Lybica	Rom.	F	1027
Magi	Christ.	M	1037
Mahapancaraja	Tib.	M	1043
Maharshis	Hin.	M	1044
Malachi	Hebr.	M	1048
Mark	Christ.	M	1068
Matthew	Christ.	M	1076
Medicine Man	N.A.I.	M	1083
Melampus	Gk.	M	1085
Melchior	Christ.	M	1085
Memnon	Gk.	M	1088
Merlin (Ambrosios)	Bryth.	M	1092
Metis	Gk.	F	1096
Micah	Hebr.	M	1097
Micaiah	Hebr.	M	1098
Michabo	Algon.	M	1098
Mimir	Norse	M	1105
Miriam	Hebr.	F	1109
Mohammed	Mos.	M	1114
Mopsus	Gk.	M	1122
Moses	Hebr.	M	1126
Nach-un	Tib.	M	1146
Nag-pa	Tib.	M	1148
Nahum	Hebr.	M	1148
Naiades	Gk.	F	1148
Navagvas	Hin.	M	1158
Nekyomanteion	Gk.	M	1161
Nereus	Gk.	M	1164
Nix	Teutonic	M	1176
Nixe	Teutonic	F	1176
Noidde	Lapp	M	1179

	Culture	Sex	Page
Nostradamus	Fr.	M	1182
Ob	Hebr.		1191
Obadiah	Hebr.	M	1191
Oceanid	Gk.	F	1193
Oedipus	Gk.	M	1198
Oenone	Gk.	F	1199
Ogma	Cel.	M	1200
Old Moore	Eng.	M	1205
Ombrophore	Gk.	M	1207
Orpheus	Gk.	M	1216
Pe-har	Tib.	M	1146
Philomela	Gk.	F	1263
Phineus	Gk.	M	1264
Picus	Rom.	M	1269
Pi Kan	Chin.	M	1271
Polyidus	Gk.	M	1284
Praepates	Rom.	M	1290
Prin-las-gyi-rgyla-po	Tib.	M	1294
Procne	Gk.	F	1294
Prometheus	Gk.	M	1295
Proteus	Gk.	M	1297
Pythia	Gk.	F	1308
Raven	N.A.I.	M	1325
Ravgga	Fin-Ug.	M	1325
Rhodope	Gk.	F	1337
Rishis	Hin.	M	1340
Ryo-to-bin	Jap.	M	1356
Samuel	Hebr.	M	1394
Selli	Gk.	M	1415
Serapis	Egy.	M	1418
Seth	Hebr.	M	1421
Seven Ancient Elders	Baby.	M	1422
Sibyl	Gk., Hebr.	F	1445
Silenii	Gk.	M	1453
Silenus	Gk.	M	1453
Simeon	Christ.	M	1454
Simurgh	Pers.	M	1456
Sin	Assyr.	M	1456
Sionite (Ellerian)	Norw. (Germ.)	M	1457
Sitnapishtim	Baby.	M	1461
Somber Warrior	Chin., Jap.	M	1474
Svantovit	Slav.	M	1514
Svarozic	Slav.	M	1514
Tages	Ital.	M	1524
Tantalus	Gk.	M	1533
Teraphim	Sem.	M	1546

	Culture	Sex	Page
Tervils	Norw.	M	1547
Themis	Gk.	F	1553
Thomas the Rhymer	Scot.	M	1560
Thoth (Hermes Trismegistus)	Egy.	M	1562
Thriae	Gk.	F	1566
Tiresias	Gk.	M/A	1576
Tohunga	Maori	M	1584
Ts'ang Chieh	Chin.	M	1602
Tsi-ku	Chin.	F	1603
Tsui Goab	Hotten.	M	1604
Ulala	Haida	M	1621
Urdawl Ben	Welsh	M	1628
Uriel	Caba.	M	1629
Vafthrudner	Norse	M	1633
Varjohaltia	Fin-Ug.	M	1639
Vipascit	Hin.	M	1651
Visvamitra	Hin.	M	1655
Xanthus	Gk.		1695
Yiddeoni	Hebr.		1707
Yiyi	Afr.	M	1708
Zadkiel	Hebr.	M	1714
Zechariah	Hebr.	M	1717
Zephaniah	Hebr.	M	1718
Zeus	Gk.	M	1719
Zoroaster	Zoro.	M	1734

DREAMS (SEE SLEEP)

DROUGHT (FAMINE)

	Culture	Sex	Page
Afrasiyab	Pers.	M	43
Agastya	Hin.	M	45
Ahi	Hin.	M	52
Aillen mac Midhna	Cel.	M	56
Akano Jewel	Jap.	M	59
Alcyoneus	Gk.	M	65
Amangons	Bryth.	M	79
Amycus	Gk.	M	89
Andhaka	Hin.	M	93
Apaosha	Zoro.	M	107
Apappus	Egy.	M	107
Arezoshamana	Pers.	M	918
Azhi Dakaha	Pers.	M	165
Blihos-Bliheris	Bryth.	M	225
Calydonian Boar	Gk.	M	279
Con	Inca	M	363
Crommyonia Sow	Gk.	F	384

	Culture	Sex	Page
Dasas	Hin.	M	416
Eochaid Ollathair	Cel.	M	513
Eteocles	Gk.	M	527
Fomor	Cel.	M	590
Frode	Dan.	M	613
Galta-ulan-tengeri	Mong.	M	624
Geryon	Gk.	M	647
Grim & Hilde	Norse	M-F	691
Gudanna	Assyr-Baby.	M	694
Houmea	Maori	F	794
Hydra	Gk.	M	810
Ith	Cel.	F	849
Itztlacoliuhqui	Mex.	M	850
Joseph of Arimathea	Christ.	M	889
Kalinak	Hin.	M	904
Kamak	Pers.	M	906
Kanook	Alas.	M	908
Kauravas	Hin.	M	913
Keresavazdah	Pers.	M	918
Koshchei	Fin.	M	943
Limos	Gk.	M	997
Lycurgus	Gk.	M	1028
Mada	Hin.	M	1035
Maelcen	Cel.	M	1036
Mahisha (Bhainsasura)	Hin.	M	1045
Marathon Bull	Gk.	M	1064
Mata	Cel.	M	1074
Mawa	Afr.	M	1078
Mordred	Bryth.	M	1122
Nahusa	Hin.	M	1148
Namuci	Hin.	M	1152
Nemean Lion	Gk.	M	1162
Ninib	Assyr-Baby.	M	1173
Paluc Cat	Bryth.	F	1230
Panis	Hin.	M	1233
Pantagruel	Fr.	M	1234
Pelops	Gk.	M	1251
Python	Gk.	M	1308
Raudalo	N. Guin.	M	1324
Rerir	Norse	M	1333
Ritho	Bryth.	M	1341
Sag	Egy.	F	1360
Sambara	Hin.	M	1393
Scythians (Arimaspi)	Gk.	M, F	1410
Sekhet	Egy.	F	1414
Senach	Cel.	M	1416

	Culture	Sex	Page
Set	Egy.	M	1420
Shwe Myet-hna	Ind. Chin.	F	1445
Siva	Hin.	M	1461
Sphinx	Gk.	F	1482
Su-shen	Hin.	M	1513
Svigdur	Norse	M	1515
Tezcatlipoca	Mex.	M	1549
Thermutis	Hebr.	F	1554
Varcin	Hin.	M	1639
Vena	Hin.	M	1644
Visvarupa	Hin.	M	1656
Vrtra	Hin.	M	1659
Xiuhcoatl	Mex.		1696
Yaotl	Mex.	M	1701
Yaotzin	Mex.	M	1701
Zamzummim	Hebr.	M	1716
Zmei Goruinich	Slav.	M	1722
Zohak	Pers.	M	1734

DRUNKENNESS (SEE WINE)
DUSK (SEE GLOAMING)

DYING GOD OR HERO

	Culture	Sex	Page
Actaeon	Gk.	M	28
Ame-Waka-Hiko	Jap.	M	85
Apam Napat	Hin.	M	107
Apollo	Gk.	M	110
Ara	Arm.	M	116
Arcas	Gk.	M	118
Balder	Norse	M	174
Christ	Christ.	M	330
Cian	Cel.	M	338
Combalus	Sem.	M	361
Dumuzi	Sum.	M	476
Eniautes Diamon	Gk.	M	+
Frode	Norse	M	613
Heitsi-Eibib	Hotten.	M	744
Heracles	Gk.	M	752
Hercules	Rom.	M	759
Hyacinthus	Gk.	M	809
Hypsistos	Gk.	M	813
Iasion	Gk.	M	816
Icarus	Gk.	M	817
Izanami	Jap.	F	853
Lahu	Burm.	M	964
Lil	Sum.	M	994

Dying God (cont.)	Culture	Sex	Page
Melkarth	Phoen.	M	1086
Myiagros	Gk.	M	1142
Ninurta	Sum.	M	1174
Oannes	Baby., Chald.	M	1190
Persephone	Gk.	F	1257
Proserpina	Rom.	F	1296
Ra	Egy.	M	1314
Tammuz	Baby.	M	1530
Tchue	Bush.	M	1540
Ushumgalanna	Sum.	M	1631
Yarilo	Rus.	M	1701
Yati	Hin.	M	1702
Yima	Pers.	M	1707
Zagreus	Cretan	M	1715
EARTH			
Acca Larentia	Rom.	F	22
Acrea	Gk.	F	27
Aeracura	Cel.	F	41
Afrasiyab	Pers.	M	43
Agraulid	Gk.	F	51
Agraulos	Gk.	F	51
Airmed	Cel.	F	57
Aker	Egy.	M	59
Akka	Fin.	F	1621
Alcmene	Gk.	F	65
Alfar	Norse	M	67
Althea	Gk.	F	77
Amalthea	Gk.	F	79
Ament	Egy.	F	84
Anatu	Sum.	F	92
Andromeda	Gk.	F	94
Anu	Cel.	F	104
Anunaki	Baby.	M	105
Aphrodite	Gk.	F	108
Ariadne	Gk.	F	123
Armat	Arm.	F	521
Aruru	Sum.	F	133
Ashi-nadzu-chi	Jap.	M	139
Ataentsic	Huron	F	147
Atira	Pawnee	F	151
Attabeira	Taino	F	154
Awitelin Tsita	Zuni	F	162
Baalath	Sem.	M	167
Baau	Phoen., Sum.	F	168
Behr (Medr)	Arab.	M	196

	Culture	Sex	Page
Belleros	Cel.	M	199
Bhumidevi	Hin.	F	209
Bhumiya	Hin.	M	209
Burkhan	Sib.	M	261
Can	Mex.	M	283
Canam-lum	Mex.	M	283
Caswallawn	Bryth.	M	296
Cecrops	Gk.	M	301
Cercopes	Gk.	M	304
Ceres	Rom.	F	305
Chaabu	Sem.	F	307
Chikisanti	Ainu	F	323
Chimalman	Mex.	F	325
Cinteotl	Mex.	F	341
Ciuateotl	Mex.	F	346
Coatlicue	Mex.	F	352
Conchobar	Cel.	M	364
Consus	Ital.	M	368
Couatlicue	Mex.	F	376
Criosphinx	Egy.	M	382
Cybele	Phryg.	F	400
Dagda	Cel.	M	405
Danae	Gk.	F	411
Demeter	Gk.	F	429
Demogorgon	Christ.	M	431
Dhara	Hin.	M	1641
Dharti Mai	Hin.	F	439
Dione	Gk.	F	446
Duergar	Norse	M	475
Dyava-Matar	Hin.	F	480
Eire	Cel.	F	496
Eithinoha	Iroq.	F	496
Elara	Gk.	F	+
Elbegast	Norse	M	+
Elberich	Norse	M	498
Elle-folk	Norse	M, F	505
Eniautes Daimon	Gk.	M	+
Enki	Assyr., Baby., Sum.	M	511
Enlil	Assyr., Baby., Sum.	M	512
Eriu	Cel.	F	521
Erkir	Arm.	F	521
Fafnir	Norse	M	544
Faknik	Papuan		546
Fjorgyn	Norse	F	578

	Culture	Sex	Earth Page
Frigg	Norse	F	612
Gaea	Gk.	F/A	621
Gahe	Apache Ind.		622
Ga'n	Apache Ind.		625
Gargamelle	Fr.	F	630
Gashan-ki	Baby.	F	633
Geb	Egy.	M	637
Gemeter	Gk.	F	643
Gnome	Med. Lit.	M	664
Goewin	Bryth.	F	669
Gorgon	Gk.	F	678
Great Turtle	N.A.I.		1610
Gyges	Gk.	M	703
Hebe	Gk.	F	739
Hecatoncheires (Centimani)	Gk.	M	741
Heke-heke-I-papa	Poly.	F	745
Hera	Gk.	F	752
Hermione	Gk.	F	761
Hertha	Norse	F	764
Hine-tuamauge	Poly.	F	1531
Hkrip Hkrawp	Burm.	M	775
Hlodyn	Norse	F	776
Hotu-papa	Poly.	F	794
Hou-t'u	Chin.	M	797
Hou-t'u nai nai	Chin.	F	797
Huang Ti	Chin.	M	801
Huayna Capac	Inca	M	801
Huemac	Mex.	M	802
Humba	Sem.	M	804
H'uraru	Pawnee	F	808
Ida	Gk.	F	818
Ilamatecutli	Mex.	F	823
Ilancueitl	Mex.	F	823
Ilat	Arab.	F	823
Ingun (Yngvi)	Norse	F	831
Innini	Sum.	F	832
Iowahine	Hawa.	F	837
Iweridd	Bryth.	F	852
Jogaoh	Iroq.	M, F	884
Jord	Norse	F/A	887
Jordegumma	Swed.	F	887
Jormungandr	Norse	M	887
Juno	Rom.	F	895
Kaiwan	Ethiop.	F	902
Karpophoros	Gk.	F	911
Khan-iki	Ostiak	M	923
Khon-ma	Tib.	F	925

	Culture	Sex	Page
Khudjana	Transvaal	M	925
Ki	Sum.	F	926
Kleo	Gk.	F	936
Kobold	Germ.	M	936
Kokyanwuqti	Pueblo	F	940
Koloowisi	Zuni	M	941
Ksetrasya	Hin.	M	947
Ksitigarbha	Bud	M	947
Kukumatz	Yuman	M	950
Kun	Hin.	F	951
Libera	Rom.	F	990
Libitina	Rom.	F	991
Libya	Gk.	F	991
Llevelys	Bryth.	M	1004
Lumimu-ut	Indo.	F	1024
Ma	As. Min.	F	1030
Maa-emae	Fin.	F	1030
Madderakka	Lapp	F	1035
Madhavi	Hin.	F	1035
Magna Mater	Phryg.	F	1040
Mah	Sem.	F	1042
Mahuika	Poly.	F	1046
Mama	Sum.	F	1050
Mama Allpa	Inca	F	1051
Mamzraumana	Pueblo	F	1052
Marzyana	Slav.	F	1072
Matres	Rom/Cel.	F	1076
Midgard Serpent (Midgardsormen)	Norse	M	1100
Mimas	Gk.	M	1105
Modron	Bryth.	F	1114
Mokkurkalfi	Norse	M	1115
Mo-li Hung (Mo-li Shou)	Chin.	M	601
Mucalinda	Bud.	M	1133
Mu Kwa	Chin.	F	1135
Mumuhango	Poly.	F	1531
Musisi	Uganda	M	1139
Muskrat	Algon.	F	1140
Nagasvaraja	Bud.	M	1148
Nana	Sum.	F	1152
Nang Pyek-kha	Ind-Chin.	F	1153
Nazit	Egy.	F	1159
Neheb-kau	Egy.	F	1160
Neith	Lib., Egy.	F	1161
Nin-ki	Baby.	F	1173
Nintu	Sum.	F	1174

	Culture	Sex	Page
Nishtigri	Hin.	F	1175
Nokomis	Algon.	F	1179
Nzambi	Congo	A	1188
Ohodowas	Iroq.		1202
Oho-ge-tsu-hime	Jap.	F	1202
Oho-iwa-daimyo-jin	Jap.	M	1202
Oho-to-no-Be	Jap.	F	1202
Oho-to-no-Ji	Jap.	M	1202
Oho-usu	Jap.	M	1202
O-kuni-nushi	Jap.	M	1204
Old Woman Who Never Dies	Siouan	F	1205
Omeciuatl	Mex.	F	1207
Oneis	Gk.	F	1209
Onitsu-nu	Jap.	M	1210
Ophion	Gk.	M	1211
Otukan (Natigai)	Asian	M	1221
Otygen	Mong.	F	1221
Oxomuco	Mex.	F	1223
Pachamama	Inca	F	1224
Papa	Poly.	F	1235
Paravataksha	Hin.	M	1237
Parvati	Hin.	F	1241
Patshak	Ostiak		1244
Pelops	Gk.	M	1251
Pilumnus	Rom.	M	1273
Pirua	Inca	F	1275
Porphyrion	Gk.	M	1287
Prthivi	Hin.	F	1297
Pwyll	Bryth.	M	1306
Pyrrha	Gk.	F	1307
Qeb (Seb)	Egy.	M	1309
Rebecca	Hebr.	F	1326
Rhea	Gk.	F	1335
Rhiannon (Rigantona)	Bryth.	F	1336
Rhoda	Gk.	F	1336
Ribhus	Hin.	M	1337
Rind	Norse	F	1339
Ruaumoko	Poly.	M	1352
Sa-bdag	Tib.		1357
Sashi-mi-rig-gilha	Tib.	M	1401
Schamir	Hebr.		1407
Semele	Gk.	F	1415
Shahapet	Arm.	M	1428
Shang-ti	Chin.	M	1430
She	Chin.		1431
Shekinah	Caba.	F	1432

	Culture	Sex	Page
Sherah	Sum.	M	1435
Shuiji	Jap.	F	1444
Sidero	Gk.	F	1391
Sif	Norse	F	1448
Sige	Baby.	F	1449
Sigyn	Norse	F	1451
Silvanus	Rom.	M	1453
Silvia	Rom.	F	1454
Sir-syv-kudegen	Chuvash	M	1459
Spantaramet	Pers.	M	1479
Spider Woman	N.A.I.	A	1482
Sprite	Eng.	M, F	1485
Staka Pas (Kuvan Pas)	Fin-Ug.	M	1489
Sualtam	Cel.	M	1503
Surabhi	Hin.	F	1511
Suvinenge	Daho.	M	1513
Sycorax	Eng.	F	1521
Tamfana	Marsi	F	1530
Tanen	Egy.	M	1531
Tari Pennu	Khond	F	1535
Tellus Mater	Ital.	F	1542
Tengys	Sib.	M	1545
Terra Mater	Ital.	F	1547
Themis	Gk.	F	1553
Termutis	Hebr.	F	1554
Tihkuyi Wuht	Hopi	F	1573
Ti-kuan	Chin.	M	1573
Tirid	Baby.		1576
Titaea	Gk.	F	1577
Titan	Gk.	M, F	1577
Ti-ya	Chin.	M	1673
Tlahuitzin	Mex.	F	1581
Tlalecutli	Mex.	M	1581
Tlalli-iyollo	Mex.	F	1581
Tlatecutli	Mex.	M	1582
Tlazolteotl	Mex.	F	1582
Toci	Mex.	F	1583
Torx	Arm.	M	1590
Toyo-uke-bime	Jap.	A	1593
Triglav	Slav.	M	1597
Triptolemus	Gk.	M	1598
Trophonius	Gk.	M	1600
Tuila	Sib.	M	1606
Tunkan	Dakota Ind.	M	1608
T'u-ti shen (Ko-lung)	Chin.	M	1610
Tuwapontumsi	Pueblo	F	1611

Earth (cont.)	Culture	Sex	Page
Typhoeus	Gk.	M	1617
Typhon	Gk.	M	1617
Uatlan	Kiche	F	1619
Uazit (Uatchet)	Egy.	F	1619
Uchtdelbh	Cel.	F	1620
Uhiji	Jap.	M	1620
Unferth	Ang-Sax.	M	1625
Usert	Egy.	F	1631
Varaha	Hin.	M	1638
Vasudhara	Hin.	F	1641
Vis	Pre-Inca		1654
Wealtitheow	Norse	F	1670
Xochiquetzal	Mex.	F	1696
Yami	Hin.	F	1700
Yanari	Jap.	M	1700
Yeibichai	Nav.	M	1703
Yellow Corn Girl	Pueblo	F	1496
Zamin	Pers.	F	1716
EARTHQUAKE			
Gyges	Gk.	M	703
Hecatoncheires (Centimani)	Gk.	M	741
Huemac	Mex.	M	802
Mahuika	Poly.	F	1046
Mo-li Hung	Chin.	M	601
Musisi	Uganda	M	1139
Paravataksha	Hin.	M	1237
Porphyrion	Gk.	M	1287
Poseidon	Gk.	M	1288
Ruaumoko	Poly.	M	1352
Tirid	Baby.		1576
Toci	Mex.	F	1583
Torx	Arm.	M	1590
Tuila	Sib.	M	1606
Typhoeus	Gk.	M	1617
Typhon	Gk.	M	1617
Varaha	Hin.	M	1638
Yanari	Jap.	M	1700
EATEN DEITY			
Arcas	Gk.	M	118
Cronids, The	Gk.	M	384
Itys	Gk.	M	850
Jesus	Christ.	M	877
Metra	Gk.	F	1096
Nyctimus	Gk.	M	1187

	Culture	Sex	Page
Pelops	Gk.	M	1251
Thyestes' sons	Gk.	M	1569

ECHO (SEE SOUND)
ECLIPSE (SEE DARKNESS)
ELF (SEE DEMON)

ELOQUENCE

Aeschines	Gk.	M	+
Baile	Cel.	M	173
Balder	Norse	M	174
Benten	Jap.	F	203
Bragi	Norse	M	240
Cermait	Cel.	M	305
Demosthenes	Gk.	M	432
Dharmacakra	Bud.	M	438
Emer	Cel.	F	508
Fabulinus	Rom.	M	542
Fergus	Cel.	M	561
Fimbulthul	Norse	M	568
Forseti	Norse	M	595
Friar John	Eng.	M	611
Gawain	Bryth.	M	635
Hermes	Gk.	M	760
Hother	Norse	M	746
Manjusri	Bud.	M	1059
Mercury	Rom.	M	1091
Mummu	Sum.	M	1136
Ogma	Cel.	M	1200
Ogmios	Cel.	M	1201
Sarasvati	Hin.	F	1400
Simhanadamanjusri	Bud.	M	1455
Sitamanjughosa	Bud.	M	1460
Zeus	Gk.	M	1719

ENCHANTMENT (SEE MAGIC)

ENDLESS TASK WORKER (ENDLESS PENANCE)

Danaides	Gk.	F	411
Grettir	Ice.	M	374a
Ixion	Gk.	M	852
Kubaiko	Tatar	F	947
Ocnus	Gk.	M	1193
Ponos	Gk.	M	1285
Sisyphus	Gk.	M	1459

Endless Task Worker (cont.)	Culture	Sex	Page
Tantalus	Gk.	M	1533
Wu Kang	Chin.	M	1693

ENVY (SEE JEALOUSY)
ENVY VICTIM (SEE JEALOUSY OR ENVY VICTIM)

EPHEMERAL DEITIES			
Myiagros	Gk.	M	1142
Ukifune	Jap.	F	1621
Zeitgeist	Germ.		536

ETERNAL, THE (THE INFINITE)			
Absolute, The	Christ.	M	19
Ala (Allah)	Mos.	M	60
Ananta	Hin.	M	91
Apis	Egy.	M	109
Aum	Hin.	M	157
Baiame	Aus.	M	173
Brahm	Hin.	M	240
Buddha	Bud.	M	255
Chaos	Baby.	F/A	312
Chaos	Gk.	M/A	312
Ch'i	Chin.	M	321
Ewigzeitgeist	Germ.		536
Fugen En-myo	Jap.	M	615
Garbh Ogh	Cel.	F	628
Guamaonocon	Taino	M	693
Io	Mex.	M	836
Iocauna	Taino	M	836
Jehovah	Hebr.	M	870
Nun	Egypt.	M	1185
Rahu	Hin.	M	1318
Resheph	Phoen.	M	1333
Sesa & Vasuki	Hin.	M-M	1420
T'ien Pao	Chin.	M	1572
Yoskeha (Sapling)	Iroq.	M	1710

EVIL			
Abtagigi	Assyr-Baby.	F	20
Ahithophel	Hebr.	M	53
Ahriman	Zoro.	M	53
Aka Manah	Zoro.	M	59
Akuman (Aka manah)	Pers.	M	59
Al Beze	Arab.	M	63
Algea	Gk.	F	68

	Culture	Sex	Page
Amestris	Pers.	F	85
Anakim	Hebr.	M	91
Andra	Pers.	M	830
Angra Mainyu	Zoro.	M	97
Apep	Egy.	M	107
Apocatequil	Inca	M	109
Apsu	Baby.	M	115
Arimans	Pers.	M	124
Arsan-Duolai	Yakut	M	130
Artavazd	Arm.	M	130
Ashura	Jap.	M	140
Athaliah	Hebr.	F	149
Balor	Cel.	M	176
Basilisk	Christ.	M	184
Bergbui	Norse	M	204
Blatant Beast	Christ.	M	225
Bres	Cel.	M	246
Cacia	Gk.	F	265
Cacodaemon	Oc.	M	265
Caena-Maergha	Pers.	M	267
Caipora	Braz.	M	270
Cerna	Cel.	M	305
Cernobog	Slav.	M	305
Charybdis & Scylla	Gk.	F-F	316
Cichol the Footless	Cel.	M	338
Cupay	Inca	M	397
Dahhak	Pers.	M	406
Daitya	Hin.	M	407
Danavas	Hin.	M	412
Darago	Philip.	F	414
Dazbog	Slav.	M	420
Dekans	Baby., Egy.	M	427
Dirce	Gk.	F	450
Doeg	Hebr.	M	455
Druhs	Hin.	M	471
Drukh	Hin.	M	472
Duhsaha (Sudurmukha)	Hin.	M	948
Eblis	Mos.	M	489
Elissa	Eng.	F	504
Erwand	Arm.	M	523
Fierabras, Sir	Eng.	M	565
Flaga	Norse		581
Gama-Sennin	Jap.	M	625
Goin	Aus.	M	670
Golagras	Eng.	M	670
Golerotheran	Bryth.	M	674

	Culture	Sex	Page
Goliath	Hebr.	M	674
Golishan	Eng.	M	674
Grep	Norse	M	690
Guecubu (Hucuva)	Chilean	M	695
Gullveig	Norse	F	697
Hahgwehdaetgah	Seneca	M	708
Hanpa	Sum.	M	722
Hati	Norse	M	731
Heid	Norse	F	743
Hobomokko	N.A.I.	M	778
Hugon	Fr.	M	803
Ibukido Nushi	Jap.	M	816
Ilu Limnu	Jap.	M	825
Jehoram	Hebr.	M	869
Kaguhana	Jap.	M	902
Kala	Bali	M	903
Kali	Hin.	F	903
Kalu Kumara Yaka	Sinhalese	M	905
Kanook	Alaskan	M	908
Karali	Hin.	F	909
Khafra	Egy.	M	922
Khufu	Egy.	M	925
Kilili	Assyr-Baby.	F	927
Koen	Aus.	M	940
Kormos	Mong.	M	943
Koshchei	Slav.	M	943
Koupai	Inca	M	944
Kul	Fin-Ug.	M	950
Kwan	Siamese		955
Likho	Slav.	F	994
Liwa	Honduras		1004
Loki	Norse	M/A	1010
Maga-tsumi	Jap.	M	1037
Mahound	Christ.	M	1046
Mailkun	Aus.	F	940
Malsum	Algon.	M	1050
Mammon	Hebr-Christ.	M	1051
Mandarangan	Philip.	M	1056
Mara	Bud.	M	1063
Maruts	Hin.	M	1071
Matchi-Manito	Algon.	M, F	1058
Maul	Eng.	M	1078
Mazainyon	Pers.		1081
Medea	Gk.	F	1082
Mengk	Fin-Ug.	M	1089
Mirume	Jap.	F	1110

	Culture	Sex	Page
Mitothin	Norse	M	1112
Mulla	Sum.	M	1135
Mummu	Baby.	M	1136
Muretsu	Jap.	M	1137
Mushussu	Sum.	M	1139
Nahema	Oc.	M	1148
Nakk	Fin.	M	1150
Nasnas	Arab.	M	1156
Nero	Rom.	M	1164
Nesreca	Serb.	F	1165
Nibhaz	Avite	M	1167
Nickar	Norse	M	545
Nickard	Germ.	M	1168
Nickneven	Scot.	F	+
Nitne Kamui	Ainu		1176
Nynnyaw & Peibaw	Cel.	M-M	1188
Obyda (Arsori)	Chuvash	F	1192
Oderic	Ital.	M	1195
Og	Hebr.	M	1200
Oh-maga-tsumi	Jap.	M	1201
Onan	Caba.	M	1208
Oni	Jap.	M	1209
Onto & Bonto	Fin-Ug.	M-F	1210
Orgoglio	Eng.	M	1214
Ovda	Fin-Ug.	M, F	1221
Owasse	Men.	M	1221
Pairika	Zoro.	F	1226
Pallas	Gk.	M	1228
Papa Purusha	Hin.	M	1235
Pari	Tatar		1237
Parne	Fin-Ug.	M	1239
Pekah	Hebr.	M	1249
Phonoi	Gk.	M	1266
Queenah	Cowich.	M	1312
Rakshasa	Hin.	M, F	1320
Ruotta	Lapp	M	1354
Rush (Bruder Rausch)	Germ.	M	1355
Satan	Hebr-Christ.	M	1402
Sauru	Zoro.	M	925
Searbhan Lochlannach	Cel.	M	1411
Sedu	Baby.	M	1413
Simon Legree	Am. Lit.	M	981
Staka Pas (Kuvan Pas)	Fin-Ug.	M	1489
Supay	Inca	M	1510
Surali	Fin-Ug.	M	1511
Talar-disir	Teut.	F	1528

Evil (cont.)	Culture	Sex	Page
Tamamo-no-maye	Jap.	F	1529
Tangaroa	Hawa.	M	1531
Tehotennhiaron	Iroq.	M	1541
Tippakalleum	Aus.	F	940
Tlaelquani	Mex.	F	1581
Tlazolteotl	Mex.	F	1582
Turkish Knight	Christ.	M	1608
Tutivillus	Med. Lit.	M	1610
Twrch Trwyth (Porcus Troit)	Bryth.	M	1616
Utgard-Loki	Norse	M	1632
Vathek	Mos.	A	1642
Vishapa	Arm., Pers.	M	1654
Vu-murt	Fin-Ug.	A	1660
Vut-oza	Fin-Ug.	M	1660
Walichu	Argen., Chile	M	1662
Wen Kamui	Ainu	M	1673
Whiro	Poly.	M	1676
Yaotl	Mex.	M	1701
Yatu	Zoro.	M	1702
Yskal-pydomurt	Fin-Ug.	M	1711
Zacchaeus	Hebr.	M	1714
Zedekiah	Hebr.	M	1717
Ziz (Ziv)	Hebr.	M	1721

EVIL GHOST (SEE DEMON)
EXORCISM (SEE MAGIC)
EXPOSED CHILD (SEE ABANDONED CHILD)
FAIRY (SEE SPIRIT)
FAITHFULNESS (SEE LOYALTY)

FALL VICTIM			
Abbadona	Germ.	M	12
Adam	Hebr-Mos.	M	29
Anunaki	Baby.	M	105
Anunnaki	Sum.	M	105
Apollyon	Gk/Hebr.	M	111
Aries	Med. Lit.	M	124
Arioch	Eng. Lit.	M	124
Ashmodel	Oc.	M	139
Aza & Azael	Caba.	M-M	164
Azazel	Hebr., Mos.	M	165
Bali	Hin.	M	175
Belial	Hebr.	M	197
Bellerophon	Gk.	M	199
Devil	Hebr-Christ.	M	435
Eka-Srga	Hin.	M	+

	Culture	Sex	Page
Etana	Sum.	M	527
Finnegan, Tim	Cel.	M	570
Gwragedd Annwn	Bryth.	F	702
Hephaestus	Gk.	M	751
Hkun Hsang L'rong	Ind-Chin.	M	775
Hsiu-Chi	Chin.	F	1711
Humpty Dumpty	Folk.	M	806
Ikkaku Sennin	Jap.	M	822
Ixion	Gk.	M	852
Jaik-Khan	Sib.	M	861
Jamshid	Pers.	M	863
Jove	Eng.	M	891
Judas Iscariot	Christ.	M	892
Kalu Kumara Yaka	Sinhalese	M	905
Kara-khan	Mong.	M	909
Kavi-Usan	Pers.	M	914
Kesil	Sem.	M	919
Kume-no-sennin	Jap.	M	951
Lucifer	Christ.	M	1020
Mammon	Eng.	M	1051
Medea	Gk.	F	1082
Mephistopheles	Med. Lit.	M	1091
Momus	Gk.	M	1116
Nasargiel	Hebr.	M	1156
Peri	Pers.		1255
Phaethon	Gk.	M	1260
Remphan	Hebr.	M	1332
Satan	Hebr-Christ.	M	1402
Scylla	Gk.	F	1409
Semjaza	Med. Lit.	M	546
Setek	Slovenian	M	1421
Susanowo	Jap.	M	1512
Tezcatlipoca	Mex.	M	1549
Thaumiel	Caba.	M	1552
Thersander	Gk.	M	1554
Tityus	Gk.	M	1580
Yappan	Mex.	M	1701
Yima	Pers.	M	1707

FALSE INFORMER (ALSO SEE WRATH)

Anpu's wife	Egy.	F	185
Antaea	Gk.	F	101
Astydamia	Gk.	F	145
Becuma	Cel.	F	192
Bikki	Norse	M	211
Gwennere	Bryth.	F	976

False Informer (cont.)	Culture	Sex	Page
Haman	Hebr.	M	714
Iago	Eng.	M	815
Idaea	Gk.	M	1264
Keresavazdak	Pers.	M	918
Phaedra	Gk.	F	1260
Philonome	Gk.	F	1263
Potiphar's wife (Rahil, Zuleika)	Hebr., Mos.	F	1289
Sharabda	Baby.		1431
Sibeche	Germ.	M	1445
Sudabah	Pers.	F	1503
Uni	Egy.	M	1625
Zuleika	Mos.	M	1735

FALSELY ACCUSED (ALSO SEE WRATH VICTIM)

Art	Cel.	M	130
Bata	Egy.	M	185
Bellerophon	Gk.	M	199
Desdemona	Eng.	F	815
Gunasarman	Hin.	M	698
Hippolytus	Gk.	M	773
Joseph (Yusuf)	Hebr., Mos.	M	888
Launfal, Sir	Bryth.	M	976
Melissa	Gk.	F	1086
Nabhanedistha	Hin.	M	1145
Naboth	Hebr.	M	1146
Oryithus & Crambis (Polydectus & Polydorous)	Gk.	M-M	1264
Peleus	Gk.	M	1250
Randver	Norse	M	1322
Siyavahsh	Hebr.	M	1463
Susanna	Hebr.	F	1512
Swanhild	Germ.	F	1517
Syavarshan	Pers.	M	1521
Tenes (Tenedos)	Gk.	M	1545
Zoroaster	Zoro.	M	1734

FAMINE (SEE DROUGHT)
FATAL CHILD (SEE ABANDONED CHILD)
FATAL SPOT OR WEAKNESS (SEE VULNERABLE)

FATE (DESTINY)

Adrastea	Gk.	F	35

	Culture	Sex	Page
Agathadaemon	Gk.	M	46
Ajysit	Sib.	F	58
Allat	Sem.	F	69
Al Moakkibat	Mos.		70
Ana	Cel.	F	90
Ananke	Gk.	F	91
Arsa	Sem.	F	130
Asha	Zoro.	M	138
Ashima	Sem.	F	139
Ashmedai	Hebr.	M	139
Atargatis	Sem.	F/A	148
Atropos	Gk.	F	153
Baau	Phoen., Sum.	F	168
Badb	Cel.	F	171
Belit-sheri	Assyr.	F	198
Bujuruktsi	Tatar	M	259
Carmenta	Rom.	F	291
Cataclothes	Gk.	F	298
Chandra	Hin.	M	310
Ch'in-kuang	Chin.	M	326
Chuvash	Rus.	M	900
Clotho	Gk.	F	349
Cromhineach	Cel.		383
Dekans	Baby., Egy.	M	427
Disir	Norse	F	451
Dolya (Sreca)	Rus.	F	460
Dzajaga	Mong.	M	481
Enlil	Sum.	M	512
Fata Morgana	Bryth.	F	550
Fates	Gk.	F	551
Fay	Fr.		553
Fomhair	Scot.	M	590
Fortuna	Rom.	F	596
Fuku	Jap.	M	616
Giptes	Norse	F	659
Hamingja	Norse	F	714
Hathor	Egy.	F	730
Husbishag	Assyr-Baby.	F	808
Hyndla	Norse	F	812
Ishtar	Assyr-Baby.	F	844
Iuchar	Cel.	M	850
Iucharba	Cel.	M	850
Jajutsi	Mong.	M	861
Jurojin	Jap.	M	898
Kaba	Fin-Ug.	M	900
Kala	Hin.	M	903

	Culture	Sex	Page
Kingu	Baby.	M	932
Kudai	Sib.	M	948
Kybai-Khotun	Yakut	F	956
Lachesis	Gk.	F	960
Liu Tsung	Chin.	M	1003
Luonnotar	Fin.	F	1025
Mamit	Sum.	F	1051
Manat	Sem.	F	1056
Matres	Rom/Cel.	F	1076
Mean	Ital.	F	1081
Meni	Assyr.	F/A	1089
Meskhenet	Egy.	F	1094
Midir	Cel.	M	1100
Moirai	Gk.	F	1114
Moros	Gk.	M	1125
Morrigu	Cel.	F	1125
Nabu	Baby.	M	1146
Narucnici	Bulg.	F	1156
Necessitas	Gk.	F	1160
Nemesis	Gk.	F	1162
Nesreca	Serb.	F	1165
Ninkasi	Sum.	F/A	1173
Nona	Rom.	F	+
Nornir	Norse	F	1180
Nunusesmea	Sem.	F	1042
Orlog	Norse	M	+
Osk-mayjar	Norse	F	1219
Pairekse	Ostiak	M	1226
Parcae	Rom.	F	1237
Pravuil	Hebr.	M	1291
Ptah-Osiris	Egy.	M	1299
Puleh	Rus.	M	1301
Rita	Hin.	M	1341
Rod & Rozanice	Rus.	M-F	1344
Rodjenice	Croa.	F	1344
Rusa	Arab.	F	1354
Sa'd	Arab.	M	1360
Sa'dan	Arab.	F	1360
Seimia	Syrian	F	1413
Sekhet	Egy.	F	1414
Selk	Egy.	F	1415
Seven Hathors	Egy.	F	1424
Shamash	Assyr-Baby.	M	1429
Shay	Egy.	M	1431
Shimti	Assyr.	F	1437
Sijil, Al	Mos.		1452

	Culture	Sex	Page
Skuld	Norse	F	1465
Spinster	Ang-Sax.	F	1483
Sreca	Serb.	M	1487
Ssu Ming	Chin.	M	1488
Surya	Hin.	M	1511
Taconius	Mos.		1524
Tai-yo Ta-ti	Chin.	M	1527
Tengri	Buriat	M	1545
Tiamat	Baby.	F	1570
T'ien Kou	Chin.	M	1571
T'ien-ming	Chin.	M	1571
Tiur	Arm.	M	1581
Tou Mu	Chin.	F	1591
Tyche	Gk.	F	1616
Urd	Norse	F	1628
Valkyrie	Norse	F	1636
Veele	Serb.	F	1643
Verdhandi	Norse	F	1645
Volva	Norse	F	1658
Wang-chug-mas	Tib.	F	1665
Wyrd	Ang-Sax.	F	1694
Zajan	Buriat	M	1715
Zu	Baby., Sum.	M	1734
FEAR (PANIC)			
Pachad	Caba	M	1224
Pan	Gk.	M	1230
Pavor	Rom.		1244
Phobos	Gk.	M	1265
Rudrani	Hin.	F	1353
Sokar	Egy.	M	1471
Tursa (Cerfius Martius)	Ital.	A	1610
Yama	Bud.	M	1699

FEMALE PRINCIPLE (SEE MOTHER)
FERRYMAN (SEE DEATH)

FERTILITY (FECUNDITY, GENERATION, ALSO SEE AGRICULTURE, EARTH)			
Acantum	Mex.	M	22
Acerbas	Rom.	M	23
Achelous	Gk.	M	24
Acrisius	Gk.	M	27
Actaeon	Gk.	M	28
Adda-Nari	Hin.	F	31
Addephagia	Rom.	F	31
Aditi	Hin.	F	32

	Culture	Sex	Page
Admetus	Gk.	M	33
Adon	Phoen.	M	33
Adonis	Gk.	M	34
Adranus	Ital.	M	35
Aeacus	Gk.	M	37
Aegir	Norse	M	38
Aeschere	Ang-Sax.	M	41
Ah	Egy.	F	144
Ah-kiuic	Mex.	M	53
Aide	Cel.	F	54
Ailill	Cel.	M	55
Aine	Cel.	F	56
Alcinous	Cel.	M	64
Aleyn	Bryth.	M	67
Amfortas	Germ.	M	85
Amphitryon	Gk.	M	88
Ana	Cel.	F	90
Anahit	Arm.	F	90
Anala	Hin.	F	91
Ancaeus	Gk.	M	92
Angus	Cel.	M	97
Anna Perenna	Rom.	F	99
Anqet	Egy.	F	100
Anu	Cel.	F	104
Aphrodite	Gk.	F	108
Apnapurna	Hin.	F	109
Apollo	Gk.	M	110
Aramazd	Arm.	M	117
Aranyani	Hin.	F	117
Arawn	Bryth.	M	117
Arbuda	Hin.	M	118
Ariadne	Gk.	F	123
Ariel	Eng.	M	124
Armais	Arm.	M	127
Artemis	Gk.	F	131
Artemis of Ephesus	Gk.	F	131
Arthur	Bryth.	M	132
Asar (Osiris)	Egyp.	M	135
Asari	Baby.	M	135
Ashera	Sem.	F	138
Asshur	Assyr.	M	143
Astarte	Phoen.	F	144
Asu-su-namir	Baby.	E	146
Asvins	Hin.	M	146
Atargatis	Sem.	F/A	148
Aten	Egy.	M	149

	Culture	Sex	Page
Athar	Arab.	M	150
Atse Estsan	Navaho	F	153
Attis	Phyrg.	M/A	154
Aud	Norse	M	156
Audhumla	Norse	F	156
Auxo	Gk.	F	786
Bacchus	Gk., Rom.	M	170
Badebec	Cel.	F	171
Bahet	Egy.	F	172
Bakula	Bud.	M	174
Baneb-ded	Egy.	M	178
Bast	Egy.	F	185
Becuma	Cel.	F	192
Bel Enlil	Baby.	M	197
Belit Itani	Assyr-Baby.	F	198
Belphegor	Assyr.	A	200
Benten	Jap.	F	203
Bhava	Hin.	M	208
Bhavani	Hin.	F	208
Blai	Cel.	F	224
Blathnat	Cel.	F	225
Bona Dea	Rom.	F	234
Bran	Bryth.	M	241
Brons	Bryth.	M	251
Brynhild	Norse	F	253
Buan-Ann	Cel.	F	254
Buarainech	Cel.	M	254
Cabiri	Phryg.	M	265
Cachimana	Orinoco	M	265
Cadmus	Gk.	M	266
Cailleach	Scot.	F	269
Cambalo	Eng.	M	280
Carpo	Gk.	F	293
Chaac	Mex.	M	307
Chandra	Hin.	M	310
Charidotes	Gk.	M	313
Charites	Gk.	F	314
Chemosh	Sem.	M	317
Chicomexochit	Mex.	M	322
Ch'i-lin	Chin.	A	325
Chiun	Hebr.	F	327
Chloe	Gk.	F	328
Christ	Christ.	M	330
Cilix	Gk.	M	339
Clothru	Cel.	F	349
Conan	Cel.	M	364

	Culture	Sex	Page
Conn	Cel.	M	367
Connla	Cel.	M	367
Cromhineach	Cel.		383
Cuculcan	Mex.	M	396
Dag	Hebr.	M	405
Dagan	Baby.	M	405
Dagda	Cel.	M	405
Dagon	Philis.	A	406
Daire mac Fiachna	Cel.	M	407
Danu	Cel.	F	414
Daonus	Baby.	M	414
Dardanus	Gk.	M	415
Dazbog	Sib.	M	420
Declunus	Ital.	M	424
Demeter	Gk.	F	429
Derceto	Sem.	F	433
Dhisana	Hin.	F	439
Diana of Ephesus	Rom.	F	441
Dionysus	Gk.	M	447
Dis	Cel.	M	450
Dithyrambos	Gk.	M	452
Diwrnach	Cel.	M	454
Donar	Germ.	M	461
Dosangma	Tib.	F	465
Draupner	Norse		470
Drona	Hin.	M	471
Dryas	Gk.	M	473
Dumuzi	Sum.	M	476
Dusura	Sem.	M	477
Du'uzu	Sum.	M	478
Ea	Assyr., Baby., Sum.	M	481
Ebisu	Jap.	M	489
Eigin	Cel.	F	496
Ekeko	Peru.	M	497
Eldhrimnir	Norse		499
Elidurus	Eng.	M	503
Elisha (Eliseus)	Hebr.	M	504
Eniautes Daimon	Gk.	M	+
Enki	Assyr., Baby., Sum.	M	511
Enti	Baby.	M	513
Eochaid Ollathair	Cel.	M	513
Eogabal	Cel.	M	513
Epona	Cel., Rom.	F	517
Epopeus	Gk.	M	517

	Culture	Sex	Page
Erichthonius	Gk.	M	519
Erikapaios	Gk.	A	520
Eriphos	Gk.	M	520
Estsanatlehi	Nav.	M	526
Fascinus	Rom.	M	549
Faunus (Inuus)	Rom.	M	552
Faustulus	Rom.	M	553
Februsus	Rom.	M	557
Fergus Fionnliat	Cel.	M	561
Finnbeara	Cel.	M	570
Finnegan, Tim	Cel.	M	570
Finvarra	Cel.	M	571
Fisher King	Bryth.	M	575
Flidais	Cel.	F	583
Flosshilda	Germ.	F	585
Fomor	Pre-Celtic	M	590
Fotla	Cel.	F	599
Frau Holle	Germ.	F	608
Frey	Norse	M	609
Freya	Norse	F	610
Fugen	Jap.	M	615
Galahad	Bryth.	M	622
Ga'n	Apache Ind.		625
Gandayah	Iroq.	M, F	884
Gandharva	Hin.	M	626
Gandreid	Norse	M	626
Ganga	Hin.	F	627
Ga-ur	Sum.	M	635
Gawain	Bryth.	M	635
Gefjon	Norse	F	637
Gersimi	Norse	F	647
Gilling	Norse	M	657
Glaucus	Gk.	M	662
Gluskap	Algon.	M	664
Golden Calf	Hebr.		672
Graces	Gk.	F	681
Groa	Norse	F	692
Gucumatz	Guate.	M	694
Gudhorn	Norse	M	694
Gwion Bach	Cel.	M	701
Gwri	Bryth.	M	702
Gyges	Gk.	M	703
Hamori	Jap.	M	716
Hanged Man	Folk.	M	721
Han Hsiang-tzu	Chin.	M	722
Hapi	Egy.	M/A	724

	Culture	Sex	Page
Harmonia	Gk.	F	727
Hastshehogan	Nav.	M	730
Hastsheyalti	Nav.	M	730
Heitsi-eibib	Hotten.	M	744
Hera	Gk.	F	752
Heracles of Oeta	Gk.	M	755
Heracles of Tiryns	Gk.	M	756
Hermes	Gk.	M	760
Hermod	Norse	M	762
Hervor	Norse	F	764
Hesione	Gk.	F	764
Hippa	Gk.	F	772
Hirugo	Jap.	M	774
Hjaalprek	Norse	M	775
Hobnil	Mex.	M	778
Holde	Germ.	F	780
Horae	Gk.	F	786
Hrothgar	Ang-Sax.	M	798
Hu	Bryth., Egy.	M	800
Hulda	Germ.	F	803
Iacchus	Gk.	M	815
Icarius	Gk.	M	817
Idakeru	Jap.	M	818
Idun	Norse	F	820
Iguana	C.A.I.	M	821
Ihi-yori-hiko	Jap.	M	822
Iku-guhi	Jap.	F	822
Ilbhreach	Cel.	M	823
Ilmarinen	Fin-Ug.	M	824
Inari-M'yojim	Jap.	F/A	827
Indrani	Hin.	F	830
Ingun (Yngvi)	Norse	F/A	831
Ingunar-Frey	Norse	M	831
Innini	Sum.	F	832
Inuus	Rom.	M	834
Ishtar	Assyr-Baby.	F	844
Isis	Egy.	F	845
Itzcuinan	Mex.	F	850
Ix-chel	Mex.	F	852
Izushio-tome	Jap.	F	854
Jack-in-Green	Folk.	M	856
Jack the Giant Killer	Folk.	M	857
Jacob	Hebr.	M	858
Jambhala	Bud.	M	862
Jehovah	Hebr.	M	870
Jesus	Christ.	M	877

	Culture	Sex	Page
Joseph (Yusuf)	Hebr., Mos.	M	888
Joseph of Arimathea	Christ.	M	889
Juju	Nigeria	M	894
Jupiter	Rom.	M	896
Kalseru	Aus.	M	904
Kamadhenu	Hin.	F	905
Karna	Hin.	M	910
Kayanu-hime	Jap.	F	915
Kelpi	Scot.	M	916
Kernababy	Eng.	F	919
Khotun	Yakut	F	925
Kicva	Bryth.	F	927
King of the May	Folk.	M	930
King of Pecheur	Bryth.	M	931
Kissos	Gk.	M	934
Kobo Daishi	Jap.	M	939
Koloowisi	Zuni	M	941
Kono-hana-Sakuya-hime	Jap.	F	941
Kore	Gk.	F	942
Korybantes	Phryg.	M	943
Kouretes	Gk.	M	944
Ksetrasya	Hin.	M	947
Kubera	Hin.	M	948
Kukulcan	Mex.	M	950
Kukunochi	Jap.	M	950
Kunhild	Germ.	F	952
Kura	Mangaia	F	952
Kushi-nada-hime	Jap.	F	953
Kwasind	N.A.I.	M	955
Lada	Slav.	F	961
Ladon	Gk.	M	962
Lahu	Burma	M	964
Landvaettir	Scan.	M	971
Lavinia	Rom.	F	977
Leodogrance	Bryth.	M	984
Leviathan	Hebr.	A	989
Liber	Rom.	M	990
Lilinau	N.A.I.	F	994
Limniades	Gk.	F	997
Limoniades	Gk.	F	997
Ling Pao	Chin.	M	998
Lityerses	Gk.	M	1003
Lludd	Bryth.	M	1005
Lupercus	Rom.	M	1026
Ma	Asia Minor	F	1030
MacCecht	Cel.	M	1033

	Culture	Sex	Page
MacCool	Cel.	M	1033
MacDatho	Cel.	M	1033
MacGreine	Cel.	M	1033
Maenad	Gk.	F	1036
Maenawr Penardd	Cel.	M	1037
Mah	Sem.	F	1042
Maid Marian	Bryth.	F/A	1046
Makh	Assyr-Baby.	F	1048
Mala Lith	Cel.	F	1049
Mama Cora	Inca	F	1051
Manabhozho	Algon.	M	1054
Manah	Arab.	F	1054
Manannan	Cel.	M	1054
Manawyddan	Bryth.	M	1056
Mani	Braz.	M	1058
Manushcithra	Pers.	M	1062
Marduk	Assy-Baby.	M	1065
Mari	Crete, As. Min.	F	1066
Mars	Ital.	M	1069
Marsyas	Gk., Phryg.	M	1070
Maruts	Hin.	M	1071
Marzyana	Slav.	F	1072
Masubi	Shinto	M	1074
Mataora	Poly.	M	1074
Matres	Rom/Cel.	F	1076
Mayauel	Mex.	F	1080
Medusa	Gk.	F	1084
Meliades	Gk.	F	1086
Melissa	Gk.	F	1086
Merlin	Bryth.	M	1092
Mermaid	Euro.	F	1093
Mesca	Cel.	F	1094
Mesgegra	Cel.	M	1094
Messbuachalla	Cel.	M	1095
Metra	Pers.	F	1096
Miach	Cel.	M	1097
Midir	Cel.	M	1100
Miketsu-oho-kami	Jap.	M	1101
Mikura-tana-no-kami	Jap.	F	1102
Mimir	Norse	M	1105
Minerva	Rom.	F	1106
Min Kyawzwa	Ind-Chin.	M	1106
Mirsi	Baby.	M	1110
Mithra	Pers.	M	1112
Mitra	Baby., Hin.	M	1112
Mo-li Hung	Chin.	M	601

	Culture	Sex	Page
Mondamin	Chip.	M	1116
Mongan	Cel.	M	1117
Monotaro	Jap.	M	1118
Mordains	Bryth.	M	1122
Morgan le Fay	Bryth.	F	1123
Moses	Hebr.	M	1126
Mu-monto	Buriat	M	1136
Mundilfore	Norse	M	1136
Mutunus	Rom.	M	1142
Muy'ingwa	Hopi	M	1142
Nadushu-Namir	Baby.	M	1147
Na-nefer-ka-Ptah	Egy.	M	1153
Nanna	Norse	F	1153
Nannar	Baby.	M/A	1153
Nari Mariama	Hin.	F	1156
Nefer-tem	Egy.	M	1160
Neheb-kau	Egy.	F	1160
Nemed	Cel.	M	1162
Nepret	Egy.	F	1163
Nepri	Egy.	M	1163
Nerio	Rom.	F	1164
Nerthus	Dan.	F	1165
Nessa	Cel.	F	1165
Nina	Baby.	F	1170
Ningishzida	Sum.	M	1172
Ninib	Assyr-Baby.	M	1173
Nisus	Gk.	M	1176
No-no-kami	Jap.	M	1179
Nornir	Norse	F	1180
Nu	Egy.	A	1184
Nu Kua	Chin.	M/A	1185
Nyakang	Egy.	M	1187
Oannes	Baby., Chald., Phoen.	M	1190
Oberon	Eng., Fr.	M	1192
Ochall Ochne	Cel.	M	1193
Odakon	Philis.	M	1194
Odin	Norse	M	1195
Oenone	Gk.	F	1199
Ogma	Cel.	M	1200
Ogyrvran	Bryth.	M	1201
Oho-ge-tsu-hime	Jap.	F	1202
O-kama-sama	Jap.	M	1203
Oki (Kiousa)	Huron	M, F	1203
Okitsuhiko (Kudo-no-kami)	Jap.	M	1203
Okitsuhime	Jap.	M	1203

	Culture	Sex	Page
Olwen	Bryth.	F	1206
Omacatl	Mex.	M	1207
Omeciuatl	Mex.	F	1207
Onatah	Iroq.	F	1209
Onchestus	Gk.	M	1209
Ops (Berecinthia)	Ital.	F	1212
Osiris	Egy.	M	1218
Pa Cha	Chin.	M	1224
Pales	Ital.	A	1228
Palici	Ital.	M	1228
Palulukon	Hopi	M	1230
Pan	Gk.	M	1230
Pandavas	Hin.	M	1232
Panquetzalitztli	Mex.	F	1234
Parjanya	Hin.	M/A	1238
Parsifal	Germ.	M	1239
Patshak	Ostiak	M, F	1244
Pekko	Fin-Ug.	M	1249
Peleus	Gk.	M	1250
Pelleas	Bryth.	M	1250
Pelles	Bryth.	M	1251
Percival	Bryth.	M	1254
Perdix	Gk.	A	1254
Pergrubrius	Baltic	M	1255
Perkunas	Baltic	M/A	1256
Phosphorus	Gk.	M	1266
Phra In	Siam.	M	1266
Phra Naret	Siam.	F	1267
Phuphlans	Ital.	M	1267
Phytalmios	Gk.	M	1268
Picumnus	Rom.	M	1269
Piers Plowman	Eng.	M	1270
Pilumnus	Rom.	M	1273
Pirithous	Gk.	M	1275
Poloznitsa	Fin-Ug.	F	1283
Poludnica	Rus.	F	1283
Polyidus	Gk.	M	1284
Polymetis	Gk.	M	1284
Polynices	Gk.	M	1284
Poseidon	Gk.	M	1288
Potrympus	Baltic	M	1289
Priapus	Gk.	M	1292
Pripegala	Slav.	M	1294
Prthu	Hin.	M	1298
Pryderi	Bryth.	M	1298
Psilas	Gk.	M	1299

	Culture	Sex	Page
Purandhi (Parendi)	Hin. (Pers.)	F	1302
Purtupita & Hula	Ital.	A	1304
Pusan	Hin.	M	1305
Pwyll	Bryth.	M	1306
Queen of the May	Folk.	F	1311
Quetzalcoatl	Mex.	M	1312
Quetzalpetlatl	Mex.	F	1313
Ra	Egy.	M/A	1314
Rama	Hin.	M	1321
Rana-neidda	Lapp	F	1322
Rangi	Poly.	M	1322
Rath	Cel.	M	1324
Razeka	Arab.	M	1326
Rehtia	Rom.	F	1331
Rem	Egy.	M	1332
Rhampsinitus	Gk.	M	1335
Rhea	Gk.	F	1335
Rhiannon	Bryth.	F	1336
Rhine Daughters	Germ.	F	1336
Ridija	Sem.	M	1338
Rigantona	Cel.	F	1338
Rimmon	Baby.	M	1339
Rishyacringa	Hin.	M	1341
Rizpah	Hebr.	F	1342
Robin Hood	Eng.	M	1343
Rongoteus	Fin-Ug.	M	1347
Rose of Sharon	Hebr.	F	1349
Rudra	Hin.	M	1353
Rumpelstiltskin	Germ.	M	1354
Sabazius	Phryg.	M	1356
Saint George	Christ.	M	1370
Sam	Pers.	M	1392
Sampsa	Fin-Ug.	M	1394
Sanda	Hittite	M	1395
Santa	Ital.	F	1397
Sao Kang	Burma	M	1398
Sara-mama	Inca	F	1399
Sarasvant	Hin.	M	1400
Sarasvati	Hin.	F	1400
Sarpanitum	Baby.	F	1401
Sarvakamadugha	Hin.	F	1401
Satet	Egy.	F	1402
Satyr	Gk.	M	1403
Savitri	Hin.	M	1404
Saxnot	Ang-Sax.	M	1404
Scef	Norse	M	1406

	Culture	Sex	Page
Scyld	Ang-Sax.	M	1409
Sebek	Egy.	M	1412
Sedna	Eskimo	F	1413
Selwanga	Bantu	M	1415
Semele	Gk.	F	1415
Semiramis	Assyr.	F	1415
Semnae	Gk.	F	1416
Semo	Rom.	M	1416
Sena	Hin.	F	1416
Shakuru (Atius)	Pawnee	M	1429
Shamash	Assyr-Baby.	M	1429
Shantanu	Hin.	M	1430
Shar Apsi	Baby.	M	1431
Sharis	Urartian	F	1431
She	Chin.		1431
Shen Nung	Chin.	M	1434
Shiwanokia	Zuni	F	1440
Shony	Hebrides	M	1442
Shulamite	Hebr.	F	1444
Shvaz	Arm.	M	1445
Shwe Pyin Nyi-Naung	Ind-Chin.	M-M	1445
Siegfried	Germ.	M	1448
Sigurd	Norse	M	1451
Silvanus	Rom.	M	1453
Sindre	Norse	M	1457
Sir-syv-kudegen	Chuvash	M	1459
Sita	Hin.	F	1460
Siton	Philis.	M	1461
Siva	Hin.	M	1461
Siward	Norse	M	1461
Siyamak	Zoro.	M	1463
Skate	Ice.	M	1464
Sohodo-no-kami	Jap.	M	1471
Solomon	Caba.	M	1472
Spenta Armaiti	Zoro.	M	1481
Sphinx	Egy., Gk.	F	1482
Stellio	Rom.	M	1493
Sterculius	Rom.	M	1494
Stercutus	Rom.	M	+
Stigande	Ang-Sax.	M	1494
Sualtam	Cel.	M	1503
Sunrta	Hin.	F	1510
Suriel	Gnostic	M	1511
Sutekh	Syrian	M	1513
Swanhild	Germ.	F	1517

	Culture	Sex	Page
Syavarshan	Pers.	M	1521
Tagtug (Tibir)	Sum.	M	1524
Tai Shan	Chin.	F	1526
Tajima-mori	Jap.	M	1527
Tammuz	Baby.	M	1530
Ta Mo (Bodhidharma)	Chin.	M	1530
Tanga Tanga	Inca	M	1532
Tannhauser	Germ.	M	1532
Tao Chun	Chin.	M	1533
Tauropolos	Gk.	F/A	132
Tawara Toda	Jap.	M	1539
Teczistecatl	Mex.	F	1541
Telchines	Gk.	M	1541
Tengri	Buriat	M	1545
Thagya Min	Ind-Chin.	M	1550
Thalaba	Asian	M	1551
Thallo	Gk.	F	1551
Thor	Norse	M	1561
Thrita Athwya	Pers.	M	1566
Thyone	Gk.	F	1569
Tibernius	Rom.	M	1570
Tigernmas	Cel.	M	1572
Tishtrya	Pers.	M/A	1577
Titurel	Bryth.	M	1580
Tlaloc Tecutli	Mex.	M	1581
Toyo-uke-bime	Jap.	F/A	1593
Troll	Norse	M, F	1600
Ts'an Nu	Chin.	F	1603
Tse-mgon	Tib.	M	1603
Tse-ring Chhenga	Tib.	F	1603
Tuan mac Cairill	Cel.	M	1605
Tuatha de Danann	Cel.	M, F	1605
Tu-metua	Herv. Is.		1607
Tvastr	Hin.	M	1611
Uka-no-kami	Jap.	M	1621
Ukeomochi	Jap.	F	1621
Umunlua	Sum.	M	1623
Ushumgalanna	Sum.	M	1631
Vairocana	Bud.	M	1634
Vajradhatvisvari	Bud.	F	1635
Vanir	Norse	M, F	1638
Vanoc	Bryth.	M	1638
Vardhamana	Hin.	M	1639
Varuna	Hin.	M	1639
Vasudhara	Bud.	F	1641
Vegtam	Norse	M	1643

Fertility (cont.)	Culture	Sex	Page
Venus	Ital.	F	1644
Veralden-Olmai	Lapp	M	1645
Verethraghna	Pers.	M	1646
Vertumnus	Rom.	M	1646
Vidyadhara	Hin.	F	1649
Vinmara	Mel.	F	1651
Vipascit	Hin.	M	1651
Virankannos	Fin-Ug.	M	1652
Vishtaspa	Pers.	M	1655
Vitzilipuztli	Mex.	M	1656
Vivasvant	Hin.	M	1656
Volund	Norse	M	1658
Wainamoinen	Fin.	M	1661
Wakyet-wa (Chinun-way-shun)	Burm.	M	1662
Wellgunde	Germ.	F	1336
William of Cloudeslee	Eng.	M	1680
William Tell	Swiss	M	1681
Woglinde	Germ.	F	1336
Xilonen	Mex.	F/A	1696
Xipe Totec	Mex.	M	1696
Xmukane	Mex.	F	1696
Xochipilli-Cinteotl	Mex.	M	1696
Xolotl	Mex.	M	1697
Yab-Yum	Bud.	M-F	1697
Yaksa	Hin.	M	1698
Yamantaka	Bud.	M	1699
Yappan	Mex.	M	1701
Yarilo	Rus.	M	1701
Yeibichai	Nav.	M	1703
Yoshi-iye	Jap.	M	1710
Yul-lha	Tib.	M	1713
Zagreus	Cretan	M	1715
Zamama	Baby.	M	1715
Zatik	Arm.	M	1716
Zephyrus	Gk.	M	1718
Ziva	Slav.	F	1721
Zocho-ten	Jap.	M	1722
Zywie	Polish	F	1735

FIDELITY (SEE LOYALTY)
FILIAL PIETY (SEE LOYALTY)
FILTH (SEE DECAY)
FINITE, THE (SEE TIME)

FIRE (FLAME, HEAT, VOLCANO)			
Ababinili	Chick.	M	11

	Culture	Sex	Page
Acala	Jap.	M	21
Aesar	Cel.	M	41
Agenor	Gk.	M	48
Agni	Hin.	M	49
Ahavaniya	Hin.	M	52
Aidne	Cel.	M	55
Aillen	Cel.	M	56
Ain	Cel.	M	56
Anael	Oc.	M	645
Anala	Hin.	F	1641
Angirases	Hin.	M	96
Areop-it-eonin	Nauru	M	120
Arges	Gk.	M	121
Asha	Zoro.	M	138
Atago-sama	Jap.		147
Atar	Zoro.	M	148
Bahram Yasht	Zoro.	M	173
Bandicoot	Aus.	M	178
Be'al	Bryth.	M	188
Ber (Bir)	Assyr.	M	203
Berecenthia	Phryg.	F	203
Bhuranyu	Hin.	M	209
Brighu	Hin.	M	249
Brigit (Bridget)	Cel., Christ.	F	249
Brynhild	Norse	F	253
Byleipt	Norse	M	264
Cacus & Caca	Rom.	M-F	265
Cearas (Daghdae)	Cel.	M	301
Chakekenapok	Pota.	M	308
Chimera	Gk.	F	325
Chu Ch'ieh	Chin.	M	335
Cinderella	Folk.	F	339
Cyclops	Gk.	M	400
Eldir	Norse	M	499
Enceladus	Gk.	M	510
Euro	Aus.		531
Feng-huang	Chin.	M	559
Figol	Cel.	M	568
Fire People	Pac. Coast		+
Fire Spirit	N.A.I.		+
Fo (Foh, Fuhi)	Chin.	M	589
Fuchi	Jap.	F	615
Futsu-nushi	Jap.	M	618
Gabriel	Christ., Hebr., Mos.	M	619
Gaki	Jap.	M, F	622

	Culture	Sex	Page
Galai-kahn	Mong.	M	623
Gali-edzin	Mong.	M	623
Galta-ulan-tengeri	Mong.	M	624
Gibil	Baby.	M	655
Gigantes	Gk.	M	655
Girru	Baby.	M	660
Goga	Massim	F	669
Gold Betheli	Swiss	F	671
Grahapati	Hin.	M	682
Greip	Norse	F	689
Hecatoncheires	Gk.	M	741
Heimdal	Norse	M	743
Hephaestus	Gk.	M	751
Hestia	Gk.	F	765
Ho-shen	Chin.	M	793
Huehueteotl	Mex.	M	802
Hueytecpatl	Mex.	M	802
Huitzilopochtli	Mex.	M	803
Imder	Norse	F	825
Ingnersuit	Eskimo		831
Intercidona	Rom.	F	+
Iolaus	Gk.	M	836
Irra	Assyr-Baby.	M	841
Issi	Germ.	M	848
Isum	Assyr.	M	848
Itzpapalotl	Mex.	F	850
Ixcocauhqui	Mex.	M	852
Jahveh	Hebr.	A	861
Kagutsuchi	Jap.	M	902
Kay, Sir	Bryth.	M	914
Krishna	Hin.	M	945
Laki-oi	Borneo	M	965
Loder	Norse	M	1007
Loge	Fin.	M	1008
Loki	Norse	M/A	1010
Lucifer	Christ.	M	1020
Mafuike	Poly.	F/A	1037
Mahuika	Poly.	F	1046
Mandarangan	Bagobo	M	1056
Masauwu	Hopi	M	1072
Matarisvan	Hin.	M	1074
Maui	Poly.	M	1077
Michael	Christ.	M	1099
Mihr	Arm.	M	1101
Mimas	Gk.	M	1105
Mitsotsozini	Pokomo	M	1113

	Culture	Sex	Page
Mizraim	Hebr.	M	1113
Moloch	Sem.	M	1115
Moo	Mex.	F	1119
Mulla	Sum.	M	1135
Muntalog	Indo.	M	1137
Nadab	Hebr.	M	1146
Nairyosangha	Pers.	M	1150
Narasamsa	Hin.	M	1155
Nergal	Assyr-Baby.	M	1164
Nerig (Uras)	Assyr.	M	1164
Nusku	Baby.	M	1187
Obagat	Caro. Is.	M	1191
Ohnivak	Slav.		1201
Pele	Hawa.	F	1249
Phanes	Cel.	M	1261
Phlegyas	Gk.	M	1264
Phoroneus	Gk.	M	1266
Pramantha	Hin.	M	1291
Prometheus	Gk.	M	1295
Puripais	Gk.	M	1303
Pyracmon	Gk.	M	1307
Pyrrha	Gk.	F	1307
Quetzalcoatl	Mex.	M	1312
Rhoetus	Gk.	M	1337
Ruaumoko	Poly.	M	1352
Sabaga	Yakut	F	1356
Saint Bridget	Christ.	F	1366
Samael	Caba.	M	1393
Sandalphon	Caba.	M	1396
Sethlaus	Ital.	M	1421
Shahan	Sum.	M	1435
Shen Nung	Chin.	M	1434
Shri	Hin.	F	1443
Siva	Hin.	M	1461
Sui Jen	Chin.	M	1504
Surtr	Norse	M	1511
Svarozic	Slav.	M	1514
Taijas	Hin.	M	1236
Tama-nuit-ite-ra	N. Zeal.	M	1529
Tamboeja	Indo.	M	1530
Tan-tad	Breton	M	1533
Tchue	Bush.	M	1540
Thraetaona (Faridun)	Pers.	M	1563
Toh	Kiche	M	1584
Torx	Arm.	M	1590
Tota	Mex.	M	1591

Fire (cont.)	Culture	Sex	Page
Typhoeus	Gk.	M	1617
Typhon	Gk.	M	1617
Ulakhany	Yakut	M	1621
Ulgen	Tatar	M	1622
Ulu-tojon	Yakut	M	1622
Uras	Assyr.	M	1628
Ut	Mong.	F	1632
Vahagn	Arm.	M	1634
Vazishta	Pers.	M	1643
Vesta	Rom.	F	1647
Virava	Fin-Ug.	A	1652
Virgo Vestalis Maxima	Rom.	F	1648
Vulcan (Mulciber)	Rom.	M	1659
Xiuhtecutli	Mex.	M	1696
Yehl	Alaskan	M	1703
Yeibichai	Nav.	M	1703
Yima	Pers.	M	1707

FISH AND FISHERMAN'S DEITY (SEE WATER)

FISH INSTRUCTED

Cuchulainn	Cel.	M	393
Finn mac Coul	Cel.	M	570
Yu	Chin.	M	1711

FLAME (SEE FIRE)
FLEETNESS (SEE SWIFTNESS)

FLIGHT (AERONAUT)

Bellerophon	Gk.	M	199
Bladud	Bryth.	M	224
Daedalus	Gk.	M	404
Etana	Sum.	M	527
Ganymede	Gk.	M	627
Icarus	Gk.	M	817
Kavi Usan	Pers.	M	914
Kesil	Sem.	M	919
Phaethon	Gk.	M	1260
Salmoneus	Gk.	M	1391

FLOCKS (SEE ANIMAL KEEPER)

FLOWERS (BLOSSOMS)

Aka-kanet	Chil.	M	59
Chloris	Gk.	F	328

	Culture	Sex	Page
Clytie	Gk.	F	351
Crocus	Gk.	M	383
Flora	Ital.	F	584
Hua Hsien	Chin.	F	801
Hyacinthus	Gk.	M	809
Ixquina	Mex.	F	852
Konohana-Sakuya-hime	Jap.	F	941
Lan Ts'ai-ho	Chin.	M/A	971
Leimoniades	Gk.	F	982
Macuilxochitl	Mex.	M	1035
Nanna	Norse	F	1153
Narcissus	Gk.	M	1155
Niete	Mex.	F	283
Payatamu	Zuni	M	1245
Persephone	Gk.	F	1257
Proserpine	Rom.	F	1296
Rafusen	Jap.	F	1317
Sengen Sama	Jap.	F	1416
Tennin	Jap.	F	1545
Tlacolteotl	Mex.	F	1581
Tlalli-iyollo	Mex.	F	1581
Xochipilli-Cinteotl	Mex.	M	1696
Xochiquetzal	Mex.	F	1696

FOE OF DEMONS & MONSTERS

Abishai	Heb.	M	16
Amadis	Med. Lit.	M	78
Amairgen	Cel.	M	79
Apollo	Gk.	M	110
Argeiphontes	Gk.	M	121
Argus	Gk.	M	122
Arion	Gk.	M	125
Artemis	Gk.	F	131
Arthur	Bryth.	M	132
Asfandujar	Zoro.	M	137
Asshur	Assyr.	M	143
Atalanta	Gk.	F	148
Atar	Zoro.	M	148
Atet	Egy.	F	149
Bel	Baby.	M	196
Bellerophon	Gk.	M	199
Beowulf	Ang-Sax.	M	203
Bes	Egy.	M	205
Bevis of Hampton	Bryth.	M	207
Bissat	Tatar	M	220
Bu	Mel.	M	254

	Culture	Sex	Page
Cadmus	Gk.	M	266
Calidore, Sir	Bryth.	M	277
Corineus	Cel.	M	371
Cuchulainn	Cel.	M	393
Daniel	Hebr.	M	413
David	Hebr.	M	417
Diarmaid	Cel.	M	442
Dietrich von Bern	Norse	M	444
Eabani (Enkidu)	Sum.	M	482
Finn macCoul	Cel.	M	570
Fraoch	Cel.	M	607
Fudo	Jap.	M	615
Ganesa	Hin.	M	627
Gargantua	Fr.	M	630
Gawain, Sir	Bryth.	M	635
Gaya Maretan	Pers.	M	636
Gilgamesh	Sum.	M	656
Grettir	Ice.	M	374a
Guy of Warwick	Bryth.	M	700
Hadding	Norse	M	705
Haitsi-aibeb	Hotten.	M	711
Haoshyangha	Pers.	M	723
Haosravah	Pers.	M	723
Heimdal	Norse	M	743
Heracles	Gk.	M	752
Hercules	Rom.	M	759
Hiawatha	N.A.I.	M	767
Hino	Iroq.	M	772
Hipponoos	Gk.	M	774
Horus	Egy.	M	792
Hsu chen-chun	Chin.	M	800
Hu	Bryth.	M	800
Huang Ti	Chin.	M	801
Huang T'ien Shang Ti	Chin.	M	801
Huitziton	Mex.	M	803
Huan-ahpu & Xbalanque	Kiche	M-M	806
Ilmarinen	Fin-Ug.	M	824
Indra	Hin.	M	829
Iolaus	Gk.	M	836
Ioskeha	Huron	M	837
Itje	Sib.	M	849
Izayemon	Jap.	M	854
Jack the Giant Killer	Folk.	M	857
Jalk	Norse	M	862
Jason	Gk.	M	866
Jokwa	Jap.	F	885

	Culture	Sex	Page
Karaty-khan	Mong.	M	910
Keresaspa	Pers.	M	918
Khepera	Egy.	M	924
Kintaro	Jap.	M	932
Kuan-ti	Chin.	M	947
Kulhwch	Welsh	M	950
Kutsa	Hin.	M	954
Laksmana & Satrughna	Hin.	M-M	1321
Lludd	Bryth.	M	1005
Lugalbanda	Sum.	M	1023
Lu Tung-pin	Chin.	M	1026
Maasewe & Uyuuyewe	Sia Ind.	M	1031
Manjusri	Bud.	M	1059
Marduk	Assyr-Baby.	M	1065
Mars	Ital.	M	1069
Maugis	Frankish	M	1077
Merlin (Ambrosius)	Bryth.	M	1092
Michael	Christ.	M	1099
Mithra	Pers.	M	1112
Monotaro	Jap.	M	1118
Moshanyana (Litaolane)	Bantu	M	1127
Muc-thaiuy	Ind-Chin.	M	1133
Na-nefer-ka-Ptah	Egy.	M	1153
Nanzo-bo	Jap.	M	1154
Narasimha	Hin.	M	1654
Nayanezgani	Nav.	M	1159
Ningirsu	Sum.	M	1172
Ninurta	Sum.	M	1174
Nu Kua	Chin.	F/A	1185
Odin	Norse	M	1195
Odysseus	Gk.	M	1196
Otshirvani	Mong.	M	1220
Pa cha	Chin.	M	1224
Pachacamac	Inca	M	1224
Padmasambhava	Tib.	M	1225
Pallas Athena	Gk.	F	1229
Parsifal	Germ.	M	1239
Peleus	Gk.	M	1250
Pellenore	Bryth.	M	1251
Percival	Bryth.	M	1254
Perkunas	Baltic	M	1256
Perseus	Gk.	M	1257
Poeas	Gk.	M	1281
Poseidon	Gk.	M	1288
Punch	Eng.	M	1301
Punchinello	Ital.	M	1301

	Culture	Sex	Page
Pythius	Gk.	M	111
Ra	Egy.	M	1314
Ragnar Lodbrog	Norse	M	1317
Rama	Hin.	M	1321
Raphael	Hebr.	M	1323
Rata	Maori	M	1323
Recaranus	Rom.	M	1327
Roland	Carol.	M	1345
Saint George	Christ.	M	1370
Sam	Pers.	M	1392
Samson	Hebr.	M	1394
Satyrane	Eng.	M	1403
Scythians (Arimaspi)	Gk.	M	1410
Seitaka	Jap.	M	1414
Shen Shu	Chin.	M	1434
Shu Yu	Chin.	M	1445
Siegfried	Germ.	M	1448
Sigurd	Norse	M	1451
Siyamak	Zoro.	M	1463
Solomon	Caba., Mos.	M	1472
Spaul	Cowich.	M	1480
Sraoscha	Zoro.	M	1487
Susa-no-wo	Jap.	M	1512
Svipdag	Norse	M	1515
Tahmurath	Pers.	M	1525
Tammuz	Baby.	M	1530
Tauni-kapi-kapi	N. Guin.	M	1538
Tawara Toda	Jap.	M	1539
Theseus	Gk.	M	1554
Thobadzistshini	Nav.	M	1560
Thor	Norse	M	1561
Thraetaona	Pers.	M	1563
Tigranes	Arm.	M	1573
Tishpak	Accadian	M	1577
Tishtrya	Pers.	M	1577
Tlaloc Tecutli	Mex.	M	1581
Tobias	Hebr.	M	1582
Trita Aptya	Hin.	M	1599
Tsui Goab	Hotten.	M	1604
Tyurunmuzykay	Tatar	M	1618
Ulu-tojon (Syga)	Yakut	M	1622
Usnisavijaya	Bud.	F	1631
Uzava Tumaspana	Pers.	M	1633
Vahagn	Arm.	M	1634
Vajrapani	Bud.	M	1635
Vali	Norse	M	1636

	Culture	Sex	Page
Vanand	Pers.	M	1638
Varaha	Hin.	M	1638
Vazishta	Pers.	M	1643
Ve	Norse	M	1643
Verethraghna	Pers.	M	1646
Vidar	Norse	M	1649
Viracocha	Inca	M	1652
Vishnu	Hin.	M	1654
Vishtaspa	Pers.	M	1655
Vrtrahanna	Hin.	M	1659
Wainamoinen	Fin.	M	1661
Yamantaka	Bud.	M	1699
Yamato-take	Jap.	M	1699
Yaw	Hebr.	M	1702
Yoishta	Pers.	M	1709
Yorimitsu	Jap.	M	1709
Yudhisthira	Hin.	M	1711
Yu Lei	Chin.	M	1713
Yu Lu	Chin.	M	1713
Zairivairi	Pers.	M	1715
Zamama	Baby.	M	1715
Zas	Chin.	M	1716
Zeus	Gk.	M	1719
Zipacna	Kiche	M	1721

FOG (SEE MOISTURE)
FOLLY (SEE IGNORANCE)

FOOL (ALSO SEE IGNORANCE)

	Culture	Sex	Page
Arlecchino	Ital.	M	726
Calandrino	Ital.	M	272
Christ	Christ.	M	330
Dagonet, Sir	Bryth.	M	406
Eulenspiegel, Tyll	Germ.	M	529
Fimbulfambe	Norse	M	568
Gahe, Gray	Apache		622
Gothamist	Am. Lit.		679
Gracioso	Span.	M	681
Harlequin	Folk.	M	726
Joshua	Hebr.	M	889
Kesil	Sem.	M	919
Nabal	Hebr.	M	1145
Parsifal	Germ.	M	1239
Pelleas	Bryth.	M	1250
Percival	Bryth.	M	1254
Peredur	Welsh	M	1254

Fool (cont.)	Culture	Sex	Page
Plutus	Gk.	M	1280
Quixote, Don	Span.	M	1314
Silenus	Gk.	M	1453
To-karvuvu	Mel.	M	1584
Tom-norry	Eng.	M	1585

FOREST (SEE WOODLAND)

FORGETFULNESS			
Lethe	Gk.	F	986
Lotophagi	Gk.	M, F	1014
Lotus Eater	Folk.	M, F	1015
Manasseh	Hebr.	M	1055
Meng-po Niang-Niang	Chin.	F	1089

FORTUNE			
Ardokhsho (good)	Pers.	F	119
Ashera (good)	Sem.	F	138
Bhaga (good)	Hin.	M	207
Bishamon (good)	Jap.	M	220
Bol Bendo (good)	Christ.	M	234
Caipora (bad)	Braz.	M	270
Ekeko (good)	Aymara Ind.	M	497
Felicitas (good)	Rom.	F	558
Fortuna or Fors Fortuna (chance)	Rom.	F	596
Fudo (good)	Jap.	M	615
Gad (good)	Hebr.	M	620
Ganesa (good)	Hin.	M	627
Hamingja (good)	Norse	F	714
Hermes (good)	Gk.	M	760
Hotei (good)	Jap.	M	794
Jurojin (good)	Jap.	M	898
Kali (chance)	Hin.	M	903
King Goldemar (chance)	Germ.	M	929
Lakshmi (good)	Hin.	F	965
Mahakala (chance)	Hin.	M	1043
Manjusri (good)	Bud.	M	1059
Meni (good)	Assyr.	F/A	1089
Nortia (good)	Ital.	F	1182
Palamedes (chance)	Gk.	M	1227
Rehtia (good)	Ital.	F	1331
Saint George (good)	Christ.	M	1370
Sani (bad)	Hin.	M	1397
Tengri, Black (bad)	Buriat	M	1545
Tengri, White (good)	Buriat	M	1545

	Culture	Sex	Page
Tirawa (good)	Pawnee	M	1576
Tyche (chance)	Gk.	F	1616
Yakushi-sama (good)	Jap.	M	1698

FOSTER PARENT OR NURSE

	Culture	Sex	Page
Acca Larentia	Rom.	F	22
Adrastea	Gk.	F	35
Aegis	Gk.	F	38
Akki	Meso.	M	1400
Amalthea	Gk.	F	79
Aresthanas	Gk.	M	136
Athamas	Gk.	M	149
Athena	Gk.	F	150
Benthesicyme	Gk.	F	530
Bes	Egy.	M	205
Bodmhall & Liath	Cel.	M-F	570
Buto	Egy.	F	263
Chiron	Gk.	M	327
Cynosura	Gk.	F	402
Deborah	Hebr.	F	422
Ector, Sir	Bryth.	M	132
Elfinn	Bryth.	M	1528
Euryclea	Gk.	F	532
Faustulus	Rom.	M	553
Grim	Mid. Lit.	M	732
Helice	Gk.	F	747
Hippa	Gk.	F	772
Ino	Gk.	F	833
Lady of the Lake	Bryth.	F	962
Lady of the Wood	Christ.	F	905
Mayadevi	Hin.	F	1290
Merope	Gk.	F	1293
Naiades	Gk.	F	1148
Nanda	Hin.	M	1152
Nephthys	Egy.	F	1163
Polybus	Gk.	M	1283
Radha	Hin.	F	910
Regin	Norse	M	1330
Renenutet	Egy.	F	1332
Shatananda	Hin.	M	910
Silenus	Gk.	M	1453
Simurgh	Pers.	M	1456
Tama-nui-ki-to-rangi	Poly.	M	1077
Teyrnon	Bryth.	M	1549
Thermutis	Hebr.	F	1554
Thriae	Gk.	F	1566

Foster Parent (cont.)	Culture	Sex	Page
Uazit	Egy.	F	1619
Vivien	Bryth.	F	962
Yasoda	Hin.	F	945

FOUNDER OF CITY OR STATE (SEE CULTURE HERO)
FOUNTAIN (SEE WATER)
FROLIC (SEE REVELRY)

FROST (COLD, ICICLE, SLEET, SNOW)

Achachila	Bol.	M	24
Aki-yama	Jap.	M	60
Andhrimner	Norse	M	93
Anguta	Eskimo	M	97
Arimans	Pers.	M	124
Azhi Dahaka	Pers.	M	165
Bergelmir	Norse	M	204
Chione	Gk.	F	326
Elivagar	Norse		505
Erymanthian Boar	Gk.	M	523
Fafnir	Norse	M	544
Frostre	Norse	M	614
Gerd	Norse	F	647
Gohone	Iroq.		670
Gondefer	Bryth.	M	675
Gwrnach	Bryth.	M	702
Hel	Norse	F	745
Hlebard	Norse	M	776
Holde	Germ.	F	780
Hrim	Norse	M	798
Hrimgrinnir	Norse	M	798
Hrimnir	Norse	M	798
Hrimthursar	Norse	M	798
Hrungnir	Norse	M	798
Hymir	Norse	M	811
Iokul	Norse	M	900
Itztlacoliuhqui	Mex.	M	850
Jack Frost	Folk.	M	856
Jenkin	Eng.	M	872
Jonakr	Norse	M	886
Jotun	Norse	M	890
Kanook	Alaskan	M	908
Kol	Ice.	M	940
Lord of Cold	Blackfeet	M	+
Mahrkusha	Pers.	M	1046

	Culture	Sex	Page
Mo-li Shou	Chin.	M	1115
Mowis	N.A.I.	M	1132
Myrtilus	Gk.	M	1143
Nipa	Algon.	F	1175
Partinal	Bryth.	M	675
Punchkin	Hin.	M	1301
Punegusse	Sib.	M	1301
Rind	Norse	F	1339
Senach	Cel.	M	1416
Skade	Norse	F	1463
Snaer	Ice.	M	1469
Snavidhka	Pers.	M	1469
Stribog	Slav.	M	1500
Taka-okami	Jap.		1527
Thaukt (Thokk)	Norse	F/A	1552
Thrivaldi	Norse	M	1566
Thrudgelmir	Norse	M	1567
Thrym	Norse	M	1567
Ullerus	Norse	M	1622
Vasud	Norse	M	1641
Vindsval	Norse	M	1650
Yima	Pers.	M	1707
Ymir	Norse	M	1708
Yuki-onne	Jap.	F	1712
Zada	Sib.	M	1714

GAIN (SEE WEALTH)

GAMBLER

Cavendish	Eng.	M	300
Hoyle, Edmund	Eng.	M	+
Kali	Hin.	M	903
Kauravas	Hin.	M	913
King Goldemar	Germ.	M	929
Lord de Ros	Eng.	M	1013
Nala	Hin.	M	1150
Palamedes	Gk.	M	1227
Pandavas	Hin.	M	1232
Pau-puk-keewis	Am. Lit.	M	1244
Poshaiyanne	Pueblo	M	1288
Rhampsinitus	Gk.	M	1335

GENERATION (SEE FERTILITY)
GHOST, EVIL (SEE DEMON)
GHOST, KINDLY (SEE SPIRIT)
GHOUL (SEE DEMON)

GIFT BEARER (ALSO SEE WEALTH DISTRIBUTOR)	Culture	Sex	Page
Balthazar	Christ.	M	177
Befana	Ital.	F	195
Belun	Rus.	M	201
Dazbog	Rus.	M	420
Dorcas	Hebr.	F	464
Emakong	Aus.	M	507
Father Christmas	Christ.	M	551
Father Nicholas	Christ.	M	1168
Fulla	Norse	F	616
Gaspar	Christ.	M	633
Govetter	Norw.	M	680
Gufittar	Lapp	M	695
Habonde	Dan.	F	705
Hotei	Jap.	M	794
Knecht Clobes	Germ.	M	937
Knecht Ruprecht	Germ.	M	937
Kriss Kringle	Christ.	M	946
Kurukulla	Tib.	F	953
Melchior	Christ.	M	1085
Mynheer Closh	Dutch	M	1142
Oberon	Eng., Fr.	M	1192
Prometheus	Gk.	M	1295
Robin Hood	Eng.	M	1343
Rob Roy	Scot.	M	1343
Rubezahl	Germ.	M	1352
Rupert	Germ.	M	1354
Saint Nicholas	Christ.	M	1378
Santa Claus	Christ.	M	1397
Silik-mulu-khi	Sum.	M	1453
Three Magi	Christ.	M	1038
Uldda	Scan.	M	1621
Ushas	Hin.	F	1631
Vidyadhara	Hin.	F	1649

GLOAMING			
Ahans	Hin.	M	52
Antaea	Gk.	F	101
Anticleia	Gk.	F	103
Antigone	Gk.	F	103
Argus	Gk.	M	122
Asvins	Hin.	M	146
Billing	Norse	M	211
Cleopatra	Gk.	F	347
Creusa	Gk., Rom.	F	381
Deinaeira	Gk.	F	425

	Culture	Sex	Page
Delilah	Hebr.	F	427
Dido	Rom.	F	444
Evadne	Gk.	F	533
Glauce	Gk.	F	662
Grainne	Cel.	F	683
Gudrun	Norse	F	694
Gutrune	Germ.	F	699
Guttorm	Norse	M	699
Gwyar	Bryth.	F	702
Hastshehogan	Nav.	M	730
Huruing Wuhti	Hopi	F	808
Huzruwauqti	Pueblo	F	808
Hyllus	Gk.	M	811
Iphigenia	Gk.	F	838
Iseult	Bryth.	F	842
Japheth	Hebr.	M	865
Kriemhild	Germ.	F	945
Lugaid	Cel.	M	1023
Lycomedes	Gk.	M	1027
Nehes	Egy.	M	1161
Nessus	Gk.	M	1165
Nwyvre	Bryth.	M	1187
Odsmaer	Norse	F	610
Phaedra	Gk.	F	1260
Polyxena	Gk.	F	+
Potiphar's Wife	Hebr., Mos.	F	1289
Protesilaus	Gk.	M	1297
Rachel	Hebr.	F	1316
Rukmini	Hin.	F	1354
Shem	Hebr.	M	1433
Shiwa	Hin.	A	1440
Sudabah	Pers.	F	1503
Telyaveli	Baltic	M	1542
Tem	Egy.	M	1542
Thum (Tmu)	Egy.	M	1568
Tithonus	Gk.	M	1578
Wiglaf	Ang-Sax.	M	1680
Xiuhtecutli	Mex.	M	1696
GLUTTON			
Bhima	Hin.	M	209
Eresichthon	Gk.	M	518
Forese Donati	Ital.	M	594
Gaki	Jap.	M, F	622
Gargamelle	Fr.	F	630
Gargantua	Fr.	M	630

Glutton (cont.)	Culture	Sex	Page
Gizo	Hausa	M	660
Harpies	Gk.	F	728
Irus	Gk.	M	841
Preta	Hin.	M	1292
Raven	N.A.I.	M	1325
Reynard	Med. Lit.	M	1334
Shara	Arm.	M	1431
Thor	Norse	A	1561
Yo	Daho.		1708

GNOME (SEE SPIRIT)
GOOD FORTUNE (SEE FORTUNE)

GOOD SHEPHERD			
Apollo	Gk.	M	110
Christ	Christ.	M	330
Daniel	Hebr.	M	413
David	Hebr.	M	417
Good Scarabaeus	Christ.	M	675
Good Shepherd	Christ., Hebr.	M	675
Horus	Egy.	M	792
Isaac	Hebr.	M	841
Krishna	Hin.	M	945
Maitreya	Bud.	M	1047
Mi-li	Chin.	M	1102
Mithra	Pers.	M	1112
Moses	Hebr.	M	1126
Orpheus	Gk.	M	1216

GOSSIP (SEE MISCHIEVOUSNESS)
GRACE (SEE SPIRIT)

GREED			
Atreus	Gk.	M	153
Gaki	Jap.	M, F	622
Gere	Norse		647
Midas	Gk.	M	1099
Mysing	Ice.	M	1143
Reynard	Med. Lit.	M	1334
Sisyphus	Gk.	M	1459
Zeus	Gk.	M	1719

GROVE (SEE WOODLAND)

GUARDIAN (ALSO SEE PROTECTOR)			
Abeona	Rom.	F	15

	Culture	Sex	Page
Acaryavajrapani	Bud.	M	22
Adrastea	Gk.	F	35
Agrotera	Gk.	F	131
Al Moakkibat	Mos.	M	70
Al Rakim	Mos.		76
Amagat	Yakut	M	78
Ama-inu	Jap.		79
Ame-no-uzume	Jap.	F	83
Amenti Genii	Egy.	M	84
Amesha Spentas	Zoro.	M	84
Amlode	Norse	M	86
Amrtadhara & Sakti	Bud.	M-F	89
Amset	Egy.	M	89
Argus	Gk.	M	122
Asgardsveor	Norse	M	+
Athena	Gk.	F	150
Bacabab	Mex.	M	170
Bato-Kwannon	Jap.	F	186
Belun	Rus.	M	201
Bertha	Norse	F	205
Bes	Egy.	M	205
Bishamon	Jap.	M	220
Brigit	Cel.	F	249
Caelestis	Rom.	F	276
Cardea	Rom.	F	290
Carvara	Hin.	M	293
Castor & Pollux	Gk.	M-M	295
Cerberus	Gk.	M	304
Chamundi	Hin.	F	310
Chang Hsien	Chin.	M	311
Ch'en Ch'i	Chin.	M	318
Ch'eng Huang	Chin.	M	318
Cheng Lung	Chin.	M	318
Chieh-po-ka	Chin.	M	322
Ch'in Shu-pao	Chin.	M	326
Chu Ch'ieh	Chin.	M	335
Cridevi	Bud.	F	382
Cuba	Rom.	F	392
Cuchaviva	Bogota	F	393
Cunda	Bud.	F	396
Da (Dab-lha)	Tib.	M	403
Dedek	Slav.	M	424
Deduska Domovoy (Diko)	Rus.	M	424
Deverra	Rom.	F	+
Dharti Mai	Hin.	F	439
Dictynna	Gk.	F	444

	Culture	Sex	Page
Dikkumari	Hin.	F	445
Dinsangma	Tib.	F	446
Djadek	Slav.	M	454
Dogs of Foh (Foo)	Chin., Jap.	M-F	458
Domiduca	Rom.	F	460
Draco (Ladon)	Gk.	M	467
Drem	Bryth.	M	470
Duamutef	Egy.	M	474
Durga	Hin.	F	477
Ehlose	Zulu	M	494
Eldir	Norse	M	499
Epet (Tueret, Uret)	Egy.	F	514
Ephestius	Gk.	M	1720
Eurytion	Gk.	M	533
Fafnir	Norse	M	544
Faunus (Lupercus)	Rom.	M	552
Feroher	Pers.	M	562
Feronia	Ital.	F	562
Fimbultyr	Norse	M	568
Fjolsvid	Norse	M	578
Flosshilda	Germ.	F	585
Fravashi	Pers.	M	608
Funafeng	Norse	M	617
Furrina	Ital.	F	618
Fu-tai-shih	Chin.	M	618
Fylgia	Norw.	M/F	619
Fylgukona	Norw.	F	619
Gabriel	Christ., Hebr., Mos.	M	619
Gandayah	Iroq.	M	626
Gandharva	Hin.	M	626
Garm	Norse		631
Geush Urvan	Pers.	A	652
Gnome	Med. Lit.	M	664
Graeae	Gk.	F	681
dGra-lha (Da-lha)	Tib.	M	683
Grim & Hilde	Germ.	M-F	691
Hanuman	Hin.	M	723
Hapi	Egy.	M	724
Hardgrep	Norse	F	725
Hariti (Kishibojin)	Hin. (Jap.)	F	726
Hastshehogan	Nav.	M	730
Hastsheyalti	Nav.	M	730
Hecate	Gk.	F	740
Hefedha	Arab.	M	742
Heimdal	Norse	M	743

	Culture	Sex	Page
Hesperides	Gk.	F	765
Hestia	Gk.	F	765
Hino	Iroq.	M	772
Hlif	Norse	F	776
Hlina	Norse	F	776
Horus's Four Sons	Egy.	M	793
Hospodaricek	Slav.	M	793
Huyen-thien	Ind-Chin.	M	808
Hyades	Gk.	F	809
Ida	Gk.	F	818
Intercidona	Rom.	F	+
Irus	Gk.	M	841
Izeds	Zoro.	M	854
Jambhala	Bud.	M	862
Janus	Ital.	M	864
Jejamo-karpo	Bud.	M	871
Jizo (Kosodate-Jizo)	Jap.	M	881
Juno	Rom.	F	895
Jupiter Capitolinus (Tarpeius)	Rom.	M	896
Kasyapa	Bud.	M	912
Kebehsenuf	Egy.	M	915
Krsnik	Slav.	M	947
Kshiti Garbha	Hin.	M	947
Kuribu	Sum.	M	952
Lady of the Lake	Eng.	F	962
Lakshmi	Hin.	F	965
Landvaettir	Scan.	M	971
Levana	Rom.	F	988
Ling-Kuan	Chin.	M	998
Lokapalas	Bud., Hind.	M	1010
Long-do	Ind-Chin.	M	1011
Magna Mater	Phryg.	F	1040
Man	Sem.	F	1042
Mahamaya	Bud.	M	1043
Mahapancaraja	Tib.	M	1043
Mahapratisara	Bud.	F	1044
Mahasahasrapramardani	Bud.	F	1044
Mahasitavati	Bud.	F	1044
Mampes	Malay.	M	1052
Manalanrakki	Fin-Ug.	M	1054
Manannan	Cel.	M	1054
Manes	Rom.		1058
Marocael	Taino	M	1068
Mars	Rom.	M	1069
Meming	Norse	M	1088
Men Shen	Chin.	M	1090

	Culture	Sex	Page
Modgudur	Norse	F	1114
Mo-li Ch'ing	Chin.	M	1115
Mo-li Hai	Chin.	M	1115
Mo-li Hung	Chin.	M	601
Mo-li Shou	Chin	M	1115
Naga	Hin.	M, F	1147
Nagual	C.A.I.		1148
Nekhebet	Egy.	F	1161
Nikolai	Rus.	M	1169
Niltshi	Nav.	M	1170
Ningishzida	Sum.	M	1172
Ninsubur	Sum.	M	1173
Nio-san	Jap.	M	1174
Oho-kuni-nushi	Jap.	M	1621
Ops (Berecinthia)	Ital.	F	1212
Ormuzd	Zoro.	M	1216
Orthros	Gk.	M	1217
Osiris	Egy.	M	1218
Otafuku	Jap.	F	1219
Pa Cha	Chin.	M	1224
Pa-hsien	Chin.	M, F	1226
Pai-hu (Bach-ho)	Chin.	M	1226
Pales	Ital.	A	1228
Palici	Ital.	M	1228
Palladium	Gk.		1228
Pancaraksa	Bud.	F	1231
Pe-har	Tib.	M	1146
Pellean	Bryth.	M	1250
Pellenore	Bryth.	M	1251
Pelles	Bryth.	M	1251
Pephredo	Gk.	F	1254
Peter Pan	Eng.	M	1259
Phosphorus	Gk.	M	1266
Picumnus	Rom.	M	1269
Pilumnus	Rom.	M	1273
Pindolabharadvaja	Bud.	M	1273
Plouton (Pylartes)	Gk.	M	1306
Pusan	Hin.	M	1305
Pylaochos	Gk.	M	1306
Rakshasa	Hin.	M, F	1320
Raphael	Hebr.	M	1323
Riihitonttu	Fin-Ug.	M	1339
Robin Goodfellow	Eng.	M	1343
Rod & Rozanice	Rus.	M-F	1344
Sadaijin	Jap.	M	1175
Salii	Rom.	M	1390

	Culture	Sex	Page
Samvara	Bud.	M	1395
Sang-dui	Bud.	M	1396
Sedu	Baby.	M	1413
Selinus	Gk.	M	1415
Seraph	Hebr., Christ.	M	1417
Setek	Slovenian	M	1421
Shahapet	Arm.	M	1428
Sharvan	Cel.	M	1431
Shedim	Chald.	M	1432
Shelah-no-gig	Cel.	F	1433
Shen Shu	Chin.	M	1434
Shoki-san	Jap.	M	1441
Shui Jung	Chin.	M	1444
Shui Shen	Chin.	M	1444
Shu Yu	Chin.	M	1445
Shvaz	Arm.	M	1445
Shvod	Arm.	M	1445
Sohodo-no-kami	Jap.	M	1471
Sphinx	Egy., Gk.	F	1482
Sraoscha	Zoro.	M	1487
Sridevi	Bud.	F	1487
Suoje-lodde	Lapp		1510
Syn	Norse	F	1522
Tagaro the Fool	Banks Is.	M	1524
Talus	Gk.	M	1529
Tamahnous	Pac. Coast	M	1529
Tara	Bud.	F	1534
Taygete	Gk.	F	1539
Thahog-chos-rgyal-po	Bud.	M	1551
Thunderbird	N.A.I.	M	1568
Tie (Ta-urt)	Egy.	F	1571
Titurel	Bryth.	M	1580
Tonal	Mex.		1586
Torem-talmas	Sib.	M	1589
Tornak	Eskimoan	M	1589
Tran-vu	Ind-Chin.	M	1593
Tratr	Hin.	M	1593
Troll	Norse	M	1600
Trung Sisters	Ind-Chin.	F	1602
T'u-ti Lao-yeh	Chin.	M	1610
T'u-ti Nai-nai	Chin.	F	1610
Udaijin	Jap.	M	1175
Ujikami	Jap.	M	1621
Vaetter	Dan.	M, F	1633
Venus	Ital.	F	1644
Vesta	Rom.	F	1647

Guardian (cont.)	Culture	Sex	Page
Vijaya Sakti	Bud.	F	1649
Virgo Vestalis Maxima	Rom.	F	1648
Virudaka	Bud.	M	1654
Virupaksa	Bud.	M	1654
Vivian (Vivienne)	Bryth.	F	1656
Vorsud	Fin-Ug.	M	1658
Wang	Chin.	M	1664
Warai-botoke	Jap.	M	1666
Wei-t'o	Chin.	M	1672
Yetl	Tlingit	M	1156
Xolotl	Mex.	M	1697
Yamantaka	Bud.	M	1699
Yi-dam	Bud.	M	1707
Yogini	Bud.	F	1708
Yris	Carib Ind.	M	1710
Yu Ch'ih Ching-te	Chin.	M	1711
Yu Lei	Chin.	M	1713
Yu Lu	Chin.	M	1713
Zadkiel	Hebr., Christ.	M	1714
Zephon	Eng.	M	1718
Zmek	Slav.	M	1722

GUIDE (SEE DEATH)
GUILE (SEE CUNNING)

HAPPINESS			
Aglaos	Gk.	M	48
Auteb	Egy.	F	159
Bacchus	Gk., Rom.	M	170
Bai-ulgon	Tatar	M	173
Benten	Jap.	F	203
Bishamon	Jap.	M	220
Cakrasamvara	Bud.	M	272
Daikoku	Jap.	M	406
Dionysus	Gk.	M	447
Ebisu	Jap.	M	489
Euphrosyne	Gk.	F	531
Euterpe	Gk.	F	533
Friar John	Eng.	M	611
Fuku	Jap.	M	616
Fukusuke	Jap.	M	616
Fu-shen	Chin.	M	618
Fu-shou-lu	Chin.	M	618
Ganymede	Gk.	M	627
Gwen	Cel.	F	701
Haurvatat	Zoro.	M	732

	Culture	Sex	Page
Hetpet	Egy.	F	766
Hotei	Jap.	M	794
Ixcuina	Mex.	F	852
Jurojin	Jap.	M	898
Kachinas	Zuni	M	900
Kompira	Jap.	M	941
Kuo-tzu-I	Chin.	M	952
Lado & Lada	Slav.	M-F	961
Lan Ts'ai-Ho	Chin.	M/A	971
Lyaeus	Gk.	M	+
Manjusri	Bud.	M	1059
Mi-li	Chin.	M	1108
Mytyle	Belgian	M	1144
O-kuni-nushi	Jap.	M	1204
Omacatl	Mex.	M	1207
Polydamna	Gk.	F	+
Roger Bontemps	Eng.	M	1345
Sacy-Perere	Braz.	M	1360
Sakadonomaki	Jap.	M	1389
Santa Claus	Christ.	M	1397
Shichi Fukujin	Jap.	M, F	1436
Silvanus	Rom.	M	1453
Sitatara	Bud.	F	1460
T'ien Kuan	Chin.	M	1571
Tiksnamanjusri	Bud.	A	1573
Toyouga	Jap.	M	1389
Tyltyl	Belgian	M	1617
Warai-botoke	Jap.	M	1666
Yakushi-sama (Bhechad)	Jap.	M	1698
Yang Ch'eng	Chin.	M	1700

HARMONY (SEE ORDER, PEACE)
HARPY (SEE DEMON)

HARVEST

	Culture	Sex	Page
Ceres	Rom.	F	305
Chinun Way Shun	Burm.	M	899
Consus	Ital.	M	368
Convector	Rom.	M	369
Corn-baby (Kernababy)	Eng.	F	372
Cueravaperi	Mex.	F	396
Danaides	Gk.	F	411
Deverra	Rom.	F	+
Eleusis	Gk.	M	502
Erigone	Gk.	F	520
Fortuna	Rom.	F	596

Harvest (cont.)	Culture	Sex	Page
Frey	Norse	M	609
Gromovit	Slav.	M	692
Gudrun	Norse	F	694
Gutrune	Germ.	F	699
Hades	Gk.	M	706
H'ativa	Pawnee	F	731
Iliya Gromovnik	Serb.	M	692
Indra	Hin.	M	829
Ka	Burm.	M	899
Karpo	Gk.	F	911
Khensu	Egy.	M	923
Kriemhild	Germ.	F	945
Mama Allpa	Inca	F	1051
Messor	Rom.	M	1095
Min	Egy.	M	1106
Mitosh-no-kami	Jap.	M	1112
Nata & Nena	Mex.	M-F	1157
Nidaba	Sum.	F	1168
Obin-murt	Fin-Ug.	M	1192
Paimosaid	N.A.I.	M	+
Pyatnitsa Prascovia	Rus.	F	1306
Renenutet	Egy.	F	1332
Rynys-aika	Rus.	M	1355
Saeter	Norse	M	1360
Saturn	Rom.	M	1403
Sif	Norse	F	1448
Sith	Norse	F	1460
Uka-no-kami	Jap.	M	1621
Uranus	Gk.	M	1627
Vis	Pre-Inca		1654
Yeibichai	Nav.	M	1703
Yum Kaax	Mex.	M	1713

HEALER (MEDICINE MAN)

Acokottamasri	Bud.	M	26
Aesculapius	Rom.	M	137
Agathadaemon	Gk.	M	46
Agrotera	Gk.	F	131
Ahau-Chamahez	Mex.	M	52
Ahmed, Prince	Arab.	M	53
Ananeas	Christ.	M	91
Angakok	Eskimo	M	95
Apollo	Gk.	M	110
Archagathus	Rom.	M	118
Asclepius	Gk.	M	136
Askefruer	Norse	F	140

	Culture	Sex	Page
Asvins	Hin.	M	146
Aswiculapa	Hin.	M	147
Belenus	Bryth.	M	197
Bhaisajyaguru	Bud.	M	208
Binzuru	Jap.	M	212
Brhaspati	Hin.	M	247
Cambalo	Eng.	M	280
Caryotis	Gk.	F	131
Ceacht	Cel.	F	301
Cerimon	Eng.	M	305
Chalchiutlicue	Mex.	F	308
Chinnigchinich	Calif. Ind.	M	326
Ch'i Po	Chin.	M	326
Chiron	Gk.	M	327
Christ	Christ.	M	330
Cit-bolon-tum	Mex.	M	344
Cosmo & Damian	Christ.	M-M	1367
Criophorus	Gk.	M	382
Damia	Gk.	F	409
Damkina	Baby.	F	410
Danwantaree	Hin.	M	414
Dhanvantari	Hin.	M	437
Diancecht	Cel.	M	442
Eir	Norse	F	496
Enmenduranna	Sum.	M	512
Eshmun	Phoen.	M	525
Gadjisa	Iroq.	M	621
Gahe	Apache		622
Gandharva	Hin.	M	626
Ganga	Hin.	F	627
Gozu-tenwo	Jap.	M	680
Gula	Assyr.	M	696
Gula	Sum.	F	697
Gwiawn	Bryth.	M	701
Hanuman	Hin.	M	723
Harits	Hin.	M	726
Hermes	Gk.	M	760
Hiawatha	N.A.I.	M	767
Hippocrates	Gk.	M	773
Hygeia	Gk.	F	811
Imhotep	Egy.	M	825
Irman	Pers.	M	839
Ishtar	Assyr-Baby.	F	844
Isis	Egy.	F	845
Itzamna	Mex.	M	850
Ix-chel	Mex.	F	852

	Culture	Sex	Page
Jesus	Christ.	M	877
Jurojin	Jap.	M	898
Kabil	Mex.	M	900
Katcinas	Pueblo	M	912
Khensu	Egy.	M	923
Kishibojin	Jap.	F	933
Korrigans	Breton		943
Kuila-moku	Hawa.	M	949
Labhar	Cel.	M	957
Lha-K'a	Tib.	M	989
Li T'ieh-kuai	Chin.	M	1002
Lug	Cel.	M	1022
Lu Tung-pin	Chin.	M	1026
Lymphae	Rom.	F	1028
Machaon	Gk.	M	1034
Mahamantranusarini	Bud.	F	1043
Mahamayuri	Bud.	F	1043
Mahapratisara	Bud.	F	1044
Manabhozho	Algon.	M	1054
Manannan	Cel.	M	1054
Mani	Braz.	M	1058
Manito	Algon.		1058
Man-la	Bud.	M	1060
Marduk	Baby.	M	1065
Maria Wainscot	Folk.	F	1067
Medicine Man	N.A.I.	M	1083
Melampus	Gk.	M	1085
Miach	Cel.	M	1097
Minerva	Rom.	F	1106
Nasatya & Dasra	Hin.	M-M	1156
Nazi	Sum.	M	1159
Ninazu	Sum.	M	1170
Ningishzida	Sum.	M	1172
Ninkarraka	Baby.	M	1173
Ninsu-utud	Sum.	F	1174
Nuye	Jap.		1187
Oannes	Baby., Chald., Phoen.	M	1190
Ogma	Cel.	M	1200
O-kuni-nushi	Jap.	M	1204
Ophiogenes	Gk.	M, F	1211
Paeon	Gk.	M	1225
Pajan Yan	Cambodian	F	1121
Panacea	Gk.	F	1131
Paracelsus	Eng.	M	1236
Parnasabari	Hin.	F	1238

	Culture	Sex	Page
Parsifal	Germ.	M	1239
Percival	Bryth.	M	1254
Peredur	Bryth.	M	1254
Phoebus	Gk.	M	1265
Piache	C.A.I.	M	1268
Podalirius	Gk.	M	1281
Polyidus	Gk.	M	1284
Princess Woodencloak	Folk.	F	1294
Prometheus	Gk.	M	1295
Psylli	Afr.	M, F	1299
Ptah	Egy.	M	1299
Punch	Eng.	M	1301
Punchinello	Ital.	M	1301
Quetzalcoatl	Mex.	M	1312
Raphael	Hebr.	M	1323
Rohina	Hin.	F	1345
Rudra	Hin.	M	1353
Sahe no kami	Jap.	M	1361
Saint Blaise	Christ.	M	1365
Salema	Arab.	M	1390
Salus	Rom.	F	1392
Sankara	Hindu	M	1397
Santa	Ital.	F	1397
Sasthi	Hin.	F	1401
Selwanga	Bantu	M	1415
Serapis	Egy.	M	1418
Sesostris	Egy.	M	1420
Shakuru	Pawnee	M	1429
Sharis	Urartian	F	1431
Shen Nung	Chin.	M	1434
Shoki-san	Jap.	M	1441
Silik-mulu-khi	Assyr-Sum.	M	+
Sol	Ital.	M	1471
Somin-shorai	Jap.	M	1474
Suku-na-biko	Jap.	M	1505
Sul	Bryth.	F	1505
Surya	Hin.	M	1511
Susa-no-wo	Jap.	M	1512
Suvetar	Hin.	F	1513
Tabarin	Eng.	M	1523
Tammuz	Baby.	M	1530
Telesphorus Euemerion (Acesius)	Gk.	M	1542
Thoth	Egy.	M	1562
Thraetaona	Pers.	M	1563
Thrita Athwya	Pers.	M	1566

Healer (cont.)	Culture	Sex	Page
Trita Aptya	Hin.	M	1599
Tsuki-yomi	Jap.	M	1604
Usnisavijaya	Bud.	F	1631
Vajrapani	Bud.	M	1635
Valetudo	Ital.	F	1636
Verethraghna	Pers.	M	1646
Vila	Serbo-Croa.	F	1650
Vitholf	Norse	M	1656
Yakushi-Sama (Bhechad)	Jap.	M	1698
Yeibichai	Nav.	M	1703
Yo Wang	Chin.	M	1710
Zoroaster	Zoro.	M	1734

HEARTH (SEE HOUSEHOLD)
HEAT (SEE FIRE)

HERO (ALSO SEE VALOR, WARRIOR)			
Acamas	Gk.	M	21
Accolon	Bryth.	M	23
Achilles	Gk.	M	25
Acolon, Sir	Bryth.	M	1351
Agamemnon	Gk.	M	44
Agrivain	Bryth.	M	51
Amadis	Span.	M	78
Amangons	Bryth.	M	79
Andret	Bryth.	M	93
Anseis	Carol.	M	1227
Antigone	Gk.	F	103
Archbishop Turpin	Carol.	M	119
Argalia	Carol.	M	1316
Artegal	Bryth.	M	130
Arthur	Bryth.	M	132
Asa	Hebr.	M	134
Ashurbanipal	Assyr.	M	140
Astolpho	Carol.	M	144
Atharna	Cel.	M	150
Athwya	Pers.	M	151
Atli	Norse	M	152
Bach-ma	Ind-Chin.	M	171
Balan (Brennius)	Bryth.	M	174
Baldwin	Carol.	M	175
Balin (Belinus)	Bryth.	M	175
Ballamore	Bryth.	M	1351
Barbarossa	Germ.	M	180
Bedivere	Bryth.	M	193
Beleobus	Bryth.	M	1351

	Culture	Sex	Page
Bellerophon	Gk.	M	199
Belvoure	Bryth.	M	1351
Beowulf	Ang-Sax.	M	203
Berengier	Carol.	M	1227
Bersunt	Bryth.	M	1351
Bors	Bryth.	M	237
Cael	Cel.	M	267
Cairbe	Cel.	M	270
Capaneus	Gk.	M	288
Cid	Span.	M	338
Cincinnatus	Rom.	M	339
Cuchulainn	Cel.	M	393
Daniel	Hebr.	M	413
David	Hebr.	M	417
Dietrich	Germ.	M	444
Dii Indigetes	Rom.	M	445
Diomedes	Gk.	M	446
Don Quixote	Span.	M	462
Doolin of Mayence	Fr.	M	463
Drem	Bryth.	M	470
Ector de Maris	Bryth.	M	+
Engelier	Carol.	M	1227
Esther	Hebr.	F	526
Etana	Sum.	M	527
Ethan Allen	Am. Lit.	M	527
Ewain	Bryth.	M	1351
Fierabras (Ferumbras)	Carol.	M	565
Finn mac Coul	Cel.	M	570
Floll	Bryth.	M	1351
Florismart	Carol.	M	585
Gaheris	Bryth.	M	622
Galahad	Bryth.	M	622
Galohalt	Bryth.	M	1351
Ganelon	Carol.	M	627
Gareth	Bryth.	M	629
Gawain	Bryth.	M	635
Geraint	Bryth.	M	646
Gerard de Rousillon	Carol.	M	1227
Gerier	Carol.	M	1227
Gerin	Carol.	M	1227
Gilgamesh	Sum.	M	656
Gimel Sin	Baby.	M	658
Gordius	Gk.	M	678
dGra-lha (Da-lha)	Tib.	M	683
Green Knight	Bryth.	M	689
Grislet	Bryth.	M	1351

	Culture	Sex	Page
Guagugiana (Vagoniona)	Taino	M	693
Guarinos	Carol.	M	694
Guido the Savage	Carol.	M	696
Gunnodoyah	Iroq.	M	698
Gurgiunt Brabtruc	Bryth.	M	699
Guy of Warwick	Bryth.	M	700
Gwalchmei	Bryth.	M	700
Gwevyl	Bryth.	M	701
Havelock the Dane	Med. Lit.	M	732
Hector	Gk.	M	741
Heracles	Gk.	M	752
Hercules	Rom.	M	759
Hiawatha	N.A.I.	M	767
Holger Danske	Dan.	M	781
Hugh de Bras	Bryth.	M	802
Huon, Sir	Bryth.	M	807
Hur	Hebr.	M	808
Idomeneus	Gk.	M	820
Ion	Eng.	M	837
Isenbras, Sir	Bryth.	M	842
Ivon	Carol.	M	1227
Ivory	Carol.	M	1227
Jabin	Hebr.	M	855
Jael	Hebr.	F	860
Jamshid	Pers.	M	863
Jason	Gk.	M	866
Jehoram	Hebr.	M	869
Jehu	Hebr.	M	871
Jeroboam	Hebr.	M	874
Joan of Ark (Maid of Orleans)	Fr.	F	881
Joshua	Hebr.	M	889
Judith	Hebr.	F	893
Juju	W. Afr.	M	894
Junak	Slav.	M	895
Kaito	Jap.	M	902
Kavah	Pers.	M	914
Kay, Sir	Bryth.	M	914
Kayak	Eskimoan	M	1256
Keresaspa	Pers.	M	918
Kuo Shang	Chin.	M	952
Kuo Tzu-I	Chin.	M	952
Lamerock, Sir	Bryth.	M	967
Lancelot	Bryth.	M	969
Lanval, Sir	Bryth.	M	972
Launfal, Sir	Bryth.	M	976
Lavaine, Sir	Bryth.	M	977

	Culture	Sex	Page
Leofric	Bryth.	M	984
Leonidas	Gk.	M	984
Li Hun	Chin.	M	994
Lionell	Bryth.	M	1351
Lizard	Bushman	M	1256
Loegaire	Cel.	M	1008
Logris	Bryth.	M	1009
Lohengrin	Germ.	M	1009
Lot	Bryth.	M	1014
Luagni	Cel.	M	1019
Lud	Eng.	M	1021
Lug	Cel.	M	1022
Lynceus	Gk.	M	1028
Mabon	Bryth.	M	1031
Macbeth	Eng.	M	1032
Maccabees	Hebr.	M	1032
MacDuff	Eng.	M	1033
Mahaitiac	Hidat.	M	1043
Malagigi	Carol.	M	1048
Mambrino	Moorish	M	1051
Manushcithra	Pers.	M	1062
Marhaus	Bryth.	M	1351
Mark	Bryth.	M	1068
Marko Kraljevic	Serb.	M	1068
Marsk Stig	Dan.	M	1070
Maugis	Carol.	M	1077
Meleager	Gk.	M	1085
Memnon	Gk.	M	1088
Menelaus	Gk.	M	1089
Menoeceus	Gk.	M	1089
Menw	Bryth.	M	1090
Mordecai	Hebr.	M	1122
Mordred	Bryth.	M	1122
Namo (Nami)	Carol.	M	1152
Neleus	Gk.	M	1161
Neoptolemus	Gk.	M	1163
Nobunaga	Jap.	M	1178
No cha	Chin.	M	1178
Oderic	Ital.	M	1195
Odrus	Cel.	M	1196
Odysseus	Gk.	M	1196
Oedipus	Gk.	M	1198
Ogier	Dan.	M	1200
Oliver	Carol.	M	1206
Orestes	Gk.	M	1214
Orlando	Ital.	M	1215

	Culture	Sex	Page
Oton	Carol.	M	1227
Otshirvani	Mong.	M	1220
Owain	Bryth.	M	1221
Paginet	Bryth.	M	1351
Paladin	Carol.	M	1227
Palamedes	Bryth.	M	1227
Parsifal	Germ.	M	1239
Peleus	Gk.	M	1250
Pelias	Gk.	M	1250
Pelleas	Bryth.	M	1250
Pellenore	Bryth.	M	1251
Pelops	Gk.	M	1251
Penelva	Span.	M	1252
Percival	Bryth.	M	1254
Peredur	Bryth.	M	1254
Perseus	Gk.	M	1257
Pharamond	Bryth.	M	1262
Podalirius	Gk.	M	1281
Polydorus	Gk.	M	1281
Priam	Gk.	M	1292
Protesilaus	Gk.	M	1297
Quixote	Span.	M	1314
Rahab	Hebr.	F	1318
Rapunze	Germ.	M	465
Regulus	Rom.	M	1331
Remus	Rom.	M	1332
Renault	Carol.	M	1332
Rinaldo	Ital.	M	1339
Robin Hood	Eng.	M	1343
Roderick	Span.	M	1344
Rogero	Ital.	M	773
Roland	Carol.	M	1345
Romulus	Rom.	M	1346
Rustam	Pers.	M	1355
Ryence	Bryth.	M	1355
Sagramour Le Desirus	Bryth.	M	1361
Sagris	Bryth.	M	1351
Salomon	Carol.	M	1391
Samson	Carol.	M	1227
Samson	Hebr.	M	1394
Samurai	Jap.	M	1394
Sandde-Bryd-Angel	Bryth.	M	1396
Shan Kuei	Chin.	M	1430
Siegfried	Germ.	M	1448
Sigurd	Norse	M	1451
Superabilis	Bryth.	M	1351

	Culture	Sex	Page
Tcikapis	N.A.I.	M	1540
Telamon	Gk.	M	1541
Theodore the Goth	Germ.	M	1553
Theseus	Gk.	M	1554
Tor	Bryth.	M	135
Tristram	Bryth.	M	1599
Tsakakaitiac	Hidat.	M	1602
Tung Chun	Chin.	M	1607
Tung Huang T'ai I	Chin.	M	1607
Turpin, Archbishop	Bryth.	M	1609
Turquine	Bryth.	M	1351
Ulysses	Rom.	M	1622
Vistauru	Pers.	M	1655
Vivanghvant	Pers.	M	1656
William Tell	Swiss	M	1680
Wo-usu	Jap.	M	1692
Xelhua	Mex.	M	1695
Yamato-take	Jap.	M	1699
Yoishta	Pers.	M	1709
Yoshitsune	Jap.	M	1710
Yun Chung Chun	Chin.	M	1713
Zerbino	Ital.	M	1718

HOPE (DESIRE)

Hope	Gnostic Aeon	F	786
Hopeful	Eng. Lit.	M	786
Hotoke	Jap.	M	794
Philotes	Gk.		1264

HORSEHERD (SEE ANIMAL KEEPER)

HOSPITALITY

Celeus	Gk.	M	302
Darby & Joan	Eng.	M-F	415
Hyrieus	Gk.	M	813
Icarius	Gk.	M	817
Iobates	Gk.	M	836
Janus	Ital.	M	864
Phaon	Gk.	M	1261
Philemon & Baucis	Rom.	M-F	1263
Pholus	Gk.	M	1266
Sancus	Ital.	M	1395
Somin-shorai	Jap.	M	1474
Sujata	Bud.	F	1504
Tsukuba	Jap.	M	1604
Xenios	Gk.	M	1695

Hospitality (cont.)	Culture	Sex	Page
Zeus	Gk.	M	1719

HOUSEHOLD (BATH, DOOR, HEARTH, KITCHEN, OVEN, PANTRY, PRIVY, SAUCEPAN, STOVE)

Balagan Ishita	Yakut	M	174
Bannik	Rus.		179
Brigit	Cel.	F	249
Ch'u Hsieh Yuan	Chin.	M	335
Chu Jung	Chin.	M	336
Chung K'uei	Chin.	M	336
Chung Liu	Chin.	M	336
Cinderella	Folk.	F	339
Deduska Domovoy (Diko)	Rus.	M	424
Dorr-karing	Swed.	F	465
Duende	Span.	M	475
Eing Saung Nat	Ind-Chin.		496
Fornax	Rom.	F	595
Furrina	Ital.	F	618
Gadjisa	Iroq.	M	621
Gardsvor	Norse		629
Gold Betheli	Swiss	F	671
Grahapati	Hin.	M	682
Gula	Sum.	F	696
Haltia	Fin-Ug.	M	713
Hastshehogan	Nav.	M	730
Hephaestus	Gk.	M	751
Hestia	Gk.	F	765
Ho-hsien-ku	Chin.	F	780
Ho-shen	Chin.	M	793
Hospodaricek	Slav.	M	793
Icheiri	Carib	M	817
Ilia	Rom.	F	1335
Intercidona	Rom.	F	+
Kaukas (Pukys)	Slav.	M	913
Kikimoras	Slav.	F	927
Kitchie Boy	Scot.	M	934
Kobe-no-kami	Jap.	M	939
Kodojeza	Esthonian	M	939
Kojin	Jap.	M/A	940
Korka-murt	Fin-Ug.	M	942
Krsnik	Slav.	M	947
Ktesios	Gk.	M	1719
Kud-ava	Fin-Ug.	F	948
Kudo-no-kami	Jap.	M	948
Kyode-jielle	Rus., Lapp		956

	Culture	Sex	Page
Labartu	Assyr.	F	957
Lares	Rom.	M	974
Manes	Rom.	M, F	1058
Muntso-murt	Fin-Ug.	M	1137
Nain Rouge	Norman	M	1149
Nan Lha	Tib.	M	1153
Nisse	Dan.	M	1176
Okitsuhime	Jap.	M	1203
Ongon (Kurmers, Tyus)	Buriat	M	1209
Para	Fin-Ug.		1236
Penates	Rom.	M, F	1251
Port-hozjin	Rus., Lapp	M	1287
Pyvsan-aika	Rus.	M	1308
Ra (Radare)	Teut.	M	1314
Riihitonttu	Fin-Ug.	M	1339
Robin Goodfellow	Eng.	M	1343
Rod & Rozanice	Rus.	M-F	1344
Sa-bdag	Jap.	M	1357
Sambo-kojin	Jap.	M	1393
Shahapet	Arm.	M	1428
Shen	Chin.	M	577
Shoki-san	Jap.	M	1441
Shvod	Arm.	M	1445
Silvanus	Rom.	M	1453
Silvia	Rom.	F	1454
Sjen	Slav.	M	1463
Smiera-gatto	Lapp		1468
Stopan	Bulg.	M	1497
Sukuyan	Trinidad	F	1505
Teleos	Gk.	M	1719
Tomte	Swed.	M	1586
Tonttu	Fin-Ug.	M	1587
Tovodu	Daho.		1591
Tsao Shen	Chin.	M	1603
Tsi-ku	Chin.	F	1603
Tunnrida	Scan.	M	1608
Uksakka	Lapp	F	1621
Vaetter	Dan.	M, F	1633
Vaksoza	Fin-Ug.	M	1635
Vastospati	Hin.	M	1641
Vesta	Rom.	F	1647
Virgo Vestalis Maxima	Rom.	F	1648
Vispati	Hin.	M	1655
Vorsud	Fin-Ug.	M	1658
Xiuhtecutli	Mex.	M	1696
Yabune	Jap.	M	1697

Household (cont.)	Culture	Sex	Page
Yanari	Jap.	M	1700
Ya'yai	Sib.		1702
Zmek	Slav.	M	1722

HUMAN FLESH EATERS (SEE CANNIBALISM)

HUMAN FLESH SERVERS			
Atreus	Gk.	M	153
Gudrun	Norse	F	694
Lycaon	Gk.	M	1027
Lycurgus	Gk.	M	1028
Philomela	Gk.	F	1263
Procne	Gk.	F	1294
Tantalus	Gk.	M	1533

HUNTER			
Acastus	Gk.	M	22
Actaeon	Gk.	M	28
Admetus	Gk.	M	33
Alpheus	Gk.	M	76
Amarud	Baby.	M	80
Amphiaraus	Gk.	M	87
Amphitryon	Gk.	M	88
Ancaeus	Gk.	M	92
Arcas	Gk.	M	118
Artemis	Gk.	F	131
Artio	Cel.	F	133
Atalanta	Gk.	F	148
Aziza	Afr. Ewes	M	166
Belphoebe	Eng.	F	200
Bendis	Gk.	F	201
Brauronian	Gk.	F	131
Bredi	Norse	M	245
Britomartis	Gk.	F	250
Callisto	Gk.	F	278
Cephalus	Gk.	M	303
Chiron	Gk.	M	327
Coba	Cel.	M	352
Curupira	Braz.	M	399
Diana	Rom.	F	441
Diarmaid	Cel.	M	442
Endymion	Gk.	M	511
Esau	Hebr.	M	524
Faunus	Rom.	M	552
Fenian	Cel.	M	559

	Culture	Sex	Page
Fu Hsi	Chin.	M	615
Gabriel	Christ., Hebr., Mos.	M	619
Gronw Pebyr	Bryth.	M	692
Heracles	Gk.	M	752
Hercules	Rom.	M	759
Herla (Hertyr)	Scan.	M	1196
Herne	Eng.	M	762
Hiko-Hohodemi	Jap.	M	769
Hittavainen	Fin.	M	775
Idas	Gk.	M	818
Kanati	Cherokee	M	1415
Kande Yake	Cey.	M	907
Khensu	Egy.	M	923
Kulhwch	Bryth.	M	950
Kynedyr Wyllt	Bryth.	M	956
Leib-olmai	Lapp	M	981
Lycurgus	Gk.	M	1028
Mabon	Welsh	M	1031
Meleager	Gk.	M	1085
Mixcoatl	Mex.	M	1113
Mopsus	Gk.	M	1122
Nergal	Assyr-Baby.	M	1164
Nimrod	Baby.	M	1170
Ninurta	Sum.	M	1174
Odin	Norse	M	1195
Old One	Thomp. Riv.	M	+
Ondoutaete	Huron	M	1209
Opochtli	Mex.	M	1212
Oreades	Gk.	F	1213
Orion	Gk.	M	1215
Oshossi	Yorubas	M	1218
Pan	Gk.	M	1230
Pay Zume	Para.	M	1245
Pwyll	Bryth.	M	1306
Saint Eustace	Christ.	M	1386
Saint Hubert	Christ.	M	1371
Saint Julian	Christ.	M	1373
Sed	Sem.	M	1412
Serosevsky	Rus.	M	1418
Sibzianna	Baby.	M	1530
Silvanus	Rom.	M	1453
Sosondowah	Iroq.	M	1476
Telamon	Gk.	M	1541
Tirawa	Pawnee	M	1576
Tristan	Bryth.	M	1599

Hunter (cont.)	Culture	Sex	Page
Troll	Norse	M	1600
Vorys-mort (Dyadya)	Fin-Ug.	M	1658
Windigo	Algon.	M	1683
Wudes Heer	Norse	M	1693
Wyungare	Aus.	M	1694
Yehwe Zogbanu	Daho.	M	1703
Yeibichai	Nav.	M	1703

HYPOCRISY (SEE DECEIT)
ICICLE (SEE FROST)

IGNORANCE (ALSO SEE FOOL, INNOCENCE)

Angra Mainyu	Zoro.	M	97
Avidya	Hin.		162
Bayard	Med. Lit.	M	187
Boeotian	Gk.	M, F	233
Epimetheus	Gk.	M	516
Gothamite	Eng.	M, F	679
Issi	Germ.	M	848
Pancrace	Fr.	M	1231
Pantaloon	Ital.	M	1234
Parpara	Kei Is.	M	1239
Peter Schlemihl	Jewish	M	1259
Polyphemus	Gk.	M	1284
Sancho Panza	Span.	M	1395
Sangrado, Dr.	Fr.	M	1396
Suqe-matua	N. Heb.	M	1511
Tao	Philip.	M, F	1533
To-Karvuvu	Mel.	M	1584

ILL FORTUNE (SEE FORTUNE)
INCEST (SEE CONSORT OF FATHER, etc., CONSORT OF MOTHER, etc.)

INFIDELITY

Alcmene	Gk.	F	65
Apollo	Gk.	M	110
Becuma	Cel.	F	192
Boann	Cel.	F	231
Briseis	Gk.	F	249
Carmen	Fr.	F	291
Clytemnestra	Gk.	F	351
Coronis	Gk.	F	374
Cressida	Eng.	F	380
Cuchulainn	Cel.	M	393

	Culture	Sex	Page
Francesca da Rimini	Ital.	F	606
Goneril	Eng.	F	675
Grainne	Cel.	F	683
Guinevere	Bryth.	F	696
Helen	Gk.	F	745
Heracles	Gk.	M	752
Hercules	Rom.	M	759
Paris	Gk.	M	1238
Sansfoy	Eng.	M	1397
Siegfried	Germ.	M	1448
Sigurd	Norse	M	1451
Theseus	Gk.	M	1554
Thetis	Gk.	F	1555
Tyro	Gk.	F	1618
Zeus	Gk.	M	1719
INHOSPITALITY			
Ahasuerus	Hebr.	M	52
Busiris	Egy.	M	262
Emathion	Gk.	M	507
Eumolpus	Gk.	M	530
Fuji	Jap.	M	615
Geirrod	Norse	M	638
Kotan	Jap.	M	638
Lycaon	Gk.	M	1027
Nabal	Hebr.	M	1145
Taurica	Gk.	F	1538
INNOCENCE (ALSO SEE FOOL)			
Adam	Hebr.	M	29
Galatea	Gk.	F	623
Pelleas	Bryth.	M	1250
Pierrot	Fr.	M	1270
Quixote, Don	Span.	M	1314
Rishyacringa	Hin.	M	1341
INSECT			
Adramaleck (fly)	Med. Lit.	M	431
Aksak (beetle)	Chaco Ind.	M	60
Anansi (spider)	Afr. Gold Coast	M	91
Andalma-muus (Mosquito)	Tatar	M	93
Arachne (spider)	Gk.	F	116
Areop-enap (spider)	Nauru Is.	M	120
Areop-it-eonin (spider)	Nauru Is.	M	120
Beelzebub (fly)	Med. Lit.	M	194
Chamos (fly)	Med. Lit.	M	431

Insect (cont.)	Culture	Sex	Page
Euronymous (fly)	Med. Lit.	M	431
Karaty-khan	Mong.	M	910
Leviathan (fly)	Med. Lit.	M	989
Loki (fly)	Norse	M	1010
Master Leonard (fly)	Med. Lit.	M	431
Meiboia (bee)	Gk.	F	1084
Melissa (bee)	Gk.	F	1086
Moloch (fly)	Med. Lit.	M	1115
Myiagros (fly)	Gk.	M	1142
Nasu (fly)	Pers.	F	472
Neskeper-ava (Musks-ort)	Fin-Ug.	F	1165
Priapus (bee)	Gk.	M	1292
Punegusse (mosquito)	Sib.	M	1301
Resheph (pests)	Phoen.	M	1333
Sien-tsan (silk worm)	Chin.	F	1448
Tyurunmuzykay (mosquito)	Tatar	M	1618

INSTRUCTOR (SEE TUTOR)

INTEMPERANCE (PRESUMPTION, SHAMELESSNESS)

Name	Culture	Sex	Page
Acrasia	Eng.	M	27
Acrates	Eng.	M	27
Ame-no-uzume	Jap.	F	83
Anaideia	Gk.	F	+
Attis	Phryg.	M	154
Divje Devojke	Slav.	F	454
Golias, Bishop	Med. Lit.	M	674
Hybris	Gk.	M	+
Salome	Christ.	M	1391

IZED (SEE SPIRIT)

JEALOUSY OR ENVY (j=jealousy; e=envy)

Name	Culture	Sex	Page
Agraulos (j)	Gk.	F	51
Aoife (j)	Cel.	F	106
Benten (j)	Jap.	F	203
Circe (j)	Gk.	F	341
Daedalus (e)	Gk.	M	404
Damocles (e)	Rom.	M	410
Deianeira (j)	Gk.	F	425
Ea (e)	Assyr., Baby., Sum.	M	481
Enki (e)	Assyr., Baby., Sum.	M	511

	Culture	Sex	Page
Fuamnach (j)	Cel.	F	615
Ganelon (e)	Carol.	M	627
Glaucus (j)	Gk.	M	662
Guendolen (j)	Eng.	F	1357
Hera (j)	Gk.	F	752
Hidakagawa (j)	Jap.	F	767
Iha-no-hime (j)	Jap.	F	822
Ino (j)	Gk.	F	833
Juno (j)	Rom.	F	895
Keresavazdah (e)	Pers.	M	918
Lord Uye-minu (j)	Jap.	M	1013
Malbecco (j)	Eng.	M	1049
Mataora (j)	Poly.	M	1074
Medea (j)	Gk.	F	1082
Nascakiyetl (j)	Tlingit Ind.	M	1156
Nessus (j)	Gk.	M	1165
Ninigi (j)	Jap.	M	1173
Othello (j)	Eng.	M	1220
Pele (j)	Poly.	F	1249
Peleus (e)	Gk.	M	1541
Polyphemus (j)	Gk.	M	1284
Potiphar's Wife (j)	Hebr., Mos.	F	1289
Rahil (j)	Mos.	F	1319
Reuben (e)	Hebr.	M	1334
Saint Julian (j)	Christ.	M	1373
Sarah (Sarai)	Hebr.	F	1399
Saul (e)	Hebr.	M	1404
Set (e)	Egy.	M	1420
Siggeir (e)	Norse	M	1449
Tangaroa (j)	Maori	M	1531
Telamon (e)	Gk.	M	1541
Yaotl (e)	Mex.	M	1701
Yega (j)	Athapascan		1703
Zuleika (j)	Mos.	F	1735

JEALOUSY OR ENVY VICTIM

	Culture	Sex	Page
Adapa	Assyr., Baby., Sum.	M	30
Callisto	Gk.	F	278
Conlaoch	Cel.	M	367
David	Hebr.	M	417
Deirdre	Cel.	F	426
Desdemona	Eng.	F	815
Estrildis	Bryth.	F	695
Etain	Cel.	F	526
Galatea	Gk.	F	623

Jealousy or Envy Victim (cont.)	Culture	Sex	Page
Glauce (Creusa)	Gk.	F	662
Hagar	Hebr.	F	707
Helle	Gk.	F	748
Heracles	Gk.	M	752
Hercules	Rom.	M	759
Herse	Gk.	F	51
Io	Gk.	F	835
Jacob	Hebr.	M	858
Lamia	Gk.	F	967
Latona	Rom.	F	975
Leto	Gk.	F	986
Locrine	Bryth.	M	695
Naoise	Cel.	M	1154
Nessus	Gk.	M	1165
Nuvarahu	Poly.	F	1074
Osiris	Egy.	M	1218
Perdix	Gk.	M	1254
Phocus	Gk.	M	154
Phrixus	Gk.	M	1267
Rangi	Poly.	M	1322
Sabrina	Bryth.	F	1357
Scylla	Gk.	F	1409
Syavarshan	Pers.	M	1521
Volsung	Norse	M	1658
Yetl	Tlingit	M	1156

JESTER (SEE REVELRY)
JINNEE (SEE SPIRIT)
JUDGE (SEE DEATH, JUSTICE)

JUSTICE			
Adad	Assyr.	M	28
Aeacus	Gk.	M	37
Allah	Arab.	M	69
Amairgen	Cel.	M	79
Amen	Egy.	M	83
Ananke	Gk.	F	91
Artegal	Eng.	M	130
Asha	Zoro.	M	138
Astraea	Gk.	F	145
Dendin, Peter	Fr.	M	432
Dendin, Tenot	Fr.	M	432
Dice (Dike)	Gk.	F	443
Elidure	Bryth.	M	503
Esar	Mos.	M	524
Forseti	Norse	M	595

	Culture	Sex	Page
Gabriel	Christ., Hebr., Mos.	M	619
Geburah	Caba.	M	637
Godh	Dan.	M	604
Hecate	Gk.	F	740
Horae	Gk.	F	786
Hosia	Gk.	F	793
Hu	Bryth.	M	800
Hudibras	Eng.	M	802
Ishar	Sum.	M	843
Ishum	Sum.	M	845
Jehovah	Hebr.	M	870
Jupiter Fidius	Rom.	M	896
Justitia	Rom.	F	899
Kaguhana	Jap.	M	902
Kettu (Sydyk)	Baby.	M	920
Lu Tung-pin	Chin.	M	1026
Maat	Egy.	F	1031
Math	Bryth.	M	1075
Minos	Gk.	M	1107
Moses	Hebr.	M	1126
Nemesis	Gk.	F	1162
Ramman	Baby.	M	1322
Rashnu	Zoro.	M	1323
Rhadamanthus	Gk.	M	1335
Rimmon	Baby.	M	1339
Ripheus	Rom.	M	1340
Samuel	Hebr.	M	1394
Sancho Panza	Span.	M	1395
Sin You	Jap.		1457
Solomon	Hebr.	M	1472
Solon	Gk.	M	1473
Soru	Pers.	M	604
Taripaca	Inca	M	1535
Themis	Gk.	F	1553
Tyche	Gk.	F	1616
Urukagina	Sum.	M	1630
Varuna	Hin.	M	1639
Yu Ti	Chin.	M	1713
Zadkiel	Hebr.	M	1714
Zeus	Gk.	M	1719
Ziu (Tiu)	Germ.	M	1721

KNIGHT (SEE HERO)
KNOWLEDGE (SEE WISDOM)
LAKE (SEE WATER)

LAME (SEE MAIMED)	Culture	Sex	Page
LAW			
Ashem Vahishtem	Zoro.	M	+
Asshur	Assyr.	M	143
Athena	Gk.	F	150
Begoe (Bergoia)	Ital.	F	195
Curicaberis	Mex.	M	398
Daramulum	Aus.	M	414
Dharma	Hin.	M	438
Dharmapala	Bud.	M	438
Eunomia	Gk.	F	530
Hammurabi	Baby.	M	716
Haoshyangha	Pers.	M	723
Horae	Gk.	F	786
Itzamna	Mex.	M	850
Jehovah	Hebr.	M	870
Jupiter Fidius	Rom.	M	896
Kubera	Bud.	M	948
Kudai	Sib.	M	948
Kulakaras	Jainism	M	950
Litae	Gk.	F	1002
Lycurgus	Gk.	M	1028
Maat	Egy.	F	1031
Maira-monan	S.A.I.	M	1047
Manu	Hin.	M	1061
Minos	Gk.	M	1107
Mithra	Pers.	M	1112
Moses	Hebr.	M	1126
Nabhi	Jainism	M	1146
Nomos	Gk.	M	1179
Numa Pompilius	Rom.	M	1185
Orlog	Norse	M	+
Palici	Ital.	M	1228
Pilos	Gk.	M	1720
Prometheus	Gk.	M	1295
Quetzalcoatl	Mex.	M	1312
Sitabrahma	Bud.	M	1460
Sitatara	Bud.	F	1460
Solon	Gk.	M	1473
Syn	Norse	F	1522
Thor	Norse	M	1561
LETTER VICTIM OR CARRIER			
Bellerophon	Gk.	M	199
Bevis of Hampton	Bryth.	M	207
Guildenstern	Eng.	M	987

	Culture	Sex	Page
Mutalammis	Arab.	M	1140
Palamedes	Gk.	M	1227
Rosencrantz	Eng.	M	987
Tarafah	Arab.	M	987
Uriah	Hebr.	M	1629

LIAR (SEE DECEIT)
LIFE (SEE FERTILITY)

LIGHT (DAY)

	Culture	Sex	Page
Ab	Sem.	M	11
Ababinili	Chick.	M	11
Abel	Hebr., Mos.	M	14
Acarnan & Amphoterus	Gk.	M	22
Adrastus	Gk.	M	35
Aegle	Gk.	F	39
Aeife	Cel.	F	39
Aglaia	Gk.	F	48
Agnar	Norse	M	49
Aham	Hin.	M	52
Ahi	Egy.	F	52
Ahura Mazda	Zoro.	M	54
Aidne	Cel.	M	55
Ainle	Cel.	M	56
Airya	Pers.	M	57
Alfar	Norse	M	67
Amida	Jap.	M	85
Amitabha	Bud.	M	86
Amphiaraus	Gk.	M	87
Anakes	Gk.	M	90
Anchises	Rom.	M	93
Androgeos	Gk.	M	94
Angantyr	Norse	M	95
Angeburga	Norse	M	95
Anu	Sum.	M	104
Ao-marama	Poly.		106
Aos (Hoa)	Chald.	M	106
Ao-tu-roa	Poly.		106
Arama	Moxos Ind.	M	117
Argeiphontes	Gk.	M	121
Arjuna	Hin.	M	126
Aruna	Hin.	M	133
Arusha	Hin.	M	134
Asmund & Asvitus	Norse	M-M	141
Asvins	Hin.	M	146
Atea	So. Is.	M	149

	Culture	Sex	Page
Athra	Gk.	F	151
Atri	Hin.	M	153
Azer Abad	Pers.	M	1042
Baba, Cassim	Arab.	M	168
Bahram Yasht	Zoro.	M	173
Baiame	Aus.	M	173
Balarama	Hin.	M	174
Bebhionn	Cel.	F	192
Bel	Baby.	M	196
Belbogh	Slav.	M	196
Berecinthia	Phryg.	F	203
Bjort	Norse	F	221
Bloedel	Norse	M	226
Bragi	Norse	M	240
Brhaspati	Hin.	M	247
Brigit	Cel.	F	249
Byelbog	Slav.	M	264
Capaneus	Gk.	M	288
Ce Acatl	Mex.	M	301
Cethe	Cel.	M	306
Chimizigagua	Chib.	M	325
Chur	Pers.	M	336
Coh, Prince	Mex.	M	355
Cormac Conlingas	Cel.	M	371
Credne	Cel.	M	379
Dag (Day)	Norse	M	405
Daire mac Fiachna	Cel.	M	407
Dasra & Nasatya	Hin.	M-M	416
Delbaeth	Cel.	M	427
Demophoon	Gk.	M	432
Deva	Bali	M	435
Dipamkara	Bud.	M	449
Dyaus	Hin.	M	479
Electra	Gk.	F	499
Elpenor	Gk.	M	506
Emathion	Gk.	M	507
Emer	Cel.	F	508
Eremon	Cel.	M	518
Eusoph	Chald., Gnostic	M	533
Eylimi	Norse	M	541
Ezra	Hebr.	M	541
Fat the Flasher & Tan the Dawn	Chin.	M-M	550
Fo-hi	Chin.	M	589
Gaheris	Bryth.	M	622

	Culture	Sex	Page
Gayomart	Pers.	M	636
Gedulah	Caba.	M	637
Gizhigooke	Algon.	M	660
Greit	Welsh	M	689
Gwalchmei	Bryth.	M	700
Hadding	Norse	M	705
Hamlet	Eng.	M	714
Hehu	Egy.	M	742
Heliades	Gk.	F	747
Hemera	Gk.	F	750
Hera	Gk.	F	752
Hippomedon	Gk.	M	774
Idas	Gk.	M	818
Illann	Cel.	M	824
Iobates	Gk.	M	836
Is	Baby.	M	841
Ishi	Phoen.	M	843
Israel	Hebr.	M	847
Izamna	Mex.	M	853
Izeds	Zoro.	M	854
Jack the Giant Killer	Folk.	M	857
Jotham	Hebr.	M	890
Juno	Rom.	F	895
Jupiter	Rom.	M	896
Kekui	Egy.	M	916
Kerh	Egy.	M	918
Khu	Egy.	M	925
Kichigonai	Kiche	M	927
Kynddelig	Bryth.	M	956
Lado & Lada	Slav.	M-F	961
Laghlaghghi-Gar	Baby.	M	964
Lampetia	Gk.	F	969
Lampetus	Gk.	M	969
Light	Gnostic Aeon		992
Ljosalfar	Norse	M	1004
Llewyd	Bryth.	M	1005
Luagni	Cel.	M	1019
Lucifer	Christ.	M	1020
Lug	Cel.	M	1022
Lugalbanda	Sum.	M	1023
Lung	Chin.	M	1025
Lyceus	Gk.	M	1027
Lycurgus	Gk.	M	1028
Lycus	Gk.	M	1028
Lyfir	Norse	M	1028
Lynceus	Gk.	M	1028

	Culture	Sex	Page
Mahora-nui-a-tea	Poly.	F	1045
Mariucella	Folk.	F	1068
Marsk Stig	Dan.	M	1070
Matali	Hin.	M	1074
Mazda	Pers.	M	1081
Melchior	Christ.	M	1085
Mengk	Norse		1089
Merlin (Ambrosius)	Bryth.	M	1092
Micaiah	Hebr.	M	1098
Michabo (Messon)	Algon.	M	1098
Mithra	Pers.	M	1112
Mopsus	Gk.	M	1122
Mulla	Sum.	M	1135
Namo	Carol.	M	1152
Nanaboojoo	Pota.	M	1152
Nemed	Cel.	M	1162
Neoptolemus	Gk.	M	1163
Nisus	Rom.	M	1176
Nuada	Cel.	M	1184
Numitor	Rom.	M	1185
Ormuzd	Zoro.	M	1216
Ortlieb	Germ.	M	1217
Owain	Bryth.	M	1221
Panemerios	Gk.	M	1233
P'an Ku	Chin.	M/A	1233
Parthenopaeus	Gk.	M	1240
Partholan	Cel.	M	1240
Pelias	Gk.	M	1250
Pelleas	Eng.	M	1250
Perithous	Gk.	M	1256
Phaethousa	Gk.	F	1260
Philandrus	Gk.	M	1262
Phineus	Gk.	M	1264
Piguero	Inca	M	109
Po-begat-te-ao	Poly.		106
Polynices	Gk.	M	1284
Prajapati (Prakriti)	Hin.	M/A	1290
Pratyusha	Hin.	M	1641
Protesilaus	Gk.	M	1297
Qat	Mel.	M	1309
Quetzalcoatl	Mex.	M	1312
Romulus	Rom.	M	1346
Rudiger	Norse	M	1353
Sangke	Fin-Ug.	M	1396
Sarpedon	Gk.	M	1401
Segda	Cel.	M	1413

	Culture	Sex	Page
Shem	Hebr.	M	1433
Shu	Egy.	M	1443
Sin	Haida	M	1453
Siyamak	Zoro.	M	1463
Svantavoit	Slav.	M	1514
Tama-nui-a-rangi	Poly.	M	1529
Te-ao-marama	N. Zeal.		1541
Te-ao-tu-roa	N. Zeal.		1541
Tennin	Jap.	F	1545
Theia	Gk.	F	1553
Tiw	Ang-Sax.	M	1581
Tow	Haida	M	1592
Tuan mac Cairill	Cel.	M	1605
Tuatha de Danann	Cel.	M, F	1605
Tuisco	Germ.	M	1606
Tydeus	Gk.	M	1616
Tyr	Teut.	M	1617
Uma	Hin.	F	1622
Vairocana	Bud.	M	1634
Vajradhatvisvari	Bud.	F	1635
Vanand	Pers.	M	1638
Vatea	Hervey Is.	M	1641
Vikramaditya	Hin.	M	1650
Vispala	Hin.	M	1655
Wahieroa	Maori	M	1661
Zeus	Gk.	M	1719
Ziu	Germ.	M	1721
Zoroaster	Zoro.	M	1734

LIGHTNING

	Culture	Sex	Page
Acestes	Gk.	M	24
Achiyalatopa	Zuni	M	26
Agni	Hin.	M	49
Aja Ekapada	Hin.	M	58
Al Borak	Mos.		63
Apam Napat	Hin.	M	107
Auuenau	Aus.	M	160
Baal-Lebanon	Sem.	M	167
Dadhyanc	Hin.	M	404
Diomedes	Gk.	M	446
Futsu-nushi	Jap.	M	618
Gabriel	Christ., Hebr., Mos.	M	619
Galta-ulan-tengeri	Buriat	M	624
Ganaskidi	Nav.		625
Gucumatz	Guate.	M	694

	Culture	Sex	Page
Haietlik	British Col.	M	708
Hino	Iroq.	M	772
Hono-ika-zuchi	Jap.	M	785
Hurakan	C.A.I.	M	808
Hyagnis	Gk.	M	1070
Indra	Hin.	M	829
Ixcocauhqui	Mex.	M	852
Jen	Fin-Ug.	M	872
Jupiter Elicius (Fulgurator, Fulminator)	Rom.	M	896
Kakaitch	Makah Ind.	M	902
Kemosh	Sem.	M	916
Kohin	Aus.	M	940
Koloowisi	Zuni	M	941
Krishna	Hin.	M	945
Latawiec	Polish	A	975
Leza	Bantu	M	989
Loki	Norse	M/A	1010
Lopter	Norse	M	1012
Lycaon	Gk.	M	1027
Matarisvan	Hin.	M	1074
Mekala	Siam.	F	1085
Mer (Ber)	Sum.	M	1091
Mergen Tengere	Altaic	M	1092
Michabo	Algon.	M	1098
Murtaznu	Baby.	M	1138
Mutabriqu	Baby.	M	1140
Nari	Jap.	A	1156
Palulukon	Hopi	M	1230
Paravataksha	Hin.	M	1237
Perun	Slav.	M	1258
Pramantha	Hin.	M	1291
Prometheus	Gk.	M	1295
Pur Dios	Gk.	M	1302
Radigast	Slav.	M	1316
Resheph	Phoen.	M	1333
Rudra	Hin.	M	1353
Shu	Egy.	M	1443
Siva	Hin.	M	1461
Steropes	Gk.	M	1494
Tabuerik	Micro.	M	1523
Taijas	Hin.	M	1236
Tarku (Teshup)	Hittite	M	1535
Tawhaki	Chath. Is.	M	1539
Tezcatlipoca	Mex.	M	1549
Thein	Burm.	M	1553

	Culture	Sex	Page
Thjalfi	Norse	M	1560
T'hlu-kluts	Makah Ind.	M	1560
T'ien Mu	Chin.	F	1571
Tiermes	Lapp	M	1572
Titan	Gk.	M, F	1577
Torem	Sib.	M	1589
Trita Aptya	Hin.	M	1599
Tulchuherris	Wintun	M	1607
Tu-tutsh	Nootkan Ind.	M	1611
Tydeus	Gk.	M	1616
Typhon	Gk.	M	1617
Ulgen	Tatar	M	1622
Ulu-tojon (Syga)	Yakut	M	1622
Vazishta	Pers.	M	1643
Vii	Serb.	M	1649
Vili	Norse	M	1650
Vulcan	Rom.	M	1659
Xolotl	Mex.	M	1697
Yehl	Alaskan	M	1703

LITERATURE (SEE POETRY, WISDOM)
LOHAN (SEE SPIRIT)

LONGEVITY

Arphaxad	Hebr.	M	129
Asuniti	Hin.	F	146
Atarhasis	Baby.	M	148
Cheou-lao	Chin.	M	318
Dinsangma	Tib.	F	446
Dosangma	Tib.	F	465
Enoch	Hebr.	M	512
Evelake	Christ.	M	534
Fuku	Jap.	M	616
Fum	Chin.		617
Fu-shou-lu	Chin.	M	618
Geras	Gk.	M	646
dGra-lha (Da Lha)	Tib.	M	683
Hahaiwuqti	Pueblo	F	708
Hildesheim	Germ.	M	770
Ho	Chin.		776
Hsi Wang Mu	Chin.	F	800
Iha-no-hime	Jap.	F	822
Inari-M' Yojim	Jap.	F/A	827
Isaac	Hebr.	M	841
Jamshid	Pers.	M	863
Jiu	Jap.	M	880

Longevity (cont.)	Culture	Sex	Page
Job	Hebr., Mos.	M	882
Jurojin	Jap.	M	898
K'Mukamtch	Klamath	M	936
Kuo-tzu-I	Chin.	M	952
Lobsangma	Tib.	F	1006
Long Life Sisters	Tib.	F	1012
Machi-pal Lha-mo	Tib.	F	1034
Ma-lha	Tib.	M	1571
Methuselah	Hebr.	M	1096
Noah	Hebr.	M	1177
Nor-lha	Tib.	M	1571
Nornagest	Norse	M	1180
Og	Hebr.	M	1200
Ogier	Dan.	M	1200
Oisin	Cel.	M	1202
Old Parr	Eng.	M	+
P'an Ku	Chin.	M/A	1233
Pano-ka	Chin.	M	1234
Peng Tsu	Chin.	M	1252
Pho-lha	Tib.	M	1571
Rsabha	Jainism	M	1352
Saeter	Norse	M	1360
Sarpedon	Gk.	M	1401
Sarvakamadugha	Hin.	F	1401
Sarvanivaranviskambhin	Bud.	M	1401
Seitaka	Jap.	M	1414
Shang-lha	Tib.	M	1571
Shen Nung	Chin.	M	1434
Shou Hsing	Chin.	M	1442
Takasago	Jap.	M-F	1527
Take-no-uji	Jap.	M	1528
Tashitsheringma	Tib.	F	1537
Thinggishalsangma	Tib.	F	1556
Tithonus	Gk.	M	1578
Tobosaku	Jap.	M	1583
Yul-lha	Tib.	M	1571

LONGING (SEE MELANCHOLY)

LOVE (ALSO SEE LOVE LUST, LOVERS)			
Aengus	Cel.	M	40
Aizenmyo-o	Jap.	M	57
Amor	Rom.	M	87
Amorini	Ital.	M	87
Amyas	Rom.	M	89

	Culture	Sex	Page
Ananga	Hin.	M	91
Anat	Sem.	F	91
Anat-Bethel	Hebr.	A	92
Andromache	Gk.	F	94
Angus	Cel.	M	97
Anteros	Gk.	M	102
Apaharavarman	Hin.	M	106
Aphrodite	Gk.	F	108
Aphrodite, Bearded	Gk.	A	109
Arcite	Eng.	M	119
Armida	Ital.	F	128
Arusyak	Arm.	F	134
Aryaman	Hin.	M	134
Ashera	Sem.	F	138
Astarte (Ashtart, Ashtoreth)	Phoen.	F	144
Astrild	Norse	M	145
Athtar	Arab.	M	151
Belili	Sum.	F	197
Benten	Jap.	F	203
Bes	Egy.	M	205
Bidúcht	Pers.	F	210
Blodeuwedd	Bryth.	F	226
Brangwaine	Bryth.	F	243
Branwen	Welsh	F	243
Brynhild	Norse	F	253
Brynwyn (Dwynwen)	Christ.	F	243
Cathena	Mojave	F	298
Celimene	Fr.	F	302
Chloe	Gk.	F	328
Cinteotl	Mex.	F	341
Cupid	Rom.	M	397
Delia	Euro. Lit.	F	427
Derceto	Philistine	F	433
Dione	Gk.	F	446
Dzydzilelya	Slav.	F	481
Eros	Gk.	M	522
Erycina	Ital.	F	523
Eshmun-Astarte	Phoen.	A	525
Freo	Bryth.	F	609
Freya	Norse	F	610
Gan Ceanach	Cel.	M	625
Hermaphrodite	Gk.	A	761
Himeros	Gk.	M	771
Horsel	Germ.	F	791
Hymen	Gk.	M	811
Iccha-Sakti	Hin.	F	817

	Culture	Sex	Page
Idalia	Gk.	F	818
Inada-hime	Jap.	F	827
Inari-M'yojim	Jap.	F/A	827
Ixquina	Mex.	F	852
Kama	Bud.	M	905
Khensu	Egy.	M	923
Kurukulla	Tib.	F	953
Lakshmi	Hin.	F	965
Libitina	Rom.	F	991
Lilinau	N.A.I.	F	994
Lochinvar	Scot.	M	1007
Lofn	Norse	F	1008
Metra	Pers.	F	1096
Mowis	N.A.I.	M	1132
Musubi	Jap.	M	1140
Oengus	Cel.	M	1198
O-kuni-nushi	Jap.	M	1204
Olwen	Bryth.	F	1206
Ono-no-yorikaze	Jap.	M	1210
Peitho	Gk.	F	1249
Perdix	Gk.	A	1254
Phra Naret	Siam.	F	1267
Pierrette (Columbine)	Fr.	F	1270
Polydamna	Gk.	F	+
Pothos	Gk.	M	1289
Pradyumna	Hin.	M	1290
Rati	Hin.	F	1342
Robin Hood	Eng.	M	1343
Saint Valentine	Christ.	M	1383
Sakti	Bud., Hin.	F	1389
Sarasvati	Hin.	F	1400
Shulamite	Hebr.	F	1444
Sjofn	Norse	F	1463
Solomon	Hebr.	M	1472
Tashmetu	Baby., Sum.	F	1537
Tilottama	Hin.	F	1574
Tlacolteotl	Mex.	F	1581
Tlalli-iyollo	Mex.	F	1581
Turan	Ital.	F	1608
Urania	Gk.	F	1627
Uzza	Arab.	F	1633
Var	Norse	F	1638
Venere	Christ.	F	1383
Venus	Rom.	F	1644
Venus, Bearded	Rom.	A	1645
Vorys-mort (Dyadya)	Fin-Ug.	M	1658

	Culture	Sex	Page
Xochipilli-Cinteotl	Mex.	M	1696
Yachihoko	Jap.	M	1204

LOVE LUST (ALSO SEE LOVE, LOVERS)

	Culture	Sex	Page
Abtagigi	Sum.	F	20
Acrasia	Eng.	F	27
Aglaope	Gk.	F	1458
Aglaopheme	Gk.	F	1458
Ahalya	Hin.	F	52
Aholah & Aholibah	Hebr.	F-F	53
Alcina	Ital.	F	64
Allat	Sem.	F	69
Amnon	Hebr.	M	87
Amoret	Eng.	F	87
Amyas	Eng.	M	89
Antinous	Gk.	M	103
Aphrodite	Gk.	F	108
Aphrodite, Bearded	Gk.	A	109
Argante	Bryth.	F	121
Armida	Ital.	F	128
Aryuputra	Hin.	M	134
Aspasia	Gk.	F	141
Astarte (Ashtart, Ashtoreth)	Phoen.	F	144
Azazel	Hebr., Mos.	M	165
Azhi-Dahaka	Pers.	M	165
Azi	Pers.	M	165
Belphegor	Med.	M	200
Beltis	Baby.	F	201
Busirane	Eng.	M	262
Butes	Gk.	M	262
Calypso	Gk.	F	279
Camille	Fr.	F	281
Campaspe	Gk.	F	282
Carmen	Fr.	F	291
Centaur	Christ.	M	303
Chie	Chibcha	F	322
Circe	Gk.	F	341
Ciuateteo	Mex.	F	346
Cleopatra	Eng.	F	347
Creusa	Gk.	F	381
Cyprian	Gk.	M, F	403
Dinah	Hebr.	F	445
Don Juan	Span.	M	462
Dorulas	Gk.	M	465
Dusio	Med.	M	477

	Culture	Sex	Page
Elle-folk	Norse	M	505
Fand	Cel.	F	548
Fata Alcina	Ital.	F	550
Fata Morgana	Ital.	F	550
Gandharva	Hin.	M	626
Ganis	Lapp	F	627
Garman	Cel.	M	631
Genji	Jap.	M	645
Goewin	Bryth.	F	669
Gomer	Hebr.	F	675
Guinevere	Bryth.	F	696
Havfrue	Dan.	F	732
Helen	Gk.	F	745
Himeros	Gk.	F	771
Indra	Hin.	M	829
Ishtar	Assyr., Baby.	F	844
Itzcuinan	Mex.	F	850
Jahi	Zoro.	F	861
Jezebel	Hebr.	F	879
Kama	Hin.	M	905
Kilili	Assyr., Baby.	F	927
Kundry	Germ.	F	952
Kunigunde	Germ.	F	952
Labe	Arab.	F	957
Lais	Gk.	F	964
Lamia	Gk., Lib.	F	967
Lempo	Fin.	M	982
Leucosia	Gk.	F	987
Ligea	Gk.	F	992
Lilith	Hebr.	F	994
Lilithu	Sum.	F	995
Lilu	Baby.	M	995
Lindabrides	Span.	F	997
Lorelei	Germ.	F	1013
Lothario	Eng.	M	1014
Lovelace	Eng.	M	1018
Magdalene	Christ.	F	1037
Malecasta	Eng.	F	1050
Maleger	Eng.	M	1050
Mara	Hin.	M	1063
Merlin	Bryth.	M	1092
Mermaid	Euro.	F	1093
Mesca	Cel.	F	1094
Messalina	Rom.	F	1095
Mordred	Bryth.	M	1122
Naamah	Caba.	F	1145

	Culture	Sex	Page
Naga	Hin.	F	1147
Nimue	Bryth.	F	1170
Pairika	Zoro.	F	1226
Pan	Gk.	M	1230
Pandemos	Gk.	F	108
Paphian	Gk.	F	+
Paphnutius	Fr.	M	1236
Paris	Gk.	M	1238
Parthenope	Gk.	F	1240
Pasiphae	Gk.	F	1241
Phaedra	Gk.	F	1260
Phaedria	Eng.	F	1260
Philander	Ital.	M	1262
Phryne	Gk.	F	1267
Pisinoe	Gk.	F	1458
Queen of Sheba	Hebr.	F	1311
Rahab	Hebr.	F	1318
Rakshasa	Hin.	M	1320
Rakshasis	Hin.	F	1320
Rhiannon	Bryth.	F	1336
Rhodopis	Gk.	F	1337
Rusalka	Rus.	F	1355
Satan	Hebr-Christ.	M	1402
Satyr	Gk.	M	1403
Sharis	Urartian	F	1431
Shechem	Hebr.	M	445
Siren	Gk.	F	1458
Skogsfru	Scan.	F	1465
Suadela	Rom.	F	1502
Succuba	Med. Lit.	F	1503
Sukkamielli	Fin.	F	1505
Suksendal	Fin-Ug.	A	1505
Tachi	Chin.	F	1523
Tachi	Tembu (Afr.)	M	1523
Tamamo-no-maye	Jap.	F	1529
Tara Bai	Hin.	F	1534
Tarquinius Sextus	Rom.	M	1536
Tereus	Gk.	M	1546
Thais	Fr., Gk.	F	1551
Thelxiepia	Gk.	F	1458
Thyamis	Eng.	F	1403
Tlazolteotl	Mex.	F	1582
Ukhat	Baby.	F	1621
Urganda	Carol.	F	1628
Vasa	Fin-Ug.	F	1640
Vatak	Zoro.	F	1641

Love Lust (cont.)	Culture	Sex	Page
Venus	Rom.	F	1644
Venus, Bearded	Rom.	A	1645
Vila	Serbo-Croa.	F	1650
Vodni-Panny	Slav.	F	1657
Warren, Mrs.	Eng.	F	+
Weisse Frauen	Norse	F	1672
Xochiquetzal	Mex.	F	1696
Yama-uba	Jap.	F	1700
Yara	Brazil	F	1701
Yatai	Ind-Chin.	F	1702
Yatawm	Ind-Chin.	M	1702
Yuki-onne	Jap.	M	1712

LOVERS (ALSO SEE LOVE, LOVE LUST)

Abelard & Heloise	Fr.	M-F	14
Abradatus & Panthea	Gk/Pers.	M-F	+
Acis & Galatea	Gk.	M-F	26
Acontinus & Cydippe	Gk.	M-F	26
Aeneas & Dido	Rom.	M-F	40
Aida & Radames	Fr.	F-M	54
Aideen & Oscar	Cel.	F-M	55
Alcestis & Admetus	Gk.	F-M	63
Alexis & Corydon	Rom.	M-M	67
Anaxarete & Iphis	Gk.	F-M	92
Anat-Bethel	Hebr.	M-F	110
Apollo & Cyparissus	Gk.	M-M	110
Apollo & Cyrene	Gk.	M-F	92
Ariadne & Theseus	Gk.	F-M	123
Arjuna & Draupadi	Hin.	M-F	470
Aucassin & Nicolette	Med.	M-F	155
Baile & Ailinn	Cel.	M-F	173
Bride & Bridegroom	Hebr.	F-M	248
Cauline & Christabelle	Eng.	M-F	300
Ch'ien Niu & Chih Nu	Chin.	M-F	322
Cinderella & Prince	Folk.	F-M	339
Cindrillot & Princess	Folk.	M-F	340
Circe & Odysseus (Ulysseus)	Gk. (Rom.)	F-M	341
Cliach & Conchenn	Cel.	M-F	348
Coronis & Ischys	Gk.	M-F	374
Crimthann & Nar	Cel.	M-F	382
Cupid & Psyche	Rom.	M-F	397
Darby & Joan	Eng.	M-F	415
Demophoon & Phyllis	Gk.	M-F	432
Diana & Endymion	Rom.	F-M	441
Diarmaid & Grainne	Cel.	M-F	442
Dornroschen & Rapunze	Germ.	F-M	465

	Culture	Sex	Page
Eos & Tithonous	Gk.	F-M	514
Eros & Psyche	Gk.	M-F	522
Eshmun & Astarte	Phoen.	M-F	525
Fer Fedail & Tuag	Cel.	A-F	561
Fraoch & Findabair	Cel.	M-F	607
Frithiof & Ingelborg	Norse	M-F	612
Fukuro & Usudori	Jap.	M-F	616
Glaucus & Scylla	Gk.	M-F	662
Gunlad & Odin	Norse	F-M	698
Haemon & Antigone	Gk.	M-F	707
Hagbart & Signe	Ice.	M-F	708
Halcyone & Ceyx	Gk.	F-M	711
Harlequin & Columbine	Folk.	M-F	726
Heracles & Hylas	Gk.	A-A	752
Heracles & Iole	Gk.	M-F	752
Heracles & Omphale	Gk.	M-M	752
Hero & Leander	Gk.	F-M	762
Hippodameia & Pelops	Gk.	F-M	773
Hippomenes & Atalanta	Gk.	M-F	774
Hoder & Nanna	Norse	M-F	778
Hyacinthus & Apollo	Gk.	M-M	809
Hyacinthus & Zephyr	Gk.	M-M	809
Hylas & Dryope	Gk.	M-F	811
Hyuki & Bil	Norse	M-F	814
Iasion & Demeter	Gk.	M-F	816
Ishullanu & Ishtar	Assyr-Baby.	M-F	845
Jack & Jill	Eng.	M-F	856
Jacob & Rachel	Hebr.	M-F	858
Junak & Sudolisa	Slav.	M-F	895
Kamalamitra & Wife	Hin.	M-F	906
Kengiu & Ori-hime	Jap.	M-F	916
King Horn & Rymenhild	Eng.	M-F	1355
Kulhwch & Olwen	Bryth.	M-F	950
Lado & Lada	Slav.	M-F	961
Lancelot & Elaine	Bryth.	M-F	969
Lancelot & Guinevere	Bryth.	M-F	969
Laodamia & Protesilaus	Gk.	F-M	972
Launfal & Tryamour	Bryth.	M-F	976
Leilah & Mejnoun	Pers.	F-M	982
Lingam & Yoni	Hin.	M-F	998
Mark & Iseult	Bryth.	M-F	1068
Medea & Jason	Gk.	F-M	1082
Meleager & Atalanta	Gk.	M-F	1085
Melk & Ashtart	Phoen.	M-F	1086
Merlin & Nimue	Bryth.	M-F	1092
Merlin & Vivien	Bryth.	M-F	1092

	Culture	Sex	Page
Mordred & Guinevere	Bryth.	M-F	1122
Nala & Damayanti	Hin.	M-F	1150
Naoise & Deirdre	Cel.	M-F	1154
Narcissus & Echo	Gk.	M-F	1155
Nase & Aze	Jap.	M-F	1156
Oengus & Derbrenn	Cel.	M-F	1198
Oengus & Etain	Cel.	M-F	1198
Ogier & Morgue la Faye	Dan/Bryth.	M-F	1200
Okame & Hyottoko	Jap.	F-M	1203
Ometecutli & Omeciuatl	Mex.	M-F	1208
Ono-no-Yorikaze & Mistress	Jap.	M-F	1210
Onto & Bonto (Staka Pas)	Fin-Ug.	M-F	1210
Orion & Merope	Gk.	M-F	1215
Orpheus & Eurydice	Gk.	M-F	1216
Osiris & Isis	Egy.	M-F	1218
Pandavas & Draupadi	Hin.	M-F	1232
Paolo & Francesca	Ital.	M-F	1235
Pasiphae & The White Bull	Gk.	F-M	1241
Pelops & Hippodameia	Gk.	M-F	1251
Perseus & Andromeda	Gk.	M-F	1257
Philemon & Baucis	Rom.	M-F	1263
Pierrot & Pierrette (Columbine)	Fr.	M-F	1270
Polyphemus & Galatea	Gk.	M-F	1284
Pontus & Melicertes	Gk.	M-M	+
Poseidon & Pelops	Gk.	M-M	1288
Punch & Judy	Folk.	M-F	1301
Punchinello & Judith	Ital.	M-F	1301
Pyramus & Thisbe	Rom.	M-F	1307
Radigund & Sir Artegal	Eng.	A-A	1316
Rama & Sita	Hin.	M-F	1321
Rogero & Bradamant	Ital.	M-F	773
Romeo & Juliet	Eng.	M-F	1346
Saint George & Cleodolinda	Bryth.	M-F	1370
Saint George & Sabra	Bryth.	M-F	1370
Selene & Endymion	Gk.	F-M	1414
Shepherd Boy & Weaver Damsel	Chin.	M-F	1435
Shite & Tsure	Jap.	M-F	1439
Sigismonda & Guiscardo	Eng.	M-F	1449
Solomon (Bridegroom) & Shulamite (Bride)	Hebr.	M-F	1472
Strephon & Chloe	Eng.	M-F	1500
Susanowo & Kushinadahime	Jap.	M-F	1512
Svipdag & Menglod	Norse	M-F	1515
Takasago	Jap.	M-F	1527

	Culture	Sex	Page
Tancred & Erminia	Ital.	M-F	522
Tanhauser & Frau Holde	Germ.	M-F	1532
Tristan & Isolde	Bryth.	M-F	1599
Troilus & Cressida	Eng.	M-F	1600
Tuna & Hina	Poly.	M-F	1607
Valerian & Cecilia	Christ.	M-F	1636
Yab-Yum	Bud.	M-F	1697
Yaksas & Yaksini	Tib.	M-F	1698
Yama & Yami	Hin.	M-F	1699
Yang & Um	Korean	M-F	1700
Yang & Yin	Chin.	M-F	1700
Yudhi shthira & Draupadi	Hin.	M-F	1711
Zairivairi & Odatis	Pers.	M-F	1715
Zeus & Alcmene	Gk.	M-F	1719
Zeus & Antiope	Gk.	M-F	1719
Zeus & Callisto	Gk.	A-F	1719
Zeus & Danae	Gk.	M-F	1719
Zeus & Europa	Gk.	M-F	1719
Zeus & Io	Gk.	M-F	1719
Zeus & Leda	Gk.	M-F	1719
Zeus & Leto	Gk.	M-F	1719
Zeus & Semele	Gk.	M-F	1719

LOYALTY (DEVOTION, FIDELITY, FILIAL PIETY, FRIENDSHIP)

Abderus	Gk.	M	13
Abishai	Hebr.	M	16
Achates	Rom.	M	24
Achilles	Gk.	M/A	25
Achish	Hebr.	M	25
Aeschere	Ang-Sax.	M	41
Ahimelech	Hebr.	M	53
Akawi-ko	Jap.	F	59
Alcestis	Gk.	F	63
Antigone	Gk.	F	103
Antilochus	Gk.	M	103
Aramati	Hin.	F	117
Arria	Rom.	F	129
Aryaman	Hin.	M	134
Aze	Jap.	F	165
Baruch	Hebr.	M	183
Benkei	Jap.	M	202
Biton	Gk.	M	220
Caius	Eng.	M	271
Cleobis	Gk.	M	220
Corin	Eng.	F	546

	Culture	Sex	Page
Cycnus	Gk.	M	401
Damon	Rom.	M	410
Darby	Eng.	M	415
David	Hebr.	M	417
Dorigen	Eng.	F	464
Ector, Sir	Bryth.	M	132
Elijah	Hebr.	M	503
Emer	Cel.	F	508
Euryalus	Rom.	M	532
Evadne	Gk.	F	533
Ferdia	Cel.	M	560
Fides	Rom.	F	565
Florismart	Carol.	M	585
Forty-Seven Ronin	Jap.	M	598
Fugen	Jap.	M	615
Galahad	Bryth.	M	622
Glaucus	Gk.	M	662
Griselda	Ital.	F	691
Gudrun	Germ.	F	694
Guru Rimpoche	Tib.	M	699
Halcyone	Gk.	F	711
Horatio	Eng.	M	787
Hypermnestra	Gk.	F	812
Joan	Eng.	F	415
Jonathan	Hebr.	M	886
Laodamia	Gk.	F	972
Llewyd	Bryth.	M	1005
Maudgalyayana & Sariputra	Bud.	M-M	1077
Mentor	Gk.	M	+
Morgiana	Arab.	F	1123
Myrmidon	Gk.	M	1142
Nanna	Norse	F	1153
Nisus	Rom.	M	1176
Ol	Bryth.	M	1204
Orpheus	Gk.	M	1216
Patroclus	Gk.	M	1244
Penelope	Gk.	F	1252
Pylades	Gk.	M	1306
Pythias	Rom.	M	1308
Rizpah	Hebr.	F	1342
Ruth	Hebr.	F	1355
Saint Roch & his dog	Christ.	M	1380
Savitri	Hin.	F	1404
Sigyn	Norse	F	1452
Silas	Christ.	M	1452
Sukanya	Hin.	F	1505

	Culture	Sex	Page
Tachibana	Jap.	F	1542
Troilus	Eng.	M	1600
Tzu Sun Niang Niang	Chin.	F	1618
Ucalegon	Gk.	M	1619
Ulfin	Bryth.	M	1621

MADNESS (CRAZINESS, INSANITY)

Alcmaeon	Gk.	M	65
Amleth	Norse	M	86
Athamas	Gk.	M	149
Cambyes	Pers.	M	280
Corybantes	Phryg.	M	375
Cuchulainn	Cel.	M	393
Dionysus	Gk.	M	447
Dund	Sum.	M	476
Frithiof	Norse	M	612
Fudo-myoo	Jap.	M	615
Glam	Norse	M	661
Hamlet	Eng.	M	714
Hera	Gk.	F	752
Heracles	Gk.	M	752
Hercules	Rom.	M	759
Hrothgar	Ang-Sax.	M	798
Luna	Rom.	F	1025
Maniae	Gk.	F	1058
Tope	Norse	M	1588

MAGIC (BEWITCHMENT, ENCHANTMENT, EXORCISM, SORCERY, WITCHERY, WIZARDRY)

Aaron	Hebr.	M	10
Akhtya	Zoro.	M	1709
Aladdin	Arab.	M	61
Alberich	Norse	M	62
Alquife	Med.		76
Amairgen	Cel.	M	79
Amarum	Quichas Ind.	M	80
Amine	Arab.	F	86
Apollonious	Gk.	M	111
Aristeas	Gk.	M	125
Atatarho	Onondaga Ind.	M	149
Aza & Azael	Caba.	M-M	164
Aziza	Ewes (Afr.)	M	166
Baba, Ali	Arab.	M	168
Bagattel	Tarot	M	172
Baru	Med.	M	183

	Culture	Sex	Page
Bhavani	Ind-Chin.	F	208
Bi-har	Bud.	M	211
Blanaid	Cel.	F	224
Brizo	Gk.	F	250
Buarainech	Cel.	M	254
Busirane	Eng.	M	262
Calatine	Cel.	M	272
Canidia	Rom.	F	285
Chang Kuo	Chin.	M	311
Chang Tao-ling	Chin.	M	311
Ch'o-je	Tib.	M	328
Chos-skyon	Tib.	M	329
Christ	Christ.	M	330
Ch'u Hsieh Yuan	Chin.	M	335
Circe	Gk.	F	341
Comizahual	Honduras	F	362
Coyote	N.A.I.	M	377
Dakinis	Bud.	F	408
Digini	Nav.	M	445
Dodo	Bush.	F	455
Duergar	Norse	M	475
Ea	Assyr., Baby., Sum.	M	481
Elf	Norse	M	502
Elijah	Hebr.	M	503
Elisha (Eliseus)	Hebr.	M	504
Enmenduranna	Sum.	M	512
En-no-ozuna	Jap.	M	512
Eochaid Ollathair	Cel.	M	513
Erichtho	Rom.	M	519
Falerina	Ital.	F	176
Fata Alcina	Ital.	F	550
Fata Morgana	Med.	F	550
Fatima	Arab.	F	552
Fei-ch'ang-fang	Chin.	M	558
Freya	Norse	F	610
Freydis	Norse	F	611
Fuamnach	Cel.	F	615
Fuda-hegashi	Jap.	M	615
Gallaeus	Holland	M	624
Gaspar	Christ.	M	633
Gorddu	Bryth.	F	678
dGra-lha	Bud.	M	683
Grid	Norse	F	690
Grimhild	Norse	F	691
Groa	Norse	F	692

	Culture	Sex	Page
Guabonito	Taino	F	693
Gwiawn	Bryth.	M	701
Gwrhyr Gwalstawt	Bryth.	M	702
Gwydion	Bryth.	M	702
Gwyn	Bryth.	M	703
Gylfe	Swed.	M	704
Hag	Scot.	F	707
Han Hsiang-tzu	Chin.	M	722
Hanuman	Hin.	M	723
Hardgrep	Norse	F	725
Harlequin	Folk.	M	726
Hecate	Gk.	F	740
Heid (Gullveig)	Norse	F	743
Heka	Egy.	M	744
Hermes	Gk.	M	760
Hildebrand	Germ.	M	770
Hiram	Freemasonry	M	13
Houssain	Arab.	M	797
Huitzilopochtli	Mex.	M	803
Hun-ahpu & Xbalanque	Kiche	M-M	806
Imhotep	Egy.	M	825
Isis	Egy.	F	845
Jambres & Jannes	Egy.	M-M	862
Jochebed	Hebr.	M	883
Joshua	Hebr.	M	889
Kay, Sir	Bryth.	M	914
Klingsor	Germ.	M	936
Klu-dban	Bud.	M	936
Kurdaitcha	Aus.		952
Kveldrida	Norse	F	954
Labe	Arab.	F	957
Lady of the Lake	Bryth.	F	962
Lamia	Gk/Lib.	F	967
Lha-k'a	Tib.	M	989
Loddfafnir	Norse	M	1007
Lohan	Chin.	M	1009
Louhi	Lapland	F	1016
Lug	Cel.	M	1022
Luipa	Bud.	M	1024
Maenawr Penardd	Cel.	M	1037
Magi	Christ.	M	1037
Mahamantranusarini	Bud.	F	1043
Mahamayuri	Bud.	F	1043
Mahapancaraja	Bud.	M	1043
Mahasiddhas	Bud.	M	1044
Mahatma	Bud.	M	1044

	Culture	Sex	Page
Makaravaktra	Bud.	F	1047
Malagigi	Frankish	M	1048
Malambruno	Span.	M	1049
Manabhozho	Algon.	M	1054
Manawyddan	Bryth.	M	1056
Manito	Algon.	M, F	1058
Math	Cymric	M	1075
Matrs	Hin.	F	1076
Maugis	Frankish	M	1077
Maui	Poly.	M	1077
Maya	Hin.	F	1080
Medea	Gk.	F	1082
Mercury	Rom.	M	1091
Merlin (Ambrosius)	Bryth.	M	1092
Mongan	Cel.	M	1117
Morgan le Fay	Bryth.	F	1123
Myrkrida	Norse	F	1142
Nabu	Baby.	M	1146
Na ch'un	Tib.	M	1146
Naropa	Bud.	M	1156
Nikolai	Rus.	M	1169
Nimue	Eng.	F	1170
No cha	Chin.	M	1178
Nornir	Norse	F	1180
Nostradamus	Fr.	M	1182
Nules Murt	Fin-Ug.	M	1185
Ob	Hebr.	M, F	1191
O-kuni-nushi	Jap.	M	1204
Orillo	Ital.	M	1215
Oski	Norse	M	1219
Padmadakini	Bud.	F	1225
Padmasambhava	Tib.	M	1225
Pa-hsien	Chin.	M, F	1226
Pairika	Zoro.	F	1226
Pancamaharaja	Tib.	M	1231
Pan-t'o-ka	Chin.	M	1235
Paracelsus	Eng.	M	1236
Pau-puk-keewis	Am. Lit.	M	1244
Piache	C.A.I.	M	1268
Pied Piper of Hamlin	Germ.	M	1269
Polydamna	Gk.	F	+
Poshaiyanne	Pueblo	M	1288
Prin-las-gyi-rgyla-po	Tib.	M	1294
Prospero	Eng.	M	1296
Rakshasa	Hin.	M, F	1320
Ratnadakini	Bud.	F	1324

	Culture	Sex	Page
Rbhus	Hin.	M	1326
Rksavaktradakini	Bud.	F	1342
Salmoneus	Gk.	M	1391
Saraha	Bud.	M	1399
Sarvabuddhadakini	Bud.	F	1401
Seidhkoma	Norse	F	1413
Seidhmadhr	Norse	M	1413
Sennin	Jap.	M	1416
Seven Ancient Elders	Baby.	M	1422
Simhavaktra	Bud.	F	1455
Simon Magus	Christ.	M	1455
Siva	Hin.	M	1461
Sukya	Honduras	M	1505
Sung-gi-gval-po	Tib.	M	1510
Svengali	Eng.	M	1515
Tahmurath	Pers.	M	1525
Tailopa	Bud.	M	1526
Tcikapis	N.A.I.	M	1540
Tei-ch'ang-fang	Chin.	M	801
Telchines	Cretan	M	1541
Thahog-chos-rgyal-po	Bud.	M	1551
Thaumas	Gk.	M	1552
Thok-chho	Tib.	M	1043
Thomas the Rhymer	Scot.	M	1560
Thoth	Egy.	M	1562
Titlacauan	Mex.	M	1578
Tlacauepan	Mex.	M	1581
Tsao Shen	Chin.	M	1603
Tsun-gyi-rgyal-po	Tib.	M	1604
Tunnrida	Scan.	M	1608
Tuno	Fin-Ug.	M	1608
Turpin, Archbishop	Carol.	M	1609
Ubyr	Fin-Ug.	M	1619
Unk-ta-he	Dakota	M	1626
Upir	Slav.	M	1627
Ushas	Hin.	F	1631
Utgard-Loki	Norse	M	1632
Vajradakini	Bud.	F	1634
Vajravarahi	Bud.	F	1635
Visvadakini	Bud.	F	1655
Vitzilopochtli	Mex.	M	1656
Vivian (Vivienne)	Bryth.	F	962
Vodu	Daho.	M	1657
Voisin	Fr.	F	1657
Vyaghravaktradakini	Bud.	F	1660
Vyasa	Hin.	M	1660

Magic (cont.)	Culture	Sex	Page
Wainamoinen	Fin.	M	1661
Wanga	E. Afr.	M	1664
Wayland	Ang-Sax.	M	1670
Winti	Du. Guia.	M	1686
Yamato-hime	Jap.	F	1699
Yamato-take	Jap.	M	1699
Yatu	Zoro.	M	1702
Yatudhanas	Hin.	M, F	1320
Yech	N.A.I.	M	1703
Yogi	Hin.	M	1708
Yon-tan-rgyal-po	Tib.	M	1709
Zinsu & Zinsi	Daho.	M-M	1720

MAIMED (DEFORMED, LAME, STERILE, ALSO SEE MUTILATED)

Name	Culture	Sex	Page
Balor	Cel.	M	176
Brons	Christ.	M	251
Chaus	Bryth.	M	316
Fisher King	Bryth.	M	575
Hadui	Iroq.	M	707
Hephaestus	Gk.	M	751
Jacob	Hebr.	M	858
Li T'ieh-kuai	Chin.	M	1002
March	Bryth.	M	1064
Maty-tapire	Hin.	M	1077
Noah	Hebr.	M	1177
Nuada	Cel.	M	1184
Occasion	Eng.	F	1193
Odin	Norse	M	1195
Odysseus	Gk.	M	1196
Oedipus	Gk.	M	1198
Pellenore	Bryth.	M	1251
Polyphemus	Bryth.	M	1284
Ptah	Egy.	M	1299
Rangi	Poly.	M	1322
Roi-mehaigne (Roi Pescheur)	Bryth.	M	1345
Salmoneus	Gk.	M	1391
Samson	Hebr.	M	1394
Savitri	Hin.	M	1404
Sharvan	Cel.	M	1431
Talus	Gk.	M	1529
Thersites	Gk.	M	1554
Thor	Norse	M	1561
Troll	Germ.	M	1600
Tsui Goab	Hotten.	M	1604
Twanjiraka	Aus.	M	1611

	Culture	Sex	Page
Ulysses	Rom.	M	1622
Vulcan	Rom.	M	1659
Wayland	Ango-Sax.	M	1670

MALE PRINCIPLE (ALSO SEE PHALLUS)

	Culture	Sex	Page
Adhyatman	Hin.	M	32
Adon	Phoen.	M	33
Adonai	Hebr.	M	33
Adoni	Sem.	M	34
Aesar	Cel.	M	41
Ama-no-minaka-nushi	Jap.	M	80
Anshar	Baby.	M	101
Anu	Sum.	M	104
Apsu	Assyr., Baby., Sum.	M	115
Areskoui	Iroq.	M	121
Ashim-Bethel	Hebr.	A	139
Asshur	Assyr.	M	143
Atahocan	Algon.	M	147
Aten	Egy.	M	149
Atlas	Gk.	M	152
Aum	Bud., Hin.	M	157
Awonawilona	Zuni	M	162
Baal	Sem.	M	167
Bel Enlil	Baby.	M	197
Belus	Baby.	M	201
Brahm	Hin.	M	240
Brahma	Hin.	M	240
Bure	Norse	M	261
Chemosh	Sem.	M	317
Chinnigchinich	Calif.	M	326
Corus	Gk.	M	374a
Coxcox	Mex.	M	377
Cronus	Gk.	M	384
Daramulum	Aus.	M	414
Ea	Assyr., Baby., Sum.	M	481
Ea-pe	Burm.	M	484
El	Sem.	M	497
Elohim	Hebr.	M	506
Esar	Mos.	M	524
Eugpamolak Manobo	Philip	M	529
Fro (Friuja)	Norse	M	613
Gitche	Algon.	M	660
Hadad	Sem.	M	705

	Culture	Sex	Page
Hehu	Egy.	M	742
Her-shef	Egy.	M	763
Hiranyagarbha	Hin.	M	774
Holy Ghost (Holy Spirit)	Christ.	M	782
Iacchus	Gk.	M	815
Icona	Mex.	M	818
Izanagi	Jap.	M	853
Jehovah	Hebr.	M	870
Jupiter	Rom.	M	896
Kekui	Egy.	M	916
Kerh	Egy.	M	918
Khem	Occult	M	923
Khen-pa	Tib.	M	923
Khnemu	Egy.	M	924
Lingam	Hin.	M	998
Mahapurusa	Bud., Hin.	M	1044
Maku	Poly.	M	1048
Mentu	Egy.	M	1090
Mercury	Theosophy	M	1091
Min	Egy.	M	1106
Moloch	Carth.	M	1115
Nenaboj	Wetucks Ind.	M	1162
Njambi (Nzambi)	Congo	A	1188
Nu	Egy.	A	1184
Ometecutli	Mex.	M	1208
Osiris	Egy.	M	1218
Pappas	Sem.	M	1236
Phallus	Gk.	M	1261
Picumnus	Rom.	M	1269
Pierrot	Fr.	M	1270
Pilumnus	Rom.	M	1273
Poseidon	Gk.	M	1288
Prajapati	Hin.	M/A	1290
Priapus	Gk.	M	1292
Pripegala	Slav.	M	1294
Protogonos	Gk.	A	1297
Ptah	Egy.	M	1299
Ptah-Sokar-Osiris	Egy.	M	1471
Purusa	Hin.	A	1305
Quetzalcoatl	Mex.	M	1312
Senx	Bella Coola	M	1416
Shu	Egy.	M	1443
Susa-no-wo	Jap.	M	1512
Sutekh	Syrian	M	1513
Tahsang Kahsi (Yatawm)	Ind-Chin.	M	1702
Takamimusubi	Jap.	M	1527

	Culture	Sex	Page
Telamon	Gk.	M	1541
Telpochtli	Mex.	M	1542
Teshup	Hittite	M	1547
Tung Wang Kung	Chin.	M	1607
Tzinteotl	Mex.	A	1618
Umashi-ashi-kabi-hiko-ji	Jap.	M	1622
Uranus	Gk.	M	1627
Vatea	Herv. Is.	M	1641
Veralden-Olmai	Lapp	M	1645
Verethraghna	Pers.	M	1646
Viraj	Hin.	A	1652
Vishnu	Hin.	A	1654
Xochipilli-Cinteotl	Mex.	M	1693
Yang	Chin.	M	1700
Yo	Jap.	M	1708
MARKSMAN (ARCHER)			
Adam Bell	Eng.	M	30
Arjuna	Hin.	M	126
Clym of the Clough	Eng.	M	351
Egil	Norse	M	493
Freishutz	Germ.	M	609
Isandros	Gk.	M	842
Odysseus	Gk.	M	1196
Pandarus	Gk.	M	1232
Philoctetes	Gk.	M	1263
Robin Hood (Dikon-Bend-the-Bow, Locksley, the Archer)	Eng.	M	1343
Sudhanvan	Hin.	M	1503
Teucer	Gk.	M	1549
Ullerus	Norse	M	1622
Ulysses	Rom.	M	1622
William of Cloudeslee	Eng.	M	1680
William Tell	Swiss	M	1680
MARRIAGE			
Cecrops	Gk.	M	301
Cinxia (Unxia)	Rom.	F	896
Domiduca	Rom.	F	896
Frey	Norse	M	609
Fricka	Germ.	F	611
Frigg	Norse	F	612
Fu Hsi	Chin.	M	615
Gamelia	Gk.	F	752
Gandharva	Hin.	M	626
Gekka-o	Jap.	M	638

Marriage (cont.)	Culture	Sex	Page
Hera Teleia	Gk.	F	752
Hermaphroditus	Gk.	A	761
Hulda	Germ.	F	803
Hymen	Gk.	M	811
Izanami	Jap.	F	853
Jugalis (Huga)	Rom.	F	896
Juno	Rom.	F	895
Lofn	Scan.	F	1008
Matrona	Rom.	F	896
Nu	Chin.	F	1184
O-kuni-nushi	Jap.	M	1204
Pronuba	Rom.	F	896
Sancus	Ital.	M	1395
Semnae	Gk.	F	1416
Shekinah	Caba.	F	1432
Sif	Norse	F	1448
Takasago	Jap.	M-F	1527
Teleia	Gk.	F	752
Ts'i-ku-niang	Chin.	F	1603
Vjofr	Norse	F	1656
Zugia	Gk.	F	752

MARSHES (SEE MOISTURE)

MASTER OF DEITY OR HERO (TASKMASTER)			
Admetus	Gk.	M	33
Bauge	Norse	M	187
Bres	Cel.	M	246
Culann	Cel.	M	396
Eochaid Airem	Cel.	M	513
Eurystheus	Gk.	M	533
Frode	Dan.	M	613
Hiko-Hohodemi	Jap.	M	769
Hjaalprek	Norse	M	775
Iobates	Gk.	M	836
Laban	Hebr.	M	957
Laomedon	Gk.	M	972
Omphale	Gk.	A	1208
Polydectes	Gk.	M	1283
Potiphar	Hebr., Mos.	M	1289
Yspaddeden Penkawr	Bryth.	M	1711

MEAD (SEE WINE)
MEDICINE (SEE HEALER)

MEDITATION (ALSO SEE WISDOM)	Culture	Sex	Page
Aksobhya	Bud.	M	60
Amitabha (Amitayus)	Bud.	M	86
Amoghasiddhi	Bud.	M	87
Dhyanibuddhas	Bud.	M	440
Gopaka	Bud.	M	677
Kanakabharadvaja	Bud.	M	907
Luipa	Bud.	M	1024
Mahasiddhas	Bud.	M	1044
Melete	Gk.	F	1138
Mila-re-pa	Tib.	M	1102
Pano-ka	Chin.	M	1234
Pan-t'o-ka	Chin.	M	1235
Rachel	Hebr.	F	1316
Ratnasambhava	Bud.	M	1324
Sennin	Jap.	M	1416
Shiwa	Hin.	A	1440
Siva	Hin.	M	1461
Tailopa	Bud.	M	1526
Ta Mo (Bodhidharma)	Chin.	M	1530
Tsaphkiel	Caba.	M	1603
Vairocana	Bud.	M	1634
Vajraheruka	Bud.	M	1635
Vajrasattva	Bud.	M	1635
MELANCHOLY (LONGING)			
Euphrosyne	Gk.	F	531
Gnomes	Folk.	M, F	664
Gwevyl	Bryth.	M	701
Himeros	Gk.	M	771
Oizys	Gk.	M	1203
Orpheus	Gk.	M	1216
Pothos	Gk.	M	1289
Sansjoy	Eng.	M	1397
Saul	Hebr.	M	1404
MEMORY			
Ananda	Bud.	M	91
Magliabecchi	Ital.	M	1040
Mimir	Norse	M	1105
Mneme	Gk.	F	1138
Mnemosyne	Gk.	F	1113
Munin	Norse		1137
Tharonhiawakon	Iroq.	M	1541
Yen-lo-Wang	Chin.	M	1705

MENIAL	Culture	Sex	Page
Agelaus	Gk.	M	48
Apollo	Gk.	M	110
Aslog	Norse	F	141
Azhi Dahaka	Pers.	F	472
Balungwana	Baronga (Afr.)		177
Bata	Egy.	M	185
Baubo	Gk.	F	187
Bedivere	Bryth.	M	193
Bedreddin Hassan	Arab.	M	193
Bellerophon	Gk.	M	199
Bevis of Hampton	Bryth.	M	207
Blid	Norse	F	225
Bolverkin	Norse	M	234
Brangwaine	Bryth.	F	243
Bushyansta	Pers.	F	472
Byggvir	Norse	M	264
Cadmus	Gk.	M	266
Caryatides	Gk.	F	293
Christ	Christ.	M	330
Cinderella	Folk.	F	339
Cindrillot	Folk.	M	340
Cuchulainn	Cel.	M	393
Dagda	Cel.	M	405
Drauga	Pers.	F	472
Druj	Pers.	F	472
Eldir	Norse	M	499
Fimafeng	Norse	M	568
Finn macCoul	Cel.	M	570
Firbolgs	Cel.	M	571
Frid	Norse	F	611
Frithiof	Norse	M	612
Fulla	Norse	F	616
Ganas	Hin.	M	625
Gareth	Bryth.	M	629
Giadruvava	Taino	M	653
Golem	Caba.	M	674
Gudrun	Germ.	F	694
Gwion Bach	Cel.	M	701
Hagar	Hebr.	M	707
Ham	Hebr.	M	713
Harlequin	Folk.	M	726
Heracles	Gk.	M	752
Hercules	Gk.	M	759
Hippodameia	Gk.	F	773
Ho-no-susori	Jap.	M	785
Hunding	Germ.	M	806

	Culture	Sex	Page
Irus	Gk.	M	841
Jacob	Hebr.	M	858
Jason	Gk.	M	866
Jesus	Christ.	M	877
John Thomas	Eng.	M	885
Joseph (Yusof)	Hebr., Mos.	M	888
Krake	Norse	F	944
Kubaiko	Tatar	F	947
Kulhwch	Bryth.	M	950
Launfal, Sir	Bryth.	M	976
Ljod	Norse	F	1004
Lopter	Norse	M	1012
Malchus	Hebr.	M	1049
Manabhozho	Algon.	M	1054
Man Friday	Eng.	M	1053
Midir	Cel.	M	1100
Naniwa	Jap.	M, F	1153
Nasu	Pers.	F	472
Nayanezgani	Nav.	M	1159
Nekedzaltara	Tinne Ind.		1161
Nera	Cel.	M	+
Ninkarnunna	Sum.	M	1173
Noogumee	Micmac Ind.	M	1180
Obadiah	Eng.	M	1191
Odin	Norse	M	1195
Odysseus	Gk.	M	1196
Ogma	Cel.	M	1200
O-kuni-nushi	Jap.	M	1204
Palinurus	Rom.	M	1228
Perseus	Gk.	M	1257
Poseidon	Gk.	M	1288
Psyche	Gk.	F	1299
Rhiannon	Bryth.	F	1336
Roskva	Norse	F	1350
Rumpelstiltskin	Germ.	M	1354
Saint Thomas	Christ.	M	1382
Samson	Hebr.	M	1394
Sargon	Meso.	M	1400
Siegfried	Germ.	M	1448
Sigurd	Norse	M	1451
Skirnir	Norse	M	1465
Solomon	Hebr.	M	1472
Sosia	Rom.	M	1476
Theseus	Gk.	M	1554
Thobadzistshini	Nav.	M	1560
Thrall	Norse	M	1563

Menial (cont.)	Culture	Sex	Page
Titlacauan	Mex.	M	1578
Ulysses	Rom.	M	1622
Uncle Tom	Am. Lit.	M	1624
Uphir	Med.	M	1627
Valmiki	Hin.	M	1637
Wang	Chin.	M	1664
Yebegan	Tatar	M	1703
Yskyrdaw & Yseudydd	Bryth.	F-F	1711
Yudhisthira	Hin.	M	1711

MERCY

Amoghapasa	Bud.	M	87
Aryavalokitesvara	Bud.	M	134
Avalokitesvara	Bud.	M	160
Chesed	Caba.	M	320
Fudo-myoo	Jap.	M	615
Fugen	Jap.	M	615
Gabriel	Christ., Hebr., Mos.	M	619
Geburah	Caba.	M	637
Gedulah	Caba.	M	637
Heruka	Bud.	M	764
Hideyoshi	Jap.	M	767
Jizo	Jap.	M	881
Karuna	Bud.	M	911
Kasyapa	Bud.	M	912
Kokuzo	Jap.	M	940
Krakucchanda	Bud.	M	945
Kwannon	Jap.	F/A	955
Kwan-yin	Chin.	F/A	955
Manusibuddha	Bud.	M	1062
Marduk	Baby.	M	1065
Nairatma	Bud.	F	1149
Nintoku	Jap.	M	1174
P'u Hsien	Chin.	M	1300
Rajah Vesali	Hin.	M	1320
Sarvanivarana-viskambhin	Bud.	M	1401
Shiphrah & Puah	Hebr.	F-F	1439
Solomon	Hebr.	M	1472
Tashmetu	Baby.	F	1537
Tipherath	Caba.	M	1575
Tlaelquani	Mex.	F	1581
Tutu	Baby.	M	1611

MERRYMAKING (SEE REVELRY)

MESSENGER	Culture	Sex	Page
Ame-waka-hiko	Jap.	M	85
Angirases	Hin.	M	96
Artorious	Cel.	M	133
Aruru	Sum.	F	133
Ashi	Hin.	F	139
Cherub	Hebr.	M	319
Chiminizagagua	Chib.	M	+
Chokmah	Caba.	M	666
Christ	Christ.	M	330
Chthonius	Gk.	M	334
Elijah	Hebr.	M	503
Gabriel	Christ., Hebr., Mos.	M	619
Gadjisa	Iroq.	M	621
Gibil	Baby., Sum.	M	512
Gijigouai	Algon.	M	656
Gnaa	Norse	F	664
Guatauva	Taino	M	694
Gwrhyr Gwalstawt	Bryth.	M	702
Hayhuaypanti	Inca	M	734
Hermes	Gk.	M	760
Hermod	Norse	M	763
Huaminca	Inca	M	801
Ili-abrat	Baby.	M	823
Iris	Gk.	F	839
Irus	Gk.	M	841
Isaiah	Hebr.	M	842
Ishum	Sum.	M	845
Israfil	Mos.	M	847
Kami-no-tsukai	Jap.		906
Karshipta	Pers.	M	911
Kengida	Baby., Sum.	M	512
Khensu	Egy.	M	923
Kingaludda	Baby., Sum.	M	512
Kitsume	Jap.	M	935
Maidere	Tatar	M	1046
Malachi	Hebr.	M	1048
Malak-Bel	Sem.	M	1048
Matarisvan	Hin.	M	1074
Melchizedek	Hebr.	M	1085
Mercury	Rom.	M	1091
Mithra	Pers.	M	1112
Moses	Hebr.	M	1126
Mrtyu	Hin.	M	1132
Nabu	Baby.	M	1146
Nairyosangha	Pers.	M	1150

Messenger (cont.)	Culture	Sex	Page
Namtaru	Assyr., Baby.	M	1152
Nanaboojoo	Pota.	M	1152
Narasamsa	Hin.	M	1155
Nekedzaltara	Tinne Ind.		1161
Ninsubur	Sum.	M	1173
Noidde	Lapp	M	1179
Nusku	Baby.	M	1187
Pairekse	Ostiak	M	1226
Pap-sukal	Assyr.	M	1236
Papukkal	Sum.	M	1236
Pelethites & Cherethites	Hebr.	M-M	1249
Pravuil	Hebr.	M	1291
Puleh	Rus.	M	1301
Raziel	Caba.	M	1326
Ruadan	Cel.	M	1352
Ryuja (Hakuja)	Jap.	M	1356
Saint George	Christ.	M	1370
Sandalphon	Caba.	M	1396
Sarama	Hin.	F	1399
Sarudahiko	Jap.	M	1401
Seraph	Christ., Hebr.	M	1417
Shakuru	Pawnee	M	1429
Shiju-gara	Jap.	M	1437
Showa	Tib.	M	1443
Sjofn	Norse	F	1463
Skirnir	Norse	M	1465
Spirit (Holy Ghost)	Christ.	M	1484
Suvinenge	Daho.	M	1513
Sylph	Med.	M, F	1521
Thoth	Egy.	M	1562
Toyo-tama-hime	Jap.	F	1593
Triton	Gk.	M	1599
Uddagubha	Baby., Sum.	M	512
Vareghna	Pers.	M	1639
Yazata	Zoro.	M	1702
Yebegen	Tatar	M	1703
Zadkiel	Christ., Hebr.	M	1714
Zephon	Eng.	M	1718

MESSIAH (SEE SAVIOR)

MIRACULOUS BIRTH			
Ama-no-minaka	Jap.	M	80
Amaterasu	Jap.	F	81
Ame-no-toko-tachi	Jap.	F	83
Ariel	Eng.	M	124

	Culture	Sex	Page
Asclepius	Gk.	M	136
Atargatis	Sem.	F/A	148
Athena	Gk.	F	150
Attis	Phryg.	M	154
Balarama	Hin.	M	174
Brahma	Hin.	M	240
Buddha	Bud.	M	255
Christ	Christ.	M	330
Daksha	Hin.	M	408
Dionysus	Gk.	M	447
Dithyrambus	Gk.	M	452
Drona	Hin.	M	471
Dudugera	N. Guin.	M	475
Enceladus	Gk.	M	510
Eve	Hebr.	F	534
Fo-Hi	Chin.	M	589
Fu-Hsi	Chin.	M	615
Gargantua	Fr.	M	630
Gaya Maretan	Pers.	M	636
Gigantes	Gk.	M	655
Gilgamesh	Sum.	M	656
Hammurabi	Baby.	M	716
Heracles	Gk.	M	752
Hercules	Rom.	M	759
Hiawatha	N.A.I.	M	767
Hine-ahu-one	Poly.	F	772
Huang Ti	Chin.	M	801
Huitzilopochtli	Mex.	M	803
Ikuguhi	Jap.	F	822
Indra	Hin.	M	829
Izanagi	Jap.	M	853
Izanami	Jap.	F	853
Jarasandha	Hin.	M	865
Jurupari	Braz.	M	898
Kaitabha	Hin.	M	902
Kamu-Mimusubi	Jap.	F	907
Kao Hsin	Chin.	M	908
Karttikeya	Hin.	M	911
Klieng	Borneo	M	936
Kvaser	Norse	M	954
Lakshmi	Hin.	F	965
Lumimu-ut	Indo.	F	1024
Macbeth	Eng.	M	1032
Macduff	Eng.	M	1033
Mahavira	Jainism	M	1045
Manjusri	Bud.	M	1059

	Culture	Sex	Page
Manu	Hin.	M	1061
Marduk	Assyr-Baby.	M	1065
Ma-riko-riko	N. Zeal.	F	1067
Marnas	Gk.	M	1720
Mary	Christ.	F	1072
Mashoyi	Pers.	F	1072
Mashya	Pers.	M	1072
Maui	Poly.	M	1077
Mimir	Norse	M	1105
Monotaro	Jap.	M	1118
Moses	Hebr.	M	1126
Orion	Gk.	M	1215
Padmasambhava	Tib.	M	1225
Palici	Ital.	M	1228
Pandavas	Hin.	M	1232
P'an Ku	Chin.	M/A	1233
Papa	Poly.	F	1235
Pelasgus	Gk.	M	1249
Perseus	Gk.	M	1257
Poshaiyanne	Pueblo	M	1288
Prthu	Hin.	M	1298
Ptah	Egy.	M	1299
Purusa	Hin.	A	1305
Quetzalcoatl	Mex.	M	1312
Ra	Egy.	M	1314
Rhoetus	Gk.	M	1337
Rigi	Micro.	M	1339
Sargon I	Meso.	M	1400
Setanta	Cel.	M	1421
Shen Nung	Chin.	M	1434
Shina-tsu-hiko	Jap.	M	1438
Shingrawa	Burm.	M	1438
Shu	Egy.	M	1443
Shun	Chin.	M	1444
Sita	Hin.	F	1460
Susa-no-wo	Jap.	M	1512
Svabhava	Hin.	M	1514
Svayambhu	Bud., Hin.	M	1515
Taaroa	Poly.	M	1522
Taka-mimusubi	Jap.	M	1527
Taliesin	Bryth.	M	1528
T'ang	Chin.	M	1531
Tefenet	Egy.	F	1541
Tilottama	Hin.	F	1574
Tiri	Brazil	M	1576
Tsuki-yomi	Jap.	M	1604

	Culture	Sex	Page
Tsunuguhi	Jap.	M	1604
Tuan mac Cairill	Cel.	M	1605
Tyurunmuzykay	Tatar	M	1618
Umashi-ashi-kabi	Jap.	M	1622
Ushas	Hin.	F	1631
Volsung	Norse	M	1658
Wyungare	Aus.	M	1694
Yang	Chin.	M	1700
Yao	Chin.	M	1701
Yin	Chin	F	1707
Yu	Chin.	M	1711
Zoroaster	Zoro.	M	1734

MIRTH (SEE HAPPINESS, REVELRY)

MISCHIEVOUSNESS (INSOLENCE, MALICIOUSNESS, GOSSIP)

Arlecchino	Ital.	M	726
Ate	Gk.	F	149
Berlic	Norse		204
Blue Jay	Chinook	M	+
Bricriu	Cel.	M	248
Chelone	Gk.	F	317
Colhuatzincatl	Mex.	M	356
Conan Maol	Cel.	M	364
Coyote	N.A.I.	M	377
Curupira	Brazil.	M	399
Deil	Scot.	M	426
Divje Devojke	Slav.	F	454
Divji Moz	Slav.	M	454
Dulachan	Cel.	M	475
Dusio	Med.	M	477
Elf	Norse	M, F	502
Eris	Gk.	F	521
Eros	Gk.	M	522
Evnissyen	Bryth.	M	536
Faunus	Rom.	M	552
Friar Rush (Bruder Rausch)	Germ.	M	611
Galatea	Gk.	F	623
Hallgerda	Ice.	F	712
Harlequin	Folk.	M	726
Hermes	Gk.	M	760
Hob	Eng.	M	776
Hobbididance	Eng.	M	777
Hobgoblin	Eng.	M	778
Huard	Brittany	M	801

Mischievousness (cont.)	Culture	Sex	Page
Imp	Folk.	M, F	826
Italapas	Calif. Ind.	M	+
Jizo	Jap.	M	881
Kaches	Arm.	M, F	900
Kay, Sir	Bryth.	M	914
Kelpi	Scot.	M	916
Kitsume	Jap.		935
Loki	Norse	M/A	1010
Lyeshy	Slav.	M	1028
Momus	Gk.	M	1116
Moquequeloa	Mex.	M	1122
Muntso-murt	Fin-Ug.	M	1137
Olofat	Carol. Is.	M	1206
Ossa	Gk.	F	1219
Pantagruel	Fr.	M	1234
Pau-puk-keewis	Am. Lit.	M	1244
Pooka	Cel.	M	1286
Puck	Eng.	M	1300
Punch	Eng.	M	1301
Punchinello	Ital.	M	1301
Pwcca	Welsh	M	1300
Robin Goodfellow	Eng.	M	1343
Rush (Bruder Rausch)	Germ.	M	1355
Satyr	Gk.	M	1403
Scapino (Scapin)	Ital. (Fr.)	M	1405
Seirim	Hebr.	M	1413
Sprite	Eng.	M, F	1485
Susa-no-wo	Jap.	M	1512
Svartalfar	Norse	M	1514
Tachi	Tembu (Afr.)	M	1523
Tengu	Jap.	M	1545
Thjasse	Norse	M	1560
Troll	Germ.	M, F	1600
Uldda	Scan.	M	1621

MIST (SEE MOISTURE)

MODESTY (PRUDENCE)			
Aidos	Gk.	F	+
Graces	Gk.	F	681
Gualdrada	Ital.	F	693
O-kuni-nushi	Jap.	M	1204

MOISTURE (c=cloud, d=dew, m=mist, mar=marshes, r=rain, rb-rainbow, s=sap)

	Culture	Sex	Page
Abakan-khan (r)	Sib.	M	11
Achachila (r)	Bol.	M	24
Adad (r)	Sem.	M	28
Aebh (m)	Cel.	F	37
Aed (r)	Cel.	M	37
Agraulos (d)	Gk.	F	51
Aiauh (m)	Mex.	F	54
Aido Hwedo (rb)	Daho.	M	55
Akbal (r)	Mex.	M	59
Alviss (d)	Norse	M	78
Angeburga (m)	Norse	M	95
Aokeu & Ake (r)	Poly.	M-M	106
Apo (r)	Pers.	M	109
Arbuda (r)	Hin.	M	118
At'amjonks (rb)	Fin-Ug.	M	148
Athena (d)	Gk.	F	150
Atoakwatje (r)	Aus.	M	153
Baal-Lebanon (r)	Sem.	M	167
Bacab (r)	Sem.	M	170
Baiyuhibi (r)	Indo.	M	173
Bajanai (r)	Yakut	M	173
Bel Enlil (m)	Baby.	M	197
Borghild (m)	Norse	F	237
Breit-hut (c)	Norse	M	246
Centaur (c)	Gk.	M	303
Chaacs (r)	Mex.	M	307
Chandra (d)	Hin.	M	310
Chasca (d)	Inca	F	316
Conn (d)	Cel.	M	367
Cuchaviva (rb)	Bogata	F	393
Cueravaperi (r)	Mex.	F	396
Cuichi Supai (rb)	Ecuador		396
Dasagvas (r)	Hin.	M	416
Dionysus (s)	Gk.	M	447
Doda (r)	Slav.	F	455
Eos (d)	Gk.	F	514
Eosphorous (d)	Gk.	M	514
Euryclea (m)	Gk.	F	532
Eurydice (m)	Gk.	F	532
Eurynome (d)	Gk.	F	532
Fiachra (m)	Cel.	M	564
Fionnuala (m)	Cel.	F	571
Frey (r)	Norse	M	609
Freya (rb)	Norse	M	610
Gaea (d)	Gk.	F/A	621
Gama-Sennin (m)	Jap.	M	625

	Culture	Sex	Page
Ganaskidi (r)	Nav.		625
Ganesa (r)	Hin.	M	627
Ganymede (d)	Gk.	M	627
Graeae (m)	Gk.	F	681
Gucumatz (r)	Guate.	M	694
Hallinskide (rb)	Norse	M	712
Havfrue (m)	Dan.	F	732
Hehu (r)	Egy.	M	742
Herse (d)	Gk.	F	763
Hnikar (r)	Norse	M	776
Hobal (r)	Arab	M	777
Horae (d)	Gk.	F	786
Hotu-papa (d)	Poly.	F	794
Huecomitl (r)	Mex.	M	802
Huitzilopochtli (r)	Mex.	M	803
Hyndla (d)	Norse	F	812
Idurmer (r)	Sem.	M	821
Indra (r)	Hin.	M	829
Iris (rb)	Gk.	F	839
Isis (d)	Egy.	F	845
Itzamna (d, r)	Mex.	M	850
Ix-chel (rb)	Mex.	F	852
Ix-tub-tun (r)	Mex.	F	853
Jupiter (r)	Rom.	M	896
Kakaitch (r)	Makah Ind.	M	902
Kalseru (r)	Aus.	M	904
Khensu (r)	Egy.	M	923
Khurannojon (r)	Buriat	M	926
Koloowisi (r)	Zuni	M	941
Kukulcan (r)	Mex.	M	950
Kura-okami (r)	Jap.		952
Kwammang-A (rb)	Afr.	M	955
Leza (r)	Bantu	M	989
Limniades (mar)	Gk.	F	994
Lityerses (d)	Gk.	M	1003
Liu Tsung (r)	Chin.	M	1003
Llacheu (d)	Bryth.	M	1004
Louhi (m)	Lapp	F	1016
Lung (r)	Chin.	M	1025
Lung-wang (r)	Chin.	M	1025
Maku (d, m)	N. Zeal	M	1048
Malkosh (r)	Pers.	M	1050
Malqos (r)	Pers.	M	1046
Matlalcueje (r)	Mex.	F	1076
Maya (r)	Mex.	M	1080
Mokkurkalfi (m)	Norse	M	1114

	Culture	Sex	Page
Mordo-khan (r)	Sib.	M	1122
Murtaznu (r)	Baby.	M	1138
Naga (r)	Hin.	M, F	1147
Nanihehecatli (r)	Mex.	M	1153
Navagvas (r)	Hin.	M	1158
Neptune (d, m)	Ital.	M	1163
Nibelungen (m)	Norse	M, F	1167
Nicor (r)	Eng.	M	1168
Niflungs (m)	Norse	M, F	1169
Notus (m)	Gk.	M	1183
Nyakang (r)	Egy.	M	1187
Oceanid (m)	Gk.	F	1193
Ombrios (r)	Gk.	M	1720
Ombrophore (r)	Gk.	M	1207
Oreithyia (d)	Gk.	F	1213
Oshunmare (rb)	Yoruba (Afr.)		1218
Pandrosos (d)	Gk.	F	1233
Pegasus (m)	Gk.		1248
Perkunas (r)	Baltic	M	1256
Philomela (d)	Gk.	F	1263
Phra In (r)	Siam.	M	1266
Pluvius (r)	Rom.	M	897
Procne (d)	Gk.	F	1294
Procris (d)	Gk.	F	1294
Rem (r)	Egy.	M	1332
Ridija (r)	Sem.	M	1338
Rorik (d)	Dan.	M	1347
Ryu-wo (r)	Jap.	M	1356
Sabazius (d, m)	Phryg.	M	1353
Saint Gervais (r)	Fr.	M	1370
Saint Godelieve (r)	Flanders	M	1371
Saint Martin (r)	Scot.	M	1375
Saint Medard (r)	Fr.	M	1377
Saint Swithin (r)	Eng.	M	1382
Sakia (r)	Arab.	M	1389
Salmoneus (r)	Gk.	M	1391
Schilbung (m)	Norse	M	1407
Sebek (r)	Egy.	M	1412
Segesta (d)	Gk.	F	1413
Sgilti Lightfoot (d)	Bryth.	M	1427
Shiwanni (r)	Zuni	M	1440
Signe-Alveig (m)	Norse	F	1451
Sigrun (m)	Norse	F	1451
Sisiutl (r)	Kwakiutl	M	1459
Stutly, Will (d)	Eng.	M	1502
Sun Tear (d)	Cel.	F	564

Moisture (cont.)	Culture	Sex	Page
Surupa (r)	Hin.	F	1511
Susa-no-wo (r)	Jap.	M	1512
Swanhild (d)	Germ.	F	1517
Syavarshan (r)	Pers.	M	1521
Tai Shan (r)	Chin.	F	1526
Taygete (r)	Gk.	F	1539
Tefenet (r)	Egy.	F	1541
Tengu (r)	Jap.	M	1545
Thein (r)	Burm.	M	1553
Thonenli (r)	Nav.	M	1560
Thunderbird (r)	Am. Ind.	M	1568
Ticci (r)	Inca	M	1571
Tiermes (rb)	Lapp	M	1572
Tishtrya (r)	Pers.	M	1577
Tlaloc Tecutli (r)	Mex.	M	1581
Trung Sisters (r)	Ind-Chin.	F	1602
Tumo-pas (r)	Fin-Ug.	M	1607
Ua (r)	Poly.	M	1619
Uddushunamir (r)	Assyr-Baby.	M	1620
Untar (m)	Fin.	F	1626
Uzava Tumaspana (r)	Pers.	M	1633
Vajrapani (r)	Bud.	M	1635
Varuna (r)	Hin.	M	1639
Vasuki (r)	Hin.	M	1641
Vinayaka (r)	Bud.	M	1650
Vishtaspa (r)	Pers.	M	1655
Yaai (m)	Vancouver	M, F	1697
Yobanua-Borna (r)	Taino		1708
Yu Shih (r)	Chin.	M	1713
Zada (r)	Sib.	F	1714

MONSTER SLAYER (SEE FOE OF DEMONS)

MOON			
Aa (A, Ai)	Sum.	F	9
Ab	Sem.	M	1428
Agli-bel	Sem.	M	49
Ah (Aah)	Egy.	M	51
Ai	Sum.	F	54
Aine	Cel.	F	56
Aithuia	Gk.	F	57
Aku	Sum.		60
Amarga	Baby.		80
Amm	Sem.	F	86
Anammelech	Hebr.	M	91

	Culture	Sex	Page
Anchimallen	Araucanian	F	93
Anukt	Egy.	F	105
Anumati	Hin.	F	105
Aphrodite	Gk.	F	108
Ariadne	Gk.	F	123
Arianrhod	Cel.	F	123
Artemis	Gk.	F	131
Astarte	Phoen.	F	144
Asterodia	Gk.	F	144
Ataentsic (Eagentci)	Huron	F	147
Atargatis	Sem.	F/A	148
Baal	Sem.	M	167
Baal-Peor	Sem.	A	167
Baloo	Aus.	M	176
Bekotshidi	Nav.	M	196
Belili	Sum.	F	197
Belphoebe	Eng.	F	200
Bendis	Gk.	F	201
Bil	Norse	F	211
Blodeuwedd	Bryth.	F	226
Branwen	Bryth.	F	243
Brisaya	Hin.	F	249
Briseis	Gk.	F	249
Britomartis	Gk.	F	250
Brizo	Gk.	F	250
Cain	Christ.	M	269
Candaules	Gk.	F	284
Candra	Hin.	M	285
Cessair	Cel.	F	306
Chalchiutlicue	Mex.	F	308
Chandra	Hin.	M	310
Ch'ang-o	Chin.	A	311
Chia	Colombian Ind.	F	321
Cinderella	Folk.	F	339
Circe	Gk.	F	341
Ciuateotl	Mex.	F	346
Coyolxauhqui	Mex.	F	377
Creusa	Gk., Rom.	F	381
Cynthia	Gk.	F	402
Dechtire	Cel.	F	423
Deirdre	Cel.	F	426
Delia	Gk.	F	427
Delilah	Hebr.	F	427
Diana	Rom.	F	441
Diarmaid	Cel.	M	442
Dione	Gk.	F	446

	Culture	Sex	Page
Dubh Lacha	Cel.	F	474
Dzewana	Slav.	F	481
El	Sem.	M	497
Elaine	Bryth.	F	497
Endymion	Gk.	M	511
En-zu	Baby.	M	513
Eriphyle	Hebr.	M	520
Esau	Hebr.	M	524
Etain	Cel.	F	526
Ethne	Cel.	F	528
Europa	Gk.	F	531
Eurynome	Gk.	F	532
Fates (Moirai)	Gk.	F	551
Fatima	Folk.	F	552
Findabair	Cel.	F	568
Fraoch	Cel.	M	607
Garbh Ogh	Cel.	F	628
Gevar	Norse	M	652
Gina	Aus.	M	658
Hathor	Egy.	F	730
Hecate	Gk.	F	740
Hecuba	Gk.	F	741
Heifer of Anu	Assyr.	F	743
Helen	Gk.	F	745
Hera	Gk.	F	752
Hina	Poly.	F	771
Horsel	Germ.	F	791
Hyuki & Bil	Norse	M-F	814
Il	Arab	M	823
Ilmuqah	Pers.	M	824
Ina	Poly.	F	827
Ingcel	Cel.	M	831
Io	Gk.	F	835
Isa	Lapp	F	841
Ishmael	Hebr.	M	843
Ishtar	Assyr-Baby.	F	844
Isis	Egy.	F	845
Jarasandha	Hin.	M	865
Judas	Christ.	M	892
Juno	Rom.	F	895
Kaguya-hime	Jap.	F	1468
Kahil	Sem.	M	1429
Kalypso	Gk.	F	905
Kaua	Poly.	M	913
Kettu	Baby.	M	920
Ketu	Hin.	M	920

	Culture	Sex	Page
Khensu	Egy.	M	923
Klehanoai	Nav.	M	936
Kootamoinen	Fin.	M	942
Kuhu	Hin.	F	949
Kuru	Hin.	M	953
Lady of Shalott	Eng.	F	962
Latona	Rom.	F	975
Lord of Sesennu	Egy.	M	1013
Lucina	Rom.	F	1020
Luna	Rom.	F	1025
Maane	Norse	M	1031
Magar	Sum.	M	1037
Magog	Cel.	F	1041
Mama Quilla	Inca	F	1051
Mani	Norse	M	1058
Manto	Gk.	F	1061
Mashu & Mashtu	Baby.	M-F	1072
Mawa	Daho.	F	1078
Medb	Bryth.	F	1082
Meni	Assyr.	F/A	1089
Merope	Gk.	F	1093
Metra	Pers.	F	1096
Metzli	Mex.	F	1097
Misharu	Phoen.	M	1110
Morgause	Bryth.	F	1123
Morrigu	Cel.	F	1125
Naksatras	Hin.	F	1150
Nana	Sum.	F	1152
Nanna	Norse	F	1153
Nannar	Baby., Sum.	M	1153
Nephthys	Egy.	F	1163
Nimue	Bryth.	F	1170
Ningal	Assyr-Baby.	F	1172
Nini-anteh	Indo.	F	1173
Nipa	Algon.	F	1175
Osiris	Egy.	M	1218
O-tsuki-sama	Jap.	M	1220
Pah	Pawnee	F	1226
Pajan Yan	Cambodian	F	1121
Pasiphae	Gk.	F	1241
Phaedra	Gk.	F	1260
Philonome	Gk.	F	1263
Phoebe	Gk.	F	1265
Phosphorus	Gk.	A	1266
Plat-eye	W. Ind.		1279
Potiphar's wife	Hebr., Mos.	F	1289

	Culture	Sex	Moon Page
Rachel	Hebr.	F	1316
Rahkonen	Fin.	M	1318
Raka	Hin.	F	1320
Rhiannon	Bryth.	F	1336
Rona	Maori	A	1347
Sadb	Cel.	F	1360
Saint George	Christ.	M	1370
Samson	Hebr.	M	1394
Selene	Gk.	F	1414
Semiramis	Assyr.	F	1415
Shahar	Mos.	M	1428
Shakuntala	Hin.	F	1429
Shelartish	Urartian	M	1433
Shitta	Burm.		1439
Shulamite	Hebr.	F	1444
Si	Pre-Inca	M	1445
Sin	Assyr.	M	1456
Sinivali	Hin.	F	1457
Siva	Hin.	M	1461
Soma	Hin.	M	1473
Sudabah	Pers.	F	1503
Sydyk	Baby.	M	1521
Tanit	Carth.	F	1532
Tashmetu	Baby., Sum.	F	1537
Taurica	Gk.	F	1538
Techu	Egy.	M	1540
Teczistecatl	Mex.	F	1540
Telephassa	Gk.	F	1542
Termagant	Rom.	F	1546
Teteoinnan	Mex.	F	1548
Thoth	Egy.	M	1562
Titania	Rom.	F	1577
Tiv	Ital.	M	1581
Toyo-kumo	Jap.	M	1592
Trita Aptya	Hin.	M	1599
Trivia	Gk.	F	1599
Tsuki-yomi	Jap.	M	1604
Tuonetar (Manator)	Fin-Ug.	F	1608
Udo	Sumu Ind.	M	1620
Udsar	Sum.	M	1620
Urania	Gk.	F	108
Uranus	Gk.	M	1627
Ursula	Norse	F	1630
Wadd	Sem.	M	1661
Warah	Sem.	M	1665
Wu Kang	Chin.	M	1693
Yama	Hin.	M	1699

	Culture	Sex	Page
Yohualticetl	Anahuac	F	1709

MOTHER (FEMALE PRINCIPLE)

	Culture	Sex	Page
Acrea	Gk.	F	27
Aditi	Hin.	F	32
Adrastea	Gk.	F	35
Agave	Gk.	F	46
Agusaya	Baby.	F	51
Aima	Caba.	F	56
Akka	Fin.	F	1621
Albina	Gk.	F	63
Alilat	Arab.	F	68
Allat	Sem.	F	69
Ama	Sum.	F	78
Ame-no-toko-tachi	Jap.	F	83
Ament	Egy.	F	84
Aminah	Mos.	F	+
Ana	Hin.	F	90
Anahit	Arm.	F	90
Anaitis	Sem.	F	90
Anat	Sem.	F	91
Anatha-Baetyle	Arm.	F	92
Angeyja	Norse	F	96
Anna	Chald.	F	99
Anna Perenna	Rom.	F	99
Annit	Chald.	F	+
Anthat	As. Min.	F	102
Anu	Cel.	F	104
Anukt (Anouka)	Egy.	F	105
Apet	Egy.	F	107
Aphrodite	Gk.	F	108
Aranyani	Hin.	F	117
Arianrhod	Cel.	F	123
Armaiti	Hin.	F	127
Arsa	Sem.	F	130
Artemis	Gk.	F	131
Aruru	Sum.	F	133
Asaseya	Krachi (Afr.)	F	1693
Ashdar	Abys.	F	138
Ashuritu	Assyr.	F	143
Astarte (Ashtart, Ashtoreth)	Phoen.	F	144
Astronoe	Phoen.	F	145
Ataentsic (Eagentci)	Huron (Seneca)	F	147
Atargatis	Sem.	F/A	148
Ate (Atheh)	As. Min.	F	149
Atet	Egy.	F	149

	Culture	Sex	Page
Athena	Gk.	F	150
Attabeira	Taino	F	154
Audhumla	Norse	F	156
Awitelin Tsita	Zuni	F	162
Ayesha	Mos.	F	164
Baalti (Belti)	Phoen.	F	168
Baau	Phoen., Sum.	F	168
Bat	Egy.	F	185
Bau Gula	Assyr.	F	844
Belili	Assyr-Baby.	F	197
Belit	Assyr-Baby.	F	197
Belit Ilani	Sum.	F	197
Beltis	Baby.	F	201
Berecinthia	Phryg.	F	203
Beruth	Phoen.	F	205
Bestla	Norse	F	206
Binah	Caba.	F	212
Brimo	Mong.	F	249
Britomartis	Gk.	F	250
Buan-Ann	Cel.	F	254
Buddhalocana	Bud.	F	257
Caelestis	Rom.	F	267
Cailleach	Scot.	F	269
Cailleach Mor (Bheur)	Scot.	F	269
Cardea	Rom.	F	290
Cathena	Mojave	F	298
Ceres	Rom.	F	305
Cerridwen	Bryth.	F	305
Chaabu	Sem.	F	307
Chalchiutlicue	Mex.	F/A	308
Citlalinicue	Mex.	F	345
Ciuateotl	Mex.	F	346
Cotytto (Kotys)	Gk.	F	376
Cueravaperi	Mex.	F	396
Cybele	Phryg.	F	400
Damkina	Baby.	F	410
Danae	Gk.	F	411
Danu	Cel., Hin.	F	414
Deipara	Christ.	F	426
Demeter	Gk.	F	429
Derceto	Sem.	F	433
Dervonnae	Medit.	F	686
Devi	Hin.	F	435
Dhupa	Bud.	F	439
Diana	Rom.	F	441
Dindymene	Phryg.	F	445

	Culture	Sex	Page
Dione	Gk.	F	446
Dis	Norse	F	451
Don (Donnus)	Bryth.	A	461
Durga	Hin.	F	477
Dyava-matar	Hin.	F	480
Eire	Cel.	F	496
Embla	Norse	F	507
Epet (Tueret, Uret)	Egy.	F	514
Eurynome	Gk.	F	532
Eve (Hava)	Hebr.	F	534
Fauna	Rom.	F	552
Freya	Norse	F	610
Gaea (Titania)	Gk.	F/A	621
Gandha	Bud.	F	626
Gauri	Hin.	F	635
Gita	Bud.	F	660
Guacarapita	Taino	F	693
Guimazoa	Taino	F	696
Gula	Sum.	F	696
Hamsika	Hin.	F	716
Harmonia	Gk.	F	727
Hathor	Egy.	F	730
Hehut	Egy.	F	742
Hera	Gk.	F	752
Heru-pa-kaut	Egy.	F	764
Hi-asa	Admiralties	F	766
Hine-ahu-one	Poly.	F	772
Hod	Caba.	F	778
Hsi Wang Mu	Chin.	F	800
Hueytonantzin	Mex.	F	802
Ida	Gk., Hin.	F	818
Iella	Taino	F	821
Ilamatecutli	Mex.	F	823
Ilat	Arab.	F	823
In	Jap.	F	827
Iananna	Sum.	F	827
Innini	Sum.	F	832
Io	Gk.	F	835
Iowahine	Hawa.	F	837
Isa	Lapp	F	841
Ishah	Hebr.	F	843
Ishtar	Assyr-Baby.	F	844
Isis	Egy.	F	845
Itoki	Nica.	F	849
Izanami	Jap.	F	853
Juno	Rom.	F	895

	Culture	Sex	Page
Kadesh (Quedesh)	Sem.	F	901
Kaiwan	Ethiop.	F	902
Kali	Hin.	F	903
Kamu-Mimusubi	Jap.	F	907
Karali	Hin.	F	909
Karpophoros	Gk.	F	911
Kaukabhta	Sem.	F	913
Kekuit	Egy.	F	916
Kerhet	Egy.	F	918
Kerres	Ital.	F	919
Khadijah	Mos.	F	922
Khi-dimmeazaga	Baby.	F	924
Khon-ma	Tib.	F	925
Ki	Sum.	F	926
Kishar	Baby.	F	933
Kokyanwuqti	Pueblo	F	940
Kourtorophos	Gk.	F	944
Kun	Hin.	F	951
Kunti	Hin.	F	952
Kwannon	Jap.	F/A	955
Kwan-yin	Chin.	F/A	955
La'i-la'i	Poly.	F	964
Lakshmi	Hin.	F	965
Lasya	Bud.	F	975
Libya	Gk.	F	991
Ligoapup	Micro.	F	993
Locana	Bud.	F	1006
Lotis	Gk.	F	1014
Lumimu-ut	Indo.	F	1024
Ma	As. Min., Baby., Hin.	F	1030
Maa-emae	Fin.	F	1030
Maat	Egy.	F	1031
Maau	Egy.	F	1031
Machi-pal-lha-mo	Tib.	F	1034
Magna Mater	Phryg.	F	1040
Mah	Sem.	F	1042
Mahadevi	Hin.	F	1042
Maia	Gk.	F	1046
Maid Marian	Bryth.	F/A	1046
Mairae	Medit.	F	686
Maire	Cel.	F	1047
Maiso	Braz.	F	1047
Makh	Assyr-Baby.	F	1048
Mala	Bud.	F	1049
Malkuth	Caba.	F	1050

	Culture	Sex	Page
Mama	Sum.	F	1050
Mama Allpa	Inca	F	1051
Mama Cocha	Inca	F	1051
Mamona	Taino	F	1052
Manat	Sem.	F	1056
Manzan Gormo	Mong.	F	1062
Mari	As. Min., Cretan	F	1066
Ma-riko-riko	Maori	F	1067
Marjatta	Fin.	F	1068
Mary	Christ.	F	1072
Mater Doloroso	Christ.	F	1074
Mater Matuta	Rom.	F	1074
Matres (Matrae)	Rom/Cel.	F	1076
Matrs	Hin.	F	1076
Maya	Bud., Hin.	F	1080
Mayauel	Mex.	F	1080
Meni	Assyr.	F/A	1089
Mersekhnet	Egy.	F	149
Modron	Bryth.	F	1114
Muskrat	Algon.	F	1140
Mut	Egy.	F/A	1140
Muyinewumana	Pueblo	F	1142
Mylitta	Chald.	F	1142
Nana	Sum.	F	1152
Nang-pyek-kha-yeh-khi	Burm.	F	1153
Nari Mariama	Hin.	F	1156
Nashak	Pers.	F	1463
Nazit	Egy.	F	1159
Neheb-kau	Egy.	F	1160
Neith	Egy., Lib.	F	1161
Nina	Baby.	F	1170
Nin Ella	Baby.	F	1172
Ninhursag	Sum.	F	1173
Ninlil	Sum.	F	1173
Ninmah	Baby.	F	1173
Ninsun	Baby.	F	1174
Nintu	Sim.	F	1174
Nin-ur	Baby.	F	1174
Niritu	Phoen.	F	1175
Nowutset	Sia Ind.	F	1183
Nrtya	Bud.	F	1184
Nunusesmea	Sem.	F	1042
Nut	Egy.	F	1187
Nzambi	Congo	A	1188
Omeciuatl	Mex.	F	1207

	Culture	Sex	Page
Ops (Berecinthia)	Ital.	F	1212
Pachamama	Inca	F	1224
Pandara	Bud.	F	1232
Parvati	Hin.	F	1241
Pasiphae	Gk.	F	1241
Prakriti	Hin.	F/A	1291
Proximae	Rom.	F	686
Prthivi	Hin.	F	1297
Puspa	Bud.	F	1305
Quadriviae	Rom.	F	686
Pyrrha	Gk.	F	1307
Rhea	Gk.	F	1335
Rhiannon	Bryth.	F	1336
Rigantona	Cel.	F	1338
Rusa	Arab.	F	1354
Sa'dan	Arab.	F	1360
Sakti	Bud., Hin.	F	1389
Salmaone	Aegean	F	1391
Sarasvati	Hin.	F	1400
Sarvakamadugha	Hin.	F	1401
Satet	Egy.	F	1402
Sati	Hin.	F	1402
Seimia	Syrian	F	1413
Sekhet	Egy.	F	1414
Semiramis	Assyr.	F	1415
Sharis	Urartian	F	1431
Shauska	Hittite	F	1431
Shekinah	Caba.	F	1432
Shen Mu	Chin.	F	1434
Shuki	Hin.	F	1444
Siduri	Baby.	F	1447
Sirtu	Assyr-Baby.	F	1459
Sridevi	Bud.	F	1487
Subhadra	Hin.	F	1503
Surupa	Hin.	F	1511
Tai Yuan	Chin.	F/A	1527
Tamfana	Marsi	F	1530
Tashmetu	Baby., Sum.	F	1537
Ta-urt	Egy.	F	1538
Teleia	Gk.	F	1542
Tellus Mater	Ital.	F	1542
Temazcalteci	Mex.	F	346
Terra Mater	Ital.	F	1547
Teteoinnan	Mex.	F	1548
Tham	Baby.	F	1551
Themis	Gk.	F	1553

	Culture	Sex	Page
Theotokos	Christ.	F	1554
Tiamat	Baby.	F	1570
Tonacacihuatl	Mex.	F	1586
Tonacajohua	Mex.	F	1586
Tonantzin	Mex.	F	1586
Tyche	Gk.	F	1616
Tyro	Gk.	F	1618
Tzinteotl	Mex.	A	1618
Uatlan	Kiche	F	1619
Uazit	Egy.	F	1619
Uni	Ital.	F	1625
Utset	Sia.	F	1632
Vajradhatvisvari	Bud.	F	1635
Vari-ma-te-takere	Herv. Is.	F	1320
Venus	Rom.	F	1644
Viraj	Hin.	A	1652
Virgin Mary	Christ.	F	1653
Vishnu	Hin.	A	1654
Weiwobo	Jap.	F	1672
Xochiquetzal	Mex.	F	1696
Yahsang Kahsi (Yatai)	Ind-Chin.	F	1702
Yami	Hin.	F	1700
Yin	Chin.	F	1707
Y-Mamau	Welsh	F	686
Yoni	Hin.	F	1709
Zarbanit	Baby.	F	1716
Zerpanitum	Baby.	F	1718
Zikum	Accadian	F	1720
Ziva (Zywie)	Slav.	F	1721
Zizi	Norse	F	1721

MOTHER AND DAUGHTER

Anne & Mary	Christ.	F-F	1362
Ceres & Proserpina	Rom.	F-F	305
Chaabu & Dursa	Aramaic	F-F	307
Demeter & Persephone	Gk.	F-F	429
Derceto & Semiramis	Philis.	F-F	433
Fairy Godmother & Cinderella	Folk.	F-F	545

MOTHER & SON (SEE VIRGIN MOTHER & CHILD)

MOUNTAIN

Aido Hwedo	Daho.	M	55
Amurru	Baby.	M	89

	Culture	Sex	Page
Atlas	Gk.	M	152
Banshee	Cel.	F	179
Bean Sidhe	Cel.	F	189
Cybele	Phryg.	F	400
Divje Devojke	Slav.	F	454
Fer Sidhe	Cel.	M	1447
Gahe	Apache		622
Ha-wo-gang-zang	Tib.	M	1129
Himavat	Tib.	M	771
Iztac Ciuatl	Mex.	F	854
Kagutsuchi	Jap.	M	902
Kanchenjuna Brothers	Tib.	M	907
Kubera	Bud., Hin.	M	948
Kul-lha-sha-ri	Tib.	M	1129
Labartu	Assyr.	F	957
Maia	Gk.	F	1046
Mandarangan	Philip.	M	1056
Matlalcueje	Mex.	F	1076
Matrs	Hin.	F	1076
Min	Egy.	M	1106
Nagasena	Bud.	M	1147
Naka-hsi-na	Chin.	M	1150
Nemda Prince	Fin-Ug.	M	1161
Niang Niang	Chin.	F	1167
Ninhursag	Sum.	F	1173
Noijin	Bud.	M	1179
Oh-yama-tsumi	Jap.	M	1202
Oreades	Gk.	F	1213
Pan	Gk.	M	1230
Parvati	Hin.	F	1241
Ptah-tanen	Egy.	M	1299
Ragnhild	Norse	F	705
Rana-neidda	Lapp	F	1322
Sengen Sama	Jap.	F	1416
Sennin	Jap.	M	1416
Shan Kuei	Chin.	M	1430
Shuten Doji	Jap.	M	1444
Shvaz	Arm.	M	1445
Silenus	Gk.	M	1453
Sjen	Slav.	M	1463
Skade	Norse	F/A	1463
Tai Shan	Chin.	F	1526
Tai-yo Ta-ti	Chin.	M	1527
Tengu	Jap.	M	1545
Thang-lha	Tib.	M	1129
Tobosaku	Jap.	M	1583

	Culture	Sex	Page
Tow & Tow-us-tussin	Haida	M-M	1592
Trow	Scot.	M	1600
Tse-ring Chhe-nga	Tib.	F	1603
Twanjiraka	Aus.	M	1611
Valtam	Norse	M	1643
Vegtam	Norse	M	1643
Vulcan	Rom.	M	1659
Wakonyingo	Afr.	M	1662
Yaai	Van. Is.		1697
Yamano-kami	Jap.		1699
Yama-uba	Jap.	F	1700
Yang Ching	Chin.	M	1700
Yar-lha-shang-po	Tib.	M	1129

MUSIC (SONG)

	Culture	Sex	Page
Aeolus (Eolus)	Gk.	M	40
Amphion	Gk.	M	88
Angus	Cel.	M	97
Aoide	Gk.	F	1138
Apollo	Gk.	M	110
Arche	Gk.	F	1138
Arion	Gk.	M	125
Asaph	Hebr.	M	135
Benten	Jap.	F	203
Bes	Egy.	M	205
Bragi	Norse	M	240
Bran	Bryth.	M	241
Bromius	Gk.	M	251
Camenae	Rom.	F	281
Canente	Rom.	F	285
Carmenta	Rom.	F	291
Chibiabos	Algon.	M	321
Chiron	Gk.	M	327
Ch'ui-niu	Chin.	M	335
Cleta	Gk.	F	348
Cliach	Cel.	M	348
Dactyli	Gk.	M	404
Dagda	Cel.	M	405
David	Hebr.	M	417
Demodocus	Gk.	M	430
Doon Buidhe	Cel.	F	463
Dunga	Sum.	M	482
Egder	Norse	M	491
Elf	Norse	M, F	502
Elle-folk	Norse	M, F	505
Erato	Gk.	F	518

	Culture	Sex	Page
Euterpe	Gk.	F	533
Fjorner	Norse	M	578
Gandharva	Hin.	M	626
Gunadhya	Hin.	M	698
Gweir	Bryth.	M	701
Han Hsiang-tzu	Chin.	M	722
Hermes	Gk.	M	760
Hyuki & Bil	Norse	M, F	814
Israfil	Mos.	M	847
Iuturna	Ital.	F	850
Jubal	Hebr.	M	891
Kalivinka	Jap.	M	904
Khuri Edzhin	Mong.	M	926
King Goldemar	Germ.	M	929
Kinnaras	Hin.	M	932
Krishna	Hin.	M	945
Lamech	Hebr.	M	967
Lan Ts'ai-ho	Chin.	M/A	971
Ludki (Krasnoludi)	Serb.	M, F	1021
Lug	Cel.	M	1022
Macuilxochitl	Mex.	M	1035
Marsyas	Gk.	M	1070
Melete	Gk.	F	1138
Melpomene	Gk.	M	1087
Memnon	Gk.	M	1088
Miach	Cel.	M	1097
Minerva	Rom.	F	1106
Mo-li Hai	Chin.	M	1115
Musagetes	Gk.	M	1138
Muses	Gk.	F	1138
Nakk	Fin.	M	1150
Nix	Teut.	M	1176
Nixe	Teut.	F	1176
Nomios	Gk.	M	111
Nymph	Gk.	F	1188
Oengus	Cel.	M	1198
Orpheus	Gk.	M	1216
Palaemon	Rom.	M	1227
Pan	Gk.	M	1230
Parthenope	Gk.	F	1240
Payatamu	Zuni	M	1245
Phemios	Gk.	M	1262
Philammon	Gk.	M	1262
Pied Piper of Hamelin	Germ.	M	1269
Pierides	Gk.	F	1269
Polyhymnia	Gk.	F	1284

	Culture	Sex	Page
Rhiannon	Bryth.	F	1339
Sarasvati	Bud.	F	1400
Satyr	Gk.	M	1403
Silenii	Gk.	M	1453
Siren	Gk.	F	1458
Sivirri	Aus.	M	1461
Stromkarl	Norw.	M	1501
Suttung	Norse	M	1513
Syrinx	Gk.	F	1522
Tara Bai	Hin.	F	1534
Teirtu	Welsh	M	1541
Tennin	Jap.	F	1545
Terpsichore	Gk.	F	1547
Tezcatlipoca	Mex.	M	1549
Thamyris	Gk.	M	1551
Thelxinoe	Gk.	F	1138
Thriae	Gk.	F	1566
Tristan	Bryth.	M	1599
Troubador	Fr.	M	1600
Urien	Bryth.	M	1629
Veele	Serb.	F	1643
Viracocha	Inca	M	1652
Vodni-panny	Slav.	F	1657
Volker	Norse	M	1657
Volva	Norse	F	1658
Wainamoinen	Fin.	M	1661

MUTILATED (CRUCIFIED, DISMEMBERED, EMASCULATED. ALSO SEE DYING GOD, MAIMED)

Abednego	Hebr.	M	14
Abel	Hebr., Mos.	M	14
Absalom	Hebr.	M	19
Actaeon	Gk.	M	28
Adonis	Gk.	M	34
Amfortas	Germ.	M	85
Amilias	Norse	M	86
Andrew	Christ.	M	93
Apis	Egy.	M	109
Apsu	Baby.	M	115
Attis	Phryg.	M	154
Bata	Egy.	M	185
Bel	Baby.	M	196
Bres	Cel.	M	246
Christ	Christ.	M	330
Combalus	Sem.	M	361

	Culture	Sex	Page
Cronus	Gk.	M	384
Curetes	Gk.	M	398
Doljang	Hin.	F	458
Endymion	Gk.	M	511
Eopuco	Mex.	M	53
Eshmun	Phoen.	M	525
Frey	Norse	M	609
Gawain	Bryth.	M	635
Gaya Marten	Pers.	M	636
Hagan	Norse	M	707
Heracles of Oeta	Gk.	M	755
Hylas	Gk.	M	811
Hypsistos	Gk.	M	813
Hyuki & Bil	Norse	M-F	814
Jacob	Hebr.	M	858
Jesus	Christ.	M	877
Job	Hebr., Mos.	M	882
Kagutsuchi	Jap.	M	902
Lemmini-kainen	Fin.	M	982
Lil	Sum.	M	994
Linus	Gk.	M	998
Marsyas	Gk.	M	1070
Matthias	Christ.	M	1076
Mithra	Pers.	M	1112
Mondamin	Chip.	M	1116
Moses	Hebr.	M	1126
Narcissus	Gk.	M	1158
Noah	Hebr.	M	1177
Odin	Norse	M	1195
Orpheus	Gk.	M	1216
Osiris	Egy.	M	1218
Paris	Gk.	M	1238
Peleus	Gk.	M	1250
Pelias	Gk.	M	1250
Pentheus	Gk.	M	1253
Philoctetes	Gk.	M	1263
Prajapati (Prakriti)	Hin.	M	1290
Quetzalcoatl	Mex.	M	1312
Ra	Egy.	M	1314
Rangi	Poly.	M	1322
Rath	Cel.	M	1324
Rimmon	Baby.	M	1339
Robin Hood	Eng.	M	1343
Saint Francis	Christ.	M	1369
Saint George	Christ.	M	1370
Set	Egy.	M	1420

	Culture	Sex	Page
Shwe Pyin Nyi-Naung	Ind-Chin.	M	1445
Tammuz	Baby.	M	1530
Uranus	Gk.	M	1627
Yggr	Norse	M	1706

MUTILATOR OF KIN (SEE CHILD DEVOURER, CHILD IMMOLATOR, SLAYER OF FOREBEAR, SLAYER OF LOVER OR MATE)

NAKEDNESS

Baubo	Gk.	M	187
Digambara	Hin.	F	444
Glashan	Scot.		661
Godiva	Folk.	F	668

NIGHT (SEE DARKNESS)
NIGHTMARES (SEE SLEEP)

NOBILITY (CHIVALRY)

Bhadra	Bud.	M	207
Ch'i-lin	Chin.	A	325
Galahad	Bryth.	M	622
Isengrin	Med.	M	842
Prometheus	Gk.	M	1295
Ripheus	Rom.	M	1340
Saladin	Syrian	M	1390
Satyrane	Eng.	M	1403
Sofronia	Ital.	M	1471

NOMAD (SEE WANDERER)
NURSE (SEE FOSTER PARENT)
NYMPH (SEE SPIRIT)

OBSCENITY (DEBAUCHERY, ORGIES)

Agave	Gk.	F	46
Ame-no-uzume	Jap.	F	83
Artemis of Ephesus	Gk.	F	131
Bacchantes	Gk.	F	170
Bacchus	Gk., Rom.	M	170
Corybantes	Phryg.	M	375
Cotytto	Gk.	F	376
Cybele (Dindymene)	Phryg.	F	400
Diana of Ephesus	Rom.	F	442
Dionysus	Gk.	M	447
Lamia	Gk., Lib.	F	967

Obscenity (cont.)	Culture	Sex	Page
Ma	As. Min., Baby.	F	1030
Maenad	Gk.	F	1036
Medicine Man	N.A.I.	M	1083
Nane	Arm.	F	1153
Rebecca	Hebr.	F	1326
Salome	Christ.	F	1391
Sena	Hin.	F	1416
Siva	Hin.	M	1461
Succoth-Benoth	Baby.	F	1503
Thagya Min	Ind-Chin.	M	1550
Thyiad	Gk.	F	1569
Xochiquetzal	Mex.	F	1696
Zagreus	Cretan	M	1715

OGRE (SEE DEMON)
ORACLE (SEE DIVINATION)

ORDER (ADJUSTMENT OF UNIVERSE, HARMONY)

Ashem Vahishtem	Zoro.	M	+
Concordia	Rom.	F	365
Crios	Gk.	M	382
Dagda	Cel.	M	405
Demeter	Gk.	F	429
Ennugi	Baby.	M	512
Eros	Gk.	M	522
Eunomia	Gk.	F	530
Harmonia	Gk.	F	727
Ho-ho	Chin.	M	779
Homonoia	Gk.	F	784
Horae	Gk.	F	787
Jokwa	Jap.	F	885
Maat	Egy.	F	1031
Nrtya	Bud.	F	1184
Nu Kua	Chin.	F/A	1185
Ori-hime	Jap.	F	1215
Orlog	Norse	M	+
Penelope	Gk.	F	1252
Prometheus	Gk.	M	1295
Rita	Hin.	M	1341
Soga Brothers	Jap.	M	1471
Sphinx	Egy., Gk.	F	1482
Theia	Gk.	F	1553
Thor	Norse	M	1561
T'ien-ming	Chin.	M	1571

	Culture	Sex	Page
Tutu	Baby.	M	1611
Varuna	Hin.	M	1639
Viracocha	Inca	M	1652
Yang	Chin.	M	1700

ORGIES (SEE OBSCENITY)

OTHERWORLD VISITOR (RESURREC- TION, TWICE BORN. ALSO SEE DYING GOD)

Abednego (Azariah)	Hebr.	M	14
Adonis	Gk.	M	34
Aeneas	Rom.	M	40
Af-ra	Egy.	M	43
Alcestis	Gk.	F	63
Amaethon	Bryth.	M	78
Amaterasu	Jap.	F	81
Ame-waka-hiko	Jap.	M	85
Angakok	Eskimo	M	95
Ara	Arm.	M	116
Arta Viraf	Zoro.	M	130
Artegal, Sir	Bryth.	A	130
Arthur	Bryth.	M	132
Asclepius	Gk.	M	136
Astolpho	Carol.	M	144
Attis	Phryg.	M	154
Ayar Cachi	Inca	M	163
Balder	Norse	M	174
Bata	Egy.	M	185
Bel	Baby.	M	196
Belphegor	Assyr.	M	200
Bennu	Arab.	M	202
Beowulf	Ang-Sax.	M	203
Bolverkin	Norse	M	234
Bran	Welsh	M	241
Brandan	Christ.	M	1365
Buto	Jap.	M	263
Childe Roland	Scot.	M	324
Christ	Christ.	M	330
Christmas Fool	Christ.	M	332
Cian	Cel.	M	338
Combalus	Syrian	M	361
Conan Maol	Cel.	M	364
Connla	Cel.	M	367
Cormac mac Art	Cel.	M	371
Crimthann Nia Nair	Cel.	M	382

	Culture	Sex	Page
Cuchulainn	Cel.	M	393
Daedalus	Gk.	M	404
Daire mac Fiachna	Cel.	M	407
Danae	Gk.	F	411
Daniel	Hebr.	M	413
Dietrich Von Bern	Norse	M	444
Dionysus	Gk.	M	447
Dumuzi	Sum.	M	476
Dusura	Sem.	M	477
Elidurus	Bryth.	M	503
Elisha (Eliseus)	Hebr.	M	504
Eniautes Daimon	Gk.	M	+
Fiachna	Cel.	M	564
Finn mac Coul	Cel.	M	570
Firbolgs	Cel.	M	571
Frey	Norse	M	609
Freya	Norse	F	610
Frode	Dan.	M	613
Gangraad	Norse	M	627
Gawain	Bryth.	M	635
Gilgamesh	Sum.	M	656
Glaucus	Gk.	M	662
Golishan	Christ.	M	674
Goreu	Bryth.	M	678
Greit	Bryth.	M	689
Gucumatz	Guate.	M	694
Gudrun	Germ.	F	694
Guinevere	Bryth.	F	696
Gweir	Bryth.	M	701
Gwion Bach	Cel.	M	701
Gwydion	Bryth.	M	702
Hanuman	Hin.	M	723
Harpocrates	Gk.	M	728
Havgan	Bryth.	M	732
Heimdal	Norse	M	743
Heitsi-eibib	Hotten.	M	744
Heracles	Gk.	M	752
Hercules	Rom.	M	759
Hermod	Norse	M	762
Hiawatha	N.A.I.	M	767
Hiko-hohodemi	Jap.	M	769
Hippolytus	Gk.	M	773
Hoder	Norse	M	778
Horus	Egy.	M	792
Ishtar	Assyr-Baby.	F	844
Izanagi	Jap.	M	853

	Culture	Sex	Page
Jason	Gk.	M	866
Jesus	Christ.	M	877
Jonah	Hebr.	M	886
Joseph (Yusuf)	Hebr., Mos.	M	888
Joseph of Arimathea	Christ.	M	889
Joshua	Hebr.	M	889
Julbock (Yule Buck)	Scan.	M	894
Kayak	Eskimo	M	1256
Khepera	Egy.	M	924
Kiaklo	Zuni	M	926
Kore	Gk.	F	942
Kubaiko	Tatar	F	947
Kulhwch	Welsh	M	950
Kumush	Modoc Ind.	M	951
Kunhild	Germ.	F	952
Kura	Mangaia	F	952
Kurma	Hin.	M	952
Lancelot	Bryth.	M	969
Lanval	Bryth.	M	972
Lazarus	Christ.	M	978
Little Red Riding Hood	Folk.	F	1003
Lizard	Bush.	M	1004
Llew Llaw	Bryth.	M	1005
Loegaire	Cel.	M	1008
Lo-hu-lo	Chin.	M	1010
Loki	Norse	A	1010
Mabon	Welsh	M	1031
Maelduin	Gaelic	M	1036
Marduk	Assy-Baby.	M	1065
Mataora	Poly.	M	1074
Merlin (Ambrosius)	Bryth.	M	1092
Meshach	Hebr.	M	1094
Miled	Cel.	M	1102
Mishael	Hebr.	M	1110
Mithra	Pers.	M	1112
Monotaro	Jap.	M	1118
Moses	Hebr.	M	1126
Mu-Monto	Buriat	M	1136
Nala	Hin.	M	1150
Nemda Prince	Fin-Ug.	M	1161
Noidde	Lapp	M	1179
Nyctimus	Gk.	M	1187
Odin	Norse	M	1195
Odysseus	Gk.	M	1196
Oengus	Cel.	M	1198
Ogier	Dan.	M	1200

	Culture	Sex	Page
Oisin	Cel.	M	1202
Ometochtli	Mex.	M	1208
Onatah	Iroq.	F	1209
Orestes	Gk.	M	1214
Orion	Gk.	M	1215
Orpheus	Gk.	M	1216
Osiris	Egy.	M	1218
Owain	Bryth.	M	1221
Pa-hsien	Chin.	M, F	1226
Pan	Gk.	M	1230
Pelops	Gk.	M	1251
Pergrubrius	Baltic	M	1255
Perkunas	Baltic	M	1256
Persephone	Gk.	F	1257
Phineus	Gk.	M	1264
Pied Piper of Hamelin	Germ.	M	1269
Pradyumna	Hin.	M	1290
Proserpina	Rom.	F	1296
Protesilaus	Gk.	M	1297
Psyche	Gk.	F	1299
Pwyll	Bryth.	M	1306
Quetzalcoatl	Mex.	M	1312
Ra	Egy.	M	1314
Rama	Hin.	M	1321
Rata	Maori	M	1323
Rhampsinitus	Gk.	M	1335
Rishyacringa	Hin.	M	1341
Robin Hood	Eng.	M	1343
Saint Brandan	Christ.	M	1365
Saint George	Christ.	M	1370
Samson	Hebr.	M	1394
Semele	Gk.	F	1415
Shadrach	Hebr.	M	1428
Siegfried	Germ.	M	1448
Sigmund	Norse	M	1449
Sita	Hin.	F	1460
Sophia	Gnostic	F	1475
Stutly, Will	Eng.	M	1502
Svipdag	Norse	M	1515
Tajima-mori	Jap.	M	1527
Taliesin	Bryth.	M	1528
Tammuz	Baby.	M	1530
Tane	Poly.	M	1531
Tannhauser	Germ.	M	1532
Tezcatlipoca	Mex.	M	1549
Theseus	Gk.	M	1554

	Culture	Sex	Page
Thor	Norse	A	1561
Thorkill	Dan.	M	1561
Thyone	Gk.	F	1569
Troll	Norse	M	1600
Tsui Goab	Hotten.	M	1604
Urashima Taro	Jap.	M	1628
Vainamoinen	Fin.	M	1634
Vipascit	Hin.	M	1651
Viracocha	Inca	M	1652
Virbius	Rom.	M	1652
Votan	Mex.	M	1658
Wainamoinen	Fin.	M	1661
Xbalanque	Kiche	M	1695
Xochipilli-Cinteotl	Mex.	M	1696
Xolotl	Mex.	M	1697
Yamato-take	Jap.	M	1699
Yudhisthira	Hin.	M	1711
Zagreus	Gk.	M	1715
Zatik	Arm.	M	1716
Zoroaster	Zoro.	M	1734
OUTLAW			
Achan	Hebr.	M	24
Adam Bell	Eng.	M	30
Agamedes	Gk.	M	44
Aitherne	Cel.	M	57
Alberich	Norse	M	62
Amaethon	Bryth.	M	78
Apaches	Fr.	M, F	1114
Apaharavarman	Hin.	M	106
Arimaspians	Gk.	M	124
Armstrong, Johnnie	Scot.	M	128
Autolycus	Gk.	M	159
Azucena	Ital.	M	166
Barabras	Christ.	M	180
Berchta	Christ.	F	203
Bill Sikes	Eng.	M	211
Cacus	Rom.	M	265
Cain	Christ., Hebr., Mos.	M	269
Cercopes	Gk.	M	304
Claude Duval	Eng.	M	346
Clym of the Clough	Eng.	M	351
Continh	Anamese	F	368
Cutpurse, Moll	Eng.	F	400
Cyclops	Gk.	M	400

	Culture	Sex	Page
Cyllenius	Gk.	M	401
Diavolo (Fra Diavolo)	Ital.	M	443
Dick Turpin	Eng.	M	443
Dismas	Christ.	M	451
Don Cesar De Bazan	Fr.	M	461
Dumachus	Christ.	M	451
Dysnomie	Gk.	F	481
Fomor	Cel.	M	590
Forty Thieves	Arab.	M	598
Gestas (Gesmas)	Christ.	M	647
Ghino di Tacco	Ital.	M	652
Gilderoy	Scot.	M	656
Haiduk	Slav.	M	708
Hermes	Gk.	M	760
Jack Sheppard	Eng.	M	857
Jephthah	Hebr.	M	872
Jeremy Diddler	Eng.	M	873
Jesse James	Am. Folk.	M	876
Jonathan Wild	Eng.	M	886
Kaches	Arm.	M, F	900
Kallan	Hin.	M	904
Katipunero	Philip.	M	913
Kinmont, Willie	Scot.	M	932
Kirkrapine	Eng.	M	933
Klepht	Gk.	M	936
Laverna	Rom.	F	977
Lazarillo de Tormes	Span.	M	+
Loki	Norse	M/A	1010
Long John Silver	Eng.	M	1012
Macheath, Capt.	Eng.	M	1034
Mahu	Scot.	M	1046
Mercury	Rom.	M	1091
Mohocks	Eng.	M	1114
Molly	Eng.	F	1115
Nana Sahib	Hin.	M	+
Nanga	Poly.	M	1153
Nevison	Eng.	M	1166
Nibelungen	Norse	M	1167
Panis	Hin.	M	1233
Para	Fin-Ug.	M	1236
Peachum	Eng.	M	1246
Periphetes	Gk.	M	1256
Phansigar (Thug)	Hin.	M	1567
Poshaiyanne	Pueblo	M	1288
Punk	Esthonian	M	1305
Raffles	Eng.	M	1317

	Culture	Sex	Page
Ragnar Lodbrog	Norse	M	1317
Rephaim	Hebr.	M	1332
Rhampsinitus' Robbers	Gk.	M	1335
Riihitonttu	Fin-Ug.	M	1339
Robert Macaire	Fr.	M	1342
Robin Hood	Eng.	M	1343
Robin of Bagshot	Eng.	M	1343
Rob Roy	Scot.	M	1343
Rudra	Hin.	M	1353
Sansloy	Eng.	M	1397
Scapin	Fr.	M	1405
Sciron	Gk.	M	1407
Scythian (Arimaspi)	Gk.	M, F	1410
Set	Egy.	M	1420
Sextus	Rom.	M	1427
Shifty Lad	Scot.	M	1436
Sigi	Norse	M	1449
Sikes, Bill	Eng.	M	1452
Smiera-Gatto	Lapp		1468
Suti	Baby.	M	1513
Tezcatlipoca	Mex.	M	1549
Thrym	Norse	M	1567
Titans	Gk.	M, F	1577
Titus	Christ.	M	1580
Troll	Germ.	M	1600
Trophonius	Gk.	M	1600
Tung Fang So	Chin.	M	1607
Turpin, Dick	Eng.	M	1609
Twitcher, Jemmy	Eng.	M	1615
Vahagn	Arm.	M	1634
Vanni Fucci	Ital.	M	1638
Varangian	Norse	M	1639
Vautrin (Jacques Collin)	Fr.	M	1642
Viking	Norse	M, F	1650
William of Cloudeslee	Eng.	M	1680
Yehl	Alaskan	M	1703
Zu	Baby., Sum.	M	1734

PAIN (ANGUISH)

	Culture	Sex	Page
Angerona	Ital.	F	96
Angra Mainyu	Zoro.	M	97

PALADIN (SEE HERO)
PATHFINDER (SEE DEATH)

PEACE	Culture	Sex	Page
Balder	Norse	M	174
Concordia	Rom.	F	365
Eir	Norse	F	496
Eirene (Irene)	Gk.	F	496
Frey	Norse	M	609
Frode	Dan.	M	613
Geide	Cel.	M	638
Harmonia	Gk.	F	727
Hesychia	Gk.	F	+
Hiawatha	N.A.I.	M	767
Homonoia	Gk.	F	784
Hu	Bryth.	M	800
Janus	Rom.	M	864
Makaravaktra	Bud.	F	1047
Nerthus	Dan.	F	1165
Nissyen	Bryth.	M	1176
Nrtya	Bud.	F	1184
Pax	Rom.	F	1245
Phra In	Siam.	M	1266
Puspa	Bud.	F	1305
Quetzalcoatl	Mex.	M	1312
Shou Hsing	Chin.	M	1442
Ur-Nammu	Sum.	M	1630
Usnisavijaya	Bud.	F	1631
Vidar	Norse	M	1649

PESTILENCE (SEE DISEASE)

PHALLUS (PHALLIC WORSHIP. ALSO SEE MALE PRINCIPLE)

Chong-wang	Chin.	M	329
Frey	Norse	M	609
Iacchus	Gk.	M	815
Mul-lil	Accadian	M	1135
Nazi	Sum.	M	1159
Phallus	Gk.	M	1261
Yarilo	Rus.	M	1701

PILGRIM (SEE QUESTER, TRAVELER, WANDERER)
PITY (SEE ABSTRACTIONS)
PLANETS (SEE ASTRAL)
PLANT (SEE TREE)
PLEASURE (SEE HAPPINESS)

POETRY	Culture	Sex	Page
Aoide	Gk.	F	1138
Apollo	Gk.	M	110
Arche	Gk.	F	1138
Arion	Gk.	M	125
Aristeas	Gk.	M	125
Blihos-Bliheris	Bryth.	M	225
Bragi	Norse	M	240
Bran	Cel.	M	241
Bridget	Christ.	F	249
Brigit	Cel.	F	249
Calliope	Gk.	F	278
Camenae	Rom.	F	281
Caoilte mac Ronan	Cel.	M	287
Ch'u Yuan	Chin.	M	337
Clio	Gk.	F	348
Corpre	Cel.	M	374
Daphnis	Gk.	M	414
David	Hebr.	M	417
Demodocus	Gk.	M	430
Erato	Gk.	F	518
Euterpe	Gk.	F	533
Faunus	Rom.	M	552
Fjalar	Norse	M	578
Fjorner	Norse	M	578
Galar	Norse	M	623
Gunadhya	Hin.	M	698
Gunlad	Norse	F	698
Homer	Gk.	M	783
Kvaser	Norse	M	954
Lug	Cel.	M	1022
Melpomene	Gk.	F	1087
Minerva	Rom.	F	1106
Mneme	Gk.	F	1138
Musagetes	Gk.	M	1138
Muses	Gk.	F	1138
Odin	Norse	M	1195
Odrerer	Norse		1196
Ogma	Cel.	M	1200
Ogyrvran	Bryth.	M	1201
Oilioil	Cel.	M	1202
Oisin	Cel.	M	1202
Orpheus	Gk.	M	1216
Pierides	Gk.	F	1269
Polyhymnia	Gk.	F	1284
Raminagrobis	Fr.	M	1321
Saint Bridget	Christ.	F	1366

Poetry (cont.)	Culture	Sex	Page
Sarasvati	Bud.	F	1400
Taliesin	Welsh	M	1528
Thalia	Gk.	F	1551
Thomas the Rhymer	Scot.	M	1560
Troubador	Fr.	M	1600
Tyrtaeus	Gk.	M	1618
Urania	Gk.	F	1627
Urien	Bryth.	M	1629
Valmiki	Hin.	M	1637
Van-xuong	Ind-Chin.	M	1638
POVERTY			
Bimbogami	Jap.	M	211
Christ	Christ.	M	330
Ciuateotl	Mex.	F	346
Gautama	Bud.	M	255
Jesus	Christ.	M	877
Job	Hebr., Mos.	M	882
Nintoku	Jap.	M	1174
Sakyamuni	Bud.	M	1390
PRESUMPTION (SEE INTEMPERANCE)			
PRIDE			
Arachne	Gk.	F	116
Kandarpa	Hin.	M	905
Lucifer	Christ.	M	1020
Lucifera	Eng.	F	1020
Marsyas	Gk.	M	1070
Naonghaithya	Zoro.	M	1154
Niobe	Gk.	F	1174
Ono-no-komachi	Jap.	F	1210
Rehoboam	Hebr.	M	1331
Satan	Christ., Hebr.	M	1402
Shedad	Mos.	M	1432
Solomon	Hebr.	M	1472
Tarquinius	Rom.	M	1536
Tengu	Jap.	M	1545
Thersites	Gk.	M	1554
Thraso	Rom.	M	1563
Uzzah	Hebr.	M	1633
Zeresh	Hebr/Pers.	F	1718
PRIMORDIAL			
Adibuddha	Bud.	M	32

	Culture	Sex	Page
Aether	Rom.	F	42
Amanominaka	Jap.	M	80
Amenotoko	Jap.	F	83
Anshar	Baby.	M	101
Ao-marama	Poly.		106
Ao-tu-roa	Poly.		106
Apsu	Baby.	M	115
Atanua	So. Is.	F	148
Atea	So. Is.	M	149
Atman	Hin.	M	152
Awonawilona	Zuni	M	162
Brhaspati	Hin.	M	247
Bunjel	Aus.		261
Chaos	Baby., Gk.	M/A	312
Chinun Way Shen	Burm.	M	899
Cronus	Gk.	M	384
Dies	Rom.	M	444
Dyaus & Prithivi	Hin.	M-F	479
Echo	Poly.		489
Emen	Egy.	M	915
Haumai-Tikitiki	Maori	M	732
Hemset	Egy.	F	750
Her-shef	Egy.	M	763
Hiranya-garbha	Hin.	M	774
Hometeuli	Mex.	M	784
Hu	Bryth.	M	800
Huehueteotl	Mex.	M	802
Huitznahua	Mex.	M	803
IAO	Gnostic	M	815
Ikuguhi	Jap.	F	822
In	Jap.	F	827
Io	Mex., N. Zeal.		835
Ishi	Phoen.		843
Izanagi & Izanami	Jap.	M-F	853
Jehovah	Hebr.	M	870
Ka	Burmese	M	899
Kadru	Hin.	A	901
Kamu-mimusubi	Jap.	F	907
Keh	Egy.	M	915
Kek & Keket	Egy.	M-F	915
Kekui & Kekuit	Egy.	M-F	916
Kerh & Kerhet	Egy.	M-F	918
Khepera	Egy.	M	924
Kishar	Baby.	F	933
Kore-te-rawea	Poly.	A	942
Kore-te-tamaua	Poly.	A	942

	Culture	Sex	Page
Kore-te-whiwhia	Poly.	A	942
Kuni-toko-tachi	Jap.	M	952
Ku Shen	Chin.		953
Lachmu & Lachamu	Baby.	M-F	961
Lukelang	Caro. Is.	M	1027
Mahat	Hin.		1044
Mahora-nui-a-tea	Poly.	F	1045
Maku	Poly.	M	1048
Mashya & Mashoyi	Pers.	M-F	1072
Monad	Chin.	M-F	1116
Mutuhei	So. Is.	M	1531
Nanai	Baby.	F	1152
Narayana	Hin.	M	1155
Nau	Egy.	M	1157
Nu	Egy.	A	1184
Oceanus	Gk.	M	1193
Ogdoad	Egy.	M, F	1200
Oho-to-no-ji & Oho-to-no-be	Jap.	M-F	1202
Omo-daru & Aya-kashiko-ne	Jap.	M-F	1208
Omorka	Baby.	F	1208
Ono	So. Is.	M	1210
Ophion & Eurynome	Gk.	M-F	1212
Ormuzd	Zoro.	M	1216
Pa-hra	Egy.	M	1226
Papa	Poly.	F	1235
Phanes	Gk.	M	1261
Po	Poly.	F	1281
Po-begat-te-ao	Poly.		106
Pourushaspa	Pers.	M	1290
Prajapati (Prakriti)	Hin.	A	1290
Protogonos	Gk.	A	1297
Ptah	Egy.	M	1299
Purusa	Hin.	A	1305
Qeb (Seb)	Egy.	M	1309
Rail	Pelew Is.	M	1319
Rigi	Micro.	M	1339
Samantabdahra	Bud.	M	1393
Sesa	Hin.	M	1420
Shuhiji	Jap.	F	1444
Siyakmak & Nashak	Pers.	M-F	1463
Sophia	Gnostic	F	1475
Svabhava	Hin.	M	1514
Svayambhu	Bud., Hin.	M	1515
Taaroa	Poly.	M	1522
T'ai I Ching	Chin.	M	1525
Tai-kih	Chin.	A	1525

	Culture	Sex	Page
Tai Yuan	Chin.	F/A	1527
Taka-mimusubi	Jap.	M	1527
Tanaoa	So. Is.	M	1531
Tane	Poly.	M	1531
Tangaroa	Poly.	M	1531
Tauthe & Apason	Baby.	M-F	1539
Te-ao	Poly.	M	1540
Te-kore	N. Zeal.	A	1541
Th	Phoen.		1550
Thrita Athwya	Pers.	M	1566
Tiamat	Baby.	F	1570
Tiki	Maori	M	1573
Tiki-ahua	Marq.	M	1573
Tonacatecutli	Mex.	M	1586
Tsunu-guhi	Jap.	M	1604
Tuisco	Germ.	M	1606
Tu Metua	Herv. Is.		1607
Tzinteotl	Mex.	A	1618
Uhiji	Jap.	M	1620
Umashi-ashi-kabi-ji	Jap.	M	1622
Uranus	Gk.	M	1627
Ur-kuh	Pers.		1629
Vajradhara	Tib.	M	1634
Vari-mate-takere	Herv. Is.	F	1320
Vasuki	Hin.	M	1641
Vatea	Herv. Is.	M	1641
Viracocha	Inca	M	1652
Viraj	Hin.	A	1652
Vishnu-Narayana	Hin.	A	1655
Vivanghvant	Pers.	M	1656
Vivasvant	Hin.	M	1656
Whai-tua	N. Zeal.		1674
Woge	Yurok Ind.	M, F	1688
Wohpekumen	Yurok Ind.	M	1688
Wu-chi	Chin.	A	1693
Yama	Hin.	M	1699
Yami	Hin.	F	1700
Yang	Chin.	M	1700
Yatai	Ind-Chin.	F	1702
Yatawn	Ind-Chin.	M	1702
Yin	Chin.	F	1707
Ymir	Norse	M	1708
Yoni-Lingam	Hin.	F-M	1709

PROGENITOR (ALSO SEE CULTURE HERO)	Culture	Sex	Page
Ad	Mos.	M	28
Adam	Hebr., Mos.	M	29
Adam Kadmon	Caba.	M	30
Adapa	Baby.	M	30
Aeneas	Rom.	M	40
Aeolus	Gk.	M	40
Ag-mena	Egy.	M	49
Airya (Iraj)	Pers.	M	57
Aksak	Chaco	M	60
Alalkomeneus	Gk.	M	61
Alban	Bryth.	M	62
Alulim (Aloros)	Sum.	M	77
Ama	Sum.	F	78
Amaterasu	Jap.	F	81
Ame-waka-hiko	Jap.	M	85
Amma	Norse	F	86
Ammon	Hebr.	M	86
Anak	Hebr.	M	91
Anshar	Baby.	M	101
Apason & Tauthe	Baby.	M-F	107
Apo	Pers.	M	109
Apocatequil	Inca	M	109
Ar-soghotch	Yakut	M	130
Ashiwi	Zuni	M, F	139
Askr	Norse	M	141
Aslog	Norse	F	141
Assher	Hebr.	M	740
Ataentsic (Eagentci)	Huron	F	147
Atarhasis	Baby.	M	148
Atraioman	Carib. Ind.	M	153
Atse Hastin & Atse Estsan	Nav.	M-F	153
Benjamin	Hebr.	M	202
Bergelmir	Norse	M	204
Bhrigu	Hin.	M	209
Bile	Cel.	M	211
Boaz	Hebr.	M	232
Bor	Norse	M	236
Bregon	Cel.	M	246
Cadmus	Gk.	M	266
Cairima	Cel.	M	271
Cecrops	Gk.	M	301
Chanun & Woi-shun	Chin.	M-F	312
Chavah	Hebr.	F	317
Cipactonal & Oxomuco	Mex.	M-F	341
Closed Man	Pawnee	M	349

	Culture	Sex	Page
Comizahual	Honduras	F	362
Curetes	Gk.	M	398
Dan	Hebr.	M	410
Dazbog	Rus.	M	420
Debabou & De-ai	Gil. Is.	M-F	422
Deucalion	Gk.	M	434
Dorus	Gk.	M	465
Edda	Norse	F	490
Edji	Altaic	F	491
Edom	Hebr.	M	491
Eleusis	Gk.	M	502
Embla	Norse	F	507
Epaphus	Gk.	M	514
Ephraim	Hebr.	M	515
Erlik	Tatar	M	521
E-U	Burm.	F	529
Eve	Hebr.	F	534
Fenius Farsa	Cel.	M	560
Foam Woman	Haida Ind.	F	589
Fravak & Fravakain	Pers.	M-F	608
Gad	Hebr.	M	620
Garamas	Garamantes	M	628
Gaya Maretan	Pers.	M	636
Gayomart	Pers.	M	636
Goidel	Cel.	M	670
Guamansuri	Inca	M	693
Gurikhoisib	Hotten.	A	699
Hagar	Hebr.	F	707
Ham	Hebr.	M	713
Haoshyangha & Guzhak	Pers.	M-F	723
Harmonia	Gk.	F	727
Heber	Hebr.	M	739
Heimdal	Norse	M	743
Hellen	Gk.	M	749
Hian	Kei Is.	M	766
Hi-asa	Admir. Is.	F	766
Hina	Marq.	F	771
Huan Ching	Chin.	M	801
Hu Gadarn	Welsh	M	802
Hurakan	Kiche	M	808
Iapetus	Gk.	M	816
Ila	Hin.	F	823
Inapertwa	Aus.		827
Ingun	Norse	M/A	831
Ion	Gk.	M	837
Iowahine	Hawa.	F	837

	Culture	Sex	Page
Israel	Hebr.	M	847
Ith	Cel.	M	848
Iztac Mixcoatl	Mex.	M	854
Japheth	Hebr.	M	865
Jarl	Norse	M	865
Jesse	Hebr.	M	876
Jimmu Tennu	Jap.	M	880
Judah	Hebr.	M	892
Kaboi	Bol., Braz.	M	900
Kalinago	Carib Ind.	M	904
Karwar	Papuan	M	911
Kasyapa	Hin.	M	912
Kedar	Hebr.	M	915
Kezer-tshingis	Tatar	M	921
King Dushyanta	Hin.	M	208
Kintu	Uganda	M	932
Kisani	Nav.	M	933
Kishar	Baby.	F	933
Kybai-khotun	Yakut	F	956
La'i-La'i	Poly.	F	964
Lan-yein & A-mong	Burm.	M-F	972
Latinus	Rom.	M	975
Lelex	Gk.	M	982
Lesbos	Gk.	M	985
Levi	Hebr.	M	988
Leza	Bantu	M	989
Lif	Norse	F	992
Lifthrasir	Norse	M	992
Ligoapup	Micro.	F	993
Lingam & Yoni	Hin.	M-F	998
Louquo	Carib Ind.	M	1016
Magog	Cel.	F	1041
Maiso	Braz.	F	1047
Mama Ogllo	Inca	F	1051
Manasseh	Hebr.	M	1055
Manco Capac	Inca	M	1056
Mannus	Norse	M	1060
Manu	Hin.	M	1061
Manuai	Admir. Is.	M	1062
Ma-riko-riko	N. Zeal.	F	1067
Mashya & Mashoyi	Pers.	M-F	1072
Menaka	Hin.	M	1088
Michabo (Messon)	Algon.	M	1098
Midian	Hebr.	M	1100
Miled	Cel.	M	1102
Minyas	Gk.	M	1107

	Culture	Sex	Page
Mioya-no-kami	Jap.	M	1108
Mitsotsozini	Pokomo	M	1113
Mizraim	Hebr.	M	1113
Mogthraser	Norse	M	1114
Morna (Goll mac Morna)	Cel.	M	1124
Nambi	Uganda	F	1151
Nane Chaha	Choctaw		1153
Naphtali	Hebr.	M	1154
Ndengei	Fiji	M	1159
Nemed	Cel.	M	1162
Ninigi	Jap.	M	1173
Noah	Hebr.	M	1177
Noj	Asian	M	1179
Nowutset	Sia Ind.	F	1183
Nu Kua	Chin.	F/A	1185
Nyakang	Egy.	M	1187
Oho-kuni-nushi	Jap.	M	1621
Oilioil	Cel.	M	1202
Okikurumi (Ainu-rak-kur)	Ainu	M	1203
Oxomuco	Mex.	F	1223
Pairekse	Ostiak	M	1226
Pandora	Gk.	F	1232
Parpara	Kei Is.	M	1239
Partholan	Cel.	M	1240
Pelasgus	Gk.	M	1249
Phoroneus	Gk.	M	1266
Phut	Hebr.	M	1267
Picus	Rom.	M	1269
Piguero	Inca	M	109
Pitri	Hin.	M	1276
Pitripati	Hin.	M	1276
Prometheus	Gk.	M	1295
Pwan-choo	Chin.	M	1306
Pyrrha	Gk.	F	1307
Quoots-hooi	Chinook	F	1314
Ra	Egy.	M	1314
Rahab	Hebr.	F	1318
Rangi & Papa	Poly.	M-F	1322
Remus	Rom.	M	1332
Reuben	Hebr.	M	1334
Ribimbi	Transvaal	M	1337
Rod & Rozanice	Rus.	M-F	1344
Rongo	Mangaian	M	1347
Sakuntala	Hin.	F	1389
Scota (Beara)	Scot.	F	1408
Seming	Norse	M	1415

Progenitor (cont.)	Culture	Sex	Page
Seth	Hebr.	M	1421
Shippawn Ayawng	Burm.		1439
Simeon	Hebr.	M	1454
Singalang Burong	Borneo	M	1457
Steingud	Norse	F	1493
Sugar Cane	Mel.		1504
Tages	Ital.	M	1524
Tagtug (Tibir)	Sum.	M	1524
Tahsek-khi & Yahsek-khi	Ind-Chin.	M-F	1525
Tamoi (Tamusi)	Tupi-Guar.	M	1531
Tata	Sib.	M	1537
Tazh & Tazhak	Pers.	M-F	1539
Teharonhiawagon	Iroq.	M	1541
Thanai	Burm.	M	1551
Tii	Marq.	M	1573
Tiki-ahua	Hawa.	M	1573
Tiki-kapakapa	N. Zeal.	F	1573
Toltec	Mex.	M	1585
Torongoi	Altaic	M	1589
Tura	Pers.	M	1608
Ujikami	Jap.	M	1621
Unkulunkulu	Zulu	M	1626
Utset	Sia Ind.	F	1632
Vere	Pokomo (Afr.)	M	1646
Wiyot (Luiseno)	Calif. Ind.	M	1688
Wohpekumen	Yurok	M	1688
Xmukane	Mex.	F	1696
Yama & Yami	Hin.	M-F	1699
Yima & Yimeh	Pers.	M-F	1707
Yo & In	Jap.	M-F	1708

PROPHECY (SEE DIVINATION)
PROSPERITY (SEE WEALTH)
PROTECTIVE ANCESTOR (SEE SPIRIT)

PROTECTOR (CITY DEFENDER, SPEAKING HEAD. ALSO SEE SLEEPER)

Adam	Hebr., Mos.	M	29
Alad	Baby.	M	60
Allat	Sem.	F	69
Anat	Sem.	F	91
Apollo	Gk.	M	110
Arthur	Bryth.	M	132
Atargatis	Sem.	F/A	148
Bach-ma	Ind-Chin.	M	171
Barbarossa	Germ.	M	180

	Culture	Sex	Page
Bran	Bryth.	M	241
Cao-bien	Ind-Chin.	M	287
Charlemagne	Frankish	M	314
Conaire	Cel.	M	363
Eurystheus	Gk.	M	533
James the Great	Christ.	M	862
John the Baptist	Christ.	M	1372
Keresaspa	Pers.	M	918
Kirttimukha	Hin.	M	933
Lha-mo-kar-po	Tib.	F	989
Ma-vien (Bach-ma)	Chin.	M	1078
Memnon	Gk.	M	1088
Mimir	Norse	M	1105
Nana	Sum.	F	1152
Ops	Ital.	F	1212
Orpheus	Gk.	M	1216
Roderick	Span.	M	1344
Saint James the Great	Christ.	M	1372
Saint Januarius	Christ.	M	1373
Sebastian	Portu.	M	1381
Sol Invictus	Rom.	M	1471
Sualtam	Cel.	M	1503
Tyche	Gk.	F	1616
Urdawl Ben	Welsh	M	1628

QUESTER (ALSO SEE TRAVELER, WANDERER)

	Culture	Sex	Page
Argonauts	Gk.	M	121
Asclepius	Gk.	M	136
Balthazar	Christ.	M	1364
Castor & Pollux	Gk.	M-M	295
Cepheus	Gk.	M	304
Ceres	Rom.	F	305
Cessair	Cel.	F	306
Chung-li-ch'uan	Chin.	M	336
Cilix	Gk.	M	339
Damayanti	Hin.	F	409
Demeter	Gk.	F	429
Euphemus	Gk.	M	531
Evelake	Christ.	M	534
Finntain	Cel.	M	570
Fortunio	Folk.	F	596
Fraoch	Cel.	M	607
Freydis	Norse	F	611
Galahad	Bryth.	M	622
Gareth	Bryth.	M	629

	Culture	Sex	Page
Gargantua	Fr.	M	630
Gaspar	Christ.	M	1370
Gawain	Bryth.	M	635
Glaucus	Gk.	M	662
Hanno & Himilco	Carth.	M-M	722
Heracles	Gk.	M	752
Idas	Gk.	M	818
Isis	Egy.	F	845
Izanagi	Jap.	M	853
Jason	Gk.	M	866
Lancelot	Bryth.	M	969
Launfal	Bryth.	M	976
Lynceus	Gk.	M	1028
Maelduin	Gaelic	M	1036
Mataora	Poly.	M	1074
Melchior	Christ.	M	1085
Meleager	Gk.	M	1085
Mopsus	Gk.	M	1122
Moses	Hebr.	M	1126
Mytyl	Belg.	F	1144
Odysseus	Gk.	M	1196
Oileus	Gk.	M	1202
Orpheus	Gk.	M	1216
Percival	Bryth.	M	1254
Peredur	Bryth.	M	1254
Perithous	Gk.	M	1256
Philoctetes	Gk.	M	1263
Pirithous	Gk.	M	1275
Polyphemus	Gk.	M	1284
Psyche	Gk.	F	1299
Pururavas	Hin.	M	1304
Qat	Mel.	M	1309
Quixote, Don.	Span.	M	462
Rata	Maori	M	1323
Rogero	Ital.	M	773
Saint Brandan	Christ.	M	1365
Siegfried	Germ.	M	1448
Sigurd	Norse	M	1451
Skirnir	Norse	M	1465
Succoth-Benoth	Baby.	F	1503
Tannhauser	Germ.	M	1532
Telamon	Gk.	M	1541
Telemachus	Gk.	M	1542
Telephassa	Gk.	F	1542
Teucer	Gk.	M	1549
Theseus	Gk.	M	1554

	Culture	Sex	Page
Three Magi	Christ.	M	1565
Tyltyl	Belg.	M	1617
Ulysses	Rom.	M	1622
Vikings	Norse	M, F	1650
Wainamoinen	Fin.	M	1661

RAGE (SEE WRATH)
RAIN (SEE MOISTURE)

RASHNESS

	Culture	Sex	Page
Icarus	Gk.	M	817
Patroclus	Gk.	M	1244
Phaethon	Gk.	M	1260
Salmoneus	Gk.	M	1391

RAYS

	Culture	Sex	Page
Absyrtus	Gk.	M	20
Accolon	Bryth.	M	23
Achates	Rom.	M	24
Angantyr	Norse	M	95
Ashi	Hin.	F	139
Balaha	Bud.	M	174
Blodughofi	Norse	M	226
Chaus	Bryth.	M	316
Chrysaor	Gk.	M	334
Excalibur	Bryth.		536
Failinis	Cel.		544
Feinn	Cel.	M	558
Gandharva	Hin.	M	626
Gareth	Bryth.	M	629
Gijigouai	Algon.	M	656
Gisl	Ice.	M	660
Goibniu	Cel.	M	670
Guatauva	Taino	M	694
Gullfaxi	Norse	M	697
Gullinbursti	Norse	M	697
Gungnir	Norse		698
Gwadyn Odyeith	Bryth.	M	700
Hayhuaypanti	Inca		734
Hringhorn	Norse		798
Hrunting	Ang-Sax.		799
Huaminca	Inca	M	801
Joyeuse	Med. Lit.		891
Karshipta	Pers.	M	911
Kerkios	Gk.	M	918
Laegaire	Cel.	M	963

Rays (cont.)	Culture	Sex	Page
Lamfada	Cel.	M	967
Lampetus	Gk.	M	969
Lemminikainen	Fin.	M	982
Loegaire	Cel.	M	1008
Luchta	Cel.	M	1020
Maasewe & Uyuuyewe	Sia Ind.	M-M	1031
Menglod	Norse	F	1089
Myrmidon	Gk.	M	1142
Neamhuain Clan	Cel.	M	1159
Nusku	Baby.	M	1187
Papachtic	Mex.	M	1235
Patroclus	Gk.	M	1244
Phaethon	Gk.	M	1260
Phol (Pol)	Norse	M	1266
Ra	Egy.	M	1314
Scarlet, Will	Eng.	M	1406
Sinfjotle	Norse	M	1457
Skirnir	Norse	M	1465
Stutly, Will	Eng.	M	1502
Sudhanvan	Hin.	M	1503
Surtr	Norse	M	1511
Surya	Hin.	M	1511
Telephassa	Gk.	F	1542
Telephus	Gk.	M	1542
Teucer	Gk.	M	1549
Tiphys	Gk.	M	1575
Toltec	Mex.	M	1585
Tyr	Teut.	M	1617
Urvakshaya	Pers.	M	1630
Vareghna	Pers.	M	1639
Verethraghna	Pers.	M	1646
Vijaya Sakti	Bud.	F	1649
Vispala	Hin.	M	1655
Ychdryt Varyvdraws	Bryth.	M	1702

REJECTED (SEE RENOUNCED BY PARENT)

RENOUNCED BY PARENT (DESPISED, REJECTED, ALSO SEE ABANDONED CHILD)

Atalanta	Gk.	F	148
Danae	Gk.	F	411
David	Hebr.	M	417
Grettir	Ice.	M	690
Hippolytus	Gk.	M	773
Shakuntala	Hin.	F	1429
Tenedos	Gk.	M	1264
Tenes	Gk.	M	1545

	Culture	Sex	Page
Zeus	Gk.	M	1719

RESURRECTION (SEE OTHERWORLD VISITOR)

REVELRY (BUFFOONERY, COMIC, FROLICSOMENESS, JESTING, MERRYMAKING, RIBALDRY, RIDICULE)

	Culture	Sex	Page
Addephagia	Rom.	F	31
Aglaia	Gk.	F	48
Ame-no-uzuine (Otafuku)	Jap.	F	83
Bacchant	Gk., Rom.	M	170
Bacchante (Bacchae)	Gk., Rom.	F	170
Balmarcodes	Phoen.	M	176
Baubo	Gk.	M/F	187
Bes	Egy.	M	205
Cercopes	Gk.	M	304
Comus	Rom.	M	363
Curetes	Gk.	M	398
Dactyli	Gk.	M	404
Droll	Norse	M	471
Eulenspiegel, Tyll	Germ.	M	529
Evan	Gk.	M	533
Friar John	Fr.	M	611
Friar Tuck	Bryth.	M	611
Iambe	Gk.	F	815
Ixcuina	Mex.	F	852
Javerzaharses	Arm.	F	867
Jonathan Ploughboy	Am. Drama	M	886
Kay, Sir	Bryth.	M	914
King of Saturnalia	Rom.	M	930
Lord of Misrule	Eng.	M	1013
Lothario	Eng.	M	1014
Lot Sap Sago	Am. Drama	M	1014
Lovelace	Eng.	M	1018
Momus	Gk.	M	1116
Moquequeloa	Mex.	M	1122
Mullin	Med. Lit.	M	432
Napaeae	Gk.	F	1154
Nataraja	Hin.	M	1461
Otafuku	Jap.	F	1219
Pantagruel	Fr.	M	1234
Panurge	Fr.	M	1235
Phuphlans	Ital.	M	1267
Pierrot	Fr.	M	1270
Polichinelle	Fr.	M	1283

Revelry (cont.)	Culture	Sex	Page
Puck	Eng.	M	1300
Punch & Judy	Eng. Drama	M-F	1301
Punchinello & Judith	Ital.	M-F	1301
Pusong	Philip.	M	1305
Pwcca	Welsh	M	1300
Raven	Pac. Coast	M	1325
Robin Hood	Eng.	M	1343
Satyr	Gk.	M	1403
Scapin	Fr.	M	1405
Scapino	Ital.	M	1405
Shojo	Jap.	M	1441
Silenus	Gk.	M	1453
Silvanus	Rom.	M	1453
Siris	Baby.	A	1459
Solomon Gundy	Am. Drama	M	1473
Solomon Swap	Am. Drama	M	1473
Solon Shingle	Am. Drama	M	1473
Strenia	Rom.	F	1500
Sylvanus	Rom.	M	1521
Tannhauser	Germ.	M	1532
Thalia	Gk.	F	1551
Tuck, Friar	Bryth.	M	1606
Vice	Eng.	M	1648
Xolotl	Mex.	M	1697
Zany	Eng.	M	1716

RIBALDRY (SEE REVELRY)

RIDDLE SOLVER			
Abdemon	Hebr.	M	13
Aoshnara	Pers.	M	106
Gunasarman	Hin.	M	698
Joseph (Yusuf)	Hebr., Mos.	M	888
Oedipus	Gk.	M	1198
Rumpelstiltskin Princess	Germ.	F	1354
Vararuchi	Hin.	M	1639
Yoishta	Pers.	M	1709

RIDICULE (SEE REVELRY)
RISHIS (SEE SPIRIT)
RIVER (SEE WATER)
ROBBER (SEE OUTLAW)

RUINS			
Hambarus	Pers.		714
Ovda	Fin-Ug.	M, F	1221

SACRIFICE	Culture	Sex	Page
Agni	Hin.	M	49
Armaiti	Zoro.	F	+
Asura	Hin.	M	146
Athwya	Pers.	M	151
Celeus	Gk.	M	302
Charops	Gk.	M	315
Crom Cruaich	Cel.	M	383
Curetes	Gk.	M	398
Curtis, Marcus	Rom.	M	399
Daemons	Gk.	M	405
Deva	Bali	M	435
Golden Calf.	Hebr.		672
Hadding	Norse	M	705
Heimdal	Norse	M	743
Hestia	Gk.	F	765
Ila	Hin.	F	823
Itztli	Mex.	M	850
Maimaktes	Gk.	M	1047
Manu	Hin.	M	1061
Maruts	Gk.	M	1071
Meilichios	Gk.	M	1084
Narasamsa	Hin.	M	1155
Nezaualpilli	Mex.	M	1167
Noidde	Lapp	M	1179
Panemerios	Gk.	M	1233
Pourushaspa	Pers.	M	1290
Quetzalcoatl	Mex.	M	1312
Siward	Norse	M	1461
Suvinenge	Daho.	M	1513
Svaru	Hin.	M	1514
Tezcatlipoca (Monenequi)	Mex.	M	1549
Theseus	Gk.	M	1554
Tlamatzincatl	Mex.	M	1582
Torem	Sib.	M	1589
Vanaspati	Hin.	M	1638
Vivanghvant	Pers.	M	1656
Vivasvant	Hin.	M	1656
Xolotl	Mex.	M	1697
Zaru	Egyp.	M	1716
Ziusudra	Sum.	M	1721

SACRIFICE VICTIM (SURROGATE. ALSO SEE CHILD IMMOLATED, DYING GOD, SCAPE-GOAT)			
Anobret	Phoen.	M	100
Arcas	Gk.	M	118

Sacrifice Victim (cont.)	Culture	Sex	Page
Demophoon	Gk.	M	432
Gwern	Cel.	M	701
Icarus	Gk.	M	817
Idomeneus's son	Gk.	M	820
Iphigenia	Gk.	F	838
Isaac	Hebr.	M	841
Jephthah's daughter	Hebr.	F	872
Paris	Gk.	M	1238
Phaethon	Gk.	M	1260
Polyxena	Gk.	F	+
Procris	Gk.	F	1294
Prometheus	Gk.	M	1295
Tachibana	Jap.	F	1524
Yusoofee	Pers.	M	13

SAGE (SEE DIVINATION)
SAINT (SEE SPIRIT)

SAVIOR			
Amida	Jap.	M	85
Amin (Mohammed)	Mos.	M	114
Aryajangulitara	Bud.	F	134
Aryavalokitesvara	Bud.	M	134
Astvat-ereta	Zoro.	M	145
Asvins	Hin.	M	146
Avalokitesvara	Bud.	M	160
Berejya	Pers.	M	204
Bhrkuti	Bud.	F	209
Bodhisattva	Bud.	M	233
Bosatsu	Jap.	M	237
Buddha	Bud.	M	255
Christ	Christ.	M	330
Dag	Hebr.	M	405
Ea	Assyr., Baby., Sum.	M	481
Ekajata	Bud.	F	496
Emmanuel	Christ., Hebr.	M	509
Enki	Assyr., Baby., Sum.	M	511
Epeios	Gk.	M	514
Faruq (Mohammed)	Mos.	M	1114
Fool	World Wide	M	591
Gesu	Christ.	M	651
Gluskap	Algon.	M	664
Good Scarabaeus	Christ.	M	675
Good Shepherd	Christ.	M	675

	Culture	Sex	Page
Haakon	Norse	M	705
IHS (IHSOOS, Jesus)	Christ.	M	822
Imam Mahdi	Mos.	M	825
Inri (Jesus)	Christ.	M	833
Jehovahtzidkenu	Christ.	M	871
Jesus	Christ.	M	877
Kalki (Vishnu)	Hin.	M	904
Kanakamuni	Bud.	M	907
Kasyapa	Bud.	M	912
Khidv	Mos.	M	924
Krakucchanda	Bud.	M	945
K'ue Yu-chen T'ien-tsun	Chin.	M	949
Kurukulla	Bud.	F	953
Mahavira	Jain.	M	1045
Mahdi	Mos.	M	1045
Maidere	Tatar	M	1046
Maitreya	Bud.	M	1047
Manusibuddha	Bud.	M	1062
Melchizedek	Hebr.	M	1085
Metatron	Caba.	M	1096
Mi-li (Agita)	Chin.	M	1102
Miroku	Jap.	M	1109
Mithra	Pers.	M	1112
Mohammed	Mos.	M	1114
Moses	Hebr.	M	1126
Naaseni	Gnostic	M	1145
Ne-kilst-luss	Haida	M	1161
O-Binzuru	Jap.	M	1192
Padmapani	Bud.	M	1225
Piers Plowman	Eng.	M	1270
Prince of Light	Christ.	M	1293
Prince of Peace	Christ.	M	1293
P'usa	Chin.	M	1305
Ratnapani	Bud.	M	1324
Sakyamuni	Bud.	M	1390
Sampsa	Fin-Ug.	M	1394
Sandalphon	Caba.	M	1396
Saoshyant	Zoro.	M	1398
Seth	Hebr.	M	1421
Shepherd	Hebr.	M	1434
Siddhartha	Bud.	M	1447
Sitatapatra	Bud.	F	1460
Sitatara	Bud.	F	1460
Sommonacodum	Siam.	M	1474
Syamatara	Bud.	F	1521
Tara (sGrolmas)	Bud.	F	1534

Savior (cont.)	Culture	Sex	Page
Tarani	Hin.	M	1534
Ukhshyatereta (Hushetar)	Zoro.	M	1398
Ukhshyatnemah (Hushetar-mah)	Zoro.	M	1398
Veltro	Ital.	M	1644
Vishnu	Hin.	M	1654
Visvamitra	Hin.	M	1655
Weng-cheng	Chin.	F	1673
Yeshua (Yhs)	Christ.	M	877
Zaphnathpaaneah	Hebr.	M	1716
Zoroaster	Zoro.	M	1734

SCAPEGOAT

	Culture	Sex	Page
Azazal	Hebr.		165
Zany	Eng.	M	1716

SCORNED BY PARENT (SEE RE-NOUNCED BY PARENT)
SCRIBE (SEE WISDOM)
SEA (SEE WATER)

SEASON (a=autumn, c=seasonal changes, ny=new year, sp=spring, su=summer, w=winter)

	Culture	Sex	Page
Actaeon (su)	Gk.	M	28
Adapa (sp)	Baby.	M	30
Adonis (sp)	Gk.	M	34
Aestas (su)	Med. Art	M	+
Agnar (su)	Norse	M	49
Aki-yama (a)	Jap.	M	60
Allen-A-Dale (sp)	Bryth.	M	69
Alv (w)	Norse	M	77
Amanoro (sp)	Arm.	F	80
Angeburga (su)	Norse	F	95
Angerona (w)	Ital.	F	96
Angra Mainyu (w)	Zoro.	M	97
Angus (sp)	Cel.	M	97
Anna Perenna (sp)	Rom.	F	99
Atli (a)	Norse	M	152
Attis (sp)	Phryg.	M	154
Autumnus (a)	Med. Art	M	+
Auxo (su)	Gk.	F	786
Baba, Ali (sp)	Arab.	M	168
Balder (su)	Norse	M	174
Barbmoakka (sp)	Lapp	F	181
Belleros (w)	Gk.	M	199
Berchta (w)	Norse	F	203

	Culture	Sex	Page
Bhadra (sp)	Hin.	F	207
Bjorn (w)	Norse	M	220
Bjorno-Hoder (w)	Norse	M	221
Black Tortoise (w)	Chin.		223
Blodeuwedd (sp)	Bryth.	F	226
Bous (sp)	Ang-Sax.	M	238
Brynhild (sp)	Norse	F	253
Buinne (w)	Cel.	M	258
Caer (c)	Cel.	M	267
Ch'i lin (a)	Chin		325
Ch'ing Lung (sp)	Chin		601
Chu Ch'ieh (su)	Chin.		335
Cichol (w)	Cel.	M	338
Conn (su)	Cel.	M	367
Cora (sp)	Gk.	F	370
Cordelia (sp)	Eng.	F	371
Creudylad (sp)	Bryth.	F	381
Dagda (all)	Cel.	M	405
Dice (su)	Gk.	F	443
Draupadi (sp)	Hin.	F	470
Dursa (sp)	Aramaic	F	307
Dylan (su)	Bryth.	M	480
Eirene (a, w)	Gk.	F	786
Eostra (Ostara) (sp)	Ang-Sax.	F	514
Epona (sp)	Cel., Rom.	F	517
Etain (su)	Cel.	F	526
Eteocles (w)	Gk.	M	527
Etzel (w)	Norse	M	528
Eunomia (sp)	Gk.	F	530
Eunomos (sp)	Gk.	M	530
Fafnir (w)	Norse	M	544
Fergus mac Roy (w)	Cel.	M	561
Flora (sp)	Rom.	F	584
Fomor (w)	Cel.	M	590
Friuch (all)	Cel.	M	613
Galahad (Gwalchaved) (su)	Bryth.	M	622
Gawain (Gwalchmei) (sp)	Bryth.	M	635
Geirrod (su)	Norse	M	638
Gilvaethwy (all)	Bryth.	M	657
Gohone (w)	Iroq.		670
Goreu (sp)	Bryth.	M	678
Graces (sp)	Gk.	F	681
Green Knight (w)	Bryth.	M	689
Grismadevi (su)	Bud.	F	691
Guinevere (sp)	Bryth.	F	696
Gullveig (w)	Norse	F	697

	Culture	Sex	Page
Gwyn (w)	Bryth.	M	703
Gwyrthur (su)	Bryth.	M	703
Hagan (w)	Norse	M	707
Hama (w)	Ang-Sax.	M	714
Hamlet (sp)	Eng.	M	714
Haru-yama (sp)	Jap.	M	729
Havgan (su)	Bryth.	M	732
Haya-akihiko & Haya-Akitsu(a)	Jap.	M-F	734
Hebe (sp)	Gk.	F	739
Heimdal (su)	Norse	M	743
Hemantadevi (w)	Bud.	F	749
Hiemas (w)	Med. Art	M	+
Hoder (w)	Norse	M	778
Hogne (w)	Norse	M	779
Holler (w)	Germ.	M	781
Horae (all)	Gk.	F	786
Horus (sp)	Egy.	M	792
Hreidmar (sp)	Norse	M	797
Huitzilopochtli (su)	Mex.	M	803
Hymir (w)	Norse	M	811
Hyrokkin (w)	Norse	F	813
Idun (su)	Norse	F	820
Igerna (sp)	Bryth.	F	821
Ildico (sp)	Norse	F	823
Izushiotome (su)	Jap.	F	854
Jonakr (w)	Norse	M	886
Jormunrek (w)	Norse	M	887
Kagutsuchi (su)	Jap.	M	902
Karpo (a)	Gk.	F	911
Kauravas (w)	Hin.	M	913
Khensu (sp)	Egy.	M	923
Kore (sp)	Gk.	F	942
Kostey (w)	Slav.	M	944
Kuei Shen (w)	Chin.		949
Kukulcan (sp)	Mex.	M	950
Kulhwch (sp)	Welsh	M	950
Lado & Lada (sp)	Slav.	M-F	961
Laius (w)	Gk.	M	964
Laodamas (w)	Gk.	M	972
Lilinau (su)	N.A.I.	F	994
Linus (sp)	Gk.	M	998
Loddis-edne	Lapp	F	181
Louhi (w)	Lapp	F	1016
Marduk (sp)	Baby.	M	1065
Marpessa (sp)	Gk.	F	1068
Mars (sp)	Ital.	M	1069

	Culture	Sex	Page
Mata (w)	Cel.	M	1074
May Queen (sp)	Folk.	F	1080
Minotaur (w)	Gk.	M	1107
Miqtu (su)	Baby.	M	1108
Miranda (sp)	Eng.	F	1109
Misharu (a)	Phoen.	M	1110
Morana (w)	Slav.	F	1122
Mordred (w)	Bryth.	M	1122
Nadushu-Namir (sp)	Baby.	M	1147
Narokhachoma (all)	Bud.	F	1156
Nemean Lion (w)	Gk.		1162
Nerio (sp)	Rom.	F	1164
Niobe (w)	Gk.	F	1174
Nipinoukhe (su)	Algon.	M	1175
Nithhoggr (w)	Scan.	M	1176
Njord (su)	Norse	M	1176
Notus (a, w)	Gk.	M	1183
Nynnyaw & Peibaw (w)	Cel.	M-M	1188
Oengus (sp)	Cel.	M	1198
Oho-usu (sp)	Jap.	M	1202
Olwen (sp)	Bryth.	F	1206
Ortlieb (sp)	Germ.	M	1217
Ottar (w)	Norse	M	1220
Pai Hu (a)	Chin.	M	1226
Paluc Cat (w)	Bryth.	F	1230
Parsifal (sp)	Germ.	M	1239
Pau-puk-keewis (w)	N.A.I.	M	1244
Paynal (w)	Mex.	M	1245
Peboan (w)	N.A.I.	M	+
Perdix (sp)	Gk.	A	1254
Pergrubrius (sp)	Baltic	M	1255
Persephone (sp, su)	Gk.	F	1257
Philomela (sp)	Gk.	F	1263
Phra In (su)	Siam.	M	1266
Phyllis (sp)	Gk.	F	1267
Pipounoukhe (w)	Algon.	M	1275
Poeas (w)	Gk.	M	1281
Polydorus (w)	Gk.	M	1284
Polynices (sp)	Gk.	M	1284
Pomona (a)	Rom.	M	1285
Procne (sp)	Gk.	F	1294
Proserpina (sp, su)	Rom.	F	1296
Prthu (sp)	Hin.	M	1298
Pythias (sp)	Rom.	M	111
Randver (sp)	Norse	M	1322
Rapunze (sp)	Germ.	M	465

	Culture	Sex	Page
Rbhus (c)	Hin.		1326
Resheph (su)	Phoen.	M	1333
Rhiannon (all)	Bryth.	F	1336
Rind (w)	Norse	F	1339
Rtus (all)	Hin.		1352
Ryence (w)	Bryth.	M	1355
Saho-yama-hime (sp)	Jap.	F	1361
Samhanach (w)	Scot.	M	1393
Saraddevi (a)	Bud.	F	1399
Sati (sp)	Hin.	F	1402
Scyld (sp)	Ang-Sax.	M	1409
Sekhet (su)	Egy.	F	1414
Sharvan (w)	Cel.	M	1431
Siggeir (w)	Norse	M	1449
Sigi (w)	Norse	M	1449
Sita (sp)	Hin.	F	1460
Skate (sp)	Ice.	M	1464
Sokar (w)	Egy.	M	1471
Spenjaghrya (w)	Pers.	M	1481
Steingud (sp)	Norse	F	1493
Sthenelus (w)	Gk.	M	1494
Strenia (ny)	Rom.	F	1500
Stutly, Will (sp)	Eng.	M	1502
Sudolisa (su)	Slav.	F	895
Svanhit (su)	Norse	F	1514
Svasud (su)	Norse	M	1514
Swanhild (sp)	Germ.	F	1517
Tammuz (sp)	Baby.	M	1530
Tatsuta-hime (a)	Jap.	F	1538
Tawiscara (w)	Huron	M	1539
Telemachus (sp)	Gk.	M	1542
Thallo (sp)	Gk.	F	1551
Thebe (sp)	Gk.	F	1552
Thora (sp)	Gk.	F	1561
Thrym (w)	Norse	M	1567
Tiphys (sp)	Gk.	M	1575
Tityus (w)	Gk.	M	1580
Tobias (sp)	Hebr.	M	1582
Tung Fang So (sp)	Chin.	M	1607
Ullerus (w)	Norse	M	1622
Umma (su)	Baby.		1623
Unicorn (a)	Chin.		1625
Ura (su)	Sum.	M	1627
Urvasi (sp)	Hin.	F	1630
Utathys (sp)	Hin.	M	1632
Vali (sp, su)	Norse	M	1636

	Culture	Sex	Page
Vasantadevi (sp)	Bud.	F	1640
Venus (sp)	Ital.	F	1644
Ver (sp)	Med. Art	M	1645
Vesna (sp)	Slav.	F	1647
Vodyanik (sp)	Rus.	M	1657
Wakyet-wa (sp)	Burm.	M	1662
Wuldor (w)	Ang-Sax.	M	1693
Ya-o-gah (w)	Seneca	M	1701
Yarilo (sp)	Rus.	M	1701
Yoskeha (s)	Iroq.	M	1710
Yspaddeden Penkawr (w)	Bryth.	M	1711
Zmei Goruinich (w)	Slav.	M	1722
SECRECY (ALSO SEE SILENCE)			
Aides	Gk.	M	55
Guhya-pati	Bud.	M	695
Sang-dui	Bud.	M	1396
SEER (SEE DIVINATION)			
SELF ADORATION (ALSO SEE VANITY)			
Aniruddha	Hin.	M	98
Hallgerda	Ice.	F	712
Narcissus	Gk.	M	1155
SENSE DEITIES			
Kika-saru (deafness)	Jap.		1118
Maa (sight)	Egy.		1030
Sau (taste)	Egy.		1403
Silence	Gnostic Aeon		1452
Sozem (hearing)	Egy.	M	1479
Stentor (voice)	Egy.	M	1493
Sung-gi-gval-po (speech)	Tib.	M	1510
Tara (all)	Bud.	F	1534
T'ien-lung (deafness)	Chin.	M	1673
Ti-ya (mute)	Chin.	M	1673
Zacharias (mute)	Hebr.	M	1714
SHAMELESSNESS (SEE INTEMPERANCE)			
SHAPE CHANGER			
Achelous	Gk.	M	24
Amergin	Cel.	M	84
Arawn	Bryth.	M	117
Artemis	Gk.	F	131
Atabyrius	Gk.	M	147

	Culture	Sex	Page
Athena	Gk.	F	150
Chu-ch'a-pan-t'o-ka	Chin.	M	335
Chunuhluk	Eskimo	M	336
Cian	Cel.	M	338
Daphne	Gk.	F	414
Dionysus	Gk.	M	447
Empusa	Gk.	M	510
Eriphos	Gk.	M	520
Estsanatlehi	Nav.	F	526
Etain	Cel.	F	526
Friuch	Cel.	M	613
Gilvaethwy	Bryth.	M	657
Gluskap	Algon.	M	664
Gwion Bach	Cel.	M	701
Gwrhyr Gwalstawt	Bryth.	M	702
Gyges	Gk.	M	703
Hlakanyana	Zulu	M	775
Hlebard	Norse	M	776
Hugi	Norse	M	803
Idun	Norse	F	820
Inktonmi	Siouan	M	832
Io	Gk.	F	835
Ira-waru	Poly.	M	838
Klieng	Borneo	M	936
Korrigans	Breton	M, F	943
Llew Llaw	Bryth.	M	1005
Loki	Norse	M/A	1010
Lotis	Gk.	F	1014
Loup-garou	Fr.	M	1016
Lucian	Rom.	M	1020
Lung	Chin.	M	1025
Lyeshy	Slav.	M	1028
Mahr	Germ.	M, F	1046
Manannan	Cel.	M	1054
Marduk	Assyr-Baby.	M/A	1065
Maruts	Hin.	M	1071
Math	Cymric	M	1075
Maui	Poly.	M	1077
Menw	Bryth.	M	1090
Merlin (Ambrosius)	Bryth.	M	1092
Metra	Gk.	F	1096
Minerva	Rom.	F	1106
Mongan	Cel.	M	1117
Morrigu	Cel.	F	1125
Nemesis	Gk.	F	1162
Nimrod	Baby.	M	1170

	Culture	Sex	Page
Nules-murt	Fin-Ug.	M	1185
Odin	Norse	M	1195
Ophiogenes	Gk.	M, F	1211
Padmasambhava	Tib.	M	1225
Pa-hsien	Chin.	M, F	1226
Pairekse	Ostiak	M	1226
Pan-t'o-ka	Chin.	M	1235
Pariacaca	Inca	M	1237
Pau-puk-keewis	N.A.I.	M	1244
Periclymenus	Gk.	M	1255
Picus	Rom.	M	1269
Polyidus	Gk.	M	1284
Pooka	Cel.	M	1286
Poseidon	Gk.	M	1288
Prajapati (Prakriti)	Hin.	A	1290
Proteus	Gk.	M	1297
Pryderi (Gwri)	Bryth.	M	1298
Pwyll	Bryth.	M	1306
Rakshasa	Hin.	M, F	1320
Raven	Pac. Coast Ind.	M	1325
Rucht	Cel.	M	1353
Sadb	Cel.	M	1360
Serosevsky	Rus.	M	1418
Tamamo-no-maye	Jap.	F	1529
Tchue	Bush.	M	1540
Thetis	Gk.	F	1555
Thjasse	Norse	M	1560
Ti-tsang	Chin.	M	1580
Troll	Norse	M	1600
Tuan mac Cairill	Cel.	M	1605
Uazit	Egy.	F	1619
Utgard-Loki	Norse	M	1632
Uther Pendragon	Bryth.	M	1632
Vidyadhara	Hin.	F	1649
Vikramaditya	Hin.	M	1650
Virava (Tava-ajik)	Fin-Ug.	A	1652
Vishnu	Hin.	M	1654
Vjedogonja	Slav.	M	1656
Vodyanik	Rus.	M	1657
Xelas	Puget Sound	M	1695
Zeus	Gk.	M	1719

SHEPHERD (SEE ANIMAL KEEPER)

SILENCE (ALSO SEE SECRECY)

Harpichruti	Egy.	M	728

Silence (cont.)	Culture	Sex	Page
Harpocrates	Gk.	M	728
Iwa-saru	Jap.	M	118
Ku Shen	Chin.		953
Muta	Rom.	F	1140
Mutuhei	So. Is.	M	1141
Silence	Gnostic Aeon		1452
Sphinx	Egy., Gk.	F	1482
Vidar	Norse	M	1649

SIN (SEE EVIL)

SKY

Abdevenham	Med. Lit.	M	13
Aditi	Hin.	F	32
Aero	Gk.	F	41
Aesir	Norse	M, F	42
Ajy-tangara	Yakut	M	58
Akhtar	Zoro.	M	59
Aksobhya	Bud.	M	60
Aktaios	Gk.	M	60
Altjirra	Aus.	M	77
Ama-no-ma-hitotsu	Jap.	M	80
Amitayus	Bud.	M	86
Amma-ana-ki	Baby.	M	86
Amoghasiddhi	Bud.	M	87
An	Sum.	M	89
Ana	Baby.	M	90
Anshar	Baby.	M	101
Anu	Baby.	M	104
Apoyan Tachu	Zuni	M	112
Argus Panoptes	Gk.	M	122
Arik Anpin	Caba.	M	124
Asa	Norse	M, F	134
Assarac	Assyr.	M	143
Astraeus	Gk.	M	145
Asynjur	Norse	F	147
Asz	Slav.	M	147
Ataentsic (Eagentci)	Huron	F	147
Athtar	Assyr.	F	151
Atnatu	Aus.	M	152
Auchthon	Phoen.	M	156
Avalokitesvara	Bud.	M	160
Awonawilona	Zuni	M/A	162
Baal	Sem.	M	167
Baal-shamin	Arm.	M	168
Baau	Phoen., Sum.	F	168

	Culture	Sex	Page
Bag-Mashtu	Pers.	M	172
Bagos Papaios	Phryg.	M	172
Baiame	Aus.	M	173
Bai-ulgon	Tatar	M	173
Baneb-ded	Egy.	M	178
Batara Guru	Sumatra	M	186
Belus	Baby.	M	201
Bragi	Norse	M	240
Brigit	Cel.	F	249
Buga	Sib.	M	258
Bumba	Bushongo	M	260
Burnunta-sa	Baby.	M	262
Cakravartin	Bud.	M	272
Chak-dor-don-pa	Bud.	M	308
Chareya	Calif. Ind.	M	313
Chemin	Carib	M	317
Cipactonal	Mex.	M	341
Citallicue	Mex.	M	344
Coel	Cel.	M	355
Coelus	Rom.	M	355
Conchobar mac Nessa	Cel.	M	364
Crom Cruaich	Cel.	M	383
Cronus	Gk.	M	384
Cumhal	Cel.	M	396
Daikoku	Jap.	M	406
Damkina	Baby.	F	410
Deva	Bali	M	435
Dhyanibuddhas	Bud.	M	440
Dione	Gk.	F	446
Dios	Gk.	M	449
Diwata Magbabaya	Philip.	M	454
Don (Donnus)	Bryth.	F/A	461
Dyaus	Hin.	M	479
Dzajaga	Mong.	M	481
Ea	Assyr., Baby., Sum.	M	481
El	Sem.	M	497
El of Gebal	Sem.	M	497
Elioun (Hypsestus)	Phoen.	M	504
Emrys	Bryth.	M	510
Ennugi	Baby.	M	512
Epigeus	Phoen.	M	515
Esege-malan-tengeri	Mong.	M	524
Eusoph	Chald.	M	533
Fjorner	Norse	M	578
Frey	Norse	M	609

	Culture	Sex	Page
Freya	Norse	F	610
Frigg	Norse	F	612
Gandarewa	Pers.	M	625
Grimnir	Norse	M	691
Guamaonocon (Iocauma)	Taino	M	693
Gudatrigakwitl	Wishosk Ind.	M	694
Gulu	Uganda	M	697
Ha-nui-o-rangi	Poly.	M	722
Har	Norse	M	724
Hathor	Egy.	F	730
Hera	Gk.	F	752
Hormusda	Mong.	M	787
Huang T'ien Shang Ti	Chin.	M	801
Hurakan	C.A.I.	M	808
Ilmarinen	Fin-Ug.	M	824
Indra	Hindu	M	829
Inktonmi	Siouan	M	832
Inmar	Fin-Ug.	M	832
Innini	Sum.	F	832
Iocauna	Taino	M	836
Itzamna	Mex.	M	850
Jade Emperor (Pearly Emperor)	Chin.	M	860
Jajutsi	Mong.	M	861
Jehovah	Hebr.	M	870
Jumala	Fin.	M	895
Juno	Rom.	F	895
Jupiter	Rom.	M	896
Kaba	Fin-Ug.	M	900
Kaira-khan	Tatar	M	902
Kapipikauila	Poly.	M	913
Karnu	Assyr.	M	911
Khaldi	Urartian	M	922
Khen-pa	Tib.	M	923
Kildisin	Fin-Ug.	M	927
Knaninja	Aus.	M	936
Kokuzo	Jap.	M	940
Krishna	Hin.	M	945
Kudai	Sib.	M	948
Kukumatz	Yuman	M	950
Kuni-toko-tachi	Jap.	M	952
Kutku	Sib.	M	954
Kysan-tengere	Sib.	M	956
Lao Tze	Chin.	M	973
Leza	Bantu	M	989
Li	Chin.	M	989

	Culture	Sex	Page
Ling Pao	Chin.	M	998
Lludd (Nudd)	Bryth.	M	1005
Lug	Cel.	M	1022
Lumawig	Philip.	M	1024
Madumba	Calif. Ind.	M	1036
Mahasthamaprata	Bud.	M	1044
Mahora	N. Zeal.	F	1045
Mamaki	Bud.	F	1051
Math	Cymric	M	1075
Mathonwy	Cymric	M	1076
Mergen Tengere	Altaic	M	1092
Merlin (Ambrosius)	Bryth.	M	1092
Mitothin	Norse	M	1112
Muali	Mashonaland	M	1133
Mula Dyadi	Philip.	M	1135
Nala	Hin.	M	1150
Narokhachoma	Bud.	F	1156
Neago	Seneca	F	1159
Nepelle	Aus.	M	1163
Nisroch	Assyr.	M	1176
Nona	Poly.	F	1539
Num	Samoyed	M	1185
Numi-torem	Fin-Ug.	M	1185
Nut	Egy.	F	1187
Nwyvre	Bryth.	M	1187
Nyankopong	Ashantis	M	1187
Nzambi	Congo	M	1188
Odin	Norse	M	1195
Okikurumi	Ainu	M	1203
Olelbis	Wintun	M	1205
Ometecutli	Mex.	M	1208
Panoptes	Gk.	M	1234
Pantecatle	Mex.	M	1234
Panthaka	Bud.	M	1234
Pan-t'o-ka	Chin.	M	1235
Parpara	Kei Is.	M	1239
Penardun	Bryth.	M	1251
Perkunas	Baltic	M	1256
Peter	Christ.	M	1259
Ptah-Seker	Egy.	M	1300
Qabauil	Kiche	M	1308
Rafnagud	Norse	M	1317
Rai-tubu	Poly.	M	1319
Rangi	Poly.	M	1322
Ratnasambhava	Bud.	M	1324
Resheph	Phoen.	M	1333

	Culture	Sex	Page
Ribimbi	Trans.	M	925
Ryo-to-bin	Jap.	M	1356
Sadakari	Bud.	M	1360
Sangke	Fin-Ug.	M	1396
Satet	Egy.	F	1402
Shamshiel	Caba.	M	1430
Shang-ti	Chin.	M	1430
Shekinah	Caba.	F	1432
Shen Pao	Chin.	M	1434
Shesemtet	Egy.	F	1435
Shingrawa	Burm.	M	1438
Shu	Egy.	M	1443
Sige	Baby.	F	1449
Sik Sawp	Burm.	F	1452
Sinlap	Burm.	M	1457
Sokar-Ptah	Egy.	M	1471
Suddhodana	Bud.	M	1503
Sume	Braz.	M	1506
Suratan-tura	Chuvash	M	1511
Sutekh	Syrian	M	1513
Svantovit	Slav.	M	1514
Taka-mimu-subi	Jap.	M	1527
Tangaroa	Poly.	M	1531
Teleia	Gk.	F	1542
Tengri	Sib.	M	1545
Thagya Min	Ind-Chin.	M	1550
Tharonhiawakon	Iroq.	M	1552
Thonga Tilo	Afr.	M	1560
T'ien (Ten)	Chin. (Jap)	A	1571
T'ien Kuan	Chin.	M	1571
T'ien Lung	Chin.	M	1673
T'ien Ming	Chin.	M	1571
T'ien Pao	Chin.	M	1572
Tilo	Baronga (Afr.)	M	1573
Tina	Ital.	M	1575
Tirawa	Pawnee	M	1576
Tirthakaras	Jain	M	1577
Tishtrya	Pers.	M	1577
Tiw	Ang-Sax.	M	1617
Tlaik	Comox Ind.	M	1581
Tochipa	N.A.I.	M	950
Tokay	Inca	M	1584
Tororut	Suk (Afr.)	M	1589
Triglav	Slav.	M	1597
Tsun-gyi-rgyal-po	Tib.	M	1604
Tuirbe Tragmar	Cel.	M	1606

	Culture	Sex	Page
Tuisco	Germ.	M	1606
Tungk-pok	Ostiak	M	1607
Tushup	Hittite	M	1610
Tyr	Teutonic	M	1617
Uggerus	Norse	M	1620
Ulgen	Tatar	M	1622
Ullerus (Holler)	Norse (Germ.)	M	1622
Urania	Gk.	F	1627
Uranus	Gk.	M	1627
Uther Pendragon	Bryth.	M	1632
Vairocana	Bud.	M	1634
Vajrapani	Bud.	M	1635
Varuna	Hin.	M	1639
Vasudeva	Hin.	M	1641
Vatea	Hervey Is.	M	1641
Veralden-Olmai	Lapp	M	1645
Vidar	Norse	M	1649
Waiiri	Aus.	M	1661
Wang	Chin.	M	1664
Wolaro	Aus.	M	1688
Wulbari	Krachi	M	1693
Wuldor	Ang-Sax.	M	1693
Yaw	Hebr.	M	1702
Yazata	Zoro.	M	1702
Yelafaz	Micro.	M	1703
Yesza	Slav.	M	1705
Yryn-ajy-tojon	Sib.	M	1710
Yuttoere	Carrier Ind.	M	1713
Zajan	Buriat	M	1715
Zan	Cretan	M	1716
Zeus	Gk.	M	1719
Zimbabwe	Mashonaland	M	1720
Ziu (Tiu)	Germ.	M	1721

SLAIN, DETHRONED OR MUTILATED BY KIN

Acrisius	Gk.	M	27
Adrammelech	Hebr.	M	35
Aegisthus	Gk.	M	39
Arthur	Bryth.	M	132
Atreus	Gk.	M	153
Balor	Cel.	M	176
Brangemore	Bryth.	F	243
Cronus	Gk.	M	384
Cuchulainn	Cel.	M	393
Dagda	Cel.	M	405

Slain, Dethroned, etc. (cont.)	Culture	Sex	Page
Frode	Dan.	M	613
Halfdan	Norse	M	712
Hueytonantzin	Mex.	F	802
Kamsa	Hin.	M	907
Laius	Gk.	M	964
Nisus	Gk.	M	1176
Pelias	Gk.	M	1250
Phocus	Gk.	M	1541
Polydectes	Gk.	M	1283
Salmoneus	Gk.	M	1391
Saul	Hebr.	M	1404
Seuechorus	Sum.	M	656
Sichaeus	Rom.	M	1446
Sigbrygg	Norse	M	1451
Sigi	Norse	M	1449
Sychaeus	Rom.	M	1521
Tiamat	Baby.	F	1570
Uranus	Gk.	M	1627
Urukagina	Sum.	M	1630
Yspaddeden Penkawr	Bryth.	M	1711

SLAIN BY MATE OR LOVER (ALSO SEE BETRAYED)

Name	Culture	Sex	Page
Adonis	Gk.	M	34
Agamemnon	Gk.	M	44
Ascalaphus	Gk.	M	135
Curoi mac Daire	Cel.	M	398
Desdemona	Eng.	F	433
Heracles	Gk.	M	752
Iasion	Gk.	M	816
Mariamne	Christ.	F	763
Melissa	Gk.	F	1086
Octavia	Rom.	F	1194
Orion	Gk.	M	1215
Phyllis	Gk.	F	432
Procris	Gk.	F	1294
Stellio	Rom.	M	1493
Swanhild	Norse	F	1517
Tammuz	Assyr-Baby.	M	1530
Uriens	Bryth.	M	1123

SLAYER, DETHRONER, OR MUTILATOR OF KIN

Name	Culture	Sex	Page
Aegisthus	Gk.	M	39
Alcmaeon	Gk.	M	65
Althemenes	Gk.	M	77

	Culture	Sex	Page
Brute	Bryth.	M	253
Cronus	Gk.	M	384
Cyrus	Pers.	M	403
Ea	Assyr., Baby., Sum.	M	481
Espinogres	Bryth.	M	525
Gilgamesh	Sum.	M	656
Halfdan	Norse	M	712
Ixion	Gk.	M	852
Joshua	Hebr.	M	889
Jupiter	Rom.	M	896
Krishna	Hin.	M	945
Kulhwch	Bryth.	M	950
Lug	Cel.	M	1022
Lugaid	Cel.	M	1023
Medea	Gk.	F	1082
Meleager	Gk.	M	1085
Melusina	Fr.	F	1087
Minerva	Ital.	F	1106
Neleus	Gk.	M	1161
Oeidpus	Gk.	M	1198
Oengus	Cel.	M	1198
Orestes	Gk.	M	1214
Pelias	Gk	M	1250
Perseus	Gk.	M	1257
Pradyumna	Hin.	M	1290
Pygmalion	Gk.	M	1306
Romulus & Remus	Rom.	M-M	1346
Saint Julian	Christ.	M	1373
Siggeir	Norse	M	1449
Telegonus	Gk.	M	1541
Theseus	Gk.	M	1554
Thyestes	Gk.	M	1569
Titans	Gk.	M, F	1577
Zeus	Gk.	M	1719

SLAYER OF LOVER OR MATE

Aphrodite	Gk.	F	108
Artemis	Gk.	F	131
Blathnat	Cel.	F	225
Cephalus	Gk.	M	303
Ceres	Rom.	F	305
Clytemnestra	Gk.	F	351
Deianeira	Gk.	F	425
Demeter	Gk.	F	429
Demophoon	Gk.	M	432

Slayer of Lover or Mate (cont.)	Culture	Sex	Page
Herod	Christ.	M	763
Ishtar	Assyr-Baby.	F	844
Jormunrek	Norse	M	887
Kyohime	Jap.	F	956
Morgan le Fay	Bryth.	F	1123
Nero	Rom.	M	1194
Othello	Eng.	M	1220
Periander	Gk.	M	1086

SLEEP (DREAMS, NIGHTMARES)

Bushyasta	Zoro.	M	262
Damu	Baby.	M	410
Ephialtes	Gk.	M	515
Evaki	Braz.	F	533
Faunus	Rom.	M	552
Fjalar	Norse	M	578
Gallu	Sum.	M	624
Hepiales	Gk.	M	752
Hermes	Gk.	M	760
Hine-maki-moe	Poly.	F	772
Hugon	Fr.	M	803
Hypnus	Gk.	M	813
Icelos	Gk.	M	817
Korka-murt	Fin-Ug.	M	942
Kostey	Slav.	M	944
Krisky	Rus.	F	946
Lilith	Hebr.	F	994
Lilithu	Sum.	F	995
Lilu	Baby.	M	995
Mab	Eng.	F	1031
Mahr	Germ.	M, F	1046
Mara	Scan.	F	1063
Mora (Kikimora)	Slav.	F	1122
Morpheus	Gk.	M	1125
Naamah	Caba.	F	1145
Nipa	Algon.	F	1175
Nocnitz	Rus.	F	1179
Oneiros	Gk.	M	1209
Phantasos	Gk.	M	1261
Phemios	Gk.	M	1262
Phobetor	Gk.	M	1265
Proserpina	Rom.	F	1296
Rhiannon	Bryth.	F	1336
Sandman	Germ.	M	1395
Sin	Assyr.	M	1456
Somnus	Rom.	M	1474

	Culture	Sex	Page
Succuba	Med.	F	1503
Suksendal	Fin-Ug.	A	1505
Tentetemic	Mex.	M	1546
Tharonhiaouagon	Iroq.	M	1541
Tiur	Arm.	M	1581
Uni	Fin.	M	1625
Unk-ta-he	Dakota	M	1626
Untamo	Fin.	M	1626
Yris	Carib	M	1710
Yu Huang	Chin.	M	1712

SLEEPER (ALSO SEE PROTECTOR)

Arthur	Bryth.	M	132
Boabdil	Moorish	M	1467
Bran	Cel.	M	1467
Brian Boroihme	Cel.	M	1467
Brynhild	Norse	F	253
Cairbe	Cel.	M	270
Charlemagne	Frankish	M	1467
Dobocz	Slav.	M	929
Dornroschen	Germ.	F	465
Earl Gerald	Irish	M	929
Endymion	Gk.	M	1467
Epimenides	Gk.	M	1467
Feng-kan	Chin.	M	601
Finn mac Coul (Fionn)	Cel.	M	929
Frederick of Barbarossa	Germ.	M	1467
Han Shan	Chin.	M	601
Harold	Eng.	M	1467
Helge of Sogn	Norse	M	1467
Heracles of Oeta	Gk.	M	755
Keresaspa	Pers.	M	918
Kuan-ti	Chin.	M	947
Mahdi	Mos.	M	1467
Ma-vien	Ind-Chin.	M	1078
Meher	Arm.	M	929
Merlin (Ambrosius)	Bryth.	M	1467
Mucukunda	Hin.	M	929
Nemda Prince	Fin-Ug.	M	1161
Nera	Cel.	M	+
Ogier	Dan.	M	1467
Oisin	Cel.	M	1202
Olaf Tryggvesson	Norw.	M	929
Peter Klaus	Germ.	M	1467
Rip Van Winkle	Am. Lit.	M	1467
Robert Bruce	Scot.	M	929

Sleeper (cont.)	Culture	Sex	Page
Roderick	Span.	M	1467
Sebastian	Portu.	M	1467
Seven Champions	Christ.	M	1467
Seven Manes of Leinster	Irish	M	1467
Seven Rishis	Hin.	M	1425
Seven Youths of Ephesus	Christ.	M	1467
Shih-te	Chin.	M	601
Sleeping Beauty	Folk.	F	1467
Sualtam	Cel.	M	1503
Tannhauser	Germ.	M	1467
Tharonhiaouagon	Iroq.	M	1541
Thomas of Ercildoune	Scot.	M	1467
Ts'ai Lwan (Wen Siao)	Chin.	M	601
Uasar	Egy.	M	1619
Urashima Taro	Jap.	M	1628
Vodyanik	Rus.	M	1657
Wenzel (Wenceslaus)	Bohemian	M	929
William Tell	Swiss	M	1467

SLEET (SEE FROST)
SMITH (SEE ARTISAN)
SNOW (SEE FROST)
SOLAR (SEE SUN)
SONG (SEE MUSIC)
SOOTHSAYER (SEE DIVINATION)
SORCERY (SEE MAGIC)

SOUND (ALSO SEE MUSIC)			
Akasa	Hin.		59
Cleta	Gk.	F	348
Echo	Gk.	F	489
Feith Fiada (Faet Fiada, Manannan)	Cel.		544
Ganis	Lapp	F	627
Geide	Cel.	M	638
Keidomos	Gk.	M	915
Klu-dban	Tib.	M	936
Ko-dama	Jap.	M	939
Ono	So. Is.	M	1210
Ra	Teut.	M	1314
Sozem	Egy.	M	1479
Stentor	Gk.	M	1493
Sung-gi-gval-po	Tib.	M	1510
Svaha (Agnayi)	Hin.	F	1514
Thunderbird	Am. Ind.	M	1568
Tithonus	Gk.	M	1578

	Culture	Sex	Page
Tu-mute-anaoa	Herv. Is.		1607
Vagtanus	Rom.	M	1633

SPEAKING HEAD (SEE PROTECTOR, SLEEPER)
SPECTRAL FIEND (SEE DEMON)
SPINNER (SEE WEAVER)

SPIRIT (AEON, ANGEL, ARHAT, ELF, FAIRY, GNOME, GRACE, IZED, JINNEE, KOBOLD, LOHAN, MAGI, NYMPH, PROTECTIVE ANCESTOR, RISHIS, SAINT, SOUL)

	Culture	Sex	Page
Abans	Pers.		12
Abdiel	Eng.	M	13
Abheda	Bud.	M	15
Abosom	Afr.		17
Adrastea	Gk.	F	35
Advocate, The	Christ.	M	36
Aegle	Gk.	F	39
Aeon	Gnostic		41
Aes Sidhe	Cel.	M, F	42
Aganippe	Gk.	F	45
Agape	Eng.	F	45
Aglaia	Gk.	F	48
Agraulid	Gk.	F	51
Ahnfrau	Norse	F	53
Aine	Cel.	F	56
Ajita	Bud.	M	58
Akalo	Solom. Is.	M, F	999
Akasagarbha	Bud.	M	59
Alfar	Norse	M, F	67
Al Ussa	Arab.	F	77
Alvor	Norse	M, F	78
Amagat	Yakut	M	78
Amesha Spentas	Zoro.	M	84
Andrew	Christ.	M	1362
Angaja	Bud.	M	95
Angel	Hebr-Christ.	M-F	95
Angida	Chin.	M	96
Anna	Christ.	F	1362
Anunaki	Baby.	M, F	105
Apsaras	Bud.	F	115
Aralim	Cab.	F	1705
Archangel	Christ., Hebr., Mos.	M	119

	Culture	Sex	Page
Argante	Bryth.	F	121
Arhat	Bud.	M	123
Ariel	Cabal.	M	124
Arlez	Arm.		127
Artemidos	Christ.	F	1363
Asha	Zoro.	M	138
A-shih	Chin.	M	139
Asia	Mos.	F	140
Asura	Pers.	M	146
Asvaghosa	Bud.	M	146
Atisa	Bud.	M	151
Atlantides	Gk.	F	152
Atua-noto-whare	Poly.	M	155
Aura	Gk.	F	158
Auxo	Gk.	F	160
Avo	Norse	M	162
Ayllu	Inca	M	164
Azariel	Hebr.	M	165
Azrael	Mos.	M	166
Bakula	Bud.	M	174
Balthazar	Christ.	M	1364
Banshee (Banschi)	Christ.	M	179
Barachiel	Christ.	M	1364
Bartholomew	Christ.	M	183
Beansidhe	Cel.	F	189
Befana	Ital.	F	195
Bendegeit Vran	Christ.	M	201
Beni-Elohim	Caba.	M	1705
Bertha	Norse	F	205
Berylune	Belg.	F	205
Bhadra	Bud.	M	207
Brownie	Norse	M	252
Burkhans	Buriat	M	261
Bwbachod	Scot.	M, F	263
Caemhoc	Christ.	M	1366
Calliope	Gk.	F	278
Callirhoe	Gk.	F	278
Camenae	Rom.	F	281
Cauld-lad	Scot.	M	300
Chamuel	Hebr.	M	310
Chen Jen	Chin.	M	1564
Chenresi	Tib.	M	318
Cherub	Hebr-Christ.	M	319
Chieh-po-ka	Chin.	M	322
Chnuphis	Gnostic	M	328
Chu-ch'a-pan-t'o-ka	Chin.	M	335

	Culture	Sex	Page
Chur	Pers.	M	336
Cleta	Gk.	F	348
Clio	Gk.	F	348
Cluracan	Cel.	M	351
Coblynau	Bryth.	M	352
Corrigan	Breton	F	374a
Dasse	Bush.	F	416
Dedek	Slav.	M	424
Deduska Domovoy	Rus.	M	424
Delling	Norse	M	427
Devatas	Hin.	F	435
Dharmakaya	Bud.	M	438
Dharmaraja	Bud.	M	438
Dharmatrala	Bud.	M	438
Dii Manes	Rom.	M, F	445
Djadek	Slav.	M	454
Dokkalfar	Norse	M	458
Domovik (Iskrychi, Susetka, Tsmok)	Rus.	M	461
Dopkalfar	Norse	M	464
Dzhe Manito	Chip.	M	481
Dziady (Zadusnica)	Rus.	M, F	481
Elf	Scan.	M, F	502
Elijah	Hebr.	M	503
El Koudr	Mos.	M	505
Elle Folk	Norse	M, F	505
Ellyllon	Eng.		506
Erathaoth	Gnostic	M	1423
Esclairmond	Fr.	F	807
Fairy	Cel.	M, F	545
Fa-na-p'o-ssu (Vanavasa)	Chin.	M	548
Fantine	Swiss	M, F	548
Fashena-futo	Chin.	M	549
Fata	Ital.	F	550
Fay	Eng.	M, F	553
Feroher	Pers.		562
Finnbeara	Cel.	M	570
Finvarra	Cel.	M	571
Fravashi	Pers.	M	608
Gabriel	Hebr., Mos.	M	619
Galatea	Gk.	F	623
Gan Ceanach	Cel.	M	625
Gaspar	Christ.	M	1370
Genius	Rom.	M	645
Gian Ben Gian	Arab.	M	653
Gitche-Manito	Algon.	M, F	1058

	Culture	Sex	Page
Gnome	Med.	M	664
Gob	Med.	M	664
Goldemar	Germ.	M	672
Gopaka	Bud.	M	677
Gwragedd Annwn	Bryth.	F	702
Gyalin	Tib.	M	703
Haniel	Hebr.	M	722
Hashmalin	Caba.	M	1705
Haurvatat	Zoro.	M	732
Hayyoth Ha Kadosh	Caba.	M	1705
Hegemone	Gk.	F	742
Heinzelmannchen	Germ.		744
Hellekin	Fr.	M	749
Herfjotur	Norse	F	759
Hesperides	Gk.	F	765
Hill Folk	Irish	M, F	771
Hitogaki	Jap.		775
Hodeken	Germ.	M	778
Holdiken	Germ.	M	781
Holy Ghost	Christ.	M	782
Houri	Mos.	M	795
Hsien	Chin.	M	799
Hulderfolk	Norse	M, F	803
Huon, Sir	Bryth.	M	807
Huyen-thien	Ind-Chin.	M	1167
Hva-sang	Bud.	M	809
Hyades	Gk.	F	809
Idisi	Norse	M	819
Igigi	Baby.	M, F	821
Ili-abrat	Baby.	M	823
Immovable	Gnostic Aeon		826
Inua	Eskimo		834
Iodhi	Slav.		836
Israfil	Mos.	M	847
Ithuriel	Eng.	M	849
Izeds	Zoro.	M	854
James the Great	Christ.	M	1372
James the Less	Christ.	M	1372
Javerzaharses	Arm.	F	867
Jinn & Jinniyeh	Mos.	M-F	880
Jiva	Hin.	M	880
Joachim	Christ.	M	881
John the Baptist	Christ.	M	1372
John the Divine	Christ.	M	1373
Jophiel	Hebr.	M	887
Joseph, the Carpenter	Christ.	M	1373

	Culture	Sex	Page
Judas (Jude)	Christ.	M	892
Judas Iscariot	Christ.	M	892
Judy	Gk.	F	893
Kaches	Arm.	M, F	900
Kachinas	Zuni	M	900
Kadosh	Hebr.	M, F	901
Ka-li-ha	Chin.	M	904
Kalika	Bud.	M	904
Kaluk	Burm.	M	905
Kanakabharadvaja	Bud.	M	907
Kanakavatsa	Bud.	M	907
Kande Yake	Cey.	M	907
Kanokafatso	Chin.	M	908
Katcinas	Pueblo	M	912
Kewpie	Folk.	M	920
Khshathra Vairya	Zoro.	M	925
Kimpurushas	Hin.	M	928
King Goldemar (Vollmar)	Germ.	M	929
Kinnaras	Hin.	M	932
Klaboterman	Germ.	M	935
Knaninja	Aus.		936
Kobold	Germ.	M	939
Korka-murt	Fin-Ug.	M	942
Korrigans	Breton	F	943
Korybantes	Phryg.	M	943
Kra (Kla)	Gold Coast		944
Krsnik	Slav.	M	947
Kubera	Hin.	M	948
Kudai	Sib.	M	948
Labismina	Folk.	F	957
Laica	Inca		964
Lares	Rom.	M, F	974
Lase	Tib.		974
Leprechaun	Cel.	M	985
Limniades	Gk.	F	997
Limoniades	Gk.	F	997
Li'oa	Solom. Is.	M	999
Lohan	Chin.	M	1009
Lo-hu-lo	Chin.	M	1010
Lud	Fin-Ug.	M	1021
Luke	Christ.	M	1374
Mab	Eng.	F	1031
MacMoineanta	Cel.	M	1034
Madali Wi-hsa-Kyung	Burm.	M	1035
Maenad	Gk.	F	1036
Mahagiri	Ind-Chin.	M	1042
Maia	Gk.	F	1046

	Culture	Sex	Page
Man	Gnostic Aeon	M	1052
Manah	Arab.	F	1054
Manes	Rom.	M, F	1058
Manitogitche	Algon.	M, F	1058
Marabout	Mos.	M	1063
Mark	Christ.	M	1375
Mar-pa	Tib.	M	1068
Mary	Mos.	F	1375
Matthew	Christ.	M	1377
Matthias	Christ.	M	1377
Ma Vien (Bach-ma)	Chin.	M	1078
Maziqim	Hebr.	M, F	1081
Medb	Bryth.	F	1082
Melachim	Caba.	M	1705
Melchior	Christ.	M	1377
Melchizedek	Hebr.	M	1085
Melpomene	Gk.	F	1087
Melusina	Fr.	F	1087
Menaka	Hin.	M	1088
Mercouris	Christ.	M	1377
Metatron	Caba.	M	1096
Michael	Christ., Hebr., Mos.	M	1377
Mila-re-pa	Tib.	M	1102
Mind	Gnostic Aeon	M	1106
Mintha	Gk.	F	1107
Mmoatia	Gold Goast	M, F	1113
Mondoro	Mashonaland	M	1116
Monker	Moslem	M	1117
Morgan le Fay	Bryth.	F	1123
Mother	Gnostic Aeon	F	1128
Munkar & Nakir	Mos.	M-M	1137
Murgi	Baltic	M, F	1137
Muses	Gk.	F	1138
Nagarjuna	Bud.	M	1147
Nagasena	Bud.	M	1147
Naiades	Gk.	F	1148
Nain Rouge	Norman	M	1149
Naka-hsi-na	Chin.	M	1150
Nakir	Mos.	M	1150
Nan-t'i-mitolo-ch'ing-yu	Chin.	M	1154
Napaeae	Gk.	F	1154
Narucnici	Bulg.	F	1156
Nasatya & Dasra	Hin.	M	1156
Nat	Burm.	M, F	1157
Nathaniel	Christ.	M	183

	Culture	Sex	Page
Nguyen-hu'u-do	Ind-Chin.	M	1167
Nguyen-quan	Ind-Chin.	M	1167
Nicholas	Christ.	M	1378
Nintoku	Jap.	M	1174
Nissa	Gk.	F	1176
Nucleolus	Mystic	M	1184
Number Nip	Eng.	M	1352
Numina	Rom.	M, F	1185
Nymph	Gk.	F	1188
Nysa Nymph	Gk.	F	1188
Ob	Hebr.	M, F	1191
Oberon	Eng., Fr.	M	1192
O-Binzuru	Jap.	M	1192
Ochall Ochne	Cel.	M	1193
Oenone	Gk.	F	1199
Ogdoad	Gnostic Aeon	M, F	1200
Oho-kuni-nushi	Jap.	M	1621
Oki (Kiousa)	Huron	M, F	1203
Oneis	Gk.	F	1209
Ongon (Kurmes, Tyus)	Buriat	M	1209
Only Begotten	Gnostic Aeon	M	1210
Onoel	Gnostic	M	1423
Ophanim	Hebr.	M	1211
Orenda	Iroq.	M, F	1214
Orisnici (Uresici)	Bulg.	F	1156
Ort	Fin-Ug.	M, F	1217
Ovakuru	Ashanti		1221
Pacarina	Inca		1224
Padmasambhava	Tib.	M	1225
Pa-hsien	Chin.	M, F	1226
Pan Chhen Rinpo Chhe	Tib.	M	1231
Pano-ka (Nakula)	Chin.	M	1234
Panthaka	Bud.	M	1234
Pan-t'o-ka	Chin.	M	1235
Patrick	Christ.	M	1378
Patshak	Ostiak	M, F	1244
Paul	Christ.	M	1379
Peitho	Gk.	F	1249
Penates	Rom.	M, F	1251
Peri	Pers.	M, F	1255
Peter	Christ.	M	1379
Phaenna	Gk.	F	1260
Philip	Christ.	M	1380
Pierides	Gk.	F	1269
Pigwiggen	Eng.	M	1271
Pi Kan	Chin.	M	1271

	Culture	Sex	Page
Pindolabharadvaja	Bud.	M	1273
Pinto-lo-po-lo-t'o-she	Chin.	M	1274
Pitri	Hin.	M	1276
Pixy	Eng.	M, F	1277
Pneuma	Christ.	M	1280
Pokunt	Soshonean	M	1282
Profundity	Gnostic Aeon	M	1295
P'u Hsien	Chin.	M	1300
Pukwudjies	N.A.I.	M, F	1300
Rafusen	Jap.	F	1317
Rahula	Bud.	M	1318
Raphael	Hebr.	M	1323
Rasiel	Hebr.	M	1323
Rhodope	Gk.	F	1337
Ridija	Sem.	M	1338
Robin Goodfellow	Eng.	M	1343
Rsabha	Jain	M	1352
Rubezahl	Germ.	M	1352
Sa-bdag	Tib.		1357
Sadhyas	Hin.	M, F	1360
Sagaris	Gk.	F	1360
Santaraksita	Bud.	M	1398
Santiago	Span.	M	1398
Satta-kuro-dzusagai-ai	Yakut	M	1402
Saul of Tarsus	Christ.	M	1404
Self-born	Gnostic Aeon	M	1414
Sennin	Jap.	M, F	1416
Seraph	Hebr-Christ.	M	1417
Sheng Jen	Chin.		1434
Shih Kan Tang	Chin.	M	1437
Shin	Jap.		1437
Shin Ne Mi	Ind-Chin.	F	1438
Shu Yu	Chin.	M	1445
Shwe Myethna	Ind-Chin.	F	1445
Shwe Na Be	Ind-Chin.	F	1445
Sidh (Shee)	Cel.	M, F	1447
Silas	Christ.	M	1452
Silence	Gnostic Aeon		1452
Simeon	Christ.	M	1381
Simon Zelotes	Christ.	M	1381
Si Wang Mu	Christ.	F	1461
Skritek	Slav.	M	1465
Spenta Armaiti	Zoro.	M	1481
Sprite	Folk.	M, F	545
Sraoscha	Zoro.	M	1487
Sthavira	Bud.	M	1494

	Culture	Sex	Page
Subhinda	Chin.	M	1503
Sulton	Fin-Ug.	M	1505
Suriel	Gnostic	M	1511
Tan-mo-lo-po-t'o	Chin.	M	1532
Taran	Gaelic	M, F	1534
Tautabaoth	Gnostic	M	1539
Temperance	Gnostic Aeon		1543
Tennin	Jap.	F	1545
Thagyas	Ind-Chin.		1551
Thelxinoe	Gk.	F	1138
Thierry	Eng.	M	700
Thomas	Christ.	M	1382
T'ien Tsu	Chin.	M	1572
Tirthakaras	Jain	M	1577
Titania	Rom.	F	1577
Tobosaku	Jap.	M	1583
Tornak	Eskimoan	M	1589
Tran-vu	Ind-Chin.	M	1167
Truth	Gnostic Aeon		1602
Tryanon	Bryth.	F	1602
Tsadkiel	Caba.	M	1602
Ts'ao Kuo-chiu	Chin.	M	1603
Tsaphkiel	Caba.	M	1603
Tsong-kha-pa	Tib.	M	1604
Tulugal	Aus.	M	1607
Tylwyth Teg	Welsh	M, F	1617
Udelinicy	Bulg.	F	1156
Ujikami	Jap.	M	1621
Unfading	Gnostic Aeon		1625
Unity	Gnostic Aeon		1626
Upadhyaya	Bud.	M	1626
Upali	Bud.	M	1626
Urganda	Carol.	F	1628
Uriel	Caba.	M	1383
Uzziel	Caba.	M	1633
Vajraputra	Bud.	M	1635
Vakula	Bud.	M	1635
Vanasa	Bud.	M	1638
Varjohaltia	Fin-Ug.	M	1639
Vidyadhara	Hin.	F	1649
Vila	Serbo-Croa.	F	1650
Vinmara	Mel.	F	1651
Wakan	Siouan		1662
Weisse Frauen	Norse	F	1672
Weiwobo	Jap.	F	1672
Wisdom	Gnostic Aeon		1686

Spirit (cont.)	Culture	Sex	Page
Xin	Chin.	M	+
Yaka	Cey.	M	1698
Yaksas & Yaksini	Tib.	M-F	1698
Yazata	Zoro.	M	1702
Yeibichai	Nav.	M	1703
Yin-chieh-t'o	Chin.	M	1708
Y-Mamau	Welsh	F	686
Zadkiel	Hebr.	M	1384
Zduh	Slav.	M, F	1717
Zemi	Carib		1717
Zephon	Eng.	M	1718
Zi	Sum.	M, F	1720
Zophiel	Eng.	M	1734

SPY

Agrivain	Bryth.	M	51
Al Jassasa	Mos.		69
Caleb	Hebr.	M	276
Citragupta	Hin.	M	345
Diomedes	Gk.	M	446
Dolon	Gk.	M	459
Igal	Hebr.	M	821
Ingcel	Cel.	M	831
Joshua	Hebr.	M	889
Odysseus	Gk.	M	1196
Pairekse	Ostiak	M	1226
Ruadan	Cel.	M	1352
Sukophantai	Gk.	M, F	1505
Walsingham	Eng.	M	1664
Zophiel	Eng.	M	1734

STAR DEITY (SEE ASTRAL)
STERILE (SEE MAIMED)

STORM

Adad	Sem.	M	28
Aegeon	Gk.	M	38
Ahl At-tral	Mos.		53
Aloidae	Gk.	M	71
Ame-no-uzume	Jap.	F	83
Amlode	Norse	M	86
Antiphates	Gk.	M	104
Apa-hau	Poly.		107
Apep	Egy.	M	107
Ara-tiatia	Poly.		117
Ares	Gk.	M	120

	Culture	Sex	Page
Atlacamani	Mex.	F	152
Auuenau	Aus.	M	160
Avagddu	Cel.	M	160
Azhi Dahaka	Pers.	M	165
Baba Yaga	Rus.	F	168
Bacchantes (Bacchae)	Gk., Rom.	F	170
Badb	Cel.	F	171
Baduhenna	Norse	F	172
Bana	Hin.	M	178
Bechard	Oc.	M	192
Bel Enlil	Baby.	M	197
Beli	Norse	M	197
Berserker	Norse	M	204
Brave-Swift-Impetuous-Male	Jap.	M	244
Briareus (Aegeon)	Gk.	M	247
Bricriu	Cel.	M	248
Buto	Jap.	M	263
Cailleach Mor (Bheur)	Scot.	F	269
Caliban	Eng.	M	277
Camaxtli	Mex.	M	279
Chokanipok	Algon.	M	328
Ciris	Gk.	F	344
Coatrischic	Taino	M	352
Corus	Rom.	M	374a
Corvus	Gk.	F	374a
Cottus	Gk.	M	375
Cuchi	Aus.	M	393
Curoi mac Daire	Cel.	M	398
Cyclops	Gk.	M	400
Cyhiraeth	Bryth.	F	401
Dadu	Baby.	M	404
Dhuni	Hin.	M	439
Dino	Gk.	F	446
Divje Devojke	Slav.	F	454
Divji Moz	Slav.	M	454
Dornolla	Cel.	F	464
Dsovean	Arm.	M	474
Dsovinar	Arm.	F	474
Dub	Cel.	F	474
Ecke	Norse	M	490
Egder	Norse	M	491
Egil	Norse	M	493
Emathion	Gk.	M	507
Empusa	Gk.	M	510
Enceladus	Gk.	M	510
Enlil	Baby.	M	512

	Culture	Sex	Page
Ephialtes	Gk.	M	515
Euryale	Gk.	F	532
Faknik	Papuan		546
Fomor	Cel.	M	590
Fornjot	Fin.	M	595
Furies	Gk.	F	617
Gabriel	Christ.	M	1680
Gallu	Sum.	M	624
Gargantua	Cel.	M	630
Gava-Griva	Hin.	M	635
Gere	Norse		647
Gri-bdog (Di-do)	Tib.	M	690
Gulban	Cel.		697
Gullveig	Norse	F	697
Gurgiunt Brabtruc	Bryth.	M	699
Gustr	Norse	M	699
Gymir	Norse	M	704
Hag	Scot.	F	707
Harald	Norse	M	725
Hecatoncheires	Gk.	M	741
Herfather (Herla, Hertyr)	Scan.	M	1196
Herne	Eng.	M	1680
Hitaspa	Pers.	M	918
Hraesvelg	Norse	M	797
Humbaba	Baby.	M	804
Hunding	Germ.	M	806
Hurakan	C.A.I.	M	808
Hyrokkin	Norse	F	813
Idiptu	Baby.	M	819
Imgig	Sum.	M	825
Indra	Hin.	M	829
Jormungandr	Norse	M	887
Kaput (Pehin)	Pers.	M	909
Kare	Norse	M	910
Kaua	Poly.	M	913
Kayak	Eskimoan	M	1256
Kayurankuba	Zulu		915
Keu Woo	Chin.		920
Koyorowen (Yaho)	Aus.	M	944
Krishna	Hin.	M	945
Kui	N. Zeal.	F	949
Kynedyr Wyllt	Bryth.	M	956
Lady of T'ai Shan	Chin.	F	962
Laestrygones	Gk.	M	963
Lamus	Gk.	M	969
Loki	Norse	M/A	1010

	Culture	Sex	Page
Maboya	Carib.	M	1031
Macha	Cel.	F	1033
Maenad	Gk.	F	1036
Maga-tsumi	Jap.	M	1037
Maimaktes	Gk.	M	1047
Makutu	N. Zeal.	M	1048
Manticore	Gk.	M	1060
Mars	Rom.	M	1069
Maruts	Hin.	M	1071
Meg (Long Meg, Mons Meg)	Eng.	F	1084
Mo-li Hung	Chin.	M	601
Morgan le Fay	Bryth.	F	1123
Morrigu	Cel.	F	1125
Morvran	Bryth.	M	1126
Mul-lil	Accadian	M	1135
Nemon	Gaelic	F	1162
No Cha	Chin.	M	1178
Oh-maga-tsumi	Jap.	M	1201
Otus	Gk.	M	1221
Periphetes	Gk.	M	1256
Podarge	Gk.	F	1281
Polybotes	Gk.	M	1283
Polyphemus	Gk.	M	1284
Poseidon	Gk.	M	1288
Prsni	Hin.	F	1297
Ramman	Baby.	M	1322
Ran	Norse	F	1322
Rimmon	Baby.	M	1339
Rodasi	Hin.	F	1071
Rudra	Hin.	M	1353
Rudrami	Hin.	F	1353
Ryu-wo	Jap.	M	1356
Saint Hubert	Christ.	M	1680
Salmoneus	Gk.	M	1391
Samael	Hebr.	M	1393
Set	Egy.	M	1420
Shala	Canaanite	F	1429
Shara	Arm.	M	1431
Shargaz	Sum.	M	1431
Shedim	Chald.	M	1432
Shikome	Jap.	F	1437
Shu	Egy.	M	1443
Shuqamuna	Baby.	M	1444
Shura	Jap.	M	1444
Shurale	Tatar	M	1444
Si	Pre-Inca	M	1445

Storm (cont.)	Culture	Sex	Page
Sinis	Gk.	M	1457
Sneneik	W.U.S. Ind.	F	1470
Sojo-bo	Jap.	M	1471
Solymoi	Gk.	M	1473
Spityura	Pers.	M	1484
Srvara	Pers.	M	1488
Sthenelus	Gk.	M	1494
Stymphalides	Gk.		1502
Sume	Braz.	M	1506
Susa-no-wo	Jap.	M	1512
Tanngnjost & Tanngrisnir	Norse	M-M	1532
Tapio (Vir-ava)	Fin.	A	1534
Tengu	Jap.	M	1545
Thalassa	Gk.	F	1551
Thrud	Norse	M	1567
Tirid	Baby.		1576
Tlacauepan	Mex.	M	1581
Trita Aptya	Hin.	M	1599
Typhoeus	Gk.	M	1617
Typhon	Gk.	M	1617
Tzitzimime	Mex.	F	1618
Umiarissat Women	Eskimoan	F	1623
Umi Bozo	Jap.	M	1623
Umkovu	Afr.	M, F	1623
Umu-dapruti	Baby.		1623
Vasolt	Norse	M	1641
Vetala	Hin.	F	1648
Vikhor	Slav.	M	1649
Virabhadra	Hin.	M	1652
Vozdushnuie	Slav.	M	910
Wallace	Scot.	M	1663
Whaitari	Maori	F	1674
Wudes Heer (Wade, Wode)	Norse	M	1693
Yamutbal	Sum.		1700
Zainigav	Arab.	M	1715
Zeus	Gk.	M	1719
Ziu (Tiu)	Germ.	M	1721
Zu	Baby., Sum.	M	1734

STREAM (SEE WATER)

STRENGTH (POWER)			
Achilles	Gk.	M/A	25
Ajax the Great	Gk.	M	58
Ajax the Lesser	Gk.	M	58
Alce	Gk.	M	63
Alcides	Gk.	M	64

	Culture	Sex	Page
Antaeus	Gk.	M	101
Apollo	Gk.	M	110
Arsaphes	Gk.	M	130
Asfandujar	Zoro.	M	137
Baidrama	Taino	M	173
Belus	Gk.	M	201
Beowulf	Ang-Sax.	M	203
Bia	Gk.	M	209
Canil	Mex.	M	853
Cratos	Gk.	M	378
Cyclopes	Gk.	M	400
Cymochles	Eng.	M	402
Dwendi	Philip.	M	479
Dynamis	Gnostic.	M	480
Dyne	Rom.	F	481
Fenian	Cel.	M	559
Gahonga	Iroq.	M	622
Gallaeus	Dutch	M	624
Ganga	Hin.	F	627
Geburah	Caba.	M	637
Gilgamesh	Sum.	M	656
Goll mac Morna (Aodh)	Cel.	M	674
Grettir	Ice.	M	374a
Hadding	Norse	M	705
Harpocrates	Gk.	M	728
Heracles	Gk.	M	752
Hercules	Rom.	M	759
Idas	Gk.	M	818
Indra	Hin.	M	829
Ischys	Gk.	M	136
Issachar	Hebr.	M	848
Kaua	Poly.	M	913
Kwasind	N.A.I.	M	955
Laodamas	Gk.	M	972
Levarcham	Cel.	F	988
Llew Llaw Gyffes	Cel.	M	1005
Long Meg (Mongs Meg)	Bryth.	F	1012
Lug	Cel.	M	1022
Magni	Norse	M	1040
Mahaitiac	Hidatsa	M	1043
Marduk	Assyr-Baby.	M	1065
Masauwu	Hopi	M	1072
Meg (Long Meg, Mons Meg)	Bryth.	F	1084
Michabo	Algon.	M	1098
Nudimmud	Baby.	M	1184
O-binzuru	Jap.	M	1192

Strength (cont.)	Culture	Sex	Page
Owasse	Men.	M	1221
Palesmurt	Fin-Ug.	M	1228
Pallas	Gk.	M	1228
Pantagruel	Fr.	M	1234
Paul Bunyan	Folk.	M	1244
Perseus	Gk.	M	1257
Pollente	Eng.	M	1283
Roma	Rom.	F	1346
Rustam	Pers.	M	1355
Samson	Hebr.	M	1394
Sanda	Hittite	M	1395
Seraph	Hebr.-Christ.	M	1417
Shakuru	Pawnee	M	1429
Siegfried	Germ.	M	1448
Siegmund	Germ.	M	1448
Sigmund	Norse	M	1449
Sphinx	Egy., Gk.	F	1482
Stheno	Gk.	F	1494
Susa-no-wo	Jap.	M	1512
Tarzan	Am. Lit.	M	1536
Theseus	Gk.	M	1554
Thrudugr	Norse	M	1561
Titans	Gk.	M, F	1577
Togakushi	Jap.	M	1584
Tsakaka-Itiac	Hidatsa	M	1602
Vareghna	Pers.	M	1639
Verethraghna	Pers.	M	1646
Vyasa	Hin.	M	1660
Zal	Pers.	M	1715
Zethus	Gk.	M	1718
Zeus	Gk.	M	1719
Zmay	Serb.	M	1722

STRIFE (CONTENTION, DISCORD, DISORDER)

Amphilogeai	Gk.	F	88
Andret	Med. Lit.	M	93
Anrta	Hin.	M	101
Astaroth	Caba.	M	139
Bildad	Hebr.	M	211
Cudoemus	Gk.	M	396
Dasim	Mos.	M	416
Discordia	Rom.	F	450
Dysnomie	Gk.	F	481
Eris	Gk.	F	521
Eros	Gk.	M	522

	Culture	Sex	Page
Eurytion	Gk.	M	533
Evnissyen	Bryth.	M	536
Friuch	Cel.	M	613
Gamchicoth (Gog-sheklah)	Caba.	M	625
Harlequin	Folk.	M	723
Ioce	Gk.		836
Iris	Gk.	F	839
Jahi	Zoro.	F	861
Manmatha	Hin.	M	905
Neikea	Gk.	F	1161
Numitor & Amulius	Rom.	M-M	1185
Picrochole	Fr.	M	1268
Rahu & Ketu	Hin.	M	1318
Raka	Herv. Is.		1320
Ratatosk	Norse	M	1324
Robigus (Averuncus)	Rom.	M	1343
Ruaumoko	Poly.	M	1352
Rucht	Cel.	M	1353
Saltu	Baby.	F	1392
Tiamat	Baby.	F	1570
Togarini	Caba.	M	1584
Vari-mate-takere	Herv. Is.	F	1320
Yaotlnecoc	Mex.	M	1701

STRONG DRINKS (SEE WINE)
STUPIDITY (SEE IGNORANCE)

SUN (SOLAR)

	Culture	Sex	Page
Aaron	Hebr.	M	10
Aarvak	Norse		10
Ababinili	Chick.	M	11
Abaeus	Gk.	M	11
Abednego	Hebr.	M	14
Abraham	Hebr., Mos.	M	17
Absalom	Hebr.	M	19
Achilles	Gk.	M/A	25
Adam-Bell	Eng.	M	30
Adapa	Baby.	M	30
Adekagagwaa	Iroq.	M	31
Adi-daivata	Hin.	M	32
Aditya	Hin.	M	33
Adityabandhu	Bud.	M	33
Adon	Phoen.	M	33
Adonai	Hebr.	M	33
Adrammelech	Sem.	M	35
Aeneas	Rom.	M	40

	Culture	Sex	Page
Aepytus	Gk.	M	41
Af-ra	Egy.	M	43
Agag	Hebr.	M	44
Agamemnon	Gk.	M	44
Agni	Hin.	M	49
Agohya	Hin.	M	50
Aharyu	Hin.	M	52
Alcmaeon	Gk.	M	65
Alsvid	Norse		11
Amarud	Baby.	M	80
Amaruduk	Baby.	M	80
Amaterasu	Jap.	F	81
Ambres	Cel.	M	82
Amen (Amen-Ra)	Egy.	M	83
Amitabha	Bud.	M	86
Amleth	Norse	M	86
Ammon	Egy.	M	86
Anhoret	Egy.	M	87
Ansa	Hin.	M	101
Apis	Egy.	M	109
Apollo	Gk.	M	110
Ara	Arm.	M	116
Ariel	Eng.	M	124
Arthur	Bryth.	M	132
Artinis	Urartians	M	133
Arusha	Hin.	M	134
Aryaman	Hin.	M	134
Asari	Baby.	M	135
Asclepius	Gk.	M	136
Asshur	Assyr.	M	143
Atabyrius	Hebr.	M	147
Aten	Egy.	M	149
Athamas	Gk.	M	149
Aton	Mex.	M	153
Atreus	Gk.	M	153
Attis	Phryg.	M	154
Atum	Egy.	M	155
Aum	Hin.	M	157
Avo	Norse	M	162
Azariah	Hebr.	M	164
Baal	Sem.	M	167
Baal-Peor	Sem.	A	167
Baal-Tamar	Phoen.	M	168
Baba, Ali	Arab.	M	168
Babbar	Sum.	M	169
Bacchus	Gk.	M	170

	Culture	Sex	Page
Bacis	Egy.	M	171
Balder	Norse	M	174
Balin	Bryth.	M	176
Bata	Egy.	M	185
Belenus	Bryth.	M	197
Beli	Bryth.	M	197
Bellerophon	Gk.	M	199
Bennu	Baby.	M	202
Beowulf	Ang-Sax.	M	203
Bevis of Hampton	Bryth.	M	207
Bhaga	Hin.	M	207
Bheki	Hin.	M	208
Bissat	Tatar	M	220
Bjelbog	Slav.	M	220
Bors (Emrys, Myrddin)	Bryth.	M	237
Brahm	Hin.	M	240
Bres	Cel.	M	246
Buddha	Bud.	M	255
Cadmus	Gk.	M	266
Canute	Norse	M	287
Capac	Inca	M	288
Catha	Ital.	M	298
Caut & Cautopat	Pers.	M-M	300
Cephalus	Gk.	M	303
Chalchiutlicue (Altcanals)	Mex.	F/A	308
Chandragupta	Hin.	M	310
Chemosh	Sem.	M	317
Cheop	Egy.	M	318
Chors	Slav.	M	329
Christ	Christ.	M	330
Chrysaor	Gk.	M	334
Cian	Cel.	M	338
Cinderella	Folk.	F	339
Cindrillot	Folk.	M	340
Clym of the Clough	Eng.	M	351
Conall Cernach	Cel.	M	363
Conlaoch	Cel.	M	367
Corineus	Cel.	M	371
Cretan Bull	Gk.	M	381
Cu	Cel.	M	392
Cuchulainn	Cel.	M	393
Curoi mac Daire	Cel.	M	398
Cymbeline	Cel.	M	402
Dadhikra	Hin.	M	404
Daedalus	Gk.	M	404
Dagda	Cel.	M	405

	Culture	Sex	Page
Dainichinyorai	Jap.	A	407
Daksha	Hin.	M	408
Dan	Assyr.	M	410
David	Hebr.	M	417
Dazbog	Rus.	M	420
Deimne	Cel.	M	570
Demophoon	Gk.	M	432
Dianus	Rom.	M	442
Dietrich von Bern	Norse	M	444
Dionysus	Gk.	M	447
Dioscuri	Gk.	M-M	449
Dudugera	N. Guin.	M	475
Dusura	Sem.	M	477
Dyumani	Hin.		481
Ef	Egy.	M	491
Egli-yahu (Yaw)	Samaria	M	1702
El	Sem.	M	497
Eleleus	Gk.	M	500
El-Gebal	Sem.	M	497
El Hidr	Arab.	M	503
Elijah	Hebr.	M	503
Elisha (Eliseus)	Hebr.	M	504
Elissa	Arab., Rom.	F	504
Endymion	Gk.	M	511
Enoch	Hebr.	M	512
Epunamun	Argen., Chil. Ind.	M	517
Eravan	Siam.	M	518
Eri	Arm.	M	519
Eros	Gk.	M	522
Eshmun	Phoen.	M	525
Esus	Cel.	M	526
Euphemus	Gk.	M	531
Fer Fedail	Cel.	M/A	561
Fiachadh	Cel.	M	564
Fiachna	Cel.	M	564
Fingal	Cel.	M	568
Finn	Norse	M	570
Finn mac Coul	Cel.	M	570
Fo (Foh, Fuhi)	Chin.	M	589
Frey	Norse	M	609
Frithiof	Norse	M	612
Fuchi	Jap.	F	615
Fum	Chin.		617
Galahad	Bryth.	M	622
Gareth	Bryth.	M	629

	Culture	Sex	Page
Gawain	Bryth.	M	635
Gilgamesh	Sum.	M	656
Gish Bar	Baby.	M	660
Glaucus	Gk.	M	662
Golden Egg	World Wide		672
Golden Fleece	Gk.		673
Grettir	Ice.	M	374a
Guy of Warwick	Bryth.	M	700
Gwawl	Bryth.	M	700
Gwion Bach	Cel.	M	701
Gwydion	Bryth.	M	702
Gwyrthur	Bryth.	M	703
Hahgweldiyu	Iroq.	M	708
Haosravah	Pers.	M	723
Hari	Hin.	M	726
Harmachis	Egy.	M	727
Harpichruti	Egy.	M	728
Harpocrates	Gk.	M	728
Hathor	Egy.	F	730
Hecatos	Gk.	M	741
Helios	Gk.	M	747
Heol	Cel.	M	751
Heracles	Gk.	M	752
Hercules	Rom.	M	759
Hesus	Cel.	M	765
Hippolytus	Gk.	M	773
Hippomenes	Gk.	M	774
Hor-akhi	Egy.	M	787
Horus	Egy.	M	792
Horvendil	Dan.	M	793
Ho-Wo	Jap.		797
Hu	Bryth., Egy.	M	800
Hu Gadarn	Welsh	M	800
Huitzilopochtli	Mex.	M	803
Humber	Germ.	M	805
Hvar	Zoro.	M	809
Hyperion	Gk.	M	812
Hypsistos	Gk.	M	813
Ichabod	Hebr.	M	817
Ilat	Arab.	F	823
Immanuence	Bryth.	M	826
Indra	Hin.	M	829
Ini-init	Philip.	M	831
Intu	Inca	M	834
Ioskeha	Huron	M	837
Ipalnemohuani	Mex.	M	+

	Culture	Sex	Page
Iruwa	Afr.	M	841
Isaac	Hebr.	M	841
Isandros	Gk.	M	842
Itylus	Gk.	M	849
Itys	Gk.	M	850
Itzamna	Mex.	M	850
Ixion	Gk.	M	852
Izdubar	Chald.	M	854
Jacob	Hebr.	M	858
Jan	Burm.		863
Janus	Ital.	M	864
Jason	Gk.	M	866
Jehovah	Hebr.	M	870
Jephthah	Hebr.	M	872
Jesus	Christ.	M	877
Joseph (Yusuf)	Hebr., Mos.	M	888
Joshua	Hebr.	M	889
Junak	Slav.	M	895
Kalyb	Christ.	M	905
Kamalamitra	Hin.	M	906
Kane	Poly.	M	908
Ka-nub	Egy.	M	908
Kao Hsin	Chin.	M	908
Karna	Hin.	M	910
Karnu	Assyr.	M	911
Karoon	Mos.	M	911
Katcinas	Pueblo	M	912
Keneu	Iroq.		916
Keresaspa	Pers.	M	918
Kettu	Baby.	M	920
Khambaba	Pers.	M	922
Khepera	Egy.	M	924
Khidr	Arab.	M	924
King Bruin	Bryth.	M	929
King Lud	Bryth.	M	929
Kinich-ahau	Mex.	M	932
Kintaro	Jap.	M	932
Kitshi Manitou	Chip.	M	935
Korah	Hebr.	M	942
Kowwituma	Zuni	M	944
Krishna	Hin.	M	945
Kuhlwch	Welsh	M	950
Kumush	Modoc	M	951
Kwasind	N.A.I.	M	955
Lado & Lada	Slav.	M-F	961
Laertes	Gk.	M	963

	Culture	Sex	Page
Lancelot	Bryth.	M	969
Leander	Gk.	M	979
Lisa	Daho.	M	1001
Llew Llaw Gyffes	Welsh	M	1005
Llwch Llawwynnawc	Welsh	M	1006
Lohengrin	Germ.	M	1009
Lug	Cel.	M	1022
Lugus	Gaelic	M	1024
Mabon	Welsh	M	1031
Maelduin	Gaelic	M	1036
Maha-ben-ach	Sem.	M	1042
Malak-Bel	Sem.	M	1048
Manabhozho	Algon.	M	1054
Maponos	Gaulish	M	1063
Marathon Bull	Gk.	M	1064
Mardoll	Norse	F	1065
Marduk (Merodach)	Baby.	M	1065
Marttanda	Hin.	M	1071
Matholwych	Welsh	M	1076
Meleager	Gk.	M	1085
Melicertes	Gk.	M	1086
Melkarth	Phoen.	M	1086
Menes	Egy.	M	1089
Mentu	Egy.	M	1090
Meriadek	Breton	M	1092
Michabo	Algon.	M	1098
Michael	Christ.	M	1099
Mikura-tana-no-kami	Jap.	F	1102
Milanion	Rom.	M	1102
Minos	Gk.	M	1107
Misharu	Phoen.	M	1110
Mithra	Pers.	M	1112
Mitra	Baby., Hin.	M	1112
Mnevis	Egy.	M	1113
Molc	Cel.	M	1115
Moloch	Sem.	M	1115
Mongan	Cel.	M	1117
Moses	Hebr.	M	1126
Mumba'an	Indo.	M	1136
Nabu	Baby.	M	1146
Nala	Hin.	M	1150
Naoise	Cel.	M	1154
Nayanezgani	Nav.	M	1159
Nefer-tem	Egy.	M	1160
Nephthys	Egy.	F	1163
Nergal	Assyr-Baby.	M	1164

	Culture	Sex	Page
Ninazu	Sum.	M	1170
Ningirsu (En-mersi)	Sum.	M	1172
Ninib	Assyr-Baby.	M	1173
Nin-shach	Baby.	M	1173
Ninurta (Sakut)	Sum.	M	1174
Noah	Hebr.	M	1177
Noman (Outis)	Gk.	M	1179
Nonuragmi	Mex.	M	1179
Nornagest	Norse	M	1180
Nusku	Baby.	M	1187
Nyambe	Cong.	A	1188
Od	Norse	M	1194
Odysseus	Gk.	M	1196
Oedipus	Gk.	M	1198
Ogma	Cel.	M	1200
Oisin	Cel.	M	1202
Okikurumi	Ainu	M	1203
Old Sol	Folk.	M	1205
Om	Hin.	M	1207
Onouris	Egy.	M	97
Orestes	Gk.	M	1214
Orion	Gk.	M	1215
Orlando	Ital.	M	1215
Ormuzd	Pers.	M	1216
Orpheus	Gk.	M	1216
Ortlieb	Germ.	M	1217
Osiris	Egy.	M	1218
Oxylus	Gk.	M	1223
Paeivae	Fin.	M	1225
Papachtic	Mex.	M	1235
Parashurama	Hin.	M	1655
Paris	Gk.	M	1238
Parsifal	Germ.	M	1239
Paynal	Mex.	M	1245
Pay Zume	Para.	M	1245
Pegasus	Gk.		1248
Peleus	Gk.	M	1250
Perdix (Kalos, Talus)	Gk.	M/A	1254
Peredur	Bryth.	M	1254
Periclymenus	Gk.	M	1255
Perkunas	Baltic	M	1256
Perses	Gk.	M	1257
Perseus	Gk.	M	1257
Phaethon	Gk.	M	1260
Philoctetes	Gk.	M	1263
Phoebus	Gk.	M	1265

	Culture	Sex	Page
Phoenix	Arab.		1265
Phol (Pol)	Norse	M	1266
Phra Narai	Siam.	M	1267
Piltzintecutlitonatiuh	Mex.	M	1273
Pirhua & Manca	Inca	M-M	1275
Poludnica	Rus.	F	1283
Polymetis	Gk.	M	1284
Prince Charming	Folk.	M	1293
Prince Slugobyl	Slav.	M	1042
Pryderi	Bryth.	M	1298
Pururavas	Hin.	M	1304
Pusan	Hin.	M	1305
Pyramus	Rom.	M	1307
Qat	Mel.	M	1309
Quetzalcoatl	Mex.	M	1312
Ra (Rhe)	Egy.	M	1314
Ragnar Lodbrog	Norse	M	1317
Rakib El	Sem.	M	1320
Rama	Hin.	M	1321
Randver	Norse	M	1322
Rata	Maori	M	1323
Rerir	Norse	M	1333
Resheph	Phoen.	M	1333
Ribhus	Hin.	M	1337
Robin Hood	Eng.	M	1343
Roc (Rekh)	Arab.		1343
Roderick	Span.	M	1344
Roland (Orlando)	Carol.	M	1345
Romulus	Rom.	M	1346
Rustam (Frangrasyan)	Pers.	M	1355
Saint George	Christ.	M	1370
Sakuru	Pawnee	M	1389
Salma	Sem.	M	1391
Samas (Utuki)	Baby.	M	1393
Samson	Hebr.	M	1394
Sandaliarius	Rom.	M	1392
Sandde-bryd-angel	Bryth.	M	1396
Sargon I	Meso.	M	1400
Savitri	Hin.	M	1404
Scyld	Ang-Sax.	M	1409
Sebek-tum-ra	Egy.	M	1412
Sed	Sem.	M	1412
Senx	Bella Coola	M	1416
Setanta	Cel.	M	1421
Shahan	Sum.	M	1435
Snakuru	Pawnee	M	1429

	Culture	Sex	Page
Shalman	Sem.	M	1429
Shamash	Assyr-Baby.	M	1429
Shamshu	Arab.	F	1430
Short Shanks	Scot.	M	1442
Shri (Anushayini)	Hin.	F	1443
Siegfried	Germ.	M	1448
Siegmund	Germ.	M	1448
Sigmund	Norse	M	1449
Sigurd	Norse	M	1451
Sisyphus	Gk.	M	1459
Siyavahsh	Pers.	M	1463
Skate	Ice.	M	1464
Smintheus	Gk.	M	1468
Sobk	Egy.	M	1470
Sokar	Egy.	M	1471
Sol	Ital., Bryth.	M	1471
Sol (Sunna)	Norse	F	1471
Solomon	Hebr., Mos.	M	1472
Stigande	Ang-Sax.	M	1494
Stone Giant	Yaghan Ind.	M	1496
Sua	Bogata Ind.	M	232
Suhrab	Pers.	M	1504
Sume	Braz.	M	1506
Sunna	Norse	F	1510
Surya	Hin.	M	1511
Surya-bai	Hin.	F	1512
Susravas	Hin.	M	1513
Sutekh	Syrian	M	1513
Svar	Hin.	M	1514
Svipdag	Norse	M	1515
Sydyk	Baby.	M	1521
Tahmurath	Pers.	M	1525
Taliesin	Cymric	M	1528
Talus	Gk.	M	1529
Tama-nuit-ite-ra	N. Zeal.	M	1529
Tammuz	Baby.	M	1530
Ta Mo (Bodhidharma)	Chin.	M	1530
Tamoi	Tupi-Guar.	M	1531
Tannhauser	Germ.	M	1532
Tantalus	Gk.	M	1533
Tarani	Hin.	M	1534
Tarksya	Hin.		1535
Telegonus	Gk.	M	1541
Tem	Egy.	M	1542
Tenes (Tenedos)	Gk.	M	1545
Tensho	Jap.	F	1545

	Culture	Sex	Page
Tereus	Gk.	M	1546
Tezcatlipoca	Mex.	M	1549
Thalaba	Oriental	M	1551
Thersander	Gk.	M	1554
Theseus	Gk.	M	1554
Thobadzistshini	Nav.	M	1159
Thorkill	Dan.	M	1561
Thraetaona	Pers.	M	1563
Thum (Tmu)	Egy.	M	1568
Tigranes	Arm.	M	1573
Titan	Gk.	M	1577
Tlaloc Tecutli	Mex.	M	1581
Tobit	Hebr.	M	1583
Tonatiuh	Mex.	M	1586
Topiltcin	Mex.	M	1588
Tortor	Gk.	M	1590
Tristan	Bryth.	M	1599
Tshohanoi	Nav.	M	1603
Tung Chun	Chin.	M	1607
Tyurunmuzykay	Tatar	M	1618
Ubastet	Egy.	F	1619
Uhubaput	Sumu Ind.	M	1621
Ulysses	Rom.	M	1622
Umunla & Umunesiga	Sum.	M-M	1623
Unas	Egy.	M	1623
Unbu	Egy.	M	1623
Unelanuhi	Cherokee	F	1624
Unnefer	Egy.	M	1625
Uriel	Christ.	M	1383
Utnapishtim	Baby.	M	1632
Utu	Sum.	A	1632
Vahagn	Arm.	M	1634
Vali	Norse	M	1636
Varuna	Hin.	M	1639
Vindlir	Norse	M	744
Viracocha	Inca	M	1652
Virbius	Rom.	M	1652
Vishnu	Hin.	M	1654
Vistauru	Pers.	M	1655
Visvakarman	Hin.	M	1655
Vivasvant	Hin.	M	1656
Volsung	Norse	M	1658
Votan	Mex.	M	1658
Wabasso	Pota.	M	1660
Wabun	Algon.	M	1660
Wainamoinen	Fin.	M	1661

Sun (cont.)	Culture	Sex	Page
William Tell	Swiss	M	1681
Xipe Totec	Mex.	M	1696
Yama	Hin.	M	1699
Yamato-take (Wo-uso)	Jap.	M	1699
Yao	Chin.	M	1701
Yaw	Hebr.	M	1702
Yima	Pers.	M	1707
Yimantuwingyai	Calif. Ind.	M	1707
Yo	Daho.		1708
Yoishta	Pers.	M	1709
Yorimitsu	Jap.	M	1709
Yoskeha	Iroq.	M	1710
Yu	Chin.	M	1711
Yudhisthira	Hin.	M	1711
Zairivairi	Pers.	M	1715
Zal	Pers.	M	1715
Zaleukos	Locrian	M	1715
Zamama	Baby.	M	1715
Zas	Chin.	M	1716
Zechariah	Hebr.	M	1717
Zimbabwe	Mashonaland	M	1720
Ziusudra (Xisuthros)	Sum.	M	1721
Zoroaster	Zoro.	M	1734
SUPREME (ALSO SEE CREATOR, MALE PRINCIPLE)			
Ab	Hebr.	M	11
Aba	Choctaw	M	11
Ababinili	Chick.	M	11
Abba	Caba.	M	12
Abraxas	Gnostic	M	18
Absolute, The	Christ.	M	19
Adad	Assyr., Baby., Sum.	M	28
Addu	Arm.	M	31
Adhyatman	Hin.	M	32
Adibuddha	Bud.	M	32
Adi-daivata	Hin.	M	32
Adon	Phoen.	M	33
Adonai	Hebr.	M	33
Adoni	Sem.	M	34
Adrammelech & Anammelech	Sem.	M-M	35
Aesar	Cel.	M	41
Ahi (Ahu)	Sem.	M	52
Ahsonnutli	Nav.	A	54
Ahura Mazda	Zoro.	M	54

	Culture	Sex	Page
Aiapaec	Inca	M	54
Ain Soph	Caba.	M	56
Ajy-tangara	Yakut	M	58
Ala	Mos.	M	60
Alfadir	Norse	M	67
Alif	Arab.	M	68
Alilah	Arab.	M	68
Alkuntam	Bella Coola	M	69
Allah	Mos.	M	69
All-Father	World-wide	M	69
Ama-no-minaka-nushi	Jap.	M	80
Amarud	Baby.	M	80
Amaruduk	Baby.	M	80
Amaterasu	Jap.	F	81
Amen (Amen-Ra)	Egy.	M	83
Amida	Jap.	M	85
Amitabha	Bud.	M	86
Amitayus	Bud.	M	86
Amma-ana-ki	Baby.	M	86
Ammon	Egy.	M	86
Ancient of Days	Gnostic	M	93
Androgyne	Tarot	A	94
Anshar	Baby.	M	101
Antipater	Gnostic	M	104
Anu	Sum.	M	104
Apsu	Assyr., Baby., Sum.	M	115
Aramazd	Arm.	M	117
Areop-enap	Nauru Is.	M	120
Areskoui	Iroq.	M	121
Ar-tojon	Yakut	M	133
Ashima	Hamath	M	139
Ashim-Bethel	Hebr.	A	139
Asshur	Assyr.	M	143
Atahocan	Algon.	M	147
Atala	Borneo	M	147
Aten	Egy.	M	149
Athi	Ind-Chin.	M	151
Atman	Hin.	M	152
Attabeiro	Taino	F	154
Au-aa	Sem.	M	155
Aum	Bud., Hin.	M	157
Author	Gnostic	M	159
Awonawilona	Zuni	M/A	162
Baal	Sem.	M	167
Baalberith	Sem.	M	167

	Culture	Sex	Page
Bag-mashtu	Pers.	M	172
Baiame	Aus.	M	173
Be'al	Bryth.	M	188
Bel	Baby.	M	196
Bel Enlil	Baby.	M	197
Bel-Marduk	Baby.	M	200
Belus	Baby.	M	201
Bhagavan	Hin.	M	208
Binah	Caba.	F	212
Bir	Assyr.	M	212
Bongabong	Indo.	M	235
Brahm	Hin.	M	240
Brahma	Hin.	M	240
Buddha	Bud.	M	255
Bure	Norse	M	261
Carios	Gk.	M	1300
Chemosh	Sem.	M	317
Chesed	Caba.	M	320
Chimizigagua	Chib.	M	325
Chinnigchinich	Calif. Ind.	M	326
Chnoumis	Egy.	M	328
Chokmah	Caba.	M	328
Chuku	Ibo (Afr.)	M	336
Coelus	Rom.	M	355
Confucius	Chin.	M	366
Countenance, The	Gnostic	M	667
Coxcox	Mex.	M	377
Cronus	Gk.	M	384
Daath	Caba.	M	404
Dadu	Baby.	M	404
Danu	Cel.	F	104
Daramulum	Aus.	M	414
Deus (Devus)	Gk., Rom.	M	434
Dharmakara	Bud.	M	438
Dipamkara	Bud.	M	449
Diwata Magbabaya	Philip.	M	454
Don	Bryth.	F/A	461
Dyaus (Dyu)	Hin.	M	479
Ea	Assyr., Baby., Sum.	M	481
Ea-pe	Ind-Chin.	M	481
Eheieh (Ehyeh)	Caba.	M	494
Ei	Hebr.	M	494
El	Sem.	M	497
El Chai	Caba.	M	498
Elioun	Phoen.	M	504

	Culture	Sex	Page
Elohim (Eloah)	Hebr.	M	506
El Shaddai	Caba.	M	506
Enki	Assyr.	M	511
Enlil	Baby., Sum.	M	512
Esar	Mos.	M	524
Eternal, The	Gnostic	M	527
Eugpamolak Manobo	Philip.	M	529
Father	Gnostic	M	551
Fatherly	Gnostic	M	551
Fo (Foh)	Chin.	M	589
Foo	Jap.	M	590
Fro (Friuja)	Norse	M	613
Gadiri	Mos.	M	621
Gaea (Ga)	Gk.	F	621
Galligantua	Folk.	M	624
Gautama Siddartha	Bud.	M	255
Geburah (Pachad)	Caba.	M	637
Gedulah	Caba.	M	637
Gitche	Algon.	M	660
Gluskap	Algon.	M	664
God	Hebr-Christ.	M	666
Great Spirit	N.A.I.	M	687
Guamaonocon (Iocauna)	Taino	M	693
Hadad	Sem.	M	705
Hatuibwari	Mel.	M	732
Her-shef	Egy.	M	763
Hod	Caba.	F	778
Huaca	Inca	M	801
Huang T'ien Shang Ti	Chin.	M	801
Huhi	Egy.	M	803
Hypsistos	Gk.	M	813
Iao (Iaw, Jao)	Caba.	M	815
Icona	Mex.	M	818
Ihoh (Ihvh)	Caba.	M	822
Ilex	Bryth.	M	823
Illa Ticci	Inca	M	824
Ilmarinen	Fin-Ug.	M	824
Ilu	Assyr.	M	825
Imana	Warundi	M	825
Indra	Hin.	M	829
Infinite One	Gnostic	M	831
Invisible, The	Gnostic	M	835
I-O	Gnostic	M	835
Io (Ihoh)	Universal	M	836
Iocauna	Taino	M	836
Ioskeha	Huron	M	837

	Culture	Sex	Page
Ipalnemohuani	Mex.	M	+
Irmin	Germ.	M	839
Isvara	Hin.	M, F	848
Izanagi & Izanami	Jap.	M-F	853
Jah (Au, Ya, Ya'u)	Hebr.	M	861
Jahveh	Hebr.	A	861
Janus	Ital.	M	864
Jaoth	Baby.	M	865
Jehovah	Hebr.	M	870
Jehovah Elohim	Caba.	M	870
Jessis	Slav.	M	876
Jina	Bud.	M	880
Jove	Rom.	M	891
Juggernaut	Hin.	M	894
Jumala	Fin.	M	895
Jupiter	Rom.	M	896
Ka	Hin.	M	899
Kala	Hin.	M	903
Kala-siva	Hin.	M	903
Kami	Jap.	M	906
Kane	Poly.	M	908
Karu	Gk.	M	1309
Kether	Caba.	A	919
Khaira Khan	Tatar	M	922
Khaldi	Urartian	M	922
Khoda	Pers.	M	925
Kiara	Wankonde	M	926
King of Kings	Christ.	M	930
Kitshi Manitou	Chip.	M	935
Kneph	Egy.	M	937
Koloowisi (Palulukon)	Zuni	M	941
Ku	Hawa.	M	947
Laki Oi	Borneo	M	965
Lao Tze (Shen Pao)	Chin.	M	973
Li	Chin.	M	989
Lord of Israel	Caba.	M	667
Lukelang	Caro. Is.	M	1024
Lumawig	Philip.	M	1024
Macroprosopus	Caba.	M	1034
Mahadeva	Hin.	M	1042
Mahadevi	Hin.	F	1042
Maho-peneta	Iroq.	M	1045
Malkuth	Caba.	F	1050
Manama	Philip.	M	1054
Manitou	Algon.	M	1058
Marduk (Merodach)	Assyr-Baby.	M	1065

	Culture	Sex	Page
Mauli	Mashonaland	M	1078
Mawa-Lisa	Daho.	A	1078
Mawr Pen Aethir	Welsh	M	1079
Mazda	Pers.	M	1081
Mbamba	Wankonde	M	1081
Meriadek	Breton	M	1092
Messou	Pota.	M	1095
Mexitli	Mex.	M	1097
Michabo (Messon)	Algon.	M	1098
Microprosopus	Caba.	M	1099
Milcom	Sem.	M	1102
Min	Egy.	M	1106
Missibizi	Algon.	M	1111
Moloch	Ammonite	M	1115
Monan	Braz.	M	1116
Monenequi	Mex.	M	1116
Moyocoyatzin	Mex.	M	1132
Mulungu	Zulu	M	1135
Mushtari	Pers.	M	1139
Nadimmud	Baby.	M	1146
Nannar	Baby.	A	1153
Narayana	Hin.	M	1155
Nareau	Gil. Is.	M	1156
Nenaboj	Wetucks Ind.	M	1162
Nergal	Assyr-Baby.	M	1164
Nesaru	Caddoan Ind.	M	1165
Netzach	Caba.	M	1166
Ngai	Masai (Afr.)	M	1167
Niezguinek	Slav.	M	1168
Nimrod (Kozi)	Baby.	M	1592
Ning Sang	Burm.	M	1173
Nphan Wa	Burm.	M	1184
Nuada	Cel.	M	1184
Nudimmud (Ninigkug)	Baby.	M	1184
Nyankopong (Nyame)	Ashanti (Afr.)	M	1187
Nzambi (Zambi)	Congo	M	1188
Oannes	Baby., Chald., Phoen.	M	1190
Obassi	Ekoi, Ibibio	M	1191
Odin	Norse	M	1195
Om (Aum)	Hin.	M	1207
Omit'o-Fo	Chin.	M	1208
Ophion & Eurynome	Gk.	M	1211
Ormuzd	Zoro.	M	1216
Ormzdakan	Arm.	M	1480
Oshala	Yoruba	M	1218

	Culture	Sex	Page
Othinus	Dan.	M	1220
Pachacamac	Inca	M	1224
Pachad	Caba.	M	1224
Padmaheruka	Bud.	M	1225
Pallantios	Gk.	M	1228
P'an Ku	Chin.	M/A	1233
Papaeus	Rom.	M	1235
Pappas	Sem.	M	1236
Perkunas	Baltic	M/A	1256
Perun	Slav.	M	1258
Phanes	Gk.	M	1261
Pillan	Chil.	M	1271
Pita	Brahman	M	1276
Porenutius	Slav.	M	1514
Ptah-Sokar-Osiris	Egy.	M	1471
Pundjel	Aus.	M	1301
Purushottama	Hin.	M	1305
Qamate	Afr.	M	1309
Qeb (Seb)	Egy.	M	1309
Q're	Hebr.	M	1309
Ra	Egy.	M	1314
Radgost	Dan.	M	1316
Radigast	Slav.	M	1316
Ribimbi	Transvaal	M	1337
Sabaoth	Hebr.	M	1356
Sadai	Caba.	M	667
Sakyamuni	Bud.	M	1390
San Ch'ing	Chin.	M	1395
Saturn	Rom.	M	1403
Settin-ki-jash	Haida Ind.	M	1421
Shaddai	Hebr.	M	667
Shamash & Sin	Assyr.	M-M	1429
Shang-ti	Chin.	M	1430
Shen Pao	Chin.	M	1434
Shepherd (Good Shepherd)	Christ.	M	1434
Shepherd of Israel	Hebr.	M	1435
Shin	Chin., Jap.	M	1437
Si	Pre-Inca	M	1445
Sibu	Antilles	M	1445
Simurgh	Pers.	M	1456
Siyakmak	Pers.	M	1463
Solomon	Hebr.	M	1472
Sor	Hebr.	M	1476
Spaul	Cowich.	M	1480
Succothbenoth	Baby.	F	1503
Sussistinnako	Sia Ind.	M	1513

	Culture	Sex	Page
Sutekh	Syrian	M	1513
Svabhava	Hin.	M	1514
Svafnir	Norse	M	1514
Svarog	Slav.	M	1514
Svayambhu	Bud., Hin.	M	1515
Sydyk	Phoen.	M	1521
Symbetylos	Hebr.	A	139
Taaroa	Poly.	M	1522
Tai-kih	Chin.	A	1525
Tane	Poly.	M	1531
Tangaroa	Poly.	M	1531
Tarku (Teshup)	Hittite	M	1535
Taronhiawagon	Onondaga Ind.	M	1535
Tartak	Avite		1536
Tat	Theosophy		1537
Tengri	Sib.	M	1545
Teotl	Mex.	M	1546
Teshup	Hittite	M	1547
Tezcatlipoca	Mex.	M	1549
Tezpi	Mex.	M	377
Th	Phoen.	M	1550
Thaah	Mayan	M	1550
Thagya Min	Ind-Chin.	M	1550
Thau	Cel.	M	1552
Theos	Gk.	M	1554
Thonga Tilo	Afr.	M	1560
Thor	Norse	M	1561
Thride (Odin)	Norse	M	1566
Tiamat	Assyr., Baby., Sum.	F	1570
T'ien (Ten)	Chin. (Jap)	A	1571
T'ien Pao	Chin.	M	1572
Tii	Marq.	M	1573
Tiki	Maori	M	1573
Tina	Ital.	M	1575
Tipherath	Caba.	M	1575
Tirawa	Pawnee	M	1576
Tiu	Teut.	M	1617
Tiw	Ang-Sax.	M	1617
Tixe	Zulu	M	1581
Tloque Nahuaque	Mex.	M	1582
Tonacatecutli	Mex.	M	1586
Tornarsuk	Eskimo	M	1589
Tororut	Suk (Afr.)	M	1589
Tshan-pa	Tibet.	M	1603
Tupan	Braz.	M	1608

Supreme (cont.)	Culture	Sex	Page
Tyr	Norse	M	1617
Uggerus	Norse	M	1620
Uhubaput	Sumu Ind.	M	1621
Ukko	Fin.	M	1621
Uranus	Gk.	M	1627
Urge	Gnostic	M	1629
Vajradhara	Tib.	M	1634
Varuna	Hin.	M	1639
Vasu	Hin.	M	1641
Vatea	Herv. Is.	M	1641
Ve	Norse	M	1643
Veralden-Olmai	Lapp	M	1648
Visvakarman	Hin.	M	1655
Vodu	Daho.	M	1657
Wabun	Algon.	M	1660
Wak	Galla (Afr.)	M	1662
Walleyneup	Aus.	M	1663
Wisakketjak	Micmac	M	1686
Wohpekumen	Yurok	M	1688
Wotan	Germ.	M	1692
Xax-coc-ahmut	Mex.	M	853
Yah (Yahweh)	Caba.	M	1698
Yesod	Caba.	M	1705
Yu Huang	Chin.	M	1712
Yuttoere	Carrier Ind.	M	1713
Zabaoth	Gnostic	M	1714
Zakar	Assyr.	M	1715
Zan	Cretan	M	1716
Zanahary	Madagascan	M	1716
Zapala	Inca	M	1652
Zarathustra	Zoro.	M	1734
Zebaot	Caba.	M	1425
Zeus	Gk.	M	1719
Ziu (Tiu)	Germ.	M	1721
Zoroaster	Zoro.	M	1734
Ztak	Hittite	M	1734

SURROGATE (SEE SACRIFICE VICTIM)

SWIFTNESS (FLEETNESS)			
Ajax the Lesser	Gk.	M	58
Anakes	Gk.	M	90
Asahel	Hebr.	M	134
Asvins	Hin.	M	146
Atalanta	Gk.	F	148
Bayard	Med. Lit.	M	187

	Culture	Sex	Page
Bedivere	Bryth.	M	193
Byat Ta	Ind-Chin.	M	264
Camilla	Rom.	F	281
Caoilte mac Ronan	Cel.	M	287
Centaur	Gk.	M	303
Cherub	Hebr.	M	319
Con	Inca	M	363
Dornolla	Cel.	F	464
Dorulas	Gk.	M	465
Enbarr	Cel.		510
Garide	Mong.		630
Garuda	Hin.		633
Hippomenes	Gk.	M	774
Hoener	Norse	M	779
Ho Hsien-Ku	Chin.	F	780
Hugi	Norse	M	803
Kasenko	Jap.	F	911
Levarcham	Cel.	F	988
Medyr	Bryth.	M	1084
Milanion	Rom.	M	1102
Morgan Le Fay	Bryth.	F	1123
Paynal	Mex.	M	1245
Pelops	Gk.	M	1251
Podarge	Gk.	F	1281
Priam (Podarces)	Gk.	M	1292
Rhiannon	Bryth.	F	1336
Seraph	Hebr-Christ.	M	1417
Thjalfi	Norse	M	1560
Vareghna	Pers.	M	1639
Vayu	Hin.	M	1642
Verethraghna	Pers.	M	1646
Yskyrdaw & Yseudydd	Bryth.		1711

SWINEHERD (SEE ANIMAL KEEPER)
SYLVAN DEITY (SEE WOODLAND)
TASK FULFILLER (SEE MENIAL)
TASKMASTER (SEE MASTER OF DEITY)
TEACHER (SEE TUTOR)

TEMPTED

	Culture	Sex	Page
Adam	Hebr.	M	29
Ananda	Hin.	M	1063
Anthony the Great	Christ.	M	1363
Buddha	Bud.	M	255
Eve	Hebr.	F	534
Keresaspa	Pers.	M	918

Tempted (cont.)	Culture	Sex	Page
Lu Tung-pin	Chin.	M	1026
Orpheus	Gk.	M	1216
Siva	Hin.	M	1461
Thorkill	Dan.	M	1561
Vathek	Mos.	A	1642
Yappan	Mex.	M	1701
Yati	Hin.	M	1702
Zagreus	Cretan	M	1715
TEMPTER			
Eblis	Mos.	M	489
Eve	Hebr.	F	534
Hidimva	Hin.	M	1511
Kama	Bud., Hin.	M	905
Khnathaiti	Pers.	F	918
Mara	Bud.	M	1063
Mrtyu	Hin.	M	1132
Namuci	Bud.	M	1152
Satan	Hebr.	M	1402
Sedit	Wintun	M	1413
Surpanakha	Hin.	F	1511
Tilottama	Hin.	F	1574
Titans	Cretan	M, F	1715
Tlazolteotl	Mex.	F	1701
THREEFOLD DEITY (SEE THREE STEPS, TRIAD)			
THREE STEPS (THREE MANIFESTATIONS)			
Agni	Hin.	M	49
Apollo	Gk.	M	1566
Artemis	Gk.	F	131
Cernunnos	Cel.	M	305
Criophorus	Gk.	M	382
Diana	Rom.	F	441
Gucumatz	Guate.	M	694
Gylfe (Gangleri)	Norse	M	704
Hari	Hin.	M	726
Hecate	Gk.	F	740
Hometeuli	Mex.	M	784
Horus	Egy.	M	1598
Indra	Hin.	M	829
Janardana	Hin.	M	863
Manannan	Cel.	M	1054
Maui	Poly.	M	1077
Odin	Norse	M	1195

	Culture	Sex	Page
Praxidice	Gk.	F	1291
Tane	Poly	M	1531
Termagant	Rom.	M	1546
Triglav	Slav.	M	1597
Trikaya	Bud.	M	1597
Trivia	Rom.	F	1599
Vamana	Hin.	M	1637
Vishnu	Hin.	M	1654
Yima	Pers.	M	1707
Zoroaster	Zoro.	M	1734

THUNDER

	Culture	Sex	Page
Acaryavajrapani	Bud.	M	22
Adad (Hadad)	Sem.	M	28
Addu	Sem.	M	31
Agbe	Daho.	M	46
Ai	Fin-Ug.	M	54
Akethor	Norse	M	59
Altjirra	Aus.	M	77
Animiki	Ojibway Ind.	M	98
Apocatequil	Inca	M	109
Asan-sagan-tengeri	Mong.	M	135
Asgaya Gigagaei	Cherokee	A	137
At'am	Fin-Ug.	M	148
Baal-Lebanon	Sem.	M	167
Balshameme	Sem.	M	177
Bromius	Gk.	M	251
Bronte	Gk.	M	251
Camaxtli	Mex.	M	279
Chaac	Mex.	M	307
Cuchi	Aus.	M	393
Dadu	Baby.	M	404
Daramulum	Aus.	M	414
Daronwy	Cel.	M	416
Diomedes	Gk.	M	446
Donar	Norse	M	461
Dyaus	Hin.	M	479
Ehlaumel	Calif. Ind.	M	494
Fjorgyn	Norse	M	578
Gabriel	Christ., Hebr., Mos.	M	619
Gromovit	Slav.	M	692
Gucumatz	Guate.	M	694
Hahness	Chinook	M	708
Haokah	Sioux Ind.	M	723
Hevajra	Bud.	M	766
Hino	Iroq.	M	772

	Culture	Sex	Page
Hisa Females	Jap.	F	775
Hloride	Norse	M	776
Hono-ika-zuchi	Jap.	M	785
Hora-galles	Fin-Ug.	M	787
Hun-pic-tek	Mex.	M	807
Hurakan	C.A.I.	M	808
Idurmer	Sem.	M	821
Iliya Gromovik	Christ.	M	692
Indra	Hin.	M	829
Jehovah	Hebr.	M	870
Jove	Rom.	M	891
Jupiter Tonans	Rom.	M	897
Kakaitch	Makah	M	902
Kaminarisan	Jap.	M	906
Karei	Malay.	M	910
Kei-kung	Chin.	M	915
Kemosh	Sem.	M	916
Keraunos	Gk.	M	917
Kineun	Men.	M	928
Kohin	Aus.	M	940
Lei Kung	Chin.	M	981
Marduk	Assyr-Baby.	M	1065
Matarisvan	Hin.	M	1074
Michabo	Algon.	M	1098
Mjollnir (Miollnir)	Norse	M	1108
Mo-li Hung	Chin.	M	601
Mororoma	Bol.	M	1125
Mulungu	Afr.	M	1135
Murtaznu	Baby.	M	1138
Nari	Jap.	A	1156
Num	Samoyed	M	1185
Odin	Norse	M	1195
O-kuni-nushi	Jap.	M	1204
Oku-thor	Norse	M	1204
P'an Ku	Chin.	M	1233
Paravataksha	Hin.	M	1237
Perkunas	Baltic	M	1256
Perun	Slav.	M	1258
Piker	Esthonian	M	1271
Pillan	Chil.	M	1271
Pitkomoinen	Fin.	M	1276
Ptah	Egy.	M	1299
Purgine	Altaic	M	1303
Radigast	Slav.	M	1316
Raijin	Jap.	M	1318
Ramasoon	Siamese	M	1321

	Culture	Sex	Page
Ramman (Rimman)	Baby.	M	1322
Resheph	Phoen.	M	1333
Sandan	As. Min.	M	1396
Saxnot	Ang-Sax.	M	1404
Shango	Yoruban	M	1430
Sivirri	Aus.	M	1461
So	Daho.	M	1695
Sogbo	Daho.	M	1471
Sphinx	Gk.	F	1482
Sucellos	Cel.	M	1503
Summanus	Ital.	M	1506
Susa-no-wo	Jap.	M	1512
Sutekh	Syrian	M	1513
Tabuerik	Micro.	M	1523
Take-mi-kazuchi	Jap.	M	1527
Tannus	Gaulish	M	1532
Taranis	Gaulish	F	1534
Tarku	Hittite	M	1535
Tengu	Jap.	M	1545
Teshup (Teshub)	Hittite	M	1547
Thein	Burm.	M	1553
Theispas	Arm.	M	1553
Theodoric	Germ.	M	1553
T'hlu-kluts	Makah	M	903
Thor (Thunor)	Norse	M	1561
Thrym	Norse	M	1567
Thunderbird	Am. Ind.	M	1568
Tiermes	Lapp	M	1572
Tina	Ital.	M	1575
Tora-galles	Fin.	M	1588
Tumo-pas	Fin-Ug.	M	1607
Tupan	Braz.	M	1608
Tu-tutsh	Nootkan Ind.	M	1611
Twanjiraka	Aus.	M	1611
Tyndareus	Gk.	M	1617
Typanom	Siam.	M	1617
Ukko	Fin.	M	1621
Ulu-tojon (Syga)	Yakut	M	1622
Vac	Hin.	F	1633
Vajradhara	Tib.	M	1634
Vajrapani	Bud.	M	1635
Xevioso	Daho.	M	1695
Yaw	Hebr.	M	1702
Yesza	Slav.	M	1705
Zeus	Gk.	M	1719

TIME (FINITE)	Culture	Sex	Page
Cronus	Gk.	M	384
Elli	Norse	F	505
Eresichthon	Gk.	M	518
Ewigzeitgeist	Germ.		536
Father Time	Folk.	M	551
Hemera	Gk.	F	750
Horae	Gk.	F	787
Kairos	Gk.	M	+
Kala	Hin.	M	903
Kalachakra	Bud.	M	903
Kala-Siva	Hin.	M	903
Khensu	Egy.	M	923
Kriya Sakti	Hin.	F	947
Lha-mo-kar-po	Tib.	F	989
Luna	Rom.	F	1025
Mani	Norse	M	1471
Ra	Sem.	M	1314
Saeter	Norse	M	1360
Saturn	Rom.	M	1403
Sol	Norse	F	1471
Tai-sui	Chin.	M	1526
Thoth	Egy.	M	1562
Uac-Metunahau	Mex.	M	853
Zarvan	Zoro.	M	1716

TRADE (SEE CRAFT)

TRAITOR (TREASON, ALSO SEE DECEIT)			
Abiathar	Hebr.	M	15
Abiram	Hebr.	M	16
Achtiophel	Hebr.	M	26
Adonijah	Hebr.	M	34
Ahimelech	Hebr.	M	53
Ahithophel	Hebr.	M	53
Dathan	Hebr.	M	417
Ephialtes	Gk.	M	515
Ganelon	Carol.	M	627
Korah	Hebr.	M	942
Mata Hari	Fr.	F	1074
Mordred	Bryth.	M	1122
Morgan le Fay	Bryth.	F	1123
Pekah	Hebr.	M	1249
Pul	Assyr.	M	1300
Quisling	Norw.	M	1314
Ugolino, Count	Ital.	M	1620

TRANSFORMER (SEE SHAPE CHANGER)	Culture	Sex	Page
TRANSITORINESS (SEE EPHEMERAL)			
TRAVELER (NAVIGATION, SEAFARER, PILGRIM. ALSO SEE QUESTER, WANDERER)			
Abeona	Rom.	F	15
Artemis	Gk.	F	131
Bernard of Menthon	Christ.	M	1365
Dosojin	Jap.	M	465
Ekchuah	Mex.	M	497
Hsing Shen	Chin.	M	800
Huard	Breton	M	801
Jizo	Jap.	M	881
Kompira	Jap.	M	941
Koshin	Jap.	M	943
Kshiti Garbha	Hin.	M	947
Lares Permarini	Rom.	M	974
Latawiec	Pol.	A	975
Lityerses	Gk.	M	1003
Mercury	Rom.	M	1091
Myojo-tenshi	Jap.	M	1142
Pan	Gk.	M	1230
Pleiades	Gk.	F	1279
Pooka	Cel.	M	1286
Ptah	Egy.	M	1299
Pusan	Hin.	M	1305
Raphael	Hebr.	M	1323
Sae-no-kami	Jap.	M	1360
Saint Julian	Christ.	M	1373
Saint Nicholas	Christ.	M	1378
Succoth-Benoth	Baby.	F	1503
Surali	Fin-Ug.	M	1511
Tacatecutli	Mex.	M	1523
Usnisavijaya	Bud.	F	1631
Yacatecutli	Mex.	M	1697
Yech	Am. Ind.	M	1703
TREACHERY (SEE DECEIT, TRAITOR)			
TREASON (SEE TRAITOR)			
TREASURE (SEE WEALTH)			
TREE (PLANT)			
Adonis	Gk.	M	34
Artemis	Gk.	F	131
Astarte	Phoen.	F	144

	Culture	Sex	Page
Attis	Phryg.	M	154
Baal Tamar	Phoen.	M	168
Balder	Norse	M	174
Bata	Egy.	M	185
Belili	Sum.	F	197
Caryotis	Gk.	F	131
Chikisanti	Jap.	F	323
Cyparissus	Gk.	M	402
Daphne	Gk.	F	414
Dascylus	Gk.	M	416
Devatas	Hin.	F	435
Dryad (Hamadryad)	Gk.	F	473
Eurydice	Gk.	F	532
Gwern	Cel.	M	701
Gwydion	Bryth.	M	702
Hamadryad	Gk.	F	714
Heliades	Gk.	F	747
Heracles	Gk.	M	752
Herne	Eng.	M	762
Hesus	Cel.	M	765
Hu	Bryth.	M	800
Hu Gadarn	Welsh	M	800
Janicot	Basque	M	863
John the Baptist	Christ.	M	1372
Kono-hana-sakuya-hine	Jap.	F	941
Kukunochi	Jap.	A	950
Laufey (Nal)	Norse	F	976
Lotis	Gk.	F	1014
Lycaon	Gk.	M	1027
Mayauel	Mex.	F	1080
Meliades	Gk.	F	1086
Meliae	Gk.	F	1086
Mintha	Gk.	F	1107
Myrrha	Gk.	F	1142
Nal	Norse	F	1150
Nari	Jap.	A	1156
Nase & Aze	Jap.	M-F	1156
Nidaba	Sum.	F	1168
Nut	Egy.	F	1187
Odendonnia	Iroq.	M	1541
Osiris	Egy.	M	1218
Patollus	Prussian	M	1243
Perkunas	Prussian	M	1256
Perun	Slav.	M	1258
Philyra	Gk.	F	1264
Phyllis	Gk.	F	1267

	Culture	Sex	Page
Pitys	Gk.	F	1276
Pomona	Rom.	F	1285
Potrympus	Baltic	M	1289
Smilax	Gk.	F	1468
Sykites	Gk.	M	1521
Syrinx	Gk.	F	1522
Tata	Sib.	M	1537
Thor	Norse	M	1561
Tomte	Swed.	M	1586
Tu	Poly.	M	1604
Tumo-pas	Fin-Ug.	M	1607
Yaksa	Hin.	M	1698
Yoskeha	Iroq.	M	1710
Zacharias	Mos.	M	1714
TRESPASSER			
Actaeon	Gk.	M	28
Endymion	Gk.	M	511
Hylas	Gk.	M	811
Narcissus	Gk.	M	1155
Odysseus	Gk.	M	1196
Orpheus	Gk.	M	1216
Pentheus	Gk.	M	1253
Tiresias	Gk.	M	1576
TRIAD (THREEFOLD DEITY)			
Aeacus-Minos-Rhadamanthus	Gk.	M-M-M	1107
Aegle-Lampetia-Phaethusa	Gk.	F-F-F	747
Aello-Celaeno-Ocypeta	Gk.	F-F-F	728
Aglaia-Euphrosyne-Thalia	Gk.	F-F-F	681
Aglaia-Pasithea-Peitho	Gk.	F-F-F	681
Aglaope-Pisinoe-Thelxiepia	Gk.	F-F-F	1458
Agni-Indra-Soma	Hin.	M-M-M	1598
Agni-Indra-Surya	Hin.	M-M-M	1598
Agni-Indra-Yama	Hin.	M-M-M	1598
Agni-Surya-Vayu	Hin.	M-M-M	1598
Agni-Trita-Surya	Hin.	M-M-M	49
Agraulid	Gk.	F-F-F	51
Agraulos-Herse-Pandrosos	Gk.	F-F-F	51
Ah Kiuic-Chaac-Hobnil	Mex.	M-M-M	1598
Airya-Cairima-Tura	Pers.	M-M-M	57
Alecto-Megaera-Tisiphone	Gk.	F-F-F	520
Algia-Euphrosyne-Thalia	Gk.	F-F-F	314
Al Lat-Al Uzzah-Manah	Arab.	M-F-F	1597
Amano Mahitotsu-Taka Mimusubi-Kamu Mimusubi	Jap.	M-M-F	1598

	Culture	Sex	Page
Amano Minaka Nushi-Taka Mimusubi-Kamu Mimusubi	Jap.	M-M-F	1598
Amaterasu-Susanowo-Tsukiyoni	Jap.	F-M-M	1598
Amen-Mut-Khonsu	Egy.	M-F-M	1598
Amita-Fugen-Monju	Jap.	M-M-M	1598
Amita-Kwannon-Seishi	Jap.	M-F-M	1598
Anu-Assher-Ea	Sum.	M-M-M	1598
Anu-Bel-Ea	Sum.	M-M-M	1598
Anu-Enlil-Ea (Enki)	Sum.	M-M-M	104
Aoide-Melete-Mneme	Gk.	F-F-F	1138
Apsu-Tiamat-Mummu	Sum.	M-F-M	1598
Aramazd-Anahit-Vahagn	Arm.	M-F-M	1597
Arthur-Guinevere-Gawain	Bryth.	M-F-M	132
Arthur-Guinevere-Lancelot	Bryth.	M-F-M	132
Arthur-Guinevere-Modred	Bryth.	M-F-M	132
Astvatereta-Ukhshyat ereta-Ukhshyat nemah	Zoro.	M-M-M	1398
Athtar-Shamshu-Shahar	Arab.	M-F-M	151
Atropos-Clotho-Lachesis	Gk.	F-F-F	153
AUM	Hin.	M-F-A	1598
Auxo-Carpo-Thallo	Gk.	F-F-F	786
Avalokitesvara-Manjusri-Vajradhara	Bud.	M-M-M	1059
Baal-Astarte-Eshmun	Phoen.	M-F-M	525
Badb-Ana-Macha	Cel.	F-F-F	171
Balthazar-Gaspar-Melchior	Christ.	M-M-M	1564
Banba-Eriu-Fotla	Cel.	F-F-F	178
Brahma-Vishnu-Rudra	Hin.	M-M-M	1598
Brahma-Vishnu-Siva	Hin.	M-M-M	1598
Bres-Lother-Nar	Cel.	M-M-M	349
Brian-Iuchar-Iuchurba	Cel.	M-M-M	247
Buddha-Confucius-LaoTze	Chin.	M-M-M	1565
Buddha-Dharma-Sangha	Bud.	M-M-M	1598
Buddha-Padmapani-Mahasthamaprata	Bud.	M-M-M	1598
Bure-Bor-Bor's Son	Norse	M-M-M	1598
Cabiri	Gk.	M-M-M	265
Cerunnos	Cel.	M-M-M	305
Charites	Gk.	F-F-F	314
Cian-Cethe-Cu	Cel.	M-M-M	338
Clotho-Lachesis-Atropos	Gk.	F-F-F	349
Clothru-Medb-Ethne	Cel.	F-F-F	349
Deverra-Intercidona-Pilumnus	Rom.	F-F-M	+
Diana-Lucina-Hecate	Rom.	M-M-M	442
Dice-Eirene-Eunomia	Gk.	F-F-F	786

	Culture	Sex	Page
Dino-Enyo-Pephredo	Gk.	F-F-F	681
Dipamkara-Sakyamuni-Maitreya	Bud.	M-M-M	1598
Ea-Damkina-Marduk	Baby.	M-F-M	1598
Ea-Marduk-Nabu	Baby.	M-M-M	1598
Eber-Eremon-Amergin	Cel.	M-M-M	488
Erinys	Gk.	F-F-F	520
Eumenides	Gk.	F-F-F	529
Fates (Moirai)	Gk.	F-F-F	551
Father-Son-Holy Ghost	Christ.	M-M-M	1598
Father-Son-Virgin	Christ.	M-M-F	551
Fer Fedail-Tuag-Manannon	Cel.	M-F-M	1605
Frey-Odin-Thor	Norse	M-M-M	609
Fu-Lu-Shou	Chin.	M-M-M	1565
Furies	Gk., Rom.	F-F-F	617
God-His Word-Wisdom	Hebr.		1598
Gorgons	Gk.	F-F-F	678
Graces	Gk.	F-F-F	681
Graeae (Phorcides)	Gk.	F-F-F	681
Gratiae	Rom.	F-F-F	681
Greit-Arthur-Mabon	Bryth.	M-M-M	1565
Greit-Ludd-Mabon	Bryth.	M-M-M	689
Gwalchmei-Llacheu-Riwallaun	Bryth.	M-M-M	700
Gweir-Llyr-Mabon	Bryth.	M-M-M	1565
Ham-Japheth-Shem	Hebr.	M-M-M	713
Har-Jafnar-Thridi	Norse	M-M-M	1598
Harpies	Gk.	F-F-F	728
Hecate in triple form	Gk.	F	740
Heliades	Gk.	F-F-F	747
Hesperides	Gk.	F-F-F	765
Holy Family	Christ.	M-F-M	782
Hometeuli	Mex.	M-M-M	784
Horae	Gk.	F-F-F	786
Horus-Ra-Atum	Egy.	M-M-M	1598
Horus-Shu-Set	Egy.	M-M-M	1598
I-He-Wei	Chin.	M-M-M	822
Janardana	Hindu	M	863
Joseph-Mary-Jesus	Christ.	M-F-M	782
Jupiter-Juno-Minerva	Rom.	M-F-F	1598
Jupiter-Mars-Minerva	Rom.	M-M-F	1598
Jupiter-Pluto-Neptune	Rom.	M-M-M	1598
Ka-Khu-Khat	Egy.		903
Kether-Chokmah-Binah	Caba.	M-M-F	1598
Khaldi-Theispas-Artinis	Urartian	M-M-F	1598
Khaybet-Ba-Sahu	Egy.		923
Khnemu-Anqet (Anukt)-Satet	Egy.	M-F-F	924

	Culture	Sex	Page
Koshin	Jap		1598
Ku-Lono-Tane	Poly.	M-M-M	947
Leucosia-Ligea-Parthenope	Gk.	F-F-F	1458
MacCecht-MacCool-MacGreine	Cel.	M-M-M	1033
Magi	Christ.	M-M-M	1565
Manannan-Tuag-Fer Fedail	Cel.	M-F-M	1605
Mark-Iseult-Tristan	Bryth.	M-F-M	842
Maui-Hina-Tuna	Poly.	M-F-M	1607
Medusa-Euryale-Stheno	Gk.	F-F-F	678
Mentu-Ra-Atum	Egy.	M-M-M	1598
Metis-Eros-Erikapaios	Orphic	F-M-A	1598
Mitra-Varuna-Indra	Hin.	M-M-M	1639
Moses-Aaron-Miriam	Hebr.	M-M-F	1598
Muses	Gk.	F-F-F	1138
Nakazutsuno-Sokozutsuno-Uwazutsuno	Jap.	M-M-M	1506
Noah's Three Sons	Hebr.	M-M-M	1598
Nornir	Norse	F-F-F	1180
Odin-Frey-Thor	Norse	M-M-M	1598
Odin-Hoener-Loki	Norse	M-M-M	1598
Odin-Ve-Vili	Norse	M-M-M	1598
Ormuzd-Ahriman-Mithra	Zoro.	M-M-M	1598
Ormuzd-Anahita-Mithra	Zoro.	M-F-M	1598
Osiris-Isis-Horus	Egy.	M-F-M	1598
Osiris-Isis-Set	Egy.	M-F-M	1218
Osiris-Kneph-Ptah	Egy.	M-M-M	1598
Osiris-Neith-Horus	Egy.	M-F-M	1161
Parcae	Rom.	F-F-F	1237
Patollus-Perkunas-Potrympus	Baltic	M-M-M	1598
Praxidikae	Gk.	F-F-F	1291
Ptah-Hapi-Virgin Cow	Egy.	M-M-F	1299
Ptah-Osiris-Sokar	Egy.	M-M-M	1471
Ptah-Sekhet-Nefertem (Imhotep)	Egy.	M-F-M	1414
Ptah-Sokar-Asar (Osiris)	Egy.	M-M-M	1219
Ra-Horus-Tum	Egy.	M-M-M	1564
Ra-Khepera-Tum	Egy.	M-M-M	924
Ra-Mentu-Atum	Egy.	M-M-M	1314
Ra-Mentu-Sokar	Egy.	M-M-M	1314
San Ch'ing	Chin.	M-M-M	1395
San Kuan	Chin.	M-M-M	1397
Sansfoy-Sansjoy-Sansloy	Eng.	M-M-M	1397
San Sheng	Chin.	M-M-M	1564
Saoshyant	Zoro.	M-M-M	1398
Semnae	Gk.	F-F-F	1416
Shamash-Adad-Ishtar	Aramaean	M-M-F	1598

	Culture	Sex	Page
Shamash-Ishtar-Sin	Assyr., Baby.	M-F-M	1456
Sheng-Chen Jen-Hsien Jen	Chin.		1564
Sin-Shamas-Ramman	Baby.	M-M-M	1598
Sirens	Gk.	F-F-F	1458
Spirit-Breath-Water	Caba.		1598
Sumiyoshi	Jap.	M-M-M	1566
Tao Chun-Yu Huang-Lao Tze	Chin.	M-M-M	973
Tezcatlipoca-Huitzilopochtli-Quetzalcoatl	Mex.	M-M-M	1549
Thriae	Gk.	F-F-F	1566
T'ien kuan-Ti kuan-Shui kuan	Chin.	M-M-M	1397
T'ien Pao-Ling Pao-Shen Pao	Chin.	M-M-M	1598
T'ien Pao-Tao Chun-Lao Tzu	Chin.	M-M-M	1395
T'ien-Yang-Yin	Chin.	M-M-F	1598
Tinia-Uni-Menfra	Ital.	M-M-F	1598
Triglav	Slav.	M	1597
Triple Goddess	World wide	F	1598
Triple Horus	Egy.	M	1598
Tristan-Iseult-Iseult	Bryth.	M-F-F	1599
Tristan-Iseult-Mark	Bryth.	M-F-M	1599
Trivia	Gk.	F	1599
Tryambaka	Hin.	M	49
Tum-Shu-Tefenet	Egy.	M-M-F	1598
Urth-Verdani-Skuld	Norse	F-F-F	1180
Wodan (Wuotan)-Donar-Ziu	Germ.	M-M-M	461
Yahwe-El Shaddai-Elohim	Caba.	M-M-M	1598
Yu Huang-Ling Ping Pao-Shen Pao	Chin.	M-M-M	1395
Yu Huang-Tao Chun-Lao Tzu	Chin.	M-M-M	1598
Zeus-Hera-Athena	Gk.	M-F-F	1598
Zeus-Poseidon-Aides (Hades)	Gk.	M-M-M	1598
Zeus-Poseidon-Hephaestus	Gk.	M-M-M	1598
Zoroaster in triple form	Zoro.	M	1734

TRICKSTER (ALSO SEE CUNNING)

	Culture	Sex	Page
Amaethon	Bryth.	M	78
Cin-An-Ev	Ute Ind.	M	339
Coyote	N.A.I.	M	377
Estas	Athap.	M	525
Gluskap	Algon.	M	664
Guagugiana (Vagoniona)	Taino	M	693
Gwydion	Bryth.	M	702
Hlakanyana	Zulu	M	775
Inktonmi	Siouan	M	832
Jacob	Hebr.	M	858

Trickster (cont.)	Culture	Sex	Page
K'mukamtch	Klamath	M	936
Krishna	Hin.	M	945
Manabhozho	Algon.	M	1054
Maui	Poly.	M	1077
Ne-kilst-luss	Haida Ind.	M	1161
Nenaboj	Wetucko Ind.	M	1162
Nihancan	N.A.I.	M	1169
Noman (Outis)	Gk.	M	1179
Odysseus	Gk.	M	1196
Patelin	Fr.	M	1243
Paul Bunyan	Am. Folk.	M	1244
Raven	Pac. Coast	M	1325
Reynard	Med. Lit.	M	1334
Saci	Braz.	M	1358
Sitconski	Assiniboin	M	1460
Sunawavi	Ute Ind.	M	1509
Taliesin	Bryth.	M	1528
Tawiscara	Huron	M	1539
Ti Malice	Haitian	M	1574
Unktomi	Siouan	M	1626
Vamana	Hin.	M	1637
Wisakketjak	Micmac	M	1686
Yehl	Alaskan	M	1703
Yimantuwingyai	Calif. Ind.	M	1707
Yo	Daho.		1708

TRINITY (SEE TRIAD)
TRUTH (SEE VIRTUE)

TUTOR (ALSO SEE COUNSELOR)			
Agathadaemon	Gk.	M	46
Chiron	Gk.	M	327
Chu I	Chin.	M	335
Con-ticci Viracocha	Inca	M	1652
Curetes	Gk.	M	398
Eurytus	Gk.	M	533
Italapas	Chinook	M	+

TWILIGHT (SEE GLOAMING)
TWINS (SEE CORRELATIVES)

UGLINESS			
Ame-no-uzume	Jap.	F	83
Avagddu	Cel.	M	160
Befana	Ital.	F	195
Berchta	Christ.	F	203

	Culture	Sex	Page
Caliban	Eng.	M	277
Deino	Gk.	F	446
Dornolla	Cel.	F	464
Enyo	Gk.	F	513
Euryale	Gk.	F	532
Fudo	Jap.	M •	615
Gorgon	Gk.	F	678
Gorgopa	Gk.	F	679
Graeae	Gk.	F	681
Hag	Scot.	F	707
Harpies	Gk., Rom.	F	728
Heike-gani	Jap.	M	743
Hephaestus	Gk.	M	751
Hisa Females	Jap.	F	775
Hudibras	Eng.	M	802
Iha-naga-hime	Jap.	F	822
Izanami	Jap.	F	853
Lei-kung	Chin.	M	981
Lilith	Hebr.	F	994
Medusa	Gk.	F	1084
Morgan le Fay	Bryth.	F	1123
Morvran	Bryth.	M	1126
Muckle-mouth Meg	Eng.	F	1133
Munkar & Nakir	Mos.	M-M	1137
Okame & Hyottoko	Jap.	F-M	1203
Oni	Jap.	M	1209
Pephredo	Gk.	F	1254
Phaon	Gk.	M	1261
Polyphemus	Gk.	M	1284
Praxidikae	Gk.	F	1291
Priapus	Gk.	M	1292
Punch & Judy	Folk.	M-F	1301
Punchinello	Ital.	M	1301
Rakshasa	Hin.	M, F	1320
Saalah	Arab.	M	1356
Shikome	Jap.	F	1437
Shinje-chho-gyal	Tib.	M	1438
Tamamo-no-maye	Jap.	F	1529
Tisiphone	Gk.	F	1577
Tshindi	Nav.	M	1603
Tuwapontumsi	Pueblo	F	1611
Tzitzimime	Mex.	F	1618
Urgan	Folk.	M	1628
Yomo-tsu-shiko-me	Jap.	F	1709

UNDERWORLD (ENCHANTED REALM. ALSO SEE DEATH)	Culture	Sex	Page
Aeacus	Gk.	M	37
Ah Puch	Mex.	M	53
Aides	Gk.	M	55
Aker	Egy.	M	59
Alberich	Norse	M	62
Alcinous	Gk.	M	64
Allatu	Baby.	F	69
Amen-Ra	Egy.	M	83
Ammit	Egy.	F	86
Andvari	Norse	M	95
Anubis	Egy.	M	105
Arawn	Bryth.	M	117
Asar-Hapi	Egy.	M	135
Ascalaphus	Gk.	M	135
Ashura	Jap.	M	140
Asmegir	Norse	M, F	141
Avallon	Bryth.	M	160
Bali	Hin.	M	175
Balor	Cel.	M	176
Belili	Sum.	F	197
Belit-Sheri	Assyr.	F	198
Bes	Egy.	M	205
Bile	Cel.	M	211
Bodb	Cel.	M	233
Bran	Bryth.	M	241
Brandegore	Bryth.	M	243
Brave-swift-impetuous-male	Jap.	M	244
Brennius	Bryth.	M	246
Buto	Jap.	M	263
Carvara	Hin.	M	293
Cerberus	Gk.	M	304
Cernobog	Slav.	M	305
Cernunnos	Cel.	M	305
Chakdor	Tib.	M	308
Charon	Gk.	M	315
Ch'in-kuang	Chin.	M	326
Chipiapoos	Pota.	M	326
Chuan-lun Wang	Chin.	M	335
Ch'u-Chiang	Chin.	M	335
Circe	Gk.	F	341
Consus	Ital.	M	368
Cora	Gk.	F	370
Creudylad	Bryth.	F	381
Cupay	Inca	M	397
Despoina	Gk.	F	434

	Culture	Sex	Page
Dis	Cel.	M	450
Dis Pater	Rom.	M	451
Dumah	Caba.	M	476
Dwendi	Philip.	M	479
Elbegast	Norse	M	+
Emma	Jap.	M	509
Enlil	Baby., Sum.	M	512
Enmeshara	Sum.	M	512
Eo-Anu	Cel.	F	513
Eopuco	Mex.	M	53
Erebus	Gk.	M	518
Ereshkigal	Baby.	F	518
Erlik	Tatar	M	521
Erlik-khan	Mong.	M	521
Eubouteous	Rom.	M	529
Fand	Cel.	F	548
Fenius Farsa	Cel.	M	560
Fjolsvid	Norse	M	578
Funafeng	Norse	M	617
Furies	Gk.	F	617
Gaiar	Cel.	M	622
Garm	Norse		631
Geirrod	Norse	M	638
Gigim	Sum.	M	655
Gilgamesh	Sum.	M	656
Gorddu	Bryth.	F	678
Gorgon	Gk.	F	678
Govannon	Bryth.	M	680
Govetter	Norw.	M	680
Grim & Hilde	Germ.	M-F	691
Gucumatz	Guate.	M	694
Gufittar	Lapp	M	695
Gullveig	Norse	F	697
Gunlad	Norse	F	698
Gwyddneu Garanhir	Bryth.	M	702
Gwyn	Bryth.	M	703
Hades	Gk.	M	706
Hahgwehdaetgah	Seneca	M	708
Hecate	Gk.	F	740
Hecatoncheires	Gk.	M	741
Hel	Norse	F	745
Hine-I-Tau-Ira (Hine-Nui)	Poly.	F	772
Hisa Females	Jap.	F	775
Horus	Egy.	M	792
Husbishag	Assyr-Baby.	F	808
Irkalla	Assyr-Baby.	M/F	839

	Culture	Sex	Page
Izanami	Jap.	F	853
Jogaoh	Iroq.	M, F	884
Kachinas	Zuni	M	900
Kara-khan	Mong.	M	909
Karei	Malay.	M	910
Kavi Usan	Pers.	M	914
Ker	Gk.	F	917
Khnemu	Egy.	M	924
Kisani	Nav.	M	933
Kudai-bakshy	Yakut	M	948
Kukuri-hime	Jap.	M	950
Lady Ming	Chin.	F	962
Lady of the Lake	Bryth.	F	962
Laurin	Germ.	M	977
Libitina	Rom.	F	991
Loki	Norse	M	1010
Lord of Fire	Christ.	M	1013
Losy	Mong.	M	1013
Maahiset	Fin-Ug.		1030
Mafuike	Poly.	F	1037
Mahakala	Hin.	M	1043
Mahuika	Poly.	F	1046
Malcandros	Sem.	M	1049
Manannan	Cel.	M	1054
Manawyddan	Bryth.	M	1056
Mania	Ital.	F	1058
Mantus	Ital.	M	1061
March	Bryth.	M	1064
Math	Cymric	M	1075
Meilichios	Gk.	M	1084
Meliagraunce	Bryth.	M	1086
Melkarth	Phoen.	M	1086
Melwas	Bryth.	M	1087
Meng-po Niang-Niang	Chin.	F	1089
Midir	Cel.	M	1100
Milu	Hawa.	M	1105
Mimi	Germ.	M	1105
Minos	Gk.	M	1107
Miru	Hawa.	M	1110
Moqwaio	Men.	M	1122
Morc	Cel.	M	1122
Morgan le Fay	Bryth.	F	1123
Mors	Rom.	M	1125
Mundilfore	Norse	M	1136
Muta	Rom.	F	1140
Muy'ingwa	Hopi	M	1142

	Culture	Sex	Page
Nergal	Assyr-Baby.	M	1164
Nerrivik	Eskimo	F	1164
Nibelung	Norse	M	1167
Niddhogge	Norse	M	1168
Nimue	Bryth.	F	1170
Ninazu	Sum.	M/F	1170
Ningishzida	Sum.	M	1172
Ninsubur	Sum.	M	1173
Nithhoggr	Scand.	M	1176
Nornir	Norse	F	1180
Nyja	Slav.	M	1188
Nyx (Nox)	Gk.	F	1188
Ocnus	Gk.	M	1193
Ogyrvran	Bryth.	M	1201
Ohodowas	Iroq.	M, F	1202
O-kuni-nushi	Jap.	M	1204
Orcus	Rom.	M	1213
Orgagna	Ital.	M	176
Osiris	Egy.	M	1218
Owasse	Men.	M	1221
Paravataksha	Hin.	M	1237
Patollus	Baltic	M	1243
Pautiwa	Zuni	M	1244
Pellean	Bryth.	M	1250
Pellenore	Bryth.	M	1251
Pelles	Bryth.	M	1251
Pen Annwfn	Welsh	M	1251
Persephone	Gk.	F	1257
Phorcys	Gk.	M	1266
Piltzintecutli-Tonatiuh	Mex.	M	1273
Pluto	Rom.	M	1280
Plutus	Gk.	M	1280
Pohjan-akka	Fin.	M	1281
Polevik	Rus.	M	1283
Polydectes	Gk.	M	1283
Polydegmon	Gk.	M	1284
Polyidus	Gk.	M	1284
Porphyrion	Gk.	M	1287
Proserpina	Rom.	F	1296
Prospero	Eng.	M	1296
Pryderi (Gwri)	Bryth.	M	1298
Pylaochos	Gk.	M	1306
Pylartes	Gk.	M	1306
Rhadamanthus	Gk.	M	1335
Rutu	Lapp	M	1355
Sabitu	Baby.	F	1357

	Culture	Sex	Page
Satan	Hebr-Christ.	M	1402
Sbires	Mos.	M	1404
Schilbung	Norse	M	1407
Sedna	Eskimo	F	1413
Sedu	Baby.	M	1413
Semnae	Gk.	F	1416
Serapis	Egy.	M	1418
Shiwanni	Zuni	M	1440
Shiwanokia	Zuni	F	1440
Sichaeus	Rom.	M	1446
Skrymir	Norse	M	1465
Sokar	Egy.	M	1471
Spantaramet	Arm.	F	1479
Styx	Gk.	F	1502
Succellos	Cel.	M	1503
Sung-ti	Chin.	M	1510
Susa-no-wo	Jap.	M	1512
Sychaeus	Rom.	M	1521
Tai-yo Ta-ti	Chin.	M	1527
Tecolotl	Mex.	M	1540
Tegid Voel	Bryth.	M	1541
Tellus Mater	Ital.	F	1542
Te-Reinga	Poly.	M	1333
Thagya Min	Ind-Chin.	M	1550
Thjalfi	Norse	M	1560
Thoas	Gk.	M	1560
Thor	Egy.	M	1561
Tieholtsodi	Nav.	M	1571
Timi	Hebr.	M, F	1574
Titans	Gk.	M, F	1577
Ti-tsang	Chin.	M	1580
Triglav	Slav.	M	1597
Ts'in-kuan-wang	Chin.	M	1603
Tuchulcha	Ital.	M	1606
Tuila	Sib.	M	1606
Tumudurere	Poly.	M	775
Tuoni	Fin-Ug.	M	1608
Turehu	Poly.	M, F	1608
Typhoeus	Gk.	M	1617
Typhon	Gk.	M	1617
Uetonga	Poly.	M	1620
Ugarthilocus	Dan.	M	1620
Uhepono	Zuni	M	1620
Uldda	Scan.	M	1621
Unkulunkulu	Zulu	M	1626
Utgard-Loki	Norse	M	1632

	Culture	Sex	Page
Utnapishtim	Baby.	M	1632
Vaivasvata	Hin.	M	1634
Val-father	Norse	M	1636
Vediovis	Ital.	M	1643
Vibhandaka	Hin.	M	1648
Vivian	Bryth.	F	1656
Vodyanik	Rus.	M	1657
Vukub-cakix	Kiche	M	1659
Vulcan	Rom.	M	1659
Whiro	Poly.	M	1676
Wu Kuan	Chin.	M	1693
Xibalba	Kiche	M	1696
Yabme-akka	Lapp	F	1697
Yama	Hin.	M	1699
Yen-lo-Wang	Chin.	M	1705
Yomo-tsu-kami	Jap.	M	1709
Yomo-tsu-shiko-me	Jap.	F	1709
Yum Cimil	Mex.	M	1713
Yu Ti	Chin.	M	1713

UNIVERSAL RUIN (CATACLYSM, CONFLAGRATION, DELUGE)

Abaia	Mel.	M	11
Anamaqkiu	Men.	M	91
Aokeu & Ake	Poly.	M-M	106
Arikute & Ariconte	Braz.	M-M	124
Atra-Chasis	Baby.	M	153
Baiame	Aus.	M	173
Baneb-ded	Egy.	M	178
Bel	Baby.	M	196
Bugan	Philip.	F	258
Buzur-Kurgala	Baby.	M	263
Cessair	Cel.	F	429
Chalchiutlicue	Mex.	F	308
Cipactonal & Xumio	Mex.	M-F	784
Coxcox	Mex.	M	377
Deucalion & Pyrrha	Gk.	M-F	429
Enlil	Baby., Sum.	M	512
Finntain	Cel.	M	570
Hathor (Sekhet)	Egy.	F	429
Huan Ching	Chin.	M	801
Ila	Hin.	F	823
Irra	Assyr-Baby.	M	841
Jaik-khan	Sib.	M	861
Jehovah	Hebr.	M	870
Kezer-tshingis	Tatar	M	921

	Culture	Sex	Page
Kitimil & Magigi	Pelew Is.	M-F	935
Lifthrasir & Lif	Norse	M-F	992
Magni	Norse	M	1040
Mah Abad	Pers.	M	1042
Mahrkusha	Pers.	M	429
Manu	Hin.	M	429
Matsya	Hin.	M	1076
Messou	Pota.	M	1095
Modi	Norse	M	1114
Monan	Braz.	M	1116
Nama	Tatar	M	1622
Nata & Nena	Mex.	M-F	1157
Nephthys	Egy.	F	1163
Noah	Hebr.	M	1177
Noj	Asian	M	1179
Nu Kua	Chin.	M/A	1185
Og	Hebr.	M	1200
Ogygus	Gk.	M	1201
Onan	Caba.	M	1208
Pairekse	Ostiak	M	1226
Pir-na-pishtim	Baby.	M	1275
Pyrrha	Eng.	F	1307
Ra	Egy.	M	429
Ruahaku	So. Is.	M	429
Schal-jime	Tatar	M	1407
Shamash	Assyr-Baby.	M	1429
Simurgh	Pers.	M	1456
Sisythus	Gk.	M	1460
Tangaroa	Poly.	M	1531
Tawhaki	Chath. Is.	M	1539
Tishtrya	Pers.	M	1577
Ulgen	Tatar	M	1622
Ursanapi	Baby.	M	1630
Utnapishtim	Baby.	M	1632
Varaha	Hin.	M	1638
Vidar	Norse	M	1649
Viracocha	Inca	M	1652
Vishnu	Hin.	M	429
Whaitari	Maori	F	1674
Wigan	Philip.	M	1679
Xelhua	Mex.	M	1695
Xisuthrus	Gk/Baby.	M	1696
Yao	Chin.	M	1701
Yima	Pers.	M	1707
Yu	Chin.	M	1711

	Culture	Sex	Page
Ziusudra	Sum.	M	1721

UNUSUAL BIRTH (SEE MIRACULOUS BIRTH)

VALOR (ALSO SEE HERO)

Abednego	Hebr.	M	14
Achilles	Gk.	M	25
Ajax the Great	Gk.	M	58
Ajax the Lesser	Gk.	M	58
Antigone	Gk.	F	103
Arjuna	Hin.	M	126
Baal Shamin	Arm.	M	168
Caradawc	Bryth.	M	289
Castor & Pollux	Gk.	M	295
Cloelia	Rom.	F	349
Conan Maol	Cel.	M	364
Cuchulainn	Cel.	M	393
Daniel	Hebr.	M	413
Deiphobus	Gk.	M	426
Diomedes	Gk.	M	446
Dioscuri	Gk.	M	449
Don Quixote	Span.	M	462
Einheri	Norse	M	496
Esther	Hebr.	F	526
Euphorbus	Gk.	M	+
Fortitudo	Rom.	F	+
Goll mac Morna (Aodh)	Cel.	M	674
Hector	Gk.	M	741
Heracles	Gk.	M	752
Hercules	Rom.	M	759
Her Shef	Egy.	M	763
Horatius Cocles	Rom.	M	787
Jephthah	Hebr.	M	872
Jeremiah	Hebr.	M	873
Joab	Hebr.	M	881
Joan of Arc	Fr.	F	881
Jonathan	Hebr.	M	886
Judas Maccabees	Hebr.	M	893
Kastor & Polydeukes	Gk.	M	912
Lancelot	Bryth.	M	969
Laodamia	Gk.	F	972
Lavaine	Bryth.	M	977
Lord Uye-Minu	Jap.	M	1013
Meshach	Hebr.	M	1094
Modi	Norse	M	1114

Valor (cont.)	Culture	Sex	Page
O-Binzuru	Jap.	M	1192
Penthesilea	Gk.	F	1253
Poseidon	Gk.	M	1288
Priamond	Eng.	M	1292
Pyrrhus	Gk.	M	1307
Rhoetus	Gk.	M	1337
Rig	Norse	M	1338
Rinaldo	Ital.	M	1339
Rizpah	Hebr.	F	1342
Robin Hood	Eng.	M	1343
Samson	Hebr.	M	1394
Sarpedon	Gk.	M	1401
Shadrach	Hebr.	M	1428
Shih Kan Tang	Chin.	M	1437
Siegfried	Germ.	M	1448
Sigmund	Norse	M	1449
Sigurd	Norse	M	1451
Tancred	Ital.	M	1531
Tyr	Teutonic	M	1617
Uriah	Hebr.	M	1629
Xelhua	Mex.	M	1695
Yamato-take	Jap.	M	1699
Yoshitsune	Jap.	M	1710
Zmay	Serb.	M	1722
Zuzim	Hebr.	M	1735
VANITY (ALSO SEE SELF-ADORATION)			
Arachne	Gk.	F	116
Icarus	Gk.	M	817
Kay	Bryth.	M	914
Marsyas	Gk.	M	1070
Narcissus	Gk.	M	1155
Phaethon	Gk.	M	1260
Pierides	Gk.	F	1269
Salmoneus	Gk.	M	1391
Salome	Christ.	F	1391
Thamyris	Gk.	M	1551
Thraso	Rom.	M	1563
VENGEANCE			
Alecto	Gk.	F	66
Ara	Gk.	F	116
Ate	Gk.	F	149
Dag	Norse	M	405
Dice	Gk.	F	443
Dirae	Rom.	F	+

	Culture	Sex	Page
Electra	Gk.	F	499
Erinyes	Gk.	F	520
Eumenides	Gk.	F	529
Forty-seven Ronin	Jap.	M	598
Fuda-Hegashi	Jap.	M	615
Furies	Gk.	F	617
Guendoloena	Bryth.	F	695
Guinevere	Bryth.	F	696
Hamlet	Eng.	M	714
Harpies	Gk., Rom.	F	728
Hera	Gk.	F	752
Kamaima	Carib.		905
Lugal-zaggisi	Sum.	M	1023
Megaera	Gk.	F	1084
Nemesis	Gk.	F	1162
Orestes	Gk.	M	1214
Phaon	Eng.	M	1261
Poinae	Gk.	F	1281
Praxidice	Gk.	F	1291
Rerir	Norse	M	1333
Romulus & Remus	Rom.	M	1346
Salome	Christ.	F	1391
Samurai	Jap.	M	1394
Tisiphone	Gk.	F	1577
Vali	Norse	M	1636
Vidar	Norse	M	1649
Yega	Athap.		1703
Yoshitsune	Jap.	M	1710
Zeresh	Pers.	F	1718

VICE (SEE EVIL)
VICTORY (SEE WAR)
VIOLENCE (SEE STRIFE, VENGEANCE)
VIRGINITY (SEE CHASTITY)

VIRGIN MOTHER & CHILD (ALSO SEE MOTHER & DAUGHTER)

Aminah & Mohammed	Mos.	F-M	+
Aphrodite & Adonis	Gk.	F-M	108
Aruru & Enlil	Sum.	F-M	133
Astarte & Adonis	Phoen.	F-M	144
Atargatis & Athar	Sem.	F-M	148
Ate & Athar	Sem.	F-M	150
Athena & Erichthonius	Gk.	F-M	519
Brimo & Brimos	Mong.	F-M	249
Cailleach & Son	Scot.	F-M	269

	Culture	Sex	Page
Chalchiutlicue & Son	Mex.	F-M	308
Chimalman & Citlallatonac (Quetzalcoatl)	Mex.	F-M	325
Coatlicue & Huitzilopochtli	Mex.	F-M	352
Cybele & Attis	Phryg.	F-M	400
Daeira & Eleusis	Gk.	F-M	404
Danae & Perseus	Gk.	F-M	411
Dechtire & Cuchulainn	Cel.	F-M	423
Demeter & Dionysus	Gk.	F-M	429
Devaki & Krishna	Hin.	F-M	435
Dughdhova & Zoroaster	Zoro.	F-M	1734
Eirene & Plutus	Gk.	F-M	1280
Eos & Memnon	Gk.	F-M	1088
Hera & Heracles	Gk.	F-M	752
Hsiu-chi & Yu	Chin.	F-M	1711
Ilmatar & Vainamoinen	Fin.	F-M	824
Innini & Dumuzi	Sum.	F-M	832
Ishtar & Tammuz	Assyr-Baby.	F-M	844
Isis & Horus	Egy.	F-M	845
Juno & Hercules	Rom.	F-M	896
Maha & Son	Sem.	F-M	1042
Maia & Hermes	Gk.	F-M	1046
Mama & Marduk	Baby.	F-M	1051
Mama & Shulpae	Baby.	F-M	1051
Marjatta & Son	Fin.	F-M	1068
Mary & Jesus	Christ.	F-M	1375
Maya & Sakyamuni	Bud.	F-M	1080
Ninlil & Son	Sum.	F-M	1173
Ninsikilla & Nesu	Sem.	F-M	1042
Nintu & Tagtug	Sum.	F-M	1174
Perdix & Talus	Gk.	F-M	1254
Rhea & Marnas	Gk.	F-M	1720
Rhea & Zeus	Gk.	F-M	1719
Rhea Silvia & the twins Romulus & Remus	Rom.	F-M	1335
Rhiannon & Pryderi	Bryth.	F-M	1336
Semele & Dionysus	Gk.	F-M	1415
Sengen Sama & Hoderi	Jap.	F-M	1416
Sif & Ullerus	Norse	F-M	1448
T'ai Yuan & T'ien Pao	Chin.	F-M	1527
Tyche & Plutus	Gk.	F-M	1280
Uatlan & Xbalanque	Kiche	F-M	1619
Vari-ma-te-takere & Raka	Herv. Is.	F-M	1320
Vari-ma-te-takere & Timirau	Herv. Is.	F-M	1574
Venus & Cupid	Rom.	F-M	1644

VIRTUE (BENEVOLENCE, CANDOR, INTEGRITY, TRUTH. ALSO SEE MERCY)	Culture	Sex	Page
Abednego	Hebr.	M	14
Aeon	Gnostic	M, F	41
Areta	Gk.	F	121
Arjuna	Hin.	M	126
Arta Viraf	Zoro.	M	130
Asa	Hebr.	M	134
Ashem Vahishtem	Pers.	M	+
Bol Bendo	Eng.	M	234
Cambuscan	Eng.	M	280
Canace	Eng.	F	283
Ch'i-lin	Chin.	A	325
Confucius	Chin.	M	366
Cordelia	Eng.	F	371
Daniel	Hebr.	M	413
Dikaiosyne	Gk.	F	+
Durga	Hin.	F	477
Ebisu	Jap.	M	489
Elijah	Hebr.	M	503
Fudo	Jap.	M	615
Gabriel	Christ., Hebr., Mos.	M	619
Galahad	Bryth.	M	622
Guyon, Sir	Eng.	M	700
Haurvatat	Pers.	M	732
Job	Hebr.	M	882
Jupiter Fidius	Rom.	M	896
Khadijah	Mos.	F	922
Khshathra Vairya	Zoro.	M	925
Khvarenanh	Pers.		926
Konkara	Jap.	M	941
Kwannon	Jap.	F/A	955
Kwan-yin	Chin.	F/A	955
Lady Poverty	Christ.	F	963
Lucretia	Rom.	F	1021
Lung-ta	Bud.		1025
Mahapratisara	Bud.	F	1044
Mahasahasrapramardani	Bud.	F	1044
Meshach	Hebr.	M	1094
Mishael	Hebr.	M	1110
Misharu	Phoen.	M	1110
Moses	Hebr.	M	1126
Mucalinda	Bud.	M	1133
Muc-thaiuy	Ind-Chin.	M	1133
Mukasa	Uganda	M	1135

Virtue (cont.)	Culture	Sex	Page
Myojo-tenshi	Jap.	M	1142
Nanna	Norse	F	1153
Nobunaga	Jap.	M	1178
Om	Occult		1207
Paramita	Bud.		1237
Pindola (Pinto-lo-po-t'o-she)	Chin.	M	1274
Shadrach	Hebr.	M	1428
Shen Shu	Chin.	M	1434
Shih Kan Tang	Chin.	M	1437
Shun	Chin.	M	1444
Shu Yu	Chin.	M	1445
Siddhi	Hin.	M	1447
Sin	Assyr.	M	1456
Snorta	Norse	F	1470
Solomon	Hebr., Mos.	M	1472
Ssu Ming	Chin.	M	1488
Susanna	Hebr.	F	1512
Tenes	Gk.	M	1545
Trung Sisters	Ind-Chin.	F	1602
Tryamour, Sir	Eng.	M	1602
Tuatha de Danann	Cel.	M-F	1605
Tybert	Med. Lit.	M	1616
Tzu Sun Niang Niang	Chin.	F	1618
Una	Eng.	F	1623
Usnisavijaya	Bud.	F	1631
Vashti	Pers.	F	1641
Vishnu	Hin.	M	1654
Vistauru	Pers.	M	1655
Vohu Manah	Zoro.	M	1657
Yamato-take	Jap.	M	1699
Yao	Chin.	M	1701
Yazata	Zoro.	M	1702
Yima	Pers.	M	1707
Yudhishthira	Hin.	M	1711
Yu Huang	Chin.	M	1712
Yu Lei	Chin.	M	1713
Yu Lu	Chin.	M	1713
Zebedee	Christ.	M	1717
Zoroaster	Zoro.	M	1734

VOLCANO (SEE FIRE)

VULNERABLE (FATAL SPOT OR WEAKNESS)			
Abel	Hebr., Mos.	M	14
Achilles	Gk.	M	25

	Culture	Sex	Page
Agag	Hebr.	M	44
Balder	Norse	M	174
Beowulf	Ang-Sax.	M	203
Bran	Bryth.	M	241
Crimthann Nia Nair	Cel.	M	382
Cuchulainn	Cel.	M	393
Cycnus	Gk.	M	401
Dagda	Cel.	M	405
Diarmaid	Cel.	M	442
Harpocrates	Gk.	M	728
Havgan	Bryth.	M	732
Heracles	Gk.	M	752
Hercules	Rom.	M	759
Hermes	Gk.	M	760
Ixion	Gk.	M	852
Koshchei	Slav.	M	943
Krishna	Hin.	M	945
Kwasind	N.A.I.	M	955
Llew Llaw Gyffes	Cymric	M	1005
Math	Cymric	M	1075
Mopsus	Gk.	M	1122
Nisus	Gk.	M	1176
Orion	Gk.	M	1215
Ra	Egy.	M	1314
Ragnar Lodbrog	Norse	M	1317
Ravana	Hin.	M	1324
Rustam	Pers.	M	1355
Samson	Hebr.	M	1394
Siegfried	Germ.	M	1448
Sif	Norse	F	1448
Sigmund	Norse	M	1449
Sigurd	Norse	M	1451
Stone Giant	Yaghan Ind.	M	1496
Sunda & Upasunda	Hin.	M-M	1509
Tahmurath	Pers.	M	1525
Talus	Gk.	M	1529
Tiamat	Baby.	F	1570
Wantley Dragon	Eng.	M	469

WANDERER (ADVENTURER, NOMAD. ALSO SEE QUESTER, TRAVELER)

Abraham	Hebr.	M	17
Acastus	Gk.	M	22
Admetus	Gk.	M	33
Aeneas	Rom.	M	40
Ahasuerus	Med. Lit.	M	52

	Culture	Sex	Page
Amphiaraus	Gk.	M	87
Ancaeus	Gk.	M	92
Argonauts	Gk.	M	121
Aristeas	Gk.	M	125
Asfandujar	Zoro.	M	137
Butes	Gk.	M	262
Cartaphilus	Med. Lit.	M	293
Cuchulainn	Cel.	M	393
Daedalus	Gk.	M	404
Dietrich Von Bern	Norse	M	444
Eber's Sons	Hebr.	M	489
Elcmar	Cel.	M	498
Elpenor	Gk.	M	506
Fiachra	Cel.	M	564
Fionnuala	Cel.	F	571
Flying Dutchman	Folk.	M	589
Frithiof	Norse	M	612
Grimnir	Norse	M	691
Gulliver	Eng.	M	1013
Hyperion	Gk.	M	812
Io	Gk.	F	835
Isaac	Hebr.	M	841
Isaac Laquedem (Lakedion)	Fr.	M	1664
Ishmael	Hebr.	M	843
Isis	Egy.	F	845
Israel	Hebr.	M	847
Jabal	Hebr.	M	855
Jacob	Hebr.	M	858
Jason	Gk.	M	866
John Buttadaeus	Germ.	M	1664
Kedar	Hebr.	M	915
Khensu	Egy.	M	923
King Horn	Eng., Fr.	M	929
Klaboterman	Baltic	M	935
Lemminikainen	Fin.	M	982
Leto	Gk.	F	986
Lot	Hebr.	M	1014
Lynceus	Gk.	M	1028
Madoc	Welsh	M	1036
Magi	Christ.	M	1037
Mandarava	Bud.	F	1056
Manto	Gk.	F	1061
Mioya-no-kami	Jap.	M	1108
Muso-byoye	Jap.	M	1140
Nagaitcho (Kyoi)	Calif. Ind.	M	1147
Odysseus	Gk.	M	1196

	Culture	Sex	Page
Oku-thor	Norse	M	1204
Padmasambhava	Bud.	M	1056
Pairekse	Ostiak	M	1226
Paris	Gk.	M	1238
Peter Rugg	Am. Folk.	M	1259
Polymetis	Gk.	M	1284
Puck	Eng.	M	1300
Puleh	Rus.	M	1301
Pwcca	Welsh	M	1300
Pyrocles & Musidorus	Eng.	M-M	1307
Ra	Egy.	M	1314
Ragnar Lodbrog	Norse	M	1317
Rata	Maori	M	1323
Rati	Norse	M	1324
Reidartyr	Norse	M	1561
Rigir	Norse	M	1338
Saint Brandan	Christ.	M	1365
Saint Nicholas	Christ.	M	1378
Salathiel ben Sadi	Med. Lit.	M	1390
Savitri	Hin.	M	1404
Scyld	Ang-Sax.	M	1409
Scythians	Gk.	M, F	1410
Serosevsky	Rus.	M	1418
Shri	Hin.	F	1443
Siegfried	Germ.	M	1448
Sigurd	Norse	M	1451
Sindbad	Arab.	M	1456
Stigande	Ang-Sax.	M	1494
Talus	Gk.	M	1529
Tannhauser	Germ.	M	1532
Taran	Gaelic	M, F	1534
Tshohanoai	Nav.	M	1603
Tuck, Friar	Bryth.	M	1606
Ulysses	Rom.	M	1622
Valdi Kjola	Norse	M	1561
Viracocha	Inca.	M	1652
Vishnu	Hin.	M	1654
Votan	Mex.	M	1658
Warah	Sem.	M	1665
Waso-Byoye	Jap.	M	1666
Wati Kutjara (Men Iguana)	Aus.	M	1669
Wegtam	Norse	M	1672

WAR (ALSO SEE WARRIOR)

Adad	Sem.	M	28
Alecto	Gk.	F	66

	Culture	Sex	Page
Alilat	Arab.	F	68
Allat	Sem.	F	69
Amen	Egy.	M	83
Ana	Cel.	F	90
Anahit	Pers.	F	90
Anaitis	Sem.	F	90
Anat	Sem.	F	91
Anat-Bethel	Hebr.	A	92
Anthat	As. Min.	F	102
Anunit	Baby.	F	105
Areia	Gk.	F	108
Ares	Gk.	M	120
Astarte	Phoen.	F	144
Atotarho	Iroq.	M	153
Baau	Phoen., Sum.	F	168
Badb	Cel.	F	171
Baduhenna	Norse	F	172
Bast	Egy.	F	185
Begtse	Bud.	A	196
Bel Enlil	Baby.	M	197
Bellona	Rom.	F	200
Bes	Egy.	M	205
Bishamon	Jap.	M	220
Bran	Bryth.	M	241
Brun	Norse	M	253
Brynhild (Brunhilda)	Norse	F	253
Camaxtli	Mex.	M	279
Cam Srin	Tib.	M	282
Camulus (Cumhal, Coel)	Cel.	M	282
Cerfius Martius	Ital.	M	1610
Chanchu	Yura.	M	310
Cocidius	Bryth.	M	353
Coel	Cel.	M	355
Couatlicue	Mex.	F	376
Cymbeline	Cel.	M	402
Daibosatsu	Jap.	M	406
Dee	Cel.	F	424
Dino	Gk.	F	446
Dornolla	Cel.	F	464
Elen Lwyddawg	Bryth.	F	501
Elohim Tzabaoth	Caba.	M	506
Emrys	Bryth.	M	510
Enlil	Baby., Sum.	M	512
Enyo	Gk.	F	513
Epunamun	Argen., Chil.	M	517
Er	Bav., Sax.	M	517

	Culture	Sex	Page
Esus	Cel.	M	526
Fea	Cel.	F	553
Fe'e	Poly.	M	558
Gerovit	Prussian	M	647
Guan Di	Chin.	M	693
Gwyn	Bryth.	M	703
Hachiman	Jap.	M	705
Hanhau	Yucatec	M	722
Hathor	Egy.	F	730
Hermod	Norse	M	762
Huitzilopochtli	Mex.	M	803
Inanna	Sum.	F	827
Irmin	Sax.	M	839
Irra (Ira)	Assyr-Baby.	M	841
Ishtar	Assyr-Baby.	F	844
Janus	Ital.	M	864
Jehovah Tzabaoth	Caba.	M	871
Juno	Rom.	F	895
Jupiter	Rom.	M	896
Karttikeya	Hin.	M	911
Keidomos	Gk.	M	915
Ker	Gk.	F	917
Kowwituma	Zuni	M	944
Kuang-ch'eng Tzu	Chin.	M	947
Kuan-ti	Chin.	M	947
Kui	N. Zeal.	F	949
Kumara	Hin.	M	951
Kysan-tengere	Sib.	M	956
Lua	Ital.	F	1019
Lyada	Slav.	M	1027
Macha	Cel.	F	1033
Machai	Gk.	F	1034
Magna Mater	Phryg.	F	1040
Mahakala	Hin.	M	1043
Mara	Bud.	M	1063
Marishiten	Jap.	M	1067
Mars	Rom.	M	1069
Maruts	Hin.	M	1071
Masauwu	Hopi	M	1072
Mentu	Egy.	M	1090
Merlin (Ambrosius)	Bryth.	M	1092
Minerva	Rom.	F	1106
Morgan le Fay	Bryth.	F	1123
Morrigu	Cel.	F	1125
Nag-pa	Tib.	M	1148
Naith	Cel.	M	1150

	Culture	Sex	Page
Nane	Arm.	F	1153
Neith	Egy., Lib.	F	1161
Nemain	Cel.	F	1161
Nemetona	Bryth.	F	1162
Nemon	Gaelic	F	1162
Nergal	Assyr-Baby.	M	1164
Net	Cel.	M	1165
Nike	Gk.	F	1169
Ningirsu	Sum.	M	1172
Ninib	Assyr-Baby.	M	1173
Nin-shach	Baby.	M	1173
Ninurta (Zamama)	Sum.	M	1174
Nodons	Bryth.	M	1179
Odin	Norse	M	1195
Ogma	Cel.	M	1200
Ojin	Jap.	M	1203
Ondoutaete	Huron	M	1209
Pandora	Gk.	F	1232
Panquetzalitztli	Mex.	F	1234
Phra In	Siam.	M	1266
Poseidon	Gk.	M	1288
Quirinus	Ital.	M	1314
Rimmon	Baby.	M	1339
Sakra	Hin.	M	1414
Saltu	Baby.	F	1392
Sekhet	Egy.	F	1414
Sek-ya	Ind-Chin.	M	1414
Shalman	Assyr.	M	1429
Shuqamuna	Baby.	M	1444
Skanda	Hin.	M	1464
Sun Hou-tzu	Chin.	M	1510
Sutekh	Syrian	M	1513
Svantovit	Slav.	M	1514
Tarku (Teshup)	Hittite	M	1535
Tethra	Cel.	M	1548
Teutates	Rom/Gaelic	M	1549
Tezcatlipoca	Mex.	M	1549
Thraetaona (Faridun)	Pers.	M	1563
Thunderbird	Am. Ind.	M	1568
Tiu	Ang-Sax.	M	1617
Turris	Fin.	M	1609
Tursa	Ital.	F	1610
Tyr	Teutonic	M	1617
Valetudo	Ital.	F	1636
Vanainti (Uparatat)	Pers.	F	1638
Verethraghna	Pers.	M	1646

	Culture	Sex	Page
Victoria	Rom.	F	1648
Watsusi	Zuni	M	1669
Yahata	Jap.	M	1698
Yaotlnecoc	Mex.	M	1701
Yaw	Hebr.	M	1702
Zamama	Baby.	M	1715
Ziu (Tiu)	Germ.	M	1721

WARRIOR (CONQUEROR. ALSO SEE HERO, WAR)

Acestes	Gk.	M	24
Achilles	Gk.	M/A	25
Adrastus	Gk.	M	35
Agamemnon	Gk.	M	44
Agenor	Gk.	M	48
Ajax	Gk.	M	58
Alcmaeon	Gk.	M	65
Alexander	Gk.	M	66
Amazon	Gk.	F	81
Ambree, Mary	Eng.	F	82
Amorites	Hebr.	M	87
Amphiaraus	Gk.	M	87
Amphilochus	Gk.	M	88
Amphitryon	Gk.	M	88
Anhoret	Egy.	M	97
Aoife	Cel.	F	106
Arcturus	Fin-Ug.	M	119
Armenak	Arm.	M	128
Artegal, Sir	Eng.	M/A	1316
Artemisia	Gk.	F	132
Arthur	Bryth.	M	132
Asshur	Assyr.	M	143
Ata	Jap.	F	147
Atatarho	Onondaga	M	148
Athena	Gk.	A	150
Attila (Atli)	Norse	M	154
Baldwin	Carol.	M	175
Bel	Baby.	M	196
Bersrker	Norse	M	204
Black Tortoise	Chin.	M	223
Bodb	Cel.	M	232
Bracan	Cel.	M	239
Brandel, Sir	Bryth.	M	243
Bricriu	Cel.	M	248
Brynhild	Norse	F	253
Cairbe	Cel.	M	270

	Culture	Sex	Page
Camilla	Rom.	F	281
Cao-bien	Ind-Chin.	M	287
Caoilte mac Ronan	Cel.	M	287
Capaneus	Gk.	M	288
Castor & Pollux	Gk.	M-M	295
Charlemagne	Carol.	M	314
Ch'in Shu-Pao	Chin.	M	326
Chung-li-Ch'uan	Chin.	M	336
Chu Ping Ch'en	Chin.	M	1424
Cid	Span.	M	338
Conall Cernach	Cel.	M	363
Cycnus	Gk.	M	401
Cyrus	Pers.	M	403
David	Hebr.	M	417
Dhu'l Karnein	Mos.	M	439
Dietrich Von Bern	Norse	M	444
Diomedes	Gk.	M	446
Dioscuri	Gk.	M-M	449
Domnal	Cel.	M	464
Drona	Hin.	M	471
Einheri	Norse	M	496
Eirik	Norse	M	496
Epigoni	Gk.	M	515
Erminia	Ital.	F	522
Etzel	Germ.	M	134
Fenian	Cel.	M	559
Fiachadh	Cel.	M	564
Finn mac Coul	Cel.	M	570
Firbolgs	Cel.	M	571
Folkvitr	Norse	F	1637
Fomor	Cel.	M	590
Forty-Seven Ronin	Jap.	M	598
Futsu-nushi	Jap.	M	618
Geraint	Bryth.	M	646
Goll mac Morna (Aodh)	Cel.	M	674
Gorgon	Gk.	F	678
Gradivus	Rom.	M	681
dGra-lha	Tib.	M	683
Guendoloena	Bryth.	F	695
Hagan	Norse	M	707
Harald	Dan.	M	725
Harpe	Gk.	F	728
Ha-wo-gang-zang	Tib.	M	1129
Hector	Gk.	M	749
Heike-gani	Jap.	M	743
Heimdal	Norse	M	743

	Culture	Sex	Page
Helge	Norse	M	746
Helm Gunnar	Norse	M	749
Hengest	Norse	M	750
Heracles	Gk.	M	752
Hercules	Rom.	M	759
Herfather	Norse	M	759
Hideyoshi	Jap.	M	767
Hildebrand	Germ.	M	770
Hippolyta	Gk.	F	773
Hippomedon	Gk.	M	774
Hjalmmeyjar	Norse	F	1637
Hoder	Norse	M	778
Horatius Cocles	Rom.	M	787
Horvendil	Dan.	M	793
Hunding	Germ.	M	806
Hypsipyle	Gk.	F	813
Hysminai	Gk.	F	814
Ialmenus	Gk.	M	815
Idisi	Norse	F	819
Idomeneus	Gk.	M	820
Igal	Hebr.	M	821
Indra	Hin.	M	829
Iskander Beg	Hin.	M	846
Jehu	Hebr.	M	871
Jenghis Khan (Temudjin)	Mong.	M	872
Jephthah	Hebr.	M	872
Jeroboam	Hebr.	M	874
Jimmu Tennu	Jap.	M	880
Jina	Jain.	M	880
Jingu	Jap.	F	880
Joab	Hebr.	M	881
Joan of Ark (Maid of Orleans)	Fr.	F	881
Joshua	Hebr.	M	889
Kato-saemon	Jap.	M	913
Kiyomori	Jap.	M	935
Klepht	Gk.	M	936
Klieng	Borneo	M	936
Krsanu	Hin.	M	947
Kul-lha-sha-ri	Tib.	M	1129
Kuo Shang	Chin.	M	952
Kuo Tzu-I	Chin.	M	952
Kwaijitsu	Jap.	M	954
Ling Pao	Chin.	M	998
Lludd	Bryth.	M	1005
Llwch Llaw-wynnawc	Welsh	M	1006
Lokapalas	Bud., Hin.	M	1010

	Culture	Sex	Page
Lug	Cel.	M	1022
Lugaid	Cel.	M	1023
Lugaid Red Stripes	Cel.	M	1023
Lyfir	Norse	M	1028
Maasewe & Uyuuyewe	Sia Ind.	M-M	1031
Maccabees	Hebr.	M	1032
Mac Lugach	Cel.	M	1034
Maid of Saragossa	Span.	F	1046
Manabhozho	Algon.	M	1054
Mandarangan	Philip.	M	1056
Marko Kraljevic	Serb.	M	1068
Ma-vien	Chin.	M	1078
Memnon	Gk.	M	1088
Menelaus	Gk.	M	1089
Men Shen	Chin.	M	1090
Miled	Cel.	M	1102
Minos	Gk.	M	1107
Mithra	Pers.	M	1112
Mo-li Ch'ing	Chin.	M	1115
Molpadia	Gk.	F	+
Mopsus	Gk.	M	1122
Morrigu	Cel.	F	1125
Moses	Hebr.	M	1126
Myrmidon	Gk.	M	1142
Naaman	Hebr.	M	1145
Nebuchadnezzar	Baby.	M	1159
Nemda Prince	Fin-Ug.	M	1161
Neoptolemus	Gk.	M	1163
Nestor	Gk.	M	1165
Netzach	Caba.	M	1166
Nicophoros	Gk.	M	1720
Nuada	Cel.	M	1184
Octriallach	Cel.	M	1194
Odysseus	Gk.	M	1196
Ogma	Cel.	M	1200
Oileus	Gk.	M	1202
Oliver	Carol.	M	1206
Orpheus	Gk.	M	1216
Oskmeyjur	Norse	F	1637
Oxylus	Gk.	M	1223
Palamedes	Gk.	M	1227
Pandarus	Gk.	M	1232
Parthenopaeus	Gk.	M	1240
Partholan	Cel.	M	1240
Patroclus	Gk.	M	1244
Pekah	Hebr.	M	1249

Penthesilea	Gk.	F	1253
Philoctetes	Gk.	M	1263
Podalirius	Gk.	M	1281
Polydorus	Gk.	M	1284
Polynices	Gk.	M	1284
Pookonghoya & Balongahoya	Hopi.	M	1286
Prince Wijaya	Aryan	M	1455
Pryderi (Gwri)	Bryth.	M	1298
Pyrrhus	Gk.	M	1307
Radigund	Eng.	F/A	1316
Rerir	Norse	M	1333
Resheph	Phoen.	M	1333
Rinaldo	Ital.	M	1339
Roland	Carol.	M	1345
Rugievit (Rinvit)	Slav.	M	1514
Saint George	Christ.	M	1370
Saladin	Syrian	M	1390
Salii	Rom.	M	1390
Samurai	Jap.	M	1394
Sargon I	Meso.	M	1400
Sargon II	Assyr.	M	1400
Sarpedon	Gk.	M	1401
Sarvitr	Norse	F	1637
Saul	Hebr.	M	1404
Scathach	Cel.	F	1406
Sebastian	Portu.	M	1412
Semiramis	Assyr.	F	1415
Sesostris	Egy.	M	1420
Shura	Jap.	M	1444
Siegfried	Germ.	M	1448
Sigrdrifa	Norse	F	1451
Sigtyr	Norse	M	1451
Sigurd	Norse	M	1451
Sinon	Gk.	M	1457
Sisera	Hebr.	M	1459
Sitamahakala	Bud.	M	1460
Sitatara	Bud.	F	1460
Song-tsen Gam Po	Tib.	M	1475
Sreng	Cel.	M	1487
Sridevi	Bud.	F	1487
Starkath (Hross-hars-grani)	Norse	M	1492
Stentor	Gk.	M	1493
Sthenelus	Gk.	M	1494
Sugriva	Hin.	M	1504
Svava	Norse	F	1515
Syamatara	Bud.	F	1521
Take-mi-kazuchi	Jap.	M	1527

	Culture	Sex	Page
Taliesin	Bryth.	M	1528
Tancred	Ital.	M	1531
Tawara Toda	Jap.	M	1539
Telephus	Gk.	M	1542
Thang-lha	Tib.	M	1129
Thein	Burm.	M	1553
Theodoric	Germ.	M	1553
Thersander	Gk.	M	1554
Thersites	Gk.	M	1554
Theseus	Gk.	M	1554
Thraetaona	Pers.	M	1563
Thraso	Rom.	M	1563
Tibernius	Rom.	M	1570
Tonatiuh	Mex.	M	1586
Troilus	Eng.	M	1600
Tydeus	Gk.	M	1616
Typhoeus	Gk.	M	1617
Typhon	Gk.	M	1617
Ullerus	Norse	M	1622
Ulysses	Rom.	M	1622
Uriah	Hebr.	M	1629
Urien	Bryth.	M	1629
Uther Pendragon	Bryth.	M	1632
Valkyrie	Norse	F	1636
Valmeyjar	Norse	F	1637
Vispala	Hin.	M	1655
Volsung	Norse	M	1658
Wabun	Algon.	M	1660
Wei-t'o	Chin.	M	1672
Xerxes	Pers.	M	1695
Yalahau	Mex.	M	1698
Yamato-take	Jap.	M	1699
Yar-lha-shang-po	Tib.	M	1129
Yoshi-iye	Jap.	M	1710
Yu Ch'ih Ching-te	Chin.	M	1711
Zabaoth	Gnostic	M	1714
Zaru	Egy.	M	1716
Zduh	Slav.	M	1717

WATER (FOUNTAIN, LAKE, RIVER, SEA, STREAM, WELL. DEITY OF SAILORS & SEA TRAVELERS. ALSO FISH DEITY, WATER-BORN DEITY)

	Culture	Sex	Page
Achelous	Gk.	M	24
Acis	Gk.	M	26
Acuecueyotl	Mex.	F	28

	Culture	Sex	Page
Adad	Sem.	M	28
Adonis	Sem.	M	34
Aegeon	Gk.	M	38
Aegeus	Gk.	M	38
Aegina	Gk.	F	38
Aegir	Norse	M	38
Aegyptus	Gk.	M	39
Aesopus	Gk.	M	+
Aganippe	Gk.	F	45
Ahi Budhnya	Hin.	M	52
Ahti	Fin.	M	54
Akkruva	Fin-Ug.	F	60
Albion	Gk.	M	63
Alcippe	Gk.	F	64
Alpheus	Gk.	M	76
Alrinach	Eastern	F	76
Altcanals	Mex.	F	77
Amanki	Baby.	M	79
Amathaounta	Gk.	F	81
Amphitrite	Gk.	F	88
Amymone	Gk.	F	89
Anadyomene	Gk.	F	90
Anahit	Pers.	F	90
Andvari	Norse	M	95
Angeyja	Norse	F	96
Annar	Norse	M	100
Anqet	Egy.	F	100
Ao-Jun	Chin.	M	106
Ao-K'in	Chin.	M	106
Ao-Kuang	Chin.	M	106
Ao-Shun	Chin.	M	106
Ap (Apas)	Hin.	M	106
Apam Napat	Hin.	M	107
Apet	Egy.	F	107
Aphaea	Gk.	F	108
Aphrodite	Gk.	F	108
Apoconallotl	Mex.	F	110
Apollo Thyrxis	Gk.	M	111
Apsu	Baby.	M	115
Arethusa	Gk.	F	121
Ariel	Caba.	M	124
Ascalabus	Gk.	M	135
Asia	Gk.	F	140
Astarte	Phoen.	F	144
Aun	Sem.	M	157
Axius	Gk.	M	+

	Culture	Sex	Page
Azariel	Hebr.	M	165
Baau	Phoen., Sum.	F	168
Balder	Norse	M	174
Belili	Sum.	F	197
Belisama	Cel.	F	197
Benten	Jap.	F	203
Black Tortoise	Chin.		223
Blue Dragon	Chin.		468
Boann	Cel.	F	231
Branwen	Bryth.	F	243
Brave-Swift-Impetuous-Male	Jap.	M	244
Bredi	Norse	M	245
Buto	Jap.	M	263
Byblis	Rom.	F	264
Cacce-Olmai	Mong.	M	265
Camenae	Rom.	F	281
Canente	Rom.	F	285
Carmenta	Rom.	F	291
Cay	Mex.	M	283
Cebren	Gk.	M	1199
Cephissus	Gk.	M	304
Ceto	Gk.	F	306
Chalchiutlicue (Altcanals)	Mex.	F/A	308
Charybdis	Gk.	F	316
Chiang Tzu-ya	Chin.	M	321
Ching Chu'an	Chin.	M	577
Chrysor	Phoen.	M	334
Chuan Hou	Chin.	F	335
Clud	Bryth.	F	351
Clymene	Gk.	F	351
Clytie	Gk.	F	351
Crimisus	Gk.	M	24
Cymodoce	Rom.	F	402
Cythera	Gk.	F	403
Daeira	Gk.	F	404
Daitya	Hin.	M	407
Danaides	Gk.	F	411
Danwantaree	Hin.	M	414
Davy Jones	Folk.	M	418
Dee	Cel.	F	424
Delphinus	Gk.	M	111
Devatas	Hin.	F	435
Dione	Gk.	F	446
Dirce	Gk.	F	450
Dobaya	Darian Ind.	F	454
Dolphin	Gk.		459

	Culture	Sex	Page
Domnu	Cel.	F	460
Dopkalfar	Norse	M, F	464
Doris	Gk.	F	464
Draugr	Norse	M	470
Drebkuls	Rus.	M	470
Dryope	Gk.	M	473
Dsovean	Arm.	M	474
Dylan	Bryth.	M	480
Ea	Baby.	M	481
Ea-Oannes	Assyr.	M	484
Ebisu	Jap.	M	498
Egeria	Rom.	F	491
Egia (Angeyja)	Norse	F	96
Egther	Norse	M	493
Eikthyrner	Norse	M	496
Eire	Cel.	F	496
Eistla	Norse	F	496
Elatha	Cel.	M	498
Engur	Baby.	M	511
Enipeus	Gk.	M	1618
Enki	Assyr., Baby., Sum.	M	511
Eogan	Cel.	M	514
Ephka	Sem.	A	515
Epona	Cel., Rom.	F	517
Erwand	Arm.	M	523
Euryalus	Gk.	M	111
Eurybia	Gk.	F	532
Eyrgjafa	Norse	F	541
Faknik	Papuan		546
Farbauti	Norse	M	548
Fata Morgana	Ital.	F	550
Feng I	Chin.	M	559
Fenja & Menja	Norse	F-F	560
Fimafeng	Cel.	M	568
Flosshilde	Germ.	F	1336
Fomhair	Scot.	M	590
Fomor	Cel.	M	590
Fons (Fontus)	Rom.	M	850
Frey	Norse	M	609
Funadama	Jap.	M	617
Funafeng	Norse	M	617
Funa-yurei	Jap.	M, F	617
Gahonga	Iroq.	M	884
Gaiar	Cel.	M	622
Galatea	Gk.	F	623

	Culture	Sex	Page
Ganga	Hin.	F	627
Gava-Griva	Hin.	M	635
Giaiael	Taino	M	653
Gjalp	Norse	F	660
Glaucus	Gk.	M	662
Greip	Norse	F	689
Grendel	Ang-Sax.	M	689
Guabancex	Taino	F	693
Guabonito	Taino	F	693
Hadding	Norse	M	705
Halirrhothios	Gk.	M	712
Hapi	Egy.	M/A	724
Harahvaiti	Pers.	F	724
Harbard	Norse	M	725
Haurvatat	Zoro.	M	732
Havfrue	Dan.	F	732
Havmand	Dan.	M	732
Haya-akihiko & Haya-akitsu	Jap.	M-F	734
Heimdal	Norse	M	743
Helmund	Afghan.	F	749
Heqes	Egy.	M	752
Hesione	Gk.	F	764
Hesioneus	Gk.	M	765
Hiranyakasipu	Hin.	M	774
Hler	Norse	M	776
Hoener	Norse	M	779
Holde	Germ.	F	780
Ho-no-susori	Jap.	M	785
Ho Po	Chin.	M	786
Hpaung-daw-u	Ind-Chin.	M	794
Hrimgerd	Norse	F	798
Hsiang Chun	Chin.	M	799
Hsi Hai	Chin.	M	799
Hu	Egy.	M	800
Hydria	Gk.	F	810
Hymir	Norse	M	811
Hypermnestra	Gk.	F	812
Ike-no-nushi	Jap.	M	822
Imder	Norse	F	825
Inachus	Gk.	M	827
Ino	Gk.	F	835
Ira-waru	Poly.	M	838
Ishtar	Assyr-Baby.	F	844
Isis	Egy.	F	845
Itsuku-shima	Jap.	M	849
Iuturna (Juturna)	Ital.	F	850

	Culture	Sex	Page
Ivalde	Norse	M	850
Jalyogini	Hin.	M	862
Jarnsaxa	Norse	M	866
Jengk-tongk	Fin-Ug.	M	872
Jogaoh	Iroq.	M, F	884
Jumna	Hin.	F	895
Juturna (Diuturna)	Rom.	F	850
Khidr	Arab.	M	924
Ki-gulla	Baby.	M	927
Klaboterman	Germ.	M	935
Kobo Daishi	Jap.	M	939
Komokoa	Pac. Coast	M	941
Kompira	Jap.	M	941
Koshi	Jap.	M	943
Kul	Fin-Ug.	M	950
Ladon	Gk.	M	962
Lady of the Lake	Eng.	F	962
Laestrygones	Gk.	M	963
Lamus	Gk.	M	969
Ler	Cel.	M	985
Leucippus	Gk.	M/A	987
Leucothea	Gk.	F	988
Limniades	Gk.	F	997
Liwa	C.A.I.		1004
Llyr	Bryth.	M	1006
Lorelei	Germ.	F	1013
Losy	Mong.	M	1013
Luchorpain	Irish	M	1020
Lugal-ida	Sum.	M	1023
Lymphae	Rom.	F	1028
Lynceus	Gk.	M	1028
Mama Cocha	Inca.	F	1051
Manannan	Cel.	M	1054
Manawyddan	Bryth.	M	1056
Mara	Hebr.	F	1063
Mardoll	Norse	F	1065
Maritchi	Chin.	F	1067
Mariucella	Folk.	F	1068
Marsyas	Gk.	F	1070
Meht-ueret	Egypt.	F	1084
Melkarth	Phoen.	M	1086
Mem Loimis	Wintun	M	1088
Mermaid	Folk.	F	1093
Merman	Folk.	M	545
Metis	Gk.	F	1096
Midgard Serpent	Norse		1100

	Culture	Sex	Page
Mimir	Norse	M	1105
Mirsi	Baby.	M	1110
Miwi-no-kami	Jap.	M	1113
Morskoi Tzar	Slav.	M	1125
Muit	Egy.	F	1134
Mukasa	Uganda	M	1135
Mysing	Ice.	M	1143
Naiades	Gk.	F	1148
Nain Rouge	Norman	M	1149
Nakazutsuno	Jap.	M	1506
Naki-saha-me-no-kami	Jap.	F	1150
Naqbu	Baby.	M	1155
Nasnas	Arab.	M	1156
Nauplius	Gk.	M	1158
Navky	Slav.	M, F	1158
Nechtan	Cel.	M	1160
Neptune	Cel.	M	1163
Nereids	Gk.	F	1164
Nereus	Gk.	M	1164
Nerrivik	Eskimo	F	1164
Nhangs	Arm.	F	1167
Niamh	Cel.	F	1167
Nickard (Hnikar)	Germ.	M	776
Nicor	Eng.	M	776
Nikolai	Rus.	M	1169
Nikur (Hnikar)	Scan.	M	1169
Nilus	Gk/Egy.	M	1170
Nina	Baby.	F	1170
Nin-Bubu	Sum.	M	1170
Nindubarra	Sum.	M	1171
Nin Ella	Baby.	F	1172
Ningyo	Jap.	F	1173
Nin-ki (Damkina)	Baby.	F	1173
Nira	Baby.	M	1175
Niskai	Medit.	F	686
Nix	Teut.	M	1176
Nixe	Teut.	F	1176
Njord	Norse	M/A	1176
Nu	Egy.	M	1184
Numina	Rom.	M	1185
Oannes	Baby., Chald., Phoen.	M	1190
Obi	Sib.		1192
Oceanides	Gk.	F	1193
Oceanus	Gk.	M	1193
Odakon	Philis.	M	1194

	Culture	Sex	Page
Odrus	Cel.	M	1196
Oegir	Norse	M	1198
Oiagros	Gk.	M	1202
Onchestus	Gk.	M	1209
Orc	Ital.	M	1213
Oshun	Yorubas	F	1218
Osiris	Egy.	M	1218
Oto-hime	Jap.	F	1220
Ottar	Norse	M	1220
Pa'ewa	Solom. Is.	M	999
Palaemon (Melicertes)	Gk.	M	1227
Paravataksha	Hin.	M	1237
Pele Kolese	Fin-Ug.		1249
Peneus	Gk.	M	1252
Perse	Gk.	F	1257
Phaon	Gk.	M	1261
Philyra	Gk.	F	1264
Phorcys	Gk.	M	1266
Pierides	Gk.	F	1269
Pirene	Gk.	F	+
Pluto	Gk.	F	1280
Pontia	Gk.	F	108
Pontus	Gk.	M	1286
Portunus	Rom.	M	1287
Poseidon	Gk.	M	1288
Postverta	Rom.	F	1288
Potameides	Gk.	F	1289
Potrympus	Baltic	M	1289
Prospero	Eng.	M	1296
Proteus	Gk.	M	1297
Psamathe	Gk.	F	1299
Pylaochos	Gk.	M	1306
Rahab	Hebr.	F	1318
Rajah Kidar (Bir Badr)	Hin.	M	1320
Ran	Norse	F	1322
Ravgga (Meriraukka)	Fin-Ug.	M	1325
Rgvedic	Hin.	M	1335
Rhine Daughters	Germ.	F	1336
Ruahaku	So. Is.	M	1352
Rusalka	Rus.	F	1355
Ryu-wo	Jap.	M	1356
Sa-bdag	Tib.		1357
Sabitu	Baby.	F	1357
Sabrina	Eng.	F	1357
Sagara	Hin.	M	1360
Saiva-neida	Lapp	F	1355

	Culture	Sex	Page
Salamannu	Assyr.	M	1390
Salmacis	As. Min.	F	1391
Same-bito	Jap.	M	1393
Sarasvant	Hin.	M	1400
Sarasvati	Hin.	F	1400
Satet	Egy.	F	1402
Scamander	Gk.	M	1405
Scotia	Cyprian	F	1408
Scylla	Gk.	F	1409
Sedna	Eskimo	F	1413
Seewiesken	Germ.	F	1413
Segesta	Gk.	F	1413
Selinus	Gk.	M	1415
Seoritsu-hime	Jap.	F	1417
Shabriri	Hebr.	M	1428
Shar Apsi	Baby.	M	1431
Shony	Hebrides	M	1442
Shui Shen (Shui Kuan)	Chin.	M	1444
Shulamite	Hebr.	F	1444
Sidon	Phoen.	M	1447
Silanus	Rom.	M	1452
Silenii	Gk.	M	1453
Silenus	Gk.	M	1453
Sinann	Cel.	F	1456
Sirens	Gk.	F	1458
Sisiutl	Kwakiutl	M	1459
Siva	Hin.	M	1461
Sjen	Slav.	M	1463
Sjora	Swed.	F	1463
Skade	Norse	F/A	1463
Slagfin	Norse	M	1466
Sokozutsuno	Jap.	M	1506
Spercheus	Gk.	M	1481
Stella Maris	Christ.	F	1493
Stromkarl	Norw.	M	1501
Styx	Gk.	F	1502
Suijin-sama	Jap.	M	1504
Suitengu	Jap.	M	1504
Suku-na-biko	Jap.	M	1505
Sul	Bryth.	F	1505
Sumiyoshi Brothers	Jap.	M	1506
Susa-no-wo	Jap.	M	1512
Suvarnamacha	Siam.	F	1513
Tangaroa	Poly.	M	1513
Taria-nui	Poly.	M	1535
Tegid Voel	Bryth.	M	1541

	Culture	Sex	Page
Tengys	Sib.	M	1545
Tethra	Cel.	M	1548
Tethys	Gk.	F	1548
Teucer	Gk.	M	1549
Thalassa	Gk.	F	1551
Tham	Baby.	F	1551
Thaumas	Gk.	M	1552
Thetis	Gk.	F	1555
Thobadzistshini	Nav.	M	1159
Thonis (Osiris)	Egy.	M	1218
Thorstein	Ice.	M	1562
Thyrxis (Apollo)	Gk.	M	111
Tibernius	Rom.	M	1570
Tieholtsodi	Nav.	M	1571
T'ien Hou	Chin.	F	1571
Timirau	Herv. Is.	M	1574
Tomomori	Jap.	M	1586
Toyo-tama-hime	Jap.	F	1593
Trita Aptya	Hin.	M	1599
Triton	Gk.	M	1599
Trow	Scot.	M	1600
Tung Hai	Chin.	M	1607
Tzequiles	Mex.	A	1618
Ukupanio	Hawa.	M	1621
Ulfrun	Norse	F	1621
Umiarissat Women	Eskimo	F	1623
Umi Bozu	Jap.	M	1623
Undine	Med.	F	1624
Unk-ta-he	Dakota	M	1626
Usumgal	Sum.	M	1631
Uwazutsuno	Jap.	M	1506
Vaksoza	Fin-Ug.	M	1638
Vana-Mothers	Norse	F	1638
Vanir	Norse	M, F	1638
Varuna	Hin.	M	1639
Vasa	Fin-Ug.	F	1640
Vasillissa	Slav.	F	1641
Ve	Norse	M	1643
Vederaj	Fin-Ug.	M	1643
Vena	Hin.	M	1644
Venus	Rom.	F	1644
Vetehinen	Rus.		1648
Vivian (Vivienne)	Bryth.	F	1656
Vodni-panny	Slav.	F	1657
Vodyanik	Rus.	M	1657
Vourukasha	Pers.	M	1659

Water (cont.)	Culture	Sex	Page
Vu-murt	Fin-Ug.	A	1660
Vut-oza	Fin-Ug.	M	1660
Wata-tsu-mi	Jap.	M	1666
Watsusi	Zuni	M	1669
Wellamo	Fin.	F	1673
Wellgunde	Germ.	F	1336
Wels	Baltic	M	1673
Woglinde	Germ.	F	1336
Wudes Heer (Wade)	Norse	M	1693
Xixiquipilihui	Mex.	F	1696
Ya-daganu	Sem.	M	1697
Yalahau	Mex.	M	1698
Yemanja	Yoruban	F	1705
Yen Kung	Chin.	M	1705
Yolkai Estsan	Nav.	F	1709
Yu Po	Chin.	M	1713
Zaden	Iberian	M	1714
Zebedee	Christ.	M	1717

WATER BORN (SEE WATER)

WEALTH (GAIN, PROSPERITY, TREASURE. ALSO SEE WEALTH DISTRIBUTOR)

Name	Culture	Sex	Page
Ah-kiuic	Mex.	M	53
Aides	Gk.	M	55
Alberich	Norse	M	62
Andvari	Norse	M	95
Arawn	Bryth.	M	117
Bajanai	Yakut	M	173
Balthazar	Christ.	M	177
Bishamon	Jap.	M	220
Camacho	Span.	M	279
Carabas, Marquis De	Fr.	M	289
Chu Ts'ang Shen	Chin.	M	1424
Cluracan (Cluricaune)	Cel.	M	351
Coblymau	Bryth.	M	352
Consus	Ital.	M	368
Convector	Rom.	M	369
Daikoku	Jap.	M	406
Da-lha	Tib.	M	1571
Dazbog	Sib.	M	420
Dis	Cel.	M	450
Dis Pater	Rom.	M	451
Dives	Christ.	M	452
Diwrnach	Cel.	M	454
El Dorado	Folk.	M	499

	Culture	Sex	Page
Erichthonius	Gk.	M	519
Flosshilda	Germ.	F	585
Fortunatus	Med. Lit.	M	596
Frey	Norse	M	609
Frode	Norse	M	613
Fuku	Jap.	M	616
Fukusuke	Jap.	M	616
Funadama	Jap.	M	617
Fu Shen	Chin.	M	618
Fu-shou-lu	Chin.	M	618
Gad	Hebr.	M	620
Geirrod	Norse	M	638
Giukings	Norse	M, F	660
Gnome	Med. Lit.	M, F	664
dGra-lha	Tib.	M	1571
Hades	Gk.	M	706
Hermes	Gk.	M	760
Hesperides	Gk.	F	765
Hyrieus	Gk.	M	813
Jack the Giant Killer	Folk.	M	857
Jambhala	Bud.	M	862
Joseph of Arimathea	Christ.	M	889
Juno	Rom.	F	895
Karoon	Mos.	M	911
Kotan-Shorai	Jap.	M	944
Kubera	Bud., Hin.	M	948
Kuo-tzu-I	Chin.	M	952
Kurukulla	Tib.	F	953
Kwan-yin	Chin.	F/A	955
Lakshmi	Hin.	F	965
Laurin	Germ.	M	977
Leprechaun	Irish	M	985
Liu-hai	Chin.	M	1003
Mahakala	Hin.	M	1043
Ma-lha	Tib.	M	1571
Mammon	Syrian	M	1051
Mandrabul	Rom.	M	1057
Manyu	Hin.	M	1062
Math	Cymric	M	1075
Mercury	Rom.	M	1091
Midas	Gk.	M	1099
Midir	Cel.	M	1100
Minyas	Gk.	M	1107
Muyinewumana	Pueblo	F	1142
Naga	Hin.	M, F	1147
Nibelung	Norse	M	1167

Wealth (cont.)	Culture	Sex	Page
Njord	Norse	M	1176
Nor-lha	Tib.	M	1571
Nules-murt	Fin-Ug.	M	1185
O-kuni-nushi	Jap.	M	1204
Pho-lha	Tib.	M	1571
Plouton (Pylartes)	Gk.	M	1306
Pluto	Rom.	M	1280
Plutus	Gk.	M	1280
Poshaiyanne	Pueblo	M	1288
Potrympus	Baltic	M	1289
Pryderi	Bryth.	M	1298
Queen of Sheba	Hebr.	F	1311
Rakshasa	Hin.	M, F	1320
Raphael	Hebr.	M	1323
Regin	Norse	M	1330
Rhampsinitus	Gk.	M	1335
Ro-ku	Jap.	M	1345
Salus	Rom.	F	1392
Schilbung	Norse	M	1407
Shang-lha	Tib.	M	1571
Sichaeus	Rom.	M	1446
Sif	Norse	F	1448
Sindbad	Arab.	M	1456
Sitamahakala	Bud.	M	1460
Solomon	Hebr.	M	1472
Sri	Hin.	F	1487
T'ang	Chin.	M	1531
Tawara Toda	Jap.	M	1539
Tishtrya	Pers.	M/A	1577
Troll	Norse	M	1600
Ts'ai Shen Yeh	Chin.	M	1602
Turcaret	Fr.	M	1608
Tvastr	Hin.	M	1611
Upadhyaya	Bud.	M	1626
Yama	Hin.	M	1699
Yul-lha	Tib.	M	1571
Zacchaeus	Christ.	M	1714

WEALTH DISTRIBUTOR (ALSO SEE GIFT BEARER)

Apaharavarman	Hin.	M	106
Clym of the Clough	Eng.	M	351
Number Nip	Eng.	M	1352
Robin Hood	Eng.	M	1343
Rob Roy	Scot.	M	1343
Rubezahl	Germ.	M	1352

	Culture	Sex	Page
Saint Anne	Christ.	F	1362
Santa Claus (Saint Nicholas)	Christ.	M	1397
Silik-mulu-khi	Assyr., Sum.	M	1453
Sitconski	Assiniboin	M	1460
Ts'ao Kuochiu	Chin.	M	1603

WEAVER (SPINNER)

Arachne	Gk.	F	116
Athena	Gk.	F	150
Aurora	Rom.	F	158
Chih Nu	Chin.	F	323
Emer	Cel.	F	508
Frigg	Norse	F	612
Heracles	Gk.	M/A	753
Hercules	Rom.	M/A	759
Mama Ogllo	Inca	F	1051
Neith	Lib-Egy.	F	1161
Norn	Norse	F	1180
Ocnus	Gk.	M	1193
Omphale	Gk.	F/A	1208
Ori-hime	Jap.	F	1215
Pandora	Gk.	F	1232
Penelope	Gk.	F	1252
Philomela	Gk.	F	1263
Procne	Gk.	F	1294
Sandalphon	Caba.	M	1396
Skuld	Norse	F	1465
Tahmurath	Pers.	M	1525
Tatsuta-hime	Jap.	F	1538
Urd	Norse	F	1628
Uttukku	Sum.	M/F	1632
Verdandi	Norse	F	1645
Wyrd	Ang-Sax.	F	1694
Xochiquetzal	Mex.	F	1696

WELL (SEE WATER)
WICKEDNESS (SEE EVIL)

WIND (BREEZE)

Adad	Sem.	M	28
Aeife	Cel.	F	39
Aello	Gk.	F	40
Aeolus (Eolus)	Gk.	M	40
Afer	Rom.	M	43
Aferventus	Ital.	M	43
Africus	Rom.	M	44

	Culture	Sex	Page
Agoneus	Gk.	M	50
Alan	Philip.		61
Allen-a-Dale	Bryth.	M	69
Aloidae	Gk.	M	71
Amphion	Gk.	M	88
Anemoi	Gk.		514
Angerboda	Norse	F	96
Anila	Hin.	M	1641
Anu	Cel.	F	104
Aquila	Rom.	M	116
Ara-tiatia	Poly.		117
Ares	Gk.	M	120
Argestes	Gk.	M	1683
Arion	Gk.	M	125
Auna	Eskimo		601
Aura (Aurae)	Gk.	F	158
Aurboda	Norse	F	158
Auster	Rom.	M	159
Autolycus	Gk.	M	159
Ayar Aucca	Inca	M	164
Ayar Cachi	Inca	M	163
Ayar Manco	Inca	M	164
Ayar Uchu	Inca	M	164
Baba, Cassim	Arab.	M	168
Bacabab	Mex.	M	170
Bailos & Xanthos	Gk.	M	173
Bajanai	Yakut	M	173
Baneb-ded	Egy.	M	178
Banshee	Cel.	F	179
Bedivere	Bryth.	M	193
Benkei	Jap.	M	202
Bhima	Hin.	M	209
Black Annis of Leicester	Eng.	F	222
Blue Hag	Eng.	F	222
Boreadae	Gk.	M	236
Boreas	Gk.	M	236
Bozaloshtsh	Slav.	F	239
Brian	Cel.	M	247
Byat Ta & Byat Twe	Ind-Chin.	M-M	1445
Byrr	Norse	M	264
Cairbe	Cel.	M	270
Calais	Gk.	M	272
Caoilte mac Ronan	Cel.	M	287
Caurus (Corus)	Rom.	M	374a
Ce Acatl	Mex.	M	301
Cliach	Cel.	M	348

	Culture	Sex	Page
Con	Inca	M	363
Conan Maol	Cel.	M	364
Curetes	Gk.	M	398
Çwn Annwn	Bryth.	M	400
Cyhiraeth	Bryth.	F	401
Dactyli	Gk.	M	404
Dagda	Cel.	M	405
Dajoji	Iroq.	M	408
Dalhan	Arab.	M	409
Dulachan	Cel.	M	475
Dund (Dhundh)	Hin.	M	476
Duneyrr	Norse		476
Durathror	Norse		477
Dvalin	Norse		478
Eabani (Enkidu)	Sum.	M	482
Egder	Norse	M	491
El of Gebal	Sem.	M	497
Enlil	Baby., Sum.	M	512
Ephialtes	Gk.	M	515
Esaugeteh Emissee	Creek Ind.	M	524
Eurus	Gk., Rom.	M	532
Evnissyen	Bryth.	M	536
Ezekiel	Hebr.	M	541
Farbauti	Norse	M	548
Favonius	Rom.	M	553
Feng	Norse	M	559
Feng Po	Chin.	M	559
Feng Po-po	Chin.	F	559
Fergus	Cel.	M	561
Fuamnach	Cel.	F	615
Fujin	Jap.	M	616
Furies	Gk.	F	617
Gabriel's Ratches (Hounds)	Bryth.		620
Gahe	Apache	M	622
Gandharva	Hin.	M	626
Gandreid Spirits	Norse	M, F	626
Ga-oh	Seneca	M	628
Gardrofa	Norse	F	629
Garide	Mong.		630
Garuda	Hin.	M	633
Gayatri	Hin.		636
Gentle Annie	Scot.	F	645
Gnaa	Norse	F	664
Guabancex	Taino	F	693
Gucumatz	Guate	M	694
Gunadhya	Hin.	M	698

	Culture	Sex	Page
Guru Kam Balu	Tib.	M	699
Gweir	Bryth.	M	701
Gwrhyr Gwalstawt	Bryth.	M	702
Hackelberend	Norse	M	705
Harpies	Gk.	F	728
Heimer	Norse	M	744
Henk-niseau	Egy.	M	1683
Heracles	Gk.	M	752
Hercules	Rom.	M	759
Hermes	Gk.	M	760
Hermod	Norse	M	762
Herne	Eng.	M	762
Her-shef	Egy.	M	763
Hofvarpner	Norse		779
Ho Hsien-ku	Chin.	F	780
Holde	Germ.	F	780
Holy Ghost (Holy Spirit)	Christ.	M	782
Hoturu	Pawnee	M	794
Hraesvelg	Norse	M	797
Hulderfolk	Norse	M, F	804
Hurakan	C.A.I.	M	808
Hutchaiui	Egy.	M	1683
Ilmarinen	Fin-Ug.	M	824
Ishkur	Sum.	M	843
Ishum	Sum.	M	845
Itzamna	Mex.	M	850
Iuchar	Cel.	M	850
Iucharba	Cel.	M	850
Ixcuin	Mex.	M	852
John Nailor (Little John)	Eng.	M	885
Jubal	Hebr.	M	891
Judy	Gk.	F	893
Jupiter	Rom.	M	893
Kaare	Norse	M	900
Kabibonokka	Algon.	M	900
Kabun	Algon.	M	900
Kaches	Arm.	M, F	900
Kahit	Wintun	M	902
Kalachakra	Bud.	M	903
Kalais	Gk.	M	903
Kara	Norse	F	909
Kaua	Poly.	M	913
Kauna	Eskimo		601
Kezer-tshingis	Tatar	M	921
Khensu	Egy.	M	923
King Goldemar (Vollmar)	Germ.	M	929

	Culture	Sex	Page
Kingu	Baby.	M	932
Kinnaras	Hin.	M	932
Kneph	Egy.	M	937
Korrigans	Breton	M, F	943
Kynedyr Wyllt	Bryth.	M	956
La'a-maomao	Poly.	M	957
Lady of T'ai-shan	Chin.	F	962
Laelaps	Gk.		963
Langsuyar	Malay.	F	971
Lesiy	Rus.	M	986
Liban	Cel.	F	990
Lilith	Hebr.	F	994
Lilithu	Sum.	F	995
Lilu	Baby.	M	995
Linus	Gk.	M	998
Little Red Riding Hood	Folk.	F	1003
Liu Tsung	Chin.	M	1003
Ljod	Norse	F	1004
Louhi	Lapp	F	1016
Magni	Norse	M	1040
Mala Lith	Cel.	F	1049
Marduk	Assyr-Baby.	M	1065
Marsyas	Phryg.	M	1070
Maruts	Hin.	M	1071
Matarisvan	Hin.	M	1074
Mauthe	Irish		1078
Medyr	Bryth.	M	1084
Meluzina	Bohemian	F	1087
Menw	Bryth.	M	1090
Mer (Bir)	Sum.	M	1091
Mercury	Rom.	M	1091
Mets-haldijas	Esthonian	M	1097
Metsmees	Esthonian	M	1097
Meulen	Araucanian	M	1097
Michabo (Messon)	Algon.	M	1098
Modi	Norse	M	1114
Mo-li ch'ing	Chin.	M	1115
Morgan le Fay	Bryth.	M	1123
Mudjekeewis	N.A.I.	M	1133
Nanihehecatli	Mex.	M	1153
Neago	Seneca	F	1159
Niltshi	Nav.	M	1170
Njord	Norse	M	1176
Notus	Gk.	M	1183
Nules-murt	Fin-Ug.	M	1185
Obyda (Ar-sori)	Chuvash	F	1192

	Culture	Sex	Page
Ocypete	Gk.	F	1194
Odin	Norse	M	1195
Odrerer	Norse		1196
Oengus	Cel.	M	1198
Ol	Bryth.	M	1204
Orpheus	Gk.	M	1216
Otus	Gk.	M	1221
Ovda	Fin-Ug.	M, F	1221
Oyan-do-me	Seneca	M	1223
Pachacamac	Inca	M	1224
Pacolet	Fr.	M	1224
Palesmurt	Fin-Ug.	M	1228
Pan	Gk.	M	1230
P'an Ku	Chin.	M	1233
Pauna	Eskimo		601
Pau-puk-keewis	N.A.I.	M	1244
Payatamu	Zuni	M	1245
Pazuzu	Sum.	M	1245
Phemios	Gk.	M	1262
Philammon	Gk.	M	1262
Philomela	Gk.	F	1263
Phylla & Harpinna	Gk.	F-F	1267
Pied Piper	Germ.	M	1269
Pinto-lo-po-lo-t'o-she (Pindola)	Chin.	M	1274
Polyphemus	Gk.	M	1284
Procne	Gk.	F	1294
Proteus	Gk.	M	1297
Ptah-tanen	Egy.	M	1299
Qehui	Egy.	M	1683
Rakshasa	Hin.	M, F	1320
Ramman	Baby.	M	1322
Ribhus	Hin.	M	1337
Rimmon	Baby.	M	1339
Riwallaun	Bryth.	M	1342
Roskva	Norse	F	1350
Ruadan	Cel.	M	1352
Sanjaya	Hin.	M	1397
Saramaya	Hin.	M	1399
Sauna	Eskimo	M	601
Scarlet, Will	Eng.	M	1406
Sciron	Gk.	M	1407
Seachran	Cel.	M	570
Semnae	Gk.	F	1416
Set	Egy.	M	1420
Shawano	Algon.	M	1431

	Culture	Sex	Page
Shehbui	Egy.	M	1683
Shina-tsu-hiko	Jap.	M	1438
Shinta-to-be	Jap.	F	1438
Shu	Egy.	M	1443
Shutu	Baby.	F	1445
Sigrun	Norse	F	1451
Sillam	Eskimo	M	1453
Sleipner	Norse		1467
Soat-saki	Blackfeet Ind.	F	1470
Susa-no-wo	Jap.	M	1512
Suttung	Norse	M	1513
Svadilfari	Norse	M	1514
Svutaf	Ital.	M	1515
Tai Shan	Chin.	F	1526
Tajikarao (Futodam)	Jap	M	1527
Tapio (Vir-ava)	Fin.	A	1534
Tatsuta-hime	Jap.	F	1538
Tawhaki	Chath. Is.	M	1539
Tawhiri-ma-tea	Poly.	M	1539
Teirtu	Welsh	M	1541
Te-po-whawha	N. Zeal.		1541
Tezcatlipoca	Mex.	M	1549
Thamyris	Gk.	M	1551
Thersites	Gk.	M	1554
Thjasse	Norse	M	1560
Tom the Piper	Eng.	M	1585
Too-lux	Chinook Ind.	M	1587
Tritopatores	Gk.	M	1599
Tritos	Gk.	M	1720
Trophonius	Gk.	M	1600
Tsonoqoa	N.A.I.	F	1604
Tuck, Friar	Bryth.	M	1606
Tuiren	Cel.	F	1606
Turms	Ital.	M	1609
Typhoeus	Gk.	M	1617
Typhon	Gk.	M	1617
Uccaihsravas	Hin.		1620
Ukhat	Baby.	F	1621
Ulfin	Bryth.	M	1621
Umkovu	Afr.	M, F	1623
Valkyrie	Norse	F	1636
Vata	Pers.	M	1641
Vayu (Pavana)	Hin.	M	1642
Vayuarvat	Hin.	M	1642
Verethraghna	Pers.	M	1646
Vikhor	Slav.	M	1649

Wind (cont.)	Culture	Sex	Page
Vindsval	Norse	M	1650
Viracocha	Inca	M	1652
Virava	Fin-Ug.	A	1652
Voli	Norse	M	798
Volker	Norse	M	1657
Voltumna	Ital.	M	1658
Vorys-mort (Dyadya)	Fin-Ug.	M	1658
Vozdushnuie	Slav.	M	910
Wabun	Algon.	M	1660
White Tiger	Chin.		1572
Windigo	Algon.	M	1683
Winti	Dutch Guiana	M	1686
Wudes Heer	Norse	M	1693
Xanthus & Balius	Gk.		1695
Yahuallieheccatl	Mex.	M	1698
Yansan	Yoruban		1701
Ya-o-gah	Seneca	M	1701
Yen Kung	Chin.	M	1705
Yo	Daho		1708
Yoalliehecatl	Mex.	M	1708
Yskyrdaw & Yseudydd	Bryth.		1711
Zacharias	Hebr.	M	1714
Zada	Sib.	F	1714
Zephyrus	Gk.	M	1718
Zerbino	Ital.	M	1718
Zetes	Gk.	M	272
Zethus	Gk.	M	1718
Zeus	Gk.	M	1719

WINE (ALE, DRUNKENNESS, MEAD, STRONG DRINKS)

Acan	Mex.	M	21
Ancaeus	Gk.	M	92
Azag-bau	Sum.	M	164
Bacabab	Mex.	M	170
Bacchus	Gk., Rom.	M	170
Balarama	Hin.	M	174
Braciaca	Cel.	F	240
Braites	Gk.	M	241
Brimer	Norse	M	249
Bromius	Gk.	M	251
Cluracan	Cel.	M	351
Colhuatzincatl	Mex.	M	356
Comus	Rom.	M	363
Deucalion	Gk.	M	434
Dionysus	Gk.	M	447

	Culture	Sex	Page
Euphyus (Dionysus)	Gk.	M	+
Gambrinus	Folk.	M	625
Goibniu	Cel.	M	670
Hayk	Arm.	M	734
Heneb	Egy.	M	750
Hyas	Phryg.	M	810
Iacchus	Gk.	M	815
Icarius	Gk.	M	817
John Barleycorn	Folk.	M	884
Kezer-tshingis	Tatar	M	921
Liber	Rom.	M	990
Lyaeus	Gk.	M	+
Madana	Hin.	M	905
Min Kyawzwa	Ind-Chin.	M	1106
Ninkasi	Sum.	F/A	1173
Noah	Hebr.	M	1177
Oeneus	Gk.	M	1198
Oenomaus	Gk.	M	1199
Oenone	Gk.	F	1199
Ometochtli	Mex.	M	1208
Ormzdakan	Arm.	M	1217
Pantagruel	Fr.	M	1234
Patecatl	Mex.	M	1243
Phuphlans	Ital.	M	1267
Priapus	Gk.	M	1292
Psilas	Gk.	M	1299
Raijin	Jap.	M	1318
Rush (Bruder Rausch)	Germ.	M	1355
Sabazius	Phryg.	M	1356
Sakadonomaki (Saki)	Jap.	M	1389
Satyr	Gk.	M	1403
Shojo	Jap.	M	1441
Shuten Doji	Jap.	M	1444
Siduri	Baby.	F	1447
Silenii	Gk.	M	1453
Silenus	Gk.	M	1453
Siva	Hin.	M	1461
Spantaramet	Pers.	M	1479
Tenemet	Egy.	F	1544
Texcatzoncatl	Mex.	M	1550
Totochtin	C.A.I.	M	1591
Toyouga	Jap.	M	1389
Tvastr	Hin.	M	1611
Venus	Ital.	F	1644

WISDOM (CONTEMPLATION, EDUCATION, KNOWLEDGE, LITERATURE, MEDITATION, SCIENCE)	Culture	Sex	Page
Academus	Gk.	M	21
Achamoth	Gnostic	M	24
Adam	Hebr.	M	29
Adibuddha	Bud.	M	32
Agathadaemon	Gk.	M	46
Alaghom Naom	Mex.	F	61
Amen-Khnum	Egy.	M	83
Amitabha (Amitayus)	Bud.	M	86
Amphiarus	Gk.	M	87
Anakes	Gk.	M	90
Antenor	Gk.	M	102
Antero Wipunen	Fin-Ug.	M	102
Aoshnara	Pers.	M	106
Apollo	Gk.	M	110
Aramazd	Arm.	M	117
Arpacanamanjusri	Bud.	M	129
Aryavalokitesvara	Bud.	M	134
Ashi	Hin.	F	139
Asvid	Norse	M	146
Athena	Gk.	F	150
Avalokitesvara	Bud.	M	160
Balder	Norse	M	174
Balthazar	Christ.	M	1364
Beatrice	Ital.	F	191
Binah	Caba.	F	212
Bodhisattva	Bud.	M	233
Bodn & Son	Norse		233
Brahma	Hin.	M	240
Bran	Bryth.	M	241
Brigit	Cel.	F	249
Buddha	Bud.	M	255
Centaur	Gk.	M	303
Cherub	Hebr.	M	319
Ch'i-lin	Chin.	A	325
Chiron	Gk.	M	327
Chokmah	Caba.	M	1417
Chu I	Chin.	M	335
Clio	Gk.	F	348
Confucius	Chin.	M	366
Consus	Ital.	M	368
Cormac mac Art	Cel.	M	371
Daath	Caba.	M	404
Dagda	Cel.	M	405

	Culture	Sex	Page
David	Hebr.	M	417
Depth	Gnostic Aeon		433
Dhyanibodhisattva	Bud.	M	440
Dhyanibuddhas	Bud.	M	440
Dipamkara	Bud.	M	449
Domnu	Cel.	F	460
Dorulas	Gk.	M	465
Draco (Ladon)	Gk.	M	467
Dudu	Sum.	M	475
Dvalin	Norse	M	478
Elihu	Hebr.	M	503
Emer	Cel.	F	508
Esther	Hebr.	F	526
Finn mac Coul	Cel.	M	570
Forseti	Norse	M	595
Fudo-myoo	Jap.	M	615
Fugen (Jitoku)	Jap.	M	615
Fu Hsi	Chin.	M	615
Fuku	Jap.	M	616
Gabriel	Christ., Hebr., Mos.	M	619
Gamaliel	Hebr.	M	624
Ganesa	Hin.	M	627
Gangraad	Norse	M	627
Gaspar	Christ.	M	1370
Goll mac Morna (Aodh)	Cel.	M	674
Guabonito	Taino	F	693
Gwalchmei	Bryth.	M	700
Gwion Bach	Cel.	M	701
Gwrhyr Gwalstawt	Bryth.	M	702
Hanuman	Hin.	M	723
Harpichruti	Egy.	M	728
Heloise	Med.	F	749
Hermanubis	Gk.	M	761
Herukabuddhas	Bud.	M	764
Hideyoshi	Jap.	M	767
Hu	Egy.	M	800
Hugin & Munin	Norse		803
Iamus	Gk.	M	815
Imhotep	Egy.	M	825
Indra	Hin.	M	829
Irmin	Saxon	M	839
Isis	Egy.	F	845
Itonia	Gk.	F	849
Jamshid	Pers.	M	863
Janus	Ital.	M	864

	Culture	Sex	Page
Jarl	Norse	M	865
Javerzaharses	Arm.	F	867
Jedediah	Hebr.	M	868
Jehovah	Hebr.	M	870
Joseph	Hebr.	M	888
Jurojin	Jap.	M	898
Kalamahakala	Bud.	M	903
Kavya Usanas	Hin.	M	914
Kokuzo	Jap.	M	940
Krishna	Hin.	M	945
Kuei-sing	Chin.	M	949
Kvaser	Norse	M	954
Lady of the Abyss	Baby.	F	962
Llacheu	Bryth.	M	1004
Mada	Hin.	M	337
Magi	Chris.	M	1037
Mahatma	Bud.	M	1044
Mamaki	Bud.	F	1051
Manasa	Hin.	F	1055
Manjusri	Bud.	M	1059
Marduk	Assyr-Baby.	M	1065
Mar-Pa	Tib.	M	1068
Maudgalyayana	Bud.	M	1077
Maui	Poly.	M	1077
Medea	Gk.	F	1082
Melchior	Christ.	M	1085
Menrfa	Ital.	F	1090
Mermaid	Folk.	F	1093
Merman	Folk.	M	545
Meshach	Hebr.	M	1094
Metis	Gk.	F	1096
Michabo	Algon.	M	1098
Midas	Gk.	M	1099
Mimir	Norse	M	1105
Mind	Gnostic Aeon		1106
Minerva	Rom.	F	1106
Minos	Gk.	M	1107
Monju	Jap.	M	1117
Mordecai	Hebr.	M	1122
Morgiana	Arab.	F	1123
Moses	Hebr.	M	1126
Moymis	Baby.	M	1132
Mummu	Sum.	M	1136
Muses	Gk.	F	1138
Myojo-tenshi	Jap.	M	1142
Nabu	Baby.	M	1146

	Culture	Sex	Page
Nairatma	Bud.	F	1149
Naka-hsi-na	Chin.	M	1150
Nakula	Hin.	M	1150
Nane	Arm.	F	1153
Nan-t'i-mitolo-Ch'ing-yu	Chin.	M	1154
Nath	Cel.	F	1157
Neshamah	Caba.		1165
Nestor	Gk.	M	1165
Nguyen-hu'u-do	Ind-Chin.	M	1167
Nintoku	Jap.	M	1174
Nudimmud	Baby.	M	1184
Oannes	Baby., Chald., Phoen.	M	1190
Oberon	Eng., Fr.	M	1192
Odin	Norse	M	1195
Odrerer	Norse		1196
Ol	Bryth.	M	1204
Omohi-kane	Jap.	M	1208
Ormuzd	Zoro.	M	1216
Padmaheruka	Bud.	M	1225
Padmapani	Bud.	M	1225
Pa-hsien	Chin.	M, F	1226
Pallas	Gk.	F	1228
Pandara	Bud.	F	1232
Paracelsus	Eng.	M	1236
Pierrot	Fr.	M	1270
Prajnaparamita	Bud.	F	1291
Pravuil	Hebr.	M	1291
Prometheus	Gk.	M	1295
Pronoia	Gk.	F	1296
Ptah	Egy.	M	1299
Purushottama	Hin.	M	1305
Puskara	Hin.	M	1305
Qat	Mel.	M	1309
Raphael	Eng.	M	1323
Rasiel	Hebr.	M	1323
Ratnapani	Bud.	M	1324
Ratnasambhava	Bud.	M	1324
Rigir	Norse	M	1338
Riwallaun	Bryth.	M	1342
Ruach	Caba.	M	1352
Saga	Norse	F	1360
Sarasvati	Hin.	F	1400
Sariputra	Bud.	M	1401
Satyr	Gk.	M	1403
Scef	Norse	M	1406

	Culture	Sex	Page
Seishi-Bosatsu	Bud.	M	1413
Selk	Egy.	F	1415
Seraph	Hebr-Christ.	M	1417
Shulamite	Hebr.	F	1444
Shun	Chin.	M	1444
Siduri	Baby.	F	1447
Sigrdrifa	Norse	F	1451
Sigurd	Norse	M	1451
Silenii	Gk.	M	1453
Silenus	Gk.	M	1453
Sin	Assyr.	M	1456
Sinlap	Burm.	M	1457
Sisyphus	Gk.	M	1459
Sitatapatra	Bud.	F	1460
Sith	Norse	F	1460
Snorta	Norse	F	1470
Solomon	Hebr., Mos.	M	1472
Solon	Gk.	M	1473
Son	Norse		1474
Sophia	Hebr., Hellenic	F	1475
Sophrosyne	Gk.	F	1476
Spenta Armaiti	Zoro.	M	1481
Sphinx	Egy., Gk.	F	1482
Sudolisa	Slav.	F	1503
Tages	Ital.	M	1524
Take-no-uji	Jap.	M	1528
Thoth	Egy.	M	1562
Three Kings of Cologne	Christ.	M	1565
Tie (Ta-urt)	Egy.	F	1571
T'ien (Ten)	Chin., Jap.	A	1571
Tiksnamanjusri	Bud.	A	1573
Tipherath	Caba.	M	1575
Tiur	Arm.	M	1581
Tobias	Hebr.	M	1582
To-kabinana	Mel.	M	1584
Tom Thumb	Folk.	M	1585
Ts'ang Chieh	Chin.	M	1602
Tsun-gyi-rgyal-po	Tib.	M	1604
Tuatha De Danann	Cel.	M, F	1605
Uma	Hin.	F	1622
Urania	Gk.	F	1627
Vac	Hin.	F	1633
Vafthrudner	Norse	M	1633
Vajraheruka	Bud.	M	1635
Virgil	Ital.	M	1652
Vishnu	Hin.	M	1654

	Culture	Sex	Page
Visvamitra	Hin.	M	1655
Wen Ch'ang	Chin.	M	1673
Wen-shu	Chin.	M	1673
Wisdom	Gnostic Aeon		1686
Yao	Chin.	M	1701
Yeces mgon-po	Bud.	M	1703

WITCH (SEE DEMON
WITCHERY (SEE MAGIC)
WIZARDRY (SEE MAGIC)

WOODLAND (FOREST, GROVE, SYLVAN DEITY)

	Culture	Sex	Page
Ahlmakoh	Van. Is.	M	53
Alphito	Gk.	M	76
Andarta	Cel.	F	93
Apparas	Fin-Ug.	M, F	112
Aranyani	Hin.	F	117
Artemis	Gk.	F	131
Asaph	Pers.	M	135
Ashima	Sem.	M	139
Askefruer	Norse	F	140
Aziza	Ewes (Afr.)	M	166
Bajanai	Yakut	M	173
Billing	Norse	M	211
Caipora	Braz.	M	270
Caryotis	Gk.	F	131
Curupira	Braz.	M	399
Cybele	Phryg.	F	400
Diana	Rom.	F	441
Divje Devojke	Slav.	F	454
Divji Moz	Slav.	M	454
Dopkalfar	Norse	M, F	464
Dru	Gk.	F	471
Dryad	Gk.	F	473
Dus	Cel.	M	477
Erlking	Germ.	M	522
Faunus	Rom.	M	552
Fay (Fee)	Fr.	M, F	553
Ganis	Lapp	F	627
Goblin	Folk.	M	666
Govetter	Norw.		680
Gufittar	Lapp	M	695
Herne	Eng.	M	762
Hiisi	Fin-Ug.	M	769
Hittavainen	Fin.	M	775

	Culture	Sex	Page
Humbaba	Baby.	M	804
Huon, Sir	Bryth.	M	807
Hyndla	Norse	F	812
Intercidona	Rom.	F	+
Itshi	Sib.	M	849
Ivithjar	Norse	F	851
Kosla-Kuguza & Kosla-Kuva	Fin-Ug.	M-F	943
Leib-olmai	Lapp	M	981
Lesiy	Rus.	M	986
Lesni Zenka	Slav.	F	986
Liekkio	Fin.	M, F	991
Little Red Riding Hood	Folk.	F	1003
Loljerskor	Norse	M, F	1011
Luot-hozjik	Lapp	F	1025
Lupercus	Ital.	M	1026
Lyeshy	Slav.	M	1028
Mahasitavati	Bud.	F	1044
Maho-peneta	Iroq.	M	1045
Maiden of the White Mule	Bryth.	F	1046
Maid Marian	Bryth.	F/A	1046
Manoin	Papuan		+
Maui	Poly.	M	1077
Mendes	Egy.	M	+
Mengk	Fin-Ug.	M	1089
Meschamaat	Slav.	F	1094
Metsanhaltia	Fin.	M	1096
Metsanneitsyt	Fin.	F	1097
Mets-haldijas	Esthonian	M	1097
Metsmees	Esthonian	M	1097
Miehts-hozjin	Lapp	M	1101
Mielikki	Fin.	F	1101
Mimir	Norse	M	1105
Mis-khum	Fin-Ug.	M	1111
Mmoatia	Afr.	M, F	1113
Mwenembago	Uzaramo	M	1142
Napaeae	Gk.	F	1154
Nules-murt	Fin-Ug.	M	1185
Nyyrikki	Fin.	M	1534
Obyda (Ar-sori)	Chuvash	F	1192
Oshossi	Yorubas	M	1218
Ovda (Alvasta)	Fin-Ug.	M, F	1221
Palesmurt	Fin-Ug.	M	1228
Pan	Gk.	M	1230
Panisc (Pano)	Gk.	M	1233
Parne	Fin-Ug.	M	1239
Paul Bunyan	Folk.	M	1244

	Culture	Sex	Page
Pepezu	Yuracari Ind.	M	1254
Picus	Rom.	M	1269
Pots-hozjin & Pots-hozjik	Rus.	M-F	1289
Ragnhild	Norse	F	705
Rishyacringa	Hin.	M	1341
Robin Hood	Eng.	M	1343
Saalah	Arab.	M	1356
Saci	Braz.	M	1358
Sacy-perere	Braz.	M	1360
Sanjna	Hin.	F	1397
Satyr	Gk.	M	1403
Schratt	Germ.	M	1409
Scrat	Teut.	M	1409
Scritta	Ang-Sax.	M	1409
Serosevsky	Rus.	M	1418
Shurale	Tatar		1444
Shvaz	Arm.	M	1445
Silanus	Rom.	M	1452
Silenii	Gk.	M	1453
Silenus	Gk.	M	1453
Silvanus	Rom.	M	1453
Sjen	Slav.	M	1463
Skogsfru	Scan.	F	1465
Skratti	Ice.	M	1409
Surali	Fin-Ug.	M	1511
Sylvanus	Rom.	M	1512
Tane (Tani)	Poly.	M	1531
Tapio (Vir-ava)	Fin.	A	1534
Titania	Rom.	F	1577
Tityrus	Gk., Rom.	M	1580
Troll	Norse	M	1600
Tu	Poly.	M	1604
Tuulikki	Fin.	F	1534
Unt-tongk	Fin-Ug.	M	1626
Vanasa	Bud.	M	1638
Varns	Norse	M	1639
Vibhandaka	Hin.	M	1648
Vidar	Norse	M	1649
Vidfinner	Norse	M	1649
Virava (Tapio, Tava-ajjik)	Fin-Ug.	A	1652
Virbius	Rom.	M	1652
Vitholf	Norse	M	1656
Vorys-mort (Dyadya)	Fin-Ug.	M	1658
Wanga	East Afr.	M	1664
Yehwe Zogbanu	Daho.	M	1703

Woodland (cont.)	Culture	Sex	Page
Yskal-pydo-murt (Syiyr-ajak)	Fin-Ug.	M	1711

WRATH (ANGER, RAGE. ALSO SEE FALSE INFORMER)

	Culture	Sex	Page
Adicia	Eng.	F	32
Aeetes	Gk.	M	37
Aeshma	Zoro.	M	41
Ahab	Hebr.	M	52
Athena	Gk.	F	150
Cerridwen	Cel.	F	305
Creon	Gk.	M	380
Cycnus	Gk.	M	401
Eris	Gk.	F	521
Guinevere	Bryth.	F	696
Hera	Gk.	F	752
Heracles	Gk.	M	752
Hercules	Rom.	M	759
Jezebel	Hebr.	F	879
Jormunrek	Germ.	M	887
Karmaheruka	Hin.	M	910
Kavi Usan	Pers.	M	914
Lycus	Gk.	M	1028
Manyu	Hin.	M	1061
Medea	Gk.	F	1082
Modi	Norse	M	1114
Nycteus	Gk.	M	104
Occasion	Eng. Lit.	F	1193
Phineus	Gk.	M	1264
Potiphar	Hebr.	M	1289
Proteus	Gk.	M	1297
Pyrocles	Eng.	M	1307
Robigus	Rom.	M	1343
Salome	Christ.	F	1391
Saul	Hebr.	M	1404
Tan-ma (bsTan-ma)	Tib.	F	1532
Termagant	Christ.	A	1546
Theseus	Gk.	M	1554
To Wo	Tib.	M	1592
Tu-matauenga	Poly.	M	1607
Zeus	Gk.	M	1719

WRATH VICTIM (ALSO SEE FALSELY ACCUSED, JEALOUSY VICTIM)

	Culture	Sex	Page
Ahimelech	Hebr.	M	53
Antigone	Gk.	F	103

	Culture	Sex	Page
Antiope	Gk.	F	103
Auge	Gk.	F	156
Bellerophon	Gk.	M	199
David	Hebr.	M	417
Glauce (Creusa)	Gk.	F	662
Gwion Bach	Bryth.	M	701
Jason	Gk.	M	866
Joseph	Hebr.	M	888
Kulhwch	Welsh	M	950
Medea	Gk.	F	1082
Syavarshan	Pers.	M	1521

WRITING (SEE CULTURE HERO)

YOUTH

Agni	Hin.	M	49
Apollo	Gk.	M	110
Cherub	Hebr.	M	319
Graces	Gk.	F	681
Hebe	Gk.	F	739
Houri	Mos.	F	795
Idun	Norse	F	820
Indrani	Hin.	F	830
Jamshid	Pers.	M	863
Juventas	Rom.	F	899
Keresaspa	Pers.	M	918
Khidr	Arab.	M	924
Kiku-jido	Jap.	M	927
Konkara	Jap.	M	941
Kumara	Hin.	M	951
Lan Ts'ai-ho	Chin.	M/A	971
Lludd	Bryth.	M	1005
Mabon	Welsh	M	1031
Ningyo	Jap.	F	1173
Persephone	Gk.	F	1257
Peter Pan	Eng. Lit.	M	1259
Proserpina	Rom.	F	1296
Rishis	Chin.	M	1340
Setek	Slav.	M	1421
Telpochtli	Mex.	M	1542
Tezcatlipoca	Mex.	M	1549
Tobosaku	Jap.	M	1583
Ushas	Hin.	F	1631
Weiwobo	Jap.	F	1672
Yavishtha	Hin.	M	1702
Yoskeha	Iroq.	M	1710

PART B

Table of Mythological Affiliations

(Supernatural Forms, Realms, Things)

Index to
Supernatural Forms, Realms, Things

	Culture	Page
Brown Bull of Cualgne	Cel.	252
Bucephalus (horse)	Gk.	790
Buddha (deer)	Bud.	255
Bunyip (man-eater)	Aus.	261
Burto (dog)	Sib.	456
Caball (dog)	Bryth.	264
Callisto (bear)	Gk.	278
Calydonian Boar	Gk.	279
Camel of Saleh	Mos.	280
Cavall (horse)	Bryth.	265
Cerberus (dog)	Gk.	304
Cercopes (apes)	Gk.	304
Cerna (beast)	Cel.	305
Cerridwen (greyhound, etc.)	Bryth.	305
Cerynean Stag	Gk.	306
Chameleon (lizard)	Afr.	310
Ch'ang-o (toad)	Chin.	311
Cherubim (lion, ox)	Hebr.	319
Chibiabos (lynx)	Algon.	321
Chichivache (woman-eater)	Med. Lit.	322
Ch'i-lin (unicorn)	Chin.	325
Christ (hart, lion)	Christ.	330
Chrysippos (horse)	Gk.	334
Chrysomallus (ram)	Gk.	334
Cin-an-ev (wolf)	Ute Ind.	339
Clavigo (horse)	Span.	1049
Coh (leopard)	Mex.	283
Comizahual (tigress)	Honduras	362
Copenhagen (horse)	Eng.	+
Coyote	N.A.I.	377
Cretan Bull	Gk.	381
Crommyonia Sow	Gk.	384
Cwn Annwn (hounds)	Bryth.	400
Dadhikra (horse)	Hin.	404
Dainn (stag)	Norse	407
Dajoji (panther)	Iroq.	408
Dapple (donkey)	Span.	414
Dark Warrior (tortoise)	Chin., Jap.	416
Dawen (cow)	Cel.	418
Deimos (horse)	Gk.	120
Dinewan (emu)	Aus.	445
Dobhar (steed)	Cel.	790
Dogs of Foh (Foo)	Chin., Jap.	458
Donn (bull)	Cel.	613
Dormath (dog)	Bryth.	464
Drudwyn (whelp)	Welsh	951

	Culture	Page
Goldfax (horse)	Norse	673
Grane (horse)	Norse	683
Great Turtle	N.A.I.	1610
Grey of Macha (horse)	Cel.	690
Griffin	World Wide	690
Gringalet (steed)	Bryth.	636
Gudanna (bull)	Assyr-Baby.	694
Gulban (boar)	Cel.	697
Gullfaxi (steed)	Norse	697
Gullinbursti (boar)	Norse	697
Gulltop (steed)	Norse	697
Hadhayosh (ox)	Pers.	707
Haltia (cat or dog)	Fin-Ug.	713
Hanuman (monkey)	Hin.	723
Harits (steeds)	Hin.	726
Hati (wolf)	Norse	731
Hecuba (dog)	Gk.	741
Heidrun (goat)	Norse	743
Heifer of Anu	Assyr.	743
Hekt (frog)	Egy.	745
Helge (wolf)	Norse	746
Hildisivini (boar)	Norse	770
Himinbrjoter (ox)	Norse	771
Hippa (horse)	Gk.	772
Hippalcmos (horse)	Gk.	334
Hippogriff (winged horse)	Ital.	773
Hofvarpner (horse)	Norse	779
Houyhnhnms (horses)	Eng.	797
Hrim Faxi (steed)	Norse	798
Hrodvitnir (wolf)	Norse	798
Hsiang (elephant)	Chin.	1424
Iguana (lizard)	C.A.I.	821
Ija-kyl	Yakut	822
Iku (Capella the goat)	Assyr-Baby.	1066
Ilamatecutli (toad)	Mex.	823
Imgig (winged lion)	Sum.	825
Incitatus (steed)	Rom.	+
Inoshishi (boar)	Jap.	833
Io (heifer)	Gk.	835
Ira-waru (dog)	Poly.	838
Isengrin (wolf)	Med. Lit.	842
Ishullanu (hog)	Assyr-Baby.	845
Italapas (coyote)	Chinook	+
Itzpapalotl (deer)	Mex.	850
Iwazaru (monkey)	Jap.	943
Jumart (mare, bull)	Fr.	895

	Culture	Page
Kalki (horse)	Hin.	904
Kamadhena (cow)	Hin.	905
Kanook (wolf)	Alaskan	908
Kanthaka (horse)	Bud.	908
Ka-nub (bull)	Egy.	908
Kaput (wolf)	Pers.	909
Karashishi (lions)	Jap.	910
Kaswa, Al (camel)	Mos.	912
Kasyapa (tortoise)	Hin.	912
Katmir (dog)	Mos.	913
Keingala (horse)	Ice.	+
Kelpi (horse)	Scot.	916
Kere (unicorn)	Tib.	917
Kesava (boar)	Hin.	919
Kikaraqu (monkey)	Jap.	943
Kilin (unicorn)	Chin.	928
Kilkenny (cats)	Irish	928
Kitsume (cat or ox)	Jap.	935
Koshin (monkey)	Jap.	943
Kudu (totem)	Bantu	948
Kuei Lung (beast)	Chin.	949
Kuei Shen (tortoise)	Chin.	949
Kurma (torotise)	Hin.	942
Kuyuta (bull)	Mos.	954
Kuzu-no-ha (fox)	Jap.	954
Ladon (dog)	Gk.	962
Laelaps (dog)	Gk.	963
Lamastu (cow)	Sum.	966
Lampetus (horse)	Gk.	969
Liat Maca (horse)	Cel.	990
Lin (unicorn)	Chin.	997
Loup-garou (wolf)	Fr.	1016
Lu (unicorn)	Chin.	1268
Lucian (ass)	Rom.	1020
Lung-ta (horse)	Bud.	1025
Lycaon (wolf)	Gk.	1027
Ma (horse)	Chin.	1424
Maau (cat)	Egy.	1031
Maera (dog)	Gk.	1037
Magus (horse)	Slav.	1042
Mahavira (lion)	Jain.	1045
Maira (god)	Gk.	1047
Majok (ox)	Dinkas	1047
Makara (lion)	Bud.	1047
Malsum (wolf)	Algon.	1050
Manabhozho (hare)	Algon.	1054

	Culture	Page
Manalan-rakki (hound)	Fin-Ug.	1054
Mandishire (turtle)	Sib.	1057
Marathon Bull	Gk.	1064
Marengo (horse)	Fr.	+
Marocco (horse)	Eng.	1068
Masan (bear)	Hin.	1072
Mauthe (dog)	Cel.	1078
Melanippe (mare)	Gk.	1085
Menes (bull)	Egy.	1089
Menik (horse)	Pers.	790
Mentu (bull)	Egy.	1090
Mikazaru (monkey)	Jap.	943
Minotaur (bull)	Gk.	1107
Mishe-mokwa (bear)	N.A.I.	+
Mitsumine (dog)	Jap.	1113
Mizaru (monkey)	Jap.	943
Mnevis (bull)	Egy.	1113
Mondoro (lion)	Mashonaland	1116
Moqwaio (wolf)	Men.	1122
Mulla (mule)	Gaulish	1135
Muskrat	Algon.	1140
Nala (monkey)	Hin.	1150
Nandi (bull)	Hin.	1153
Nannar (bull)	Baby.	1153
Narasimha (lion)	Hin.	1155
Neago (fawn)	Seneca	1159
Nemean Lion	Gk.	1162
Nephesh (beast)	Cabala	1163
Nergal (lion)	Assyr-Baby.	1164
Nibhaz (dog)	Sem.	1167
Nicippe (mare)	Gk.	334
Ningirsu (goat or lion)	Sum.	1172
Ninsun (cow)	Baby.	1174
Nobel (lion)	Med. Lit.	1178
Nut (cow)	Egy.	1187
Nynnyaw & Peibaw (oxen)	Cel.	1188
Obeah (beast)	W. Afr.	1191
Ocean (heifer)	Cel.	406
Old Dog Tray	Ballads	1204
Orthos (hound)	Gk.	1217
Osiris (bull)	Egy.	1218
Otava & Otso (bears)	Fin.	1220
Ottar (otter)	Norse	1220
Owasse (bear)	Men.	1221
Pai Hu (tiger)	Chin.	1226
Paluc Cat	Bryth.	1230

	Culture	Page
Pandareos (dog)	Gk.	1232
Parjanya (cow or bull)	Hin.	1238
Pegasus (horse)	Gk.	1248
Pehin (wolf)	Pers.	909
Phaethon (horse)	Gk.	1260
Phobos (steed)	Gk.	1265
Phol (horse)	Norse	1266
Phylla & Harpinna (steeds)	Gk.	1267
Piao (unicorn)	Chin.	1268
Plat-eye (dog)	W. Indies	1279
Poh (unicorn)	Chin.	1268
Pooka (ass, horse, mule)	Cel.	1268
Porcus Troit (boar)	Bryth.	1616
Port-hozjin (dog)	Lapp, Rus.	1287
Prthivi (cow)	Hin.	1297
Ptah-Seker (bull)	Egy.	1300
Ra (bull)	Egy.	1314
Rab (dog)	Eng.	1315
Rabicano (horse)	Carol.	790
Rakhsh (steed)	Pers.	1355
Raminagrobis (cat)	Fr.	1321
Ratatosk (rabbit)	Norse	1324
Ridija (calf)	Sem.	1338
Roan Berbary (horse)	Eng.	+
Rohina (steeds)	Hin.	1345
Rosinante (horse)	Span.	1350
Rusksh (horse)	Pers.	1355
Sabala (dog)	Hin.	1699
Sadb (fawn)	Cel.	1360
Saehrimner (boar)	Norse	1360
Salamander (lizard)	Arab., Christ.	1390
Saleh's camel	Mos.	280
Sanjna (mare)	Hin.	1397
Sarama (dog)	Hin.	1399
Saranyu (mare)	Hin.	1400
Sarsaok (ox)	Pers.	1401
Sceolan (dog)	Cel.	1406
Sedit (coyote)	N.A.I.	1413
Sedu (goat)	Baby.	1413
Seian Horse	Rom.	1413
Seirim (goat)	Hebr.	1413
Senik (horse)	Pers.	790
Serou (unicorn)	Tib.	917
Set (boar)	Egy.	1420
Shedim (ox)	Chald.	1432
Shishchikul (beast)	Van. Is.	1439

	Culture	Page
Showa (deer)	Tib.	1443
Sin (bull)	Assyr.	1456
Sin You (unicorn)	Jap.	1457
Sirius (dog)	Astronomy	1459
Skin Foxi (steed)	Norse	1465
Sleipner (horse)	Norse	1467
Slidrugtanni (boar)	Norse	1467
Smintheus (mouse)	Gk.	1468
Snark (snake and shark)	Eng.	1469
Splendid Mane (horse)	Cel.	1484
Ssu (dog)	Korean	1488
Sueje (reindeer)	Lapp	1504
Sugriva (monkey)	Hin.	1504
Sun Hou-tzu (monkey)	Chin.	1510
Surya (bull)	Hin.	1511
Svadilfari (stallion)	Norse	1514
Syama (dog)	Hin.	1699
Tamamo-no-maye (fox)	Jap.	1529
Tanngnjost & Tanngrisnir (goats)	Norse	1532
Tarksya (horse)	Hin.	1534
Ta-urt (hippopotamus)	Egy.	1538
Techu (ibis)	Egy.	1540
Tefenet (cat)	Egy.	1541
Tethra's cattle	Cel.	1548
Thoth (Esden) (baboon)	Egy.	1562
Tishtrya (bull or horse)	Pers.	1577
Tlatecutli (toad)	Mex.	1582
Totochtin (rabbit)	C.A.I.	1591
Tragelphus (goat-stag)	Gk.	1593
Tsopo (unicorn)	Tib.	917
Tuiren (dog)	Cel.	1606
Twrch Trwyth (boar)	Bryth.	1616
Tybert (cat)	Med. Lit.	1616
Ubastet (cat)	Egy.	1619
Uccaihsravas (horse)	Hin.	1620
Ugallu (lion)	Sum.	1620
Uridimmu (lion)	Baby.	1629
Ur-kuh (cow)	Pers.	1629
Ur-mer (bull)	Egy.	1629
Vali (wolf)	Norse	1636
Varaha (boar)	Hin.	1638
Vayu (antelope)	Hin.	1642
Vayuarvat (horse)	Hin.	1642
Vegliantino (horse)	Carol.	+
Veltro (greyhound)	Ital.	1644

Animal (cont.)	Culture	Page
Wabanang (rabbit)	Men.	1660
Wabasso (hare)	Pota.	1660
White Surrey	Eng.	+
White Tiger	Chin.	1572
Wonder Horse	Slav.	791
Xanthus (steed)	Gk.	1281
Xochipilli-Cinteotl (jaguar)	Mex.	1696
Yale	Med. Lit.	1699
Yamutbal (ram)	Sum.	1700
Ya-o-gah (bear)	Seneca	1701
Yatai (tadpole)	Ind-Chin.	1702
Yatawn (tadpole)	Ind-Chin.	1702
Yech (cat)	Am. Ind.	1703
Zeus (bull)	Gk.	1719

ARTICLE (CLOTHING, IMPLEMENT, JEWEL, SEAT, UTENSIL, WEAPON. ALSO SEE DEITY THRONE, STONE)

Article	Culture	Page
Aaron's rod	Hebr.	10
Adam's jewel	Mos.	30
Aegis (shield)	Gk.	38
Akbal (vase)	Mex.	802
Aladdin's lamp or ring	Arab.	61
Alasnam's mirror	Arab.	61
Amalthea's horn	Gk.	79
Ama-no-hashidate (ladder)	Jap.	79
Amasis' ring	Gk.	80
Amaterasu's necklace	Jap.	81
Ame-no-iha-kura (throne)	Jap.	83
Ame-no-wo-ha-bari (sword)	Jap.	84
Ancile (shield)	Rom.	93
Andvarinaut (ring)	Norse	95
Angervadil (sword)	Norse	96
Ankh (cross)	Egy.	99
Ariadne's thread	Gk.	123
Arondight (sword)	Med. Lit.	128
Ascalon (sword)	Christ.	136
Ashera (pole)	Hebr.	138
Asi (sword)	Hin.	140
Asogwe (rattle)	Afr.	141
Aurea Virga (rod)	Gk.	158
Azoth (sword)	Eng.	1520
Balisarda (sword)	Ital.	176
Balmung (sword)	Norse	176
Blutgang (sword)	Norse	1520
Bodn & Son (cups)	Norse	233

	Culture	Page
Bran's Caldron	Bryth.	241
Branstock (sword)	Norse	1520
Breit-hut (hat)	Norse	246
Brisingamen (necklace)	Norse	250
Caduceus	Gk.	266
Caladbolg (sword)	Cel.	272
Caledvwlch (sword)	Welsh	636
Caliburnus (sword)	Bryth	277
Cambalo's ring	Eng.	280
Cardea's hinges	Rom.	290
Cerridwen's Pot	Bryth.	305
Cestus (girdle)	Gk.	306
Chin Lun (wheel)	Chin.	1424
Chlamys (cloak)	Gk.	327
Chrysaor (sword)	Eng.	334
Cista (basket)	Gk.	344
Clavigo (wooden horse)	Span.	1049
Colada (sword)	Span.	338
Contici (vase)	Inca	368
Cormac's branch	Cel.	371
Cormac's cup	Cel.	372
Cornucopia	Gk., Rom.	373
Corrougue (sword)	Carol.	1520
Courtain (sword)	Carol.	1520
Crux Ansata (key)	Egy.	391
Curtana (sword)	Christ.	399
Dagda's caldron	Cel.	405
Dainslef (sword)	Norse	407
Devadatta (weapon)	Hin.	830
Dharmachakra (wheel)	Hin.	1676
Draupner (ring)	Norse	470
Dromi (chain)	Norse	471
Dunlaing's shirt	Cel.	+
Durandal (sword)	Carol.	477
Eckesax (sword)	Norse	490
Eldhrimnir (caldron)	Norse	499
Eriphyle's jewels & veil	Gk.	520
Ethiopian Table	Gk.	528
Eucharist Chalice	Christ.	529
Excalibur (sword)	Bryth.	537
Fa lun (wheel)	Chin.	1676
Fianchuive's spit	Cel.	369
Floberge (Flamberge) (sword)	Carol.	1520
Fragarach (sword)	Cel.	606
Frode's quern	Norse	613
Fukusuke (doll)	Jap.	616

	Culture	Page
Furo (portal)	Jap.	618
Furo-no-yashiro (sword)	Jap.	618
Gae Bolg (spear)	Cel.	621
Gelgja (chain)	Norse	638
Gjallar Horn	Norse	660
Gleipner (chain)	Norse	662
Glorious (sword)	Carol.	1520
Gram (sword)	Norse	683
Greysteel (sword)	Norse	1520
Gridarvold (wand)	Norse	690
Grotte (mill)	Norse	692
Gungnir (spear)	Norse	698
Hauteclaire (sword)	Carol.	1520
Helsko (shoes)	Ice.	749
Hildegrim (helmet)	Germ.	770
Himation (robe)	Gk.	771
Hlidskjalf (throne)	Norse	776
Holy Grail (cup)	Christ.	782
Holy Spectacles	Christ.	783
Horn of Oberon	Med. Lit.	1192
Horn of Roland	Carol.	1345
Horn of St. Hubert	Christ.	1371
Horn of Sir Huon	Fr.	807
Hrotte (sword)	Norse	798
Hrunting (sword)	Ang-Sax.	799
Huecomitl (vase)	Mex.	802
Jacob's ladder	Hebr.	859
Jamshid's goblet	Pers.	863
Jesse's rod	Hebr.	876
Joyeuse (sword)	Carol.	891
Ju'i Chu (pearl)	Chin.	1424
Kagami (Yata-Kagami) (mirror)	Jap.	902
Kalachakra (wheel)	Bud.	903
Kanji (pearl)	Jap.	908
Kantha (gem)	Hin.	908
Kasa-nagi (sword)	Jap.	911
Kaustubha (gem)	Hin.	914
K'i-mu (bag)	Chin.	928
Krees (sword)	Oriental	1520
Kusanagi (sword)	Jap.	953
Kusti (girdle)	Parsee	954
Leding (chain)	Norse	980
Lia Fail (throne stone)	Irish	990
Loegaire's mantle	Cel.	1008
Luck of Edenhall (goblet)	Eng.	1021

	Culture	Page
Lug's chain	Cel.	1023
Mahavira (caldron)	Hin.	1045
Mambrino's helmet	Moorish	1051
Mani (jewel)	Hin.	1058
Manji (jewel)	Jap.	1059
Megingjard (belt)	Norse	+
Merveilleuse (sword)	Fr.	1094
Mimung (sword)	Germ.	1520
Miolnir (weapon)	Norse	1108
Miphletzeth (image, altar)	Canaanite	1108
Mirandoisa (sword)	Bryth.	1109
Mistelteinn (sword)	Norse	1111
Morglay (sword)	Welsh	1124
Muso-byoye's kite	Jap.	1140
Naegling (sword)	Ang-Sax.	1147
Naglering (sword)	Germ.	62
Nandaka (sword)	Hin.	1655
Nibelungen ring	Norse	1167
Obol (coin)	Gk.	1192
Odrerer (kettle)	Norse	1196
Oegishialm (helmet)	Norse	1198
Ogyrvran (caldron)	Bryth.	1201
Oiste (cup)	Bryth.	+
Olivant (horn)	Ital.	1345
Omphalos (spinning wheel)	Gk.	1208
Ophanim (wheel)	Caba.	1211
Palladium (image)	Gk.	1228
Pandora's box	Gk.	1233
Pasupata (spear)	Hin.	1461
Patara (wheel)	Hin.	1242
Pelian spear	Gk.	1250
Philippan (sword)	Rom.	1520
Pinaka (trident)	Hin.	1273
Prince Houssain's carpet	Arab.	1038
Pryderi's caldron	Cymric	1298
Quern-biter (sword)	Norse	1520
Rhabdus (wand)	Gk.	1335
Round Table	Bryth.	1351
Saegr (bucket)	Norse	1360
Sanglamore (sword)	Eng.	1520
Sangraal (cup)	Christ.	1396
Sarnga (bow)	Hin.	1655
Sauvagine (sword)	Carol.	1520
Schrit (sword)	German	1520
Seistron (rod)	Egy.	1414
Sharur (sword)	Baby.	1715

	Culture	Page
Zauberflote (flute)	Germ.	1716
Zlotababa (idol)	Fin-Ug.	1722
Zuflager (sword)	Mos.	1520

AXIS (SEE PILLARS)

BEVERAGE OR FOOD (b=beverage, f=food, n=narcotic. ALSO SEE PLANT)

Ale (b)	Norse	66
Alzitziutil (f)	Mex.	78
Ambrosia (b, f)	Gk.	82
Amrta (b, f)	Hin.	89
Bragi's apples (f)	Norse	240
Dead Sea apple (f)	Hebr.	421
Golden apple (f)	Gk.	672
Golden egg (f)	World Wide	672
Leifner's Flames (b)	Norse	981
Lyaeus (b)	Gk.	+
Mead (b)	Norse	1081
Nectar (b)	Gk.	1160
Nepenthe (n)	Gk.	+
Peyote (n)	Mex.	1260
Pulque (b)	Mex.	1301
Sudha (f)	Hin.	1503
Svadha (f)	Hin.	1514

BEWITCHED PLACE (SEE SACRED PLACE)

BIRD (FOWL)

Aderyn y Corph	Welsh	32
Aedon	Gk.	37
Aesacus	Gk.	41
Aithuia	Gk.	57
Alallu	Baby.	61
Alcithoe	Gk.	64
Alectryon	Gk.	+
Allala	Baby	69
Angeburga	Norse	95
Annis	Ang-Sax.	100
Any-any-any-ah	Cowich.	105
Ascalaphus	Gk.	135
Asho-zushta	Pers.	139
Astraea	Gk.	145
Athena	Gk.	150

	Culture	Page
Aurboda	Norse	158
Awonawilona	Zuni	162
Ayar Cachi	Inca	163
Ba	Egy.	167
Badb	Cel.	171
Bahram Yasht	Zoro.	173
Bangma (Bangmi)	Hin.	178
Bennu	Arab.	202
Bharundas	Hin.	208
Black Geese	Sib.	676
Blodeuwedd	Bryth.	226
Blue Jay	Chinook	+
Bran	Bryth.	241
Bucu	Sib.	255
Caena-maergha	Pers.	1721
Caer	Cel.	267
Camazotz	Mex.	279
Camrosh	Pers.	282
Cerridwen	Bryth.	305
Chanticleer	Med. Lit.	312
Chataka	Occult	316
Ch'en Chi & Ch'en Lung	Chin.	1090
Cherub	Hebr.	319
Chie	Chibcha	322
Chu Ch'ieh	Chin.	335
Circe	Gk.	341
Ciris	Gk.	344
Ciuateteo	Mex.	346
Comus	Eng.	363
Coronis	Gk.	374
Corvus	Gk.	374a
Cromhineach	Cel.	383
Cuchi	Aus.	393
Dadhikra	Hin.	404
Dechtire	Cel.	423
Derceto	Sem.	433
Devorgilla	Cel.	436
Dodona's Black Pigeon	Gk.	455
Dryope	Gk.	473
Egder	Norse	491
Erin-bird	Sum.	520
Feng-huang	Chin.	559
Fjalar	Norse	578
Fo (Foh)	Chin.	589
Foo	Jap.	590
Freya	Norse	610

	Culture	Page
Kalivinka	Jap.	904
Kamak	Pers.	906
Kara	Norse	909
Karshipta	Pers.	911
Kekeko	Ind-Chin.	916
Keneu	Iroq.	916
Khrut	Burm.	925
Khu	Egy.	925
Khubilgan	Mong.	925
Kineun	Men.	928
Koori	Sib.	942
Korotangi	N. Zeal.	943
Krake	Norse	944
Kukulcan	Mex.	950
Kurkil	Sib.	1313
Kusa Kap	Torres	953
Leda	Gk.	980
Leto	Gk.	986
Leucippe	Gk.	64
Liban	Cel.	990
Libyan Black Pigeon	Rom.	455
Lilith	Hebr.	994
Ljod	Norse	1004
Llew Llaw Gyffes	Cymric	1005
Loki	Norse	1010
Lord Uye-minu	Jap.	1013
Lost (Yggdrasil)	Norse	1706
Lunyu	Chin.	1025
Mahaitiac	Hidatsa	1043
Manannan	Cel.	1054
Mara	Bud.	1063
Matu'u-ta'u-ta'ua	Tahitian	1077
Maui	Poly.	1077
Men Shen	Chin.	1090
Moo	Mex.	283
Morrigu	Cel.	1025
Nankilstlas	Haida	1153
Nascakiyetl	Tlingit	1156
Nazit	Egy.	1159
Nekhebet	Egy.	1161
Ne-kilst-luss	Haida	1161
Ningirsu	Sum.	1172
Nisroch	Assyr.	1176
Nisus	Gk.	1176
Nuye	Jap.	1176
Nyx (Nox)	Gk.	1188

	Culture	Page
Odin	Norse	1195
Ohnivak	Slav.	1201
Otshirvani	Mong.	1220
Pairekse	Ostiak	1226
Pariacaca	Inca	1237
Paupukkeewis	N.A.I.	1244
P'eng Niao	Chin.	1252
Perdix	Gk.	1254
Philomela	Gk.	1263
Phoenix	Arab.	1265
Picumnus	Rom.	1269
Picus	Rom.	1269
Pierides	Gk.	1269
Pleiades	Gk.	1279
Procne	Gk.	1294
Ptah-Seker	Egy.	1299
Pundjel	Aus.	1301
Queenah	Cowich.	1312
Quikinna'qu (Kutq)	Sib.	1313
Radgost	Dan.	1316
Rafnagud	Norse	1317
Rail	Pelew Is.	1319
Raven	N.A.I.	1325
Rekh	Egy.	1332
Rinaggon	Borneo	1339
Roc (Rukh)	Arab., Pers.	1343
Rupe	N. Zeal.	1354
Sarasvati	Hin.	1400
Secretary Bird	Afr.	1412
Semiramis	Assyr.	1415
Shiju-gara	Jap.	1437
Shimbei	Jap.	1437
Shuki	Hin.	1444
Shulamite	Hebr.	1444
Signe-alveig	Norse	1451
Sigrun	Norse	1451
Simurgh	Pers.	1456
Singalang Burong	Borneo	1457
Siren	Gk.	1458
Spaul	Cowich.	1480
Strygе	Med. Lit.	1501
Stymphalides	Gk.	1502
Sueje	Lapp	1504
Suoje-lodde	Lapp	1510
Surya	Hin.	1511
Surya-bai	Hin.	1512

Bird (cont.)	Culture	Page
Tecolotl	Mex.	1540
Tereus	Gk.	1546
T'hlu-kluts	Makah	903
Thunderbird	N.A.I.	1568
Tlaloc Tecutli	Mex.	1581
To Fu	Chin.	1583
Tokoyo-naganaki-dori	Jap.	1584
Tonatiuh	Toltec	1586
Tsakaka-itiac	Hidatsa	1602
Tu-tutsh	Nootkan	1611
Uso-dori	Jap.	1631
Utkha	Buriat	1632
Vareghna	Pers.	1639
Vasillissa	Slav.	1641
Vedfolner	Norse	1643
Velchanos	Cretan	1644
Vermilion Bird	Chin., Jap.	1646
Vidyaharas	Hin.	1649
Vinmara	Mel.	1651
Voc	C.A.I.	1657
Yehl	Alaskan	1703
Yetl	Tlingit	1156
Zasis	Lithu.	1716
Ziz	Hebr.	1721

CALDRON (SEE WORLD MILL OR POT)

CAVE (WORLD NAVEL)		
Adullam	Hebr.	36
Ame-no-iwato	Jap.	83
Chimomoztoc	Mex.	166
Dicte (Dikte)	Gk.	443
Dom-daniel	Hebr-Christ.	11
Giovava	Taino	659
Gnipaheller	Norse	664
Leibethriades	Gk.	981
Machpelah	Hebr.	1034
Marocael's cave	Taino	1068
Mundi	Rom.	1136
Nane-chaha	Choctaw	1153
Paccari-tampu	Inca	1224
Saint Patrick's Purgatory	Christ.	1379
Trophonian Oracle	Gk.	1600
Vala	Hin.	1635
Wayland's stocc	Ang-Sax.	1670

	Culture	Page
CELESTIAL REALM (SEE UNDER OTHERWORLD REALMS)		
CHAOS (SEE PRIMORDIAL SEA)		
CONFLICT (FIELD OR TIME OF CONFLICT. (c=conflict, f=field, t=time)		
Aceldama (f)	Hebr.	23
Actium (f)	Rom.	28
Armageddon (f)	Hebr.	127
Camlan (f)	Bryth.	281
Campus Martius (f)	Rom.	282
Canne (f)	Rom.	286
Cath Godeu (c)	Bryth.	299
Doom of Gods (c, t)	Ice.	463
Dundagel (f)	Bryth.	476
Einherier (c)	Norse	496
Gabhra (c)	Cel.	619
Gigantomachia (c)	Gk.	655
Godeu (f)	Bryth.	667
Golgotha (f)	Hebr.	674
Gotterdammerung (c, f)	Germ.	680
Judgment Day (Doomsday) (t)	Hebr-Christ.	893
Lehi (f)	Hebr.	981
Mag Tured (c, f)	Cel.	1041
Mahanaim (f)	Hebr.	1043
Megiddo (f)	Hebr.	1084
Moytura (c, f)	Cel.	1132
Ragnarok (c, t)	Ice.	1317
Sligo (f)	Cel.	1467
Thermopylae (f)	Gk.	1554
Tintagel (f)	Bryth.	476
Titanomachia (c)	Gk.	1577
Troy (f)	Gk.	1601
Varena (f)	Pers.	1639
Vigrid (f)	Norse	1649
Waterloo (f)	Eng., Fr.	1669
COSMIC PLANT (SEE PLANT)		
DIETY THRONE		
Ame-no-iha-kura	Jap.	83
Ark of the Covenant (Mercy Seat)	Hebr.	126
Hlidskjalf	Norse	776
Lia Fail	Cel.	990
Tara Stone	Cel.	990

	Culture	Page
Vishapa	Arm., Pers.	1654
Wantley	Eng.	469
Zmay	Serb.	1722
Zu	Baby., Sum.	1734

DWARF

Abatwa	Afr.	12
Afifi	Afr.	43
Agastya	Hin.	45
Alberich	Norse	62
Alfar	Norse	67
Alviss	Norse	78
Andvari	Norse	95
Austre	Norse	479
Bes	Norse	205
Blastie	Scot.	224
Cercopes	Gk.	304
Coranians	Bryth.	370
Daenn	Norse	405
Dokkalfar	Norse	458
Domovui	Slav.	910
Dony	Eng.	462
Duergar	Norse	475
Dvalin	Norse	478
Dvergar	Norse	478
Elbegast	Norse	+
Elberich	Norse	498
Fjalar	Norse	578
Gahonga	Iroq.	622
Galar	Norse	623
Gandayah	Iroq.	626
Gnome	Med. Lit.	664
Gob	Med. Lit.	664
Groa	Norse	692
Guillen	Basque	968
Hari	Hin.	726
Hephaestus	Gk.	751
Hlebard	Norse	776
Hop-o-my-thumb	Folk.	786
Hreidmar	Norse	797
Hudson, Sir Jeffrey	Eng.	802
Hugi	Norse	803
Issunboshi	Jap.	848
Jack Sprat	Folk.	857
Jogaoh	Iroq.	884
Karliki	Slav.	910

Dwarf (cont.)	Culture	Page
Kaukas	Slav.	913
Khnemu	Egy.	924
Kuei Hsin	Chin.	1673
Laminak	Basque	968
Laurin	Germ.	977
Lilliputian	Eng.	995
Littur	Norse	1003
Ljosalfar	Norse	1004
Luchorpain	Cel.	1020
Ludki (Krasnoludi)	Serb.	1021
Lyeshie	Slav.	910
Maty-tapire	Hin.	1077
Mimi	Germ.	1105
Modsognir	Norse	1114
Nibelung	Norse	1167
Nordre	Norse	479
Oberon	Eng., Fr.	1192
Chodowas	Iroq.	1202
Pacolet	Fr.	1224
P'an Ku	Chin.	1233
Ptah	Egy.	1299
Pukys	Slav.	913
Ra (Radare)	Teutonic	1315
Regin	Norse	1330
Rumpelstiltskin	Germ.	1354
Saci	Braz.	1358
Schilbung	Norse	1407
Sebek (Sukhos)	Egy.	1412
Sindre	Norse	1457
Sudre	Norse	479
Suku-na-biko	Jap.	1505
Svartalfar	Norse	1514
Tcikapis	Can. Ind.	1540
Tom Thumb	Folk.	1585
Torx	Arm.	1590
Troll	Germ.	1600
Uldda	Scan.	1621
Vamana	Hin.	1637
Vestre	Norse	479
Vodyanui	Slav.	910
Volund	Norse	1658
Vozdushnuie	Slav.	910
Wakonyingo	Afr.	1662
Xolotl	Mex.	1697

ENCHANTED PLACE (SEE SACRED PLACE)

	Culture	Page
Anakim (m)	Hebr.	91
Angerboda (f)	Norse	96
Angeyja (Egia) (f)	Norse	743
Antaeus (m)	Gk.	654
Antero Wipunen (m)	Fin-Ug.	102
Antiphates (m)	Gk.	104
Apappus (m)	Eng.	107
Argante (f)	Bryth.	121
Ascapart (m)	Bryth.	654
Atla (f)	Norse	743
Atlas (m)	Gk.	152
Baal Shamin (m)	Arm.	168
Balan (m)	Bryth.	654
Balin (m)	Bryth.	174
Bana (m)	Hin.	178
Belleros (m)	Gk.	199
Bergbui (m)	Norse	204
Bergelmir (m)	Norse	204
Blunderbore (m)	Folk.	654
Bran (m)	Bryth.	241
Briareus (m)	Gk.	247
Bricriu (m)	Cel.	248
Brobdingnag (m, f)	Eng.	654
Bumba (m)	Afr.	260
Cacus (m)	Rom.	654
Caipora (m)	Braz.	270
Ceos (m)	Gk.	303
Chrysaor (m)	Gk.	334
Chung K'uei	Chin.	336
Cichol the Footless (m)	Cel.	338
Coeus (m)	Gk.	1577
Cormoran (m)	Folk.	654
Cottus (m)	Gk.	375
Crios (m)	Gk.	382
Cronus (m)	Gk.	384
Cuchulainn (m)	Cel.	393
Cumhal (m)	Cel.	396
Curoi mac Daire (m)	Cel.	398
Cyclops (m)	Gk.	400
Daeva (m)	Zoro.	405
Despair (m)	Christ.	654
Djin (m)	Slav.	454
Dzoavits	N.A.I.	481
Eabani (m)	Sum.	482
Eistla	Norse	743
Emin (m)	Hebr.	509

	Culture	Page
Enceladus (m)	Gk.	510
Enim (m, f)	Hebr.	511
Enkidu (m)	Sum.	512
Ephialtes (m)	Gk.	515
Eurytion (m)	Gk.	533
Evans, William (m)	Eng.	534
Eyrgjafa (f)	Norse	743
Fafnir (m)	Norse	544
Farbauti (m)	Norse	548
Fasolt (m)	Germ.	549
Fenian (m)	Cel.	559
Fenja & Menja (f)	Norse	560
Fenrir (m)	Norse	560
Ferracute (m)	Carol.	654
Ferragus (m)	Port.	654
Fierabras (m)	Carol.	654
Finn mac Coul (m)	Cel.	654
Fjolsvid (m)	Norse	578
Fomhair (m)	Scot.	590
Fomor (m)	Cel.	590
Fornjot (m)	Fin.	595
Frau Frigg (f)	Germ.	608
Gabbara (m)	Fr.	619
Gallingantua (m)	Folk.	654
Ga-oh (m)	Seneca	623
Garbh Ogh (f)	Cel.	628
Gargantua (m)	Fr.	630
Geirrod (m)	Norse	638
Gemmagog (m)	Fr.	644
Gerd (f)	Norse	647
Geryoneo (m)	Eng.	654
Gigantes (m)	Gk.	655
Gjalp (f)	Norse	743
Goemagot (m)	Cel.	371
Gog (m)	Bryth.	669
Goliath (m)	Hebr.	654
Grangousier (m)	Fr.	654
Grantorto (m)	Eng.	654
Greatheart (m)	Christ.	655
Greip (f)	Norse	743
Grendel (m)	Ang-Sax.	689
Grid (f)	Norse	690
Grim (m)	Bryth.	691
Grim & Hilde (m, f)	Germ.	691
Grumbo (m)	Folk.	693
Guy of Warwick (m)	Eng.	654

	Culture	Page
Gwadyn Ossol (m)	Bryth.	700
Gwrnach (m)	Bryth.	702
Gyges (m)	Gk.	654
Gymir (m)	Norse	704
Hardgrep (f)	Norse	725
Hayk (m)	Arm.	734
Hecatoncheires (m)	Gk.	741
Hel (f)	Norse	745
Heracles (m)	Gk.	752
Hercules (m)	Rom.	759
Hlebard (m)	Norse	776
Hler (m)	Norse	776
Hrim (m)	Norse	798
Hrimgerd (f)	Norse	798
Hrimgrimnir (m)	Norse	798
Hrimnir (m)	Norse	798
Hrimthursar (m)	Norse	798
Hrungnir (m)	Norse	798
Hugi (m)	Norse	803
Hymir (m)	Norse	811
Hyndla (f)	Norse	812
Hyperion (m)	Gk.	812
Hyrokkin (f)	Norse	813
Iapetus (m)	Gk.	816
Idris (m)	Welsh	820
Ind (f)	Norse	743
Iokul (m)	Norse	900
Ishbibenob (m)	Hebr.	843
Ivithjar (f)	Norse	851
Iztac Ciuatl (f)	Mex.	854
Jarnsaxa (f)	Norse	743
Jotun (m)	Norse	890
Jutmundus (m)	Med. Lit.	1345
Kaare (m)	Norse	900
Karei (m)	Malay.	910
Kesil (m)	Sem.	919
Kung Kung (m)	Chin.	1185
Laestrygones (m)	Gk.	963
Laufey (f)	Norse	976
Loge (m)	Fin.	1008
Loki (m)	Norse	1010
Long Meg (f)	Bryth.	1012
Long Tom (m)	Bryth.	1012
Losy (m)	Mong.	1013
Magog (m)	Bryth.	1041
Makutu (m)	N. Zeal.	1048

	Culture	Page
Malagigi (m)	Carol.	654
Malambruno (m)	Span.	1049
Maugis (m)	Fr.	1077
Maul (m)	Eng.	1078
Meg (f)	Eng.	1084
Mimas (m)	Gk.	1105
Mimir (m)	Norse	1105
Mnemosyne (f)	Gk.	1113
Mokkurkalfi (m)	Norse	1114
Moms Meg (f)	Bryth.	1084
Mummu Tiamat (f)	Baby.	1570
Mundilfore (m)	Norse	1136
Naraka (m)	Hin.	1155
Nephilim (m, f)	Hebr.	1163
Nickneven (f)	Scot.	+
Nor (m)	Norse	1180
Norn (f)	Norse	1180
Oceanus (m)	Gk.	1193
Og (m)	Hebr.	1200
Ogre (m)	Euro.	1201
Ogyrvran (m)	Bryth.	1201
Ophion (m)	Gk.	1211
Orgoglio (m)	Eng.	654
Orion (m)	Gk.	1215
Otus (m)	Gk.	1221
Pagan (m)	Christ.	654
Pallas (m)	Gk.	1229
Palleneous (m)	Gk.	1229
P'an Ku (a)	Chin.	1233
Pantagruel (m)	Fr.	1234
Paul Bunyan (m)	Folk.	1244
Peboan (m)	N.A.I.	+
Periphetes (m)	Gk.	1256
Phoebe (f)	Gk.	1265
Polybotes (m)	Gk.	1283
Polyphemus (m)	Gk.	1284
Pope (m)	Christ.	655
Porphyrion (m)	Gk.	1287
Ptah-Tanen (m)	Egy.	1299
Punchkin (m)	Hin.	1301
Punegusse (m)	Sib.	1301
Purusa (a)	Hin.	1305
Pyracmon (m)	Gk.	1307
Quoots-hooi (f)	Chinook	1314
Ran (f)	Norse	1322
Ravana (m)	Hin.	1324

	Culture	Page
Regin (m)	Norse	1330
Rephaim (m)	Hebr.	1332
Rhea (f)	Gk.	1577
Rhoetus (m)	Gk.	1337
Rind (f)	Norse	1339
Ritho (m)	Bryth.	1341
Ruadan (m)	Cel.	1352
Saint Christopher (m)	Christ.	654
Samson (m)	Hebr.	1394
Satan (m)	Hebr-Christ.	1402
Searbhan Lochlannach (m)	Cel.	1411
Seven Champions (m)	Christ.	654
Sharvan (m)	Cel.	1431
Shoki-san (m)	Jap.	1441
Shuten Doji	Jap.	1444
Sinis (m)	Gk.	1457
Skrymir (m)	Norse	1465
Skuld (f)	Norse	1465
Slaygood (m)	Christ.	655
Suttung (m)	Norse	1513
Svasud (m)	Norse	1514
Tauni-kapi-kapi (m)	N. Guin.	1538
Tethys (f)	Gk.	1548
Theia (f)	Gk.	1553
Themis (f)	Gk.	1553
Thjalfi (m)	Norse	1560
Thjasse (m)	Norse	1560
Thorir (m)	Ice.	+
Tirthakaras (m)	Jain.	1577
Titans (m, f)	Gk.	1577
Tityus (m)	Gk.	1580
Toltec (m)	Mex.	1585
Torx (m)	Arm.	1590
Tregeagle (m)	Bryth.	1595
Troll (m)	Norse	1600
Typhoeus (m)	Gk.	1617
Typhon (m)	Gk.	1617
Uar-gaeth-sceo-luachair-sceo (m)	Irish	1619
Ugarthilocus (m)	Dan.	1620
Uhepono (m)	Zuni	1620
Ulfrun (f)	Norse	743
Urania (f)	Gk.	1627
Uranus (m)	Gk.	1627
Urd (f)	Norse	1628
Utgard-Loki (m)	Norse	1632

	Culture	Page
Vafthrudner (m)	Norse	1633
Vagnhofde (m)	Norse	725
Vasud (m)	Norse	1641
Verdhandi (f)	Norse	1645
Vitholf (m)	Norse	1656
Vukub-cakix (m)	Kiche	1659
Wallace (m)	Scot.	1663
Wudes Heer (Wade) (m)	Norse	1693
Wyrd (f)	Ang-Sax.	1694
Yehwe Zogbanu (m)	Daho.	1703
Ymir (m)	Norse	1708
Yu (m)	Chin.	1711
Zamzummim (m)	Hebr.	1716
Zuzim (m)	Hebr.	1735

GROVE (FOREST, WOOD)

Altis	Gk.	77
Barri	Norse	183
Broceliande	Bryth.	250
Glasir	Norse	661
Hodminer's Forest	Norse	779
Iarnivde (Jarnvid)	Norse	816
Ithavoll	Norse	846
Khandava	Hin.	922
Kusoto	Fin-Ug.	954
Landvide	Norse	971
Lebanon	Baby.	980
Lud	Fin-Ug.	1021
Lumbini	Bud.	1024
Nemi Wood	Rom.	1162
Thrymheim	Norse	1567

HILL (SEE MOUNTAIN)
HOLY PLACE (SEE SACRED PLACE)

INSECT

Aksak (bettle)	Chaco	60
Anansi (spider)	Afr.	91
Andalma-muus (mosquitos)	Tatar	93
Arachne (spider)	Gk.	116
Areop-enap (spider)	Nauru Is.	120
Areop-it-eonin (spider)	Nauru Is.	120
Cagn (mantis)	Bush.	269
Girtablili (scorpion)	Baby.	660
Gizo (spider)	Hausa	660
Hold (various)	Germ.	780

	Culture	Page
Dund (Dhundh)	Hin.	476
Echidna	Gk.	489
Empusa	Gk.	510
Fomor	Cel.	590
Fum	Chin.	617
Furies	Gk.	617
Geryon	Gk.	647
Goin	Aus.	670
Gorgons	Gk.	678
Grendel	Ang-Sax.	689
Grylli (Griffin)	Euro.	693
Gyascutus	Folk.	+
Hecatoncheires (Centimani)	Gk.	741
Hell	Christ.	748
Hieracosphinx	Egy.	768
Hydra	Gk.	810
Jabberwock	Eng.	855
Jezinky	Slav.	879
Jinn	Mos.	880
Kappa	Jap.	909
Kholumolumo	Bantu	925
Kirttimukha	Hin.	933
Koshchei	Slav.	943
Koyorowen (Yaho)	Aus.	944
Kwen-lun	Chin.	1461
Mahisha	Hin.	1045
Manticore	Gk.	1060
Mata	Cel.	1074
Medusa	Gk.	1084
Meming	Norse	1088
Minotaur	Gk.	1107
Mushussu	Sum.	1139
Nasnas	Arab.	1156
Nuye	Jap.	1187
Oaf	Scan.	1189
Oni	Jap.	1209
Pallas	Gk., Rom.	1228
Pazuzu	Sum.	1245
Polyphemus	Gk.	1284
Rahu & Ketu	Hin.	1318
Reem	Hebr.	1330
Sag	Egy.	1360
Scylla	Gk.	1409
Sokar	Egy.	1471
Sphinx	Egy., Gk.	1482
Su	S.A.I.	1502

	Culture	Page
Drachenfels	Germ.	467
Ebal	Hebr.	647
Etna	Gk.	528
Everest	Bud.	535
Fuji	Jap.	615
Gerizim	Hebr.	647
Gibeon	Hebr.	655
Gilead	Hebr.	656
Glass Mountain	Folk.	661
Hara Berezaiti	Pers.	724
Hekkenfeldt	Dan.	745
Hekla	Ice.	745
Helg-fell	Ice.	746
Helicon	Gk.	747
Hêng Shang	Chin.	1247
Hēng Shang	Chin.	1247
Hill of Bat	Egy.	771
Hills of Bether	Christ.	771
Hills of Frankincense (or Myrrh)	Hebr.	771
Himavata (Himalaya)	Tib.	771
Himinbjorg	Norse	771
Hiyei-zan	Jap.	775
Horaisan	Jap.	787
Horeb	Hebr.	787
Horselborg	Germ.	791
Hua Shan	Chin.	1247
Hugar	Zoro.	1631
Ida	Gk.	818
Ishadhara	Chin.	843
Iztac Ciuatl	Mex.	854
Jochgrimm	Tyrolese	883
Kaf	Mos.	901
Kagu	Jap.	1389
Kailasa	Hin.	902
Kashmir	Bud.	911
Khvarism	Pers.	613
Kirishima	Jap.	1130
K'o-chu	Chin.	939
Koppelberg	Germ.	1269
Kothluwalawa	Zuni	944
Kouantun	Chin.	944
Kuang-hsieh	Chin.	947
Kuen-luen	Chin.	949
K'un-lun	Chin.	952
Latmus	Gk.	975

	Culture	Page
Loi Hsao Mong	Ind-Chin.	1010
Lycaeus	Gk.	1027
Lycorea	Gk.	1578
Maenalus	Gk.	+
Majoi	Burm.	1047
Mandara	Hin.	1056
Mashu	Baby.	1072
Mei Shan	Chin.	1693
Meru	Hin.	1094
Montsalvat	Christ.	1119
Moriah	Hebr.	1124
Muscas	Gk.	1138
Myimmo Taung	Burm.	1142
Myrtium	Gk.	1143
Nane Chaha	Choctaw	1153
Nane Waiyah	Choctaw	1153
Nebo	Hebr.	1159
Nissa	Egy.	1130
Nitsir	Baby.	429
Nonoalco	Mex.	1313
Nunne chaha	Apal. Ind.	1186
Nysa	Gk.	1130
Obasuteyama	Jap.	1191
Olivet	Hebr.	1130
Olympus	Gk.	1206
Ossa	Gk.	1219
Othrys	Gk.	1130
Oure	Gk.	1221
Oye-yama	Jap.	1444
Palatium	Rom.	1227
Pandava	Chin.	1150
Paria	Carib.	1237
Parnassus	Gk.	1238
Passe-vara	Lapp	1242
Pelion	Gk.	1250
Phra Men	Siam.	1267
Pirogonia	Maoris	1275
Pisgah	Hebr.	1276
Popocatepetl	Mex.	1286
Popoconaltepetl	Mex.	1286
Qaf	Mos.	1309
Quirinal	Rom.	1314
Revand	Pers.	262
Rhodope	Gk.	1337
Roshan	Pers.	1655
Ryojusen	Jap.	1356

	Culture	Page
Safa	Mos.	1360
Saffron Peak	Bud.	907
Samaria	Hebr.	1393
Samur	Hebr.	1394
Senkyo	Jap.	1416
Shide	Jap.	1436
Shishchikul	Van. Is.	1439
Sigtyr	Norse	1451
Sinai	Hebr.	1131
Snowdon	Bryth.	1470
Sumbur	Mong.	1505
Sumeru	Bud.	1506
Suro	Tatar	1511
Tabor	Hebr.	1523
Tai Shan	Chin.	1526
Takachiho	Jap.	1527
Tamradripa	Cey.	904
Tara	Cel.	1534
Teoculhuacan	Mex.	166
Tirna-nOg	Cel.	1576
Tithorea	Gk.	1578
Titthium	Gk.	1580
Tow	Haida	1592
Tow-us-Tussin	Haida	1592
Tsukuba	Jap.	1604
Ts'ung Shan	Chin.	1247
Tu So	Chin.	1434
Tzatzitepec	Mex.	1618
Urumunda	Bud.	1147
Valhalla	Norse	1636
Vermilion Hills	Chin.	1646
Vulture Peak	Chin.	1660
White Mountains	Nav.	1678
Wu Yo	Chin.	1694
Yauhqueme	Mex.	308
Yellow Mountains	Nav.	1705
Y-wyddea	Bryth.	1714
Zion	Hebr.	1131

OTHERWORLD REALMS:
Afterworld, neither good nor evil

Abokas	Mel.	17
Abraham's Bosom	Christ.	18
Abydos	Egy.	20
Acheron	Gk.	24
Acherusia	Gk.	25

	Culture	Page
Achren (Ochren)	Bryth.	26
Adliparmiut	Eskimoan	+
Adlivun	Eskimoan	+
Al Araf	Arab.	61
Ame-no-iwato	Jap.	83
Amenti	Egy.	84
Assiah	Caba.	143
Asura	Bud.	146
Atziloth	Caba.	155
Bilskirnir	Norse	211
Briah	Caba.	247
Chosii	Jap.	329
Deva	Bud.	435
Edinu	Baby.	1447
Erythea	Gk.	647
Godeu	Bryth.	667
Gwlad Yr Hav	Welsh	701
Hamistakan	Pers.	714
Helgoland	Norse	595
Heljar-ran	Norse	748
Heorot	Dan.	751
Horai	Jap.	787
Huaca	Inca	801
Issland	Germ.	848
Jinnistan	Arab.	880
Jotunheim	Norse	890
Land of Beulah	Christ.	970
Lebermeer	Germ.	980
Limbo	Christ.	996
Magombe	Afr.	1041
Maksameri	Esthonian	1048
Nara	Bud.	1155
Naraka	Bud.	1155
Necropolis	Egy.	1160
Nehan	Bud.	1160
Okolner	Norse	1203
Padalon	Hin.	1224
Pohjola (Tuonela)	Fin.	1281
Ponemah	N.A.I.	767
Pretaloka	Bud.	1292
Put	Hin.	1305
Qudlivun	Eskimoan	+
Sai-no-kawara	Jap.	1361
Saint Austin Chapel	Bryth.	1388
Santakrodhamandala	Bud.	1398
Scath	Cel.	1406

	Culture	Page
Gokuraku	Jap.	670
Gwynedd	Bryth.	703
Hesperides	Gk.	765
Hiklvth	Caba.	769
Himinbjorg	Norse	771
Hlidskjalf	Norse	776
Homeyoco	Mex.	784
Hsi T'ien (Sukhavati)	Chin.	800
Huang T'ien	Chin.	801
Huehuetlapallan	Mex.	802
Hyperborea	Gk.	812
Ithavoll	Norse	849
Jannet 'Adu	Mos.	1424
Jennet el Firdos	Mos.	1424
Jennet el Mawa	Mos.	1424
Jennet en Khuld	Mos.	1424
Jennet en Na'im	Mos.	1424
Kaan	Mex.	900
Kuling	Aus.	940
Kuru	Chin.	1154
Lhayul	Tib.	989
Ljosalfaheim	Norse	1004
Lycia	Gk.	1027
Mommur	Eng.	1115
Mong Hsang	Burm.	1117
Muspelheim	Norse	1140
Nehan	Jap.	1160
Nirvana	Bud.	1175
Noatun	Norse	1178
Ogdoad	Gnostic	1200
Olympus	Gk.	1206
Omeyocan	Mex.	1208
Ortygia	Gk.	1217
Paradise	Christ.	1236
Phoenicia	Gk.	1265
Purva-Videha	Chin.	1274
Qulivun	Eskimoan	1311
Radien-aimo	Lapp	1316
Rai	Slav.	1318
Rangipotiki	Poly.	1048
Revolving Castle	Bryth.	1334
Sakhavati	Bud.	1389
Sambhogakaya	Bud.	1393
Sessrynnir in Folkvang	Norse	610
Sokvabek	Norse	1471
Sudharma	Hin.	1503

	Culture	Page
Sunya	Bud.	1510
Svarga	Hin.	1514
Svithiod	Norse	1515
Takama-no-hara	Jap.	1527
Thrudheim (Thrudvang)	Norse	1567
Thrymheim	Norse	1567
Thund	Norse	1636
T'ien (T'ien Li)	Chin.	1571
Tilo	Baronga	1573
Tirawahut	Pawnee	1576
Tlapallan (Tlalocan)	Mex.	1582
Tollan	Mex.	1585
Trayastrimsat	Chin.	1235
Tung-kiao	Chin.	1607
Upsala	Norse	1627
Uttara-kuru	Hin.	1632
Vaikuntha	Hin.	1654
Valaskjalf	Norse	1635
Valhalla	Norse	1636
Vanaheim	Norse	1638
Varena	Pers.	1639
Vingolf	Norse	1651
Vingskornir	Norse	1651
Vourukasha	Pers.	1659
Waiiri	Aus.	1661
Whai-tua	Poly.	1048
Xalac	Mex.	1695
Xochitlalpan	Mex.	1696
Yasukawara	Jap.	1702
Ydalir	Norse	1703
Yetzirah	Caba.	1705
Yoru-no-wosu-kuni	Jap.	1710
Zivena Vitzcatl	Mex.	1721

Island Abode

Abatos	Egy.	12
Aeaea	Gk.	37
Atlantis	Gk.	152
Avalon (Avallon's Island)	Bryth.	161
Bardsey	Bryth.	181
Blessed Isles (Isles of the Blest)	Rom.	846
Blissful Isle	N.A.I.	225
Boicua (Bimini)	C.A.I.	234
Brittia	Byzantine	250
Cipango	Ital.	341

	Culture	Page
Aidenn	Ang-Sax.	55
Airyano Vaejo	Pers.	57
Alburz	Zoro.	326
Amaravati	Hin.	80
Amaurote	Eng., Fr.	81
Annwfn	Bryth.	100
Antilia	Euro. Lit.	103
Aotea-roa	Aus.	106
Arcadia	Gk.	118
Atlantis	Gk.	152
Avalon (Avallon's Isle)	Bryth.	161
Belet	Malay.	1052
Berenice	Gk.	204
Bermoothes	Eng.	204
Bimini	Euro.	212
Boiuca	C.A.I.	234
Brugh na Boinne	Cel.	253
Caerleon	Bryth.	268
Caer Sidi	Bryth.	268
Carbonek	Bryth.	289
Castle of Corbenic	Med. Lit.	295
Castle of Revelry	Bryth.	295
Castle of Wonders	Bryth.	295
Castle Perilous	Bryth.	295
Chalmecaciuatl	Mex.	309
Ching-tu	Chin.	326
Cockaign	Med. Lit.	354
Dilmun	Sum.	445
Elysium	Gk.	506
Emhain of Apple Trees	Cel.	1055
Erewhon	Eng.	519
Eridu	Sum.	520
Fensal	Norse	560
Fu-ti	Chin.	1397
Garden of Eden	Christ., Hebr.	629
Garotman	Pers.	632
Gimle	Norse	658
Gokuraku	Jap.	670
Grdhra-kuta	Bud.	1356
Happy Hunting Ground	N.A.I.	724
Havilah	Hebr.	732
Hesperides	Gk.	765
Hsi T'ien	Chin.	800
Hy-breasail	Cel.	810
Isatpragbhara	Hin.	842
Jodo	Jap.	882

	Culture	Page
Kailasa	Hin.	902
Kennaquhair	Scot.	916
Kshetra	Bud.	256
Kuen-luen	Chin.	949
Loegria	Cornish	1009
Lugdunensis (Lyonesse)	Bryth.	1023
Mag Mel	Cel.	1040
Mag Mor	Cel.	1040
Miya-jima	Jap.	1113
Mommur	Bryth.	1115
Nehan	Bud.	1160
New Jerusalem	Christ.	1166
Nirvana (Mahasukha)	Bud., Hin.	1175
Pryangu-dvipa	Chin.	1010
Purva-videha	Chin.	1305
Red Land	Egy., Mex.	1329
Revolving Castle	Bryth.	1334
Ryojusen	Jap.	1356
Sambhogakaya	Bud.	1393
San Hsien Shan	Chin.	1397
Senkyo	Jap.	1416
Seven Cities	Christ.	1423
Shangri-la	Tib.	1430
Shou Shan	Chin.	1442
Sidh	Cel.	1447
Sila	Jain.	1452
Srahmandazi	Afr.	1487
Sukhavati	Bud.	1505
Sunya	Bud.	1510
Tamoanchan	Mex.	346
Tir-na-mBan	Cel.	1576
Tir-na-nOg	Cel.	1576
Tir-tairngir	Cel.	1577
Tlalocan	Mex.	1582
Tokoyo-no-kuni	Jap.	1584
Tollan (Tonatlan)	Mex.	1585
Tosotsa-ten	Bud.	1591
Tushita	Bud.	1610
Utopia	Gk.	1632
Valhalla	Norse	1636
Wathi-wathi	Aus.	1669
Weissnichtwo	Eng.	1672
Xochitlalpan	Mex.	1696
Yalaing	Aus.	1698
Zion	Hebr.	1721

Road to Afterworld	Culture	Page
Al Sirat	Mos.	76
Ama-no-hashidate	Jap.	79
Ama-no-kawa (Yasu)	Jap.	79
Ama-no-uki-hashi	Jap.	80
Ame-no-yasu-kaha	Jap.	84
Balan Bacham	Malay.	1052
Beanstalk	Folk.	189
Bifrost (Asbru, Vindhjalmsbru)	Norse	210
Biggarroo	Aus.	210
Bitter Sea	Baby.	220
Black River Bridge	Fin-Ug.	1608
Caer Gwydion	Bryth.	268
Chinvatperetu	Zoro.	326
Cinvat	Zoro.	341
Citallicue	Mex.	344
Edinu	Baby.	1447
Erebus	Gk.	518
Galaxy, The	World-wide	623
Gjolbridge (Gjallar-bru)	Norse	661
Goonnear	Aus.	676
Helgrindr	Ice.	746
Helvegr	Norse	749
Hwang-ho River	Chin.	1705
Irmin's Way	Germ.	839
Jachin & Boaz	Hebr.	855
Jacob's Ladder	Hebr.	859
Jesse's Rod	Hebr.	876
Kerlaug	Norse	919
Khubur	Baby.	925
Kormet	Norse	943
Lug's Chain	Cel.	1023
Maze	Arm.	481
Milky Way	World-wide	1103
Ob	Ostiak	1191
Ormet	Norse	1216
Panoi	Banks Is.	1234
Pul Chinavad	Magian	1300
Rainbow	World-wide	1319
Rerenga-wairua	Poly.	1333
Saint Patrick's Purgatory	Christ.	1379
Sakrah	Mos.	1389
Sanzu-no-kawa	Jap.	1398
Sipapu	Pueblo	1458
Slid	Norse	1467
Stem of Jesse	Hebr.	876
Styx	Gk.	1502

	Culture	Page
Ekurra	Assyr.	497
Epirus	Gk.	516
Erebus	Gk.	518
Erez	Caba.	1423
Four-cornered Castle (Castle of Revelry, Castle of Riches)	Bryth.	604
Ge	Caba.	1423
Gehenna	Hebr.	637
Gehinnom	Caba.	638
Gimokodan	Philip.	658
Giovava	Taino	659
Gjol	Norse	661
Gnipaheller	Norse	664
Gower	Bryth.	680
Grjottungard	Norse	692
Hades	Gk.	706
Hawiyet	Mos.	1424
Helgrindr	Ice.	746
Helheim	Norse	745
Hell	Christ.	748
Hiyoyoa	N. Guin.	775
Hotama	Mos.	1424
Iberia	Cel., Gk.	816
Irkalla	Assyr-Baby.	839
Jehennam (Jahannam)	Mos.	1424
Jikoku	Jap.	879
Jotunheim	Norse	890
Khubur	Baby.	925
Kormet	Norse	943
Kuzimu	Bantu	954
Lahha	Mos.	1424
Lebermeer	Germ.	986
Lethe	Gk.	980
Lochlann	Cel.	1007
Lower Thingstead	Norse	943
Maksameri	Esthonian	1048
Malebolge	Ital.	1050
Mammondom	Hebr-Christ.	11
Manala (Tuonela)	Fin-Ug.	1054
Meido	Jap.	1084
Meslam	Sum.	1164
Mictlan	Mex.	1099
Naastrand	Norse	1145
Nadir	Arab.	1147
Naraka	Bud., Hin.	1155

	Culture	Page
Nenokatatsu-kuni	Jap.	1163
Neshiah	Caba.	1423
Niflheim	Norse	1169
Noatun	Norse	1178
Nyalwa	Tib.	1187
Ob	Ostiak	1191
Oeth & Anoeth	Bryth.	1199
Orcus	Ital.	1213
Pandemonium	Ital.	1232
Panoi	Banks Is.	1234
Patala	Hin.	1242
Peklo	Slav.	1249
Perilous Castle	Bryth.	1255
Perilous Cemetery	Bryth.	1256
Perilous Chapel	Bryth.	1256
Phlegethon	Gk.	1264
Pimentola	Swed.	1273
Po	Poly.	1281
Pretaloka (Yi-dvag)	Hin.	1292
Put	Hin.	1305
Reinga	N. Zeal.	1331
Rut-aimo	Lapp	1355
Ryugu	Jap.	1356
Sakar	Mos.	1424
Sarajas	Swed.	1399
Sheol	Hebr.	1434
Shipap	Pueblo	1439
Shualu	Baby.	1444
Sidh	Cel.	1447
Sindre's Hall	Norse	1457
Svartalfaheim	Norse	1514
Tartarus	Gk.	1536
Taurica	Gk.	1560
Te Reinga	Poly.	1546
Tibal	Caba.	1423
To-kwatsu	Jap.	1584
Tophet	Hebr.	1588
Tuonela (Pohjola)	Fin-Ug.	1608
Uffern	Bryth.	1620
Utgard	Norse	1632
Uttara-kuru	Hin.	1632
Xibalba	Kiche	1696
Yabmeaimo	Lapp	1697
Yamapura	Hin.	1699
Yidak	Bud.	1706
Yomi (Soko-no-kuni)	Jap.	1709

	Culture	Page
Ef	Egy.	491
Epet (Tueret, Ueret)	Egy.	514
Erathaoth	Gnostic	1423
Ereshkigal	Baby.	518
Eris	Gk.	521
Esdes	Egy.	524
Eurynome	Gk.	532
Faun	Rom.	552
Faunus	Rom.	552
Fomor	Cel.	590
Fu Hsi	Chin.	615
Gabriel	Gnostic	619
Ganesa	Hin.	627
Geb	Egy.	637
Gelu	Rumanian	638
Geryon	Gk.	647
Giolla Deacair	Cel.	659
Glaisrig	Manx	661
Gozu-tenwo	Jap.	680
Grismadevi	Bud.	691
Hanhau	Yucatec	722
Hapi	Egy.	724
Harinegamesi	Hin.	726
Harpies	Gk.	728
Hathor	Egy.	730
Hatuibwari	Mel.	732
Havfrue	Dan.	732
Havmand	Dan.	732
Hecate	Gk.	740
Hehu	Egy.	742
Hemantadevi	Bud.	749
Heqet	Egy.	752
Hermes-Anubis	Gk.	761
Her-shef	Egy.	763
Hippa	Gk.	772
Hippocentaur	Gk.	773
Horus	Egy.	792
Htamenmas	Tib.	800
Hu (sphinx form)	Egy.	800
Hyagnis	Phryg.	810
Jezinky	Slav.	879
Kebehsenuf	Egy.	915
Keh	Egy.	915
Khensu	Egy.	923
Khentamenti	Egy.	923
Khepera	Egy.	924

	Culture	Page
Nu Kua	Chin.	1185
Oannes	Baby., Chald., Phoen.	1190
Ocypete	Gk.	1194
Onoel	Gnostic	1423
Pa Cha	Chin.	1224
Pan	Gk.	1230
Panisc	Gk.	1233
Phanes	Gk.	1261
Pholus	Gk.	1266
Porphyrion	Gk.	1287
Qeb	Egy.	1309
Ran	Norse	1322
Raphael	Gnostic	1323
Red Devil Tiger	Tib.	1328
Rhoetus	Gk.	1337
Rksavaktradakini	Bud.	1342
Sagittary	Rom.	1361
Satan	Hebr-Christ.	1402
Satyr	Gk.	1403
Sebek	Egy.	1412
Sedu	Baby.	1413
Sekhet	Egy.	1414
Set	Egy.	1420
Shargaz	Sum.	1431
Shay	Egy.	1431
Shen Nung	Chin.	1434
Shesemtet	Egy.	1435
Shesmu	Egy.	1435
Shinje-chho-gyal	Tib.	1438
Shojo	Jap.	1441
Silenii	Gk.	1453
Siren	Gk.	1458
Sojobo	Jap.	1471
Sokar	Egy.	1471
Sphinx	Egy., Gk.	1482
Suriel	Gnostic	1511
Suvarnamacha	Siam.	1513
Suvinenge	Daho.	1513
Tautabaoth	Gnostic	1539
Tengu	Jap.	1545
Thoth	Egy.	1562
Tie (Ta-urt)	Egy.	1571
Tisiphone	Gk.	1577
Triton	Gk.	1599
Tubal Cain	Hebr.	1606

	Culture	Page
Uazale	Paressi Ind.	1619
Up-uauat	Egy.	1627
Vasantadevi	Bud.	1640
Vasuki	Hin.	1641
Vatak	Zoro.	1641
Vinayaka	Bud.	1650
Volos (Ganyklos)	Rus.	1657
Wang-chug-mas	Tib.	1665
Yogini	Bud.	1709
Yskal-pydo-murt	Fin-Ug.	1711
Yu	Chin.	1711

PILLAR (AXIS, PORTAL, WORLD SUPPORT)

Abyla & Calpe (Ape's Hill & Gilbraltar)	Arab.	20
Brigit & Patrick	Cel.	249
Irminsul	Germ.	839
Jachin & Boaz	Hebr.	855
Jebel Musa (Mountain of Moses)	Arab.	868
Mioto-seki	Jap.	1108
Na-gates	Norse	1148
Oure	Gk.	1221
Quetzalveixochitl	Mex.	1313
Veralden tshuold	Lapp	1645

PLACE (SEE SACRED PLACE)

PLANT (MAGIC PLANT, TREE OF KNOWLEDGE, TREE OF LIFE, UNIVERSE TREE)

Aaron's rod	Hebr.	10
Acotzentli	Mex.	27
Agave	Mex.	46
Ahuehuete	Mex.	54
Ailanthus	Chin.	55
Alder	Cel., Gk.	66
Alzitziutil	Mex.	78
Amygdalus (Almond)	Phrygian	89
Apples of Hesperides	Gk.	113
Apple Tree	Hebr.	114
Ash	Norse	137
Ashoka	Hin.	1237
Askr Yggdrasil	Norse	141
Asvotha	Hin.	147

	Culture	Page
Baobab	Afr.	179
Beanstalk	Folk.	189
Berroc	Ang-Sax.	204
Bo (Bodhi)	Bud.	230
Bojabi	Afr.	234
Bran	Bryth.	241
Branstock	Norse	243
Burning Bush	Hebr.	261
Cactus	Mex.	265
Djambu Baros	Sumatra	454
Emoki Tree	Jap.	509
Erica	Egy.	519
Faraguvaol	Taino	548
Flaming Bush	Hebr.	581
Fu-sang Women	Chin.	618
Gaokerena	Pers.	628
Gingko	Jap.	658
Golden Bough	Rom.	672
Haoma	Pers.	723
Harvesptokhm	Pers.	729
Hesperian Apples	Gk.	765
Ilex	Bryth.	823
Irminsul	Germ.	839
Izlucoco	Mex.	854
Jambu (Jambutrishring)	Hin.	862
Jesse's Rod	Hebr.	876
Katsura	Jap.	913
Laerad	Norse	963
Ling Chih	Chin.	617
Llagdigua	Para.	1004
Lotus Tree of Heaven	Mos.	1014
Luete-muor	Lapp	1022
Maguey	Mex.	1301
Mescal	Mex.	1094
Mesu	Sum.	1095
Mimameithr	Norse	1105
Mistletoe	Norse	1111
Moly	Gk.	1115
Mugwort	Mex.	1134
Niete	Mex.	283
Nimbu	Hin.	1170
Oak	Huniversal	1189
Omumborombongo	Bush.	1208
Palm	Christ.	1229
P'an-t'ao (Fan-I'ao)	Chin.	1234
Paradixion	Hin.	1237

	Culture	Page
Parijata	Hin.	1237
Peepul	Chin.	1248
Persea	Egy.	1257
Phoenix	Gk.	1265
Quetzalveixochitl	Mex.	1313
Sakaki	Jap.	1389
Sal	Bud.	1390
Sedrat (Lotus Tree)	Mos.	1016
Shen-t'ao	Chin.	1434
Soma	Hin.	1473
Staurus	Egy.	1492
Sterculia	Korea	1494
Tamara Pua	Hin.	1529
Taxus	Gk.	1539
Teocote	Mex.	1546
Terebinth	Hebr.	1546
Tezcaquahiutl	Mex.	1549
Tonacaquahuit	Mex.	1586
Tshog-shing	Tib.	1603
Tulasi	Hin.	1606
Ule	Braz.	1621
Unkulunkulu	Zulu	1626
Vardtrad	Swed.	1639
Veralden-tshuold	Lapp	1645
Wu-t'ung Shu	Chin.	1237
Yaxche	Mex.	1702
Yggdrasil	Norse	1706
Yo-shin-shi	Jap.	1710
Zakum	Mos.	1715
Zambu	Yakut	1715
Zampu	Tib.	1716
Zizal-xiu	Mex.	1721
Zutup	Mex.	1735

PORTAL (SEE PILLAR)

PRIMORDIAL SEA (ABYSS, CHAOS)

Aaba	Sum.	9
Abti	Egy.	20
Abydos	Egy.	20
Abyss	Gk.	20
Aztlan	Mex.	166
Bir-el-arwah	Mos.	+
Briah	Caba.	247
Chaos	Gk.	312
Ginnunga-gap	Norse	658

	Culture	Place
Emain Macha	Cel.	507
Emmaus	Christ.	509
Epirus	Gk.	516
Esagila	Baby.	523
Fu-Lin	Chin.	616
Gandercleugh	Eng.	626
Gehenna	Hebr.	637
Glubdubdrib	Eng.	664
Gnitaheath	Norse	664
Godhanga	Chin.	668
Golgotha	Christ.	674
Gomorrah	Hebr.	675
Gotham	Eng.	679
Grail Castle	Bryth.	682
Heijo	Jap.	743
Heliopolis	Egy.	747
Hronesness	Ang-Sax.	798
Huehuetlapallan	Mex.	802
Idavold (Ithavoll)	Norse	819
Idzumo	Jap.	821
Ithaca	Gk.	849
Jerusalem	Christ., Hebr., Mos.	875
Kaaba	Mos.	899
Kabah	S.A.I.	900
Kadesh	Hebr.	901
Karnac	Egy.	910
Kaseem	Arab.	911
Kennaquhair	Scot.	916
Keremet	Fin-Ug.	917
Kibroth-Hattaavah	Hebr.	926
Kitsuki	Jap.	935
Krisa	Gk.	945
Kuru	Hin.	953
Kusinara	Bud.	954
Lamayin	Tib.	966
Lehi	Hebr.	981
Lhayul	Tib.	989
Lilliput	Eng.	995
Lorbrulgrud	Eng.	1013
Lubberland	Eng.	1019
Mag Slecht	Cel.	1041
Mahanaim	Hebr.	1043
Mannaheim	Norse	1060
Manoa	Euro.	1060
Mecca	Mos.	1082

	Culture	Page
Medina	Mos.	1083
Mezzoramia	Afr.	1097
Midgard	Norse	1100
Miyul	Tib.	1113
Murias	Cel.	1137
Nara	Bud.	1155
Naubandhana	Hin.	1158
Nazareth	Christ.	1159
New Jerusalem	Christ.	1166
Nihon	Jap.	1169
Nishapur	Mos.	1175
Nova Solyma	Christ.	1183
On	Egy.	1208
Ophir	Hebr.	1212
Peniel	Hebr.	1252
Phocis	Gk.	1265
Pithom	Egy.	1276
Punt	Egy.	1302
Qahu	Egy.	1309
Quivira	Span.	1314
Rajagrha	Bud.	1320
Rephidim	Hebr.	1333
Rhamnus	Gk.	1335
Rhodes	Gk.	1336
Rome	Christ., Rom.	1346
Sais	Egy.	1389
Salem	Christ., Hebr., Mos.	1390
Schilda	Germ.	1407
Scobellum	Christ.	1407
Sen Mag	Cel.	1416
Shiloh	Hebr.	1437
Shurippah	Baby.	1444
Sicyon	Gk.	1447
Siege Perilous	Bryth.	1447
Sodom	Hebr.	1470
Stonehenge (Choir Gaur)	Gaelic	1497
Tara	Cel.	1534
Tenochtitlan	Mex.	1545
Thebes (Nu-Amon)	Egy.	1552
Thule	Gk.	1567
Tiryak	Bud.	1577
Tlalnepantla	Mex.	1581
Tophet	Hebr.	1588
Tower of Babel	Hebr.	1592
Tower of Xelhua	Mex.	1592

	Culture	Page
Coatlicue	Mex.	352
Cuchi	Aus.	393
Da	Daho.	403
Dark Warrior	Chin.	416
Dibbara (Lubara)	Baby.	443
Dipsas	Gk.	450
Draco (Ladon)	Gk.	467
Ea	Assyr., Baby., Sum.	481
Erichthonius	Gk.	519
Erinyes	Gk.	520
Fu-hsi	Chin.	615
Furies	Gk.	617
Gigantes	Gk.	655
Goonnear	Aus.	676
Gucumatz	Guate.	694
Haietlik	British Col.	708
Hatuibwari (winged)	Mel.	732
Hospodaricek	Slav.	793
Huitzilopochtli (winged)	Mex.	803
Hydra	Gk.	810
Itzamna	Mex.	850
Ix Tub Tun	Mex.	853
Iztac Mixcoatl	Mex.	854
Jormungandr	Norse	887
Kadru	Hin.	901
Kalinak	Hin.	904
Kalseru	Aus.	904
Kereth	Egy.	918
Koloowisi (winged)	Zuni	941
Koshchei	Slav.	943
Koshi	Jap.	943
Kukulcan (winged)	Mex.	950
Kundalini	Hin.	952
Kyohime	Jap.	956
Lajnan	Micro.	964
Lamia	Lib.	967
Laocoon	Gk., Rom.	972
Latawiec	Polish	975
Losy	Mong.	1013
Ma	As. Min.	1030
Maboya	Carib.	1031
Manabhozho	Algon.	1054
Manasa	Hin.	1055
Mbir	Guar.	1081
Meilichios	Gk.	1084

	Culture	Page
Thviti	Norse	1569
Tsuriel	Caba.	1604

STREAM (SEE WATER: LAKE, etc.)

TREASURE (ALSO SEE ARTICLE)

Aladdin's lamp or ring	Arab.	61
Amalthea's horn	Gk.	79
Amaterasu's necklace	Jap.	81
Andvarinaut	Norse	95
Bran's caldron	Bryth.	241
Brisingamen	Norse	250
Caduceus	Gk., Rom.	266
Cambalo's ring	Eng.	280
Cerridwen's pot	Bryth.	305
Chin Lun	Chin.	1424
Chu Ping Ch'en's image	Chin.	1424
Chu Ts'ang's image	Chin.	1424
Cornucopia	Gk., Rom.	373
Dagda's caldron	Cel.	405
Draupner	Norse	470
Eldhrimnir	Norse	499
Eriphyle's jewels & veil	Gk.	520
Ethiopian Table	Gk.	528
Golden Fleece	Gk.	673
Harmonia's jewels & veil	Gk.	727
Hesperides' apples	Gk.	765
Huecomitl	Mex.	802
Jamshid's goblet	Pers.	863
Ju'i chu	Chin.	1424
Kantha	Hin.	908
Kaustubha	Hin.	914
Luck of Edenhall	Eng.	1020
Mahavira	Hin.	1045
Mani	Hin.	1058
Manji	Jap.	1059
Matholwych's caldron	Bryth.	242
Nibelungen ring	Norse	1167
Odrerer	Norse	1196
Round Table	Bryth.	1351
Sangraal	Christ.	1396
Seistron	Egy.	1414
Thyrsus	Gk.	1570
Tympanum	Phoen.	1617
Urd's horn	Norse	1628
Well of Apollo Thyrxis	Gk.	831

Treasure (cont.)	Culture	Page
World Mill	Norse	1692
Yu Nu's Image	Chin.	1424

TREE OF KNOWLEDGE OR LIFE (SEE PLANT)
UNDERWORLD REALM (SEE UNDER OTHERWORLD REALMS)
UNIVERSE TREE (SEE PLANT)

VALLEY

Achor	Hebr.	26
Aijalon	Hebr.	55
Baca	Hebr.	170
Bagrada	Rom.	172
Berachah	Hebr.	203
Enna	Gk.	1637
Gehenna (Ge-Hinnon)	Hebr.	637
Humiliation	Christ.	1637
Jehoshaphat	Hebr.	869
Marvelous	Cel.	474
Nysa	Gk.	1188
Phlegra	Gk.	1264
Valley of Tears	Christ.	1637
Valley of the Shadow of Death	Christ.	1637
Valley of Thorns	Norse	1637
Ydaler	Norse	1703

VEHICLE (VESSEL. ALSO SEE ANIMAL FOR MAGIC STEED)

Alice Marr	Folk.	1261
Argo	Gk.	121
Ark	Hebr. & others	126
Carmilhan	Folk.	291
Delia	Gk.	427
Dubsainglend	Cel.	1039
Flying Dutchman	Folk.	589
Golden Fleece	Gk.	673
Houssain's carpet	Arab.	1038
Hringhorn	Norse	798
Iddahedu	Baby.	819
Ma-Banda-Anna	Baby.	1031
Magar	Sum.	1037
Manzet	Egy.	1063
Me'emzet	Egy.	1084
Mesenktet	Egy.	1094
Muso-byoye's kite	Jap.	1140

	Culture	Page
Naglfar	Norse	1148
Prydwn	Bryth.	1299
Semektet	Egy.	1415
Shoryobune	Jap.	1442
Simhasana	Bud.	1455
Skidbladnir	Norse	1464
Takara-bune	Jap.	1527
Umiarissat	Eskimoan	1623
Wave Sweeper	Cel.	1055
Wings of Icarus	Gk.	1039

VOLCANO (ALSO SEE FIRE, MOUNTAIN)

Chimborazo	Mex.	325
Cotopaxi	Ecuador	375
Etna	Gk.	528
Kilauea	Hawaii	1249
Okolner	Norse	1203

WATER: FOUNTAIN, SPRING, OR WELL

Abizendegani	Oriental	17
Aganippe	Gk	45
Ain Shams	Egy.	56
Alyssus	Gk.	78
Aonian Fount	Gk.	106
Apollo Thyrxis Well	Gk.	111
Bethesda	Hebr.	206
Bodilis	Breton	233
Byrgir	Norse	264
Caesar's Well	Folk	1673
Canathus	Gk.	283
Castalia	Gk.	294
Connla's Well	Cel.	367
Cordial Balsam	Folk.	1673
Czar's Well	Folk.	1673
Fons Bandusiae	Rom.	590
Fountain of Emmanuel's Blood	Christ.	599
Fountain of Ponce de Leon	Euro.	599
Hippocrene	Gk.	773
Hvergelmir	Norse	809
Living Waters	Folk.	1673
Mara	Hebr.	1063
Mimir's Well	Norse	1105
Mimis-Brunnen	Norse	1106
Pierian Spring	Gk.	1269
Shivaya Voda	Slav.	1439

	Culture	Page
Iakim (monster)	Brit. Col.	815
Jastoni (fish)	Christ.	867
Jhasa (fish)	Hin.	879
Kasyapa (tortoise)	Hin.	912
Khar (Khara) (fish)	Pers.	923
Khvarenanh (sea emanation)	Pers.	926
Kraken (monster)	Norw.	944
Kuei-lung (alligator)	Chin.	949
Kuei-shen (tortoise)	Chin.	949
Kulilu (fish)	Baby.	951
Kurma (tortoise)	Hin.	952
Kusariqqu (fish)	Baby.	953
Ku-yu (shark)	Majove	954
Kw-en (fish)	Chin.	955
Labismina (sea-serpent)	Folk.	957
Leviathan (giant fish)	Hebr.	989
Loki (salmon, seal)	Norse	1010
Lynn Feic (salmon)	Cel.	1029
Mah (fish)	Pers.	1042
Makara (monster)	Hin.	1047
Mandishire (turtle)	Sib.	1057
Mashenomak (monster)	Men.	1072
Matsya (fish)	Hin.	1076
Mermaid	Euro. Lit.	1093
Mishe-Nahma	N.A.I.	767
Namazu (fish)	Jap.	1151
Nereids (mermaids, nymphs)	Gk.	1164
Nickard (monster)	Germ.	1168
Nina (fish)	Baby.	1170
Noogumee (whale)	Micmac Ind.	1180
Nu (frog)	Egy.	1184
Oannes (fish	Baby., Chald., Phoen.	1190
Rahab (sea demon)	Hebr.	1318
Ravgga (Meriraukka) (fish)	Fin-Ug.	1325
Rem (fish)	Egy.	1332
Sebek (crocodile)	Egy.	1412
Serra (monster)	Med.	1420
Set (sea serpent)	Egy.	1420
Suvarnamacha (mermaid)	Siam.	1513
Tangaroa (seal)	N. Zeal.	1531
Tlatecutli (toad)	Mex.	1582
Toyo-Tama-Hime (shark)	Jap.	1593
Triton (fish)	Gk.	1599
Turtle	N.A.I.	1610
Ukupanio (shark)	Hawa.	1621